An
Extraordinary Mary
Australian

MacKillop

An
Extraordinary
Australian Mary

MacKillop

The Authorised Biography by
PAUL GARDINER SJ

E. J. Dwyer
David Ell Press

First published in 1994 by
E.J. Dwyer (Australia) Pty Ltd
Unit 13, Perry Park
33 Maddox Street
Alexandria NSW 2015
Australia
Ph: (02) 550 2355
Fax: (02) 519 3218

In association with
David Ell Press

National Library of Australia
Cataloguing-in-Publication data

Gardiner, Paul, 1924– .
 An extraordinary Australian : Mary MacKillop : the authorised biography.

 Includes index.
 ISBN 0 85574 038 8.

 1. MacKillop, Mary, 1842–1909. 2. Sisters of St. Joseph of the Sacred Heart – Biography. 3. Nuns – Australia – Biography.
 I. Title.

271.97602

Cover and text design by Warren Penney
Typeset in 11/13pt Goudy Old Style by Egan Reid Ltd, New Zealand
Printed in Australia by Griffin Paperbacks, Netley, S.A.

10 9 8 7 6 5
98 97 96 95

Distributed in Canada by:
 Meakin and Associates
 Unit 17
 81 Auriga Drive
 NEPEAN, ONT K2E 7Y5
 Ph: (613) 226 4381
 Fax: (613) 226 1687

Distributed in Ireland and the UK by:
 Columba Book Service
 93 The Rise
 Mount Merrion
 BLACKROCK CO. DUBLIN
 Ph: (01) 283 2954
 Fax: (01) 288 3770

Distributed in the United States by:
 Morehouse Publishing
 871 Ethan Allen Highway
 RIDGEFIELD CT 06877
 Ph: (203) 431 3927
 Fax: (203) 431 3964

CONTENTS

PREFACE

*"The Lord has done marvels for me
Holy is His Name!" (Lk 1:49)*

It is with great joy that the Church recognises in its members the creative, saving and sanctifying action of God. Such graciousness must be acclaimed. Thus it is that, throughout its history, the Church has honoured the memory of those whose lives have, in some particular way, given evidence of the Spirit's ongoing work among us.

Christian Australians recognise that the Holy Spirit has long been active in this land. For forty thousand years, its aboriginal peoples have handed on from one generation to the next an awareness of spiritual realities. Through myth, ritual and song they have celebrated humanity's relationship with its maker. So, too, with the coming of other peoples to these shores during the past two hundred years, witness to God's faithful love has been given by the lives of many. Faith nurtured against all odds; hearts, already straining under their own troubles, opening out to others; life given out of death—our families all over this land cherish such stories.

It is a matter of pride for us, then, that not only the Church in Australia but the Church worldwide has seen fit to identify in the life of Mary MacKillop a sure sign of God's presence in this country. As we praise God for Mary MacKillop and for the contribution she made to the Kingdom, we acknowledge also the grace of God still poured out into the lives of God's people. This Australian woman encapsulated qualities of character and spirit shared by many we know as "unrecognised saints". As we read her story, let us keep in mind the challenge such a life presents to us. It draws to the source of grace and calls us, too, to lay down our lives for the "life of the world". (cf Jn 10:17–18)

Sister Mary Cresp RSJ
Congregational Leader
Sisters of St Joseph

1

INTRODUCTION

Mary MacKillop was born in Melbourne on January 15th 1842, and died in Sydney as Mother Mary of the Cross on August 8th 1909.

In those August days of 1909, Sydney knew that it had lost not only a noted personage but a very holy one. Those attending her as she lay dying had noticed the unusual reverence of bishops and priests who came to visit her. Cardinal Moran, a very circumspect man, whose office had brought him into close contact with Mary for a quarter of a century, stated at the time that he thought she was worthy to be declared a saint.

There was such a crowd at her funeral that the church could not hold them all. When she had been laid to rest at Gore Hill, people provided themselves with samples of earth from the grave, just as they had previously been touching her body with various objects of devotion. This was all the more remarkable because it has never been a tradition in Australia that there are saints around. The cautious character of the people makes them slow to raise the cry, "Saint!" or "Miracle!"

As time went on, however, it became clear that the unusual display of enthusiasm at the time of Mary's death was a sign that there had indeed been a saint in the land. This led to the transfer of her remains in 1914 to a vault in the new memorial chapel of the Josephite Sisters in North Sydney.

The first step on the road to canonisation was taken in Sydney in 1925 when Archbishop Kelly set up a Tribunal of investigation. During the years 1926-1928 a number of witnesses were interrogated, but the procedure was suspended in 1931 when an important document could not be found in the Roman archives. The notary, N.T. Gilroy, was convinced that this interruption was an injustice to Mary's name, and twenty years later—now as Dr Kelly's successor, with the extra leverage of a cardinal—he took effective steps to procure the missing document and to reconstitute the Tribunal. Further sessions were held in Sydney in 1951 and 1959-1961, in Brisbane in 1959, and in Adelaide in 1961.

Pope Paul VI visited Sydney in 1970, and gave great joy to Mary's admirers when he prayed at her tomb. One old Josephite Sister there told him that although she was already past the century she did not intend to die until he had beatified Mother Mary. The Pope remarked on leaving, "We mustn't keep that old Sister out of heaven too long!" Back in Rome, he made it clear that he wanted the cause to proceed as speedily as possible.

At a meeting of cardinals and bishops in January 1973, it was agreed that the Cause might be formally introduced "if the Holy Father should think fit." Paul VI did this on February 1st 1973.

While unanimously recommending this step, the Pope's counsellors indicated that there were still some obscurities in the story, and advised that these should be clarified by further research. A full historical study of Mary's life should then be prepared under the direction of the Congregation for the Causes of Saints.

There were two main areas where "a fuller and definitive solution of the problems" was desired: Mary's difficulties with some bishops, and the estrangement of Father Woods. The bishops in question were: Dr Sheil during the 1871 excommunication episode in Adelaide, the Quinn brothers in Bathurst and Brisbane, and Dr Reynolds during and after the 1883 Adelaide Commission.

The first response to this directive was the research undertaken in Rome by Monsignor Aldo Rebeschini, a Melbourne priest who was at the time secretary to Cardinal James Knox, the former Archbishop of Melbourne. With Knox's encouragement, Rebeschini devoted many hours over a number of years to searching out, microfilming, photocopying, deciphering, evaluating and transcribing anything he could find relevant to Mary's life.

The most fruitful source of new material was the Congregation for the Propagation of the Faith. This was the department through which the Church authorities in Australia communicated with the Holy See in the nineteenth century, and documents of any significance, therefore, found their way into its archives. The Irish College, too, proved important. Mgr Tobias Kirby, Rector there for many years, acted as Roman proxy for fellow Irishmen who were bishops in Australia, and correspondence preserved in the College archives reveals much about some of the key personalities in this story. In addition, there is a good deal of material there about Mary's dealings with Kirby when she was in Rome in 1873 and 1874.

Useful documents were found also at the Scots College in Rome. The fact that two successive Rectors, Grant and Campbell, had befriended Mary during troubled times meant that some informative letters went into the College archives. Further material also came to light in Great Britain and Ireland.

But the richest deposit of documents concerning Mother Mary remains the head house of the Josephites in North Sydney. During his research, Mgr Rebeschini kept in touch with the archivists there, at first with Sister Christina Tancred and then with Sisters Evelyn Pickering and Anne Marie Power. These Sisters, and others like Callista Neagle in Adelaide, built solidly on the foundations laid by the skill and dedication of their predecessors, Columbkille Browne and Campion Roche. Because of the foresight of superiors in assigning such competent and dedicated people to this work, the Josephites have rich and well-ordered archives.

Rebeschini's research, added to the decades of labour of devoted people in Australia and New Zealand, produced the mountain of documentation on which the historical study, the *Positio*, is based. The production of this work was entrusted by the Congregation for the Causes of Saints to its Relator for Mary MacKillop's Cause— Father Peter Gumpel, a German Jesuit. The Provincial Superior of the Australian Jesuits made the present author available to be his collaborator, and the *Positio* was put together in Rome during the years 1984-1989.

The touchstone of what was included in the *Positio* was relevance to the history of what Mother Mary did and endured. The same applies to this present work, which is substantially identical with the *Positio*. Father Woods, for example, played such an important role in the story that the many pages devoted to him need no apology. If human interest had been the criterion, they could have been multiplied many times.

If ecclesiastical scandal had been wanted for its own sake, a similar multiplication could have been achieved in that domain also. Even as things stand, much of the history could be seen as a display of self-will, intrigue, and infighting on the part of people in high places. But nothing could be further from the truth as far as Mary MacKillop herself was concerned. Her view of life was simple and generous. She saw herself as challenged to carry out the will of God and to provide others with occasions to do so.

Her intimate union with the Creator enabled her to preserve her inner peace even when the going was toughest. She respected and loved people even when they were at their worst. Her love did not depend on performance. She looked beyond what she could see and hear and smell, and attended to what her faith told her of the dignity of every human person. This attitude called for a rare nobility of mind, one which would make life much easier for everybody if it were more widespread.

Mary MacKillop revered people in holy orders, and respected all authority as a derived expression of God's will. But she had problems when prelates extended their jurisdiction *ad libitum* or neglected the directives of higher authority. She endeavoured to resolve these difficulties not only justly but with undiminished respect and unaffected charity. Some of these episodes caused a stir at the time, and they make dramatic reading even now, but it would be superficial to regard them as her most momentous battles.

Mary's real battles were, rather, those in which the bishops were her unequivocal allies in a war with the ungodly forces at work in society. The pursuit of human values, full and authentic and founded on the eternal as revealed by Christian faith, was the main concern of all parties. Whatever differences there were, there was complete agreement about a common purpose.

Less edifying aspects of the characters and activities of some ecclesiastics cannot, however, be ignored. This history would be incomplete without them, as they are surely essential to any account of what Mary endured. Most charitable and patient, she was at the same time very perceptive. If what went on were not told, or if the impression were given that she did not know what was going on, her greatness of soul could not have been so strikingly revealed.

It would be impossible to name all the people to whom this work is indebted. Some mentioned above, and Dr Colin McKay of Sydney (whose unheralded contribution to the Cause in the legal sphere was immense), are the chief among the living. But without the dedication of many who have passed from this life, these more recent labourers would hardly have known where to begin. Distinguished names from the past, like Mother Laurence, Cardinal Gilroy, Father William Keane, and the authors George O'Neill and Osmund Thorpe, will ever be associated with the story.

It is fitting also to recall with honour those many nameless ones who worked quietly in the hope that God's achievements in the soul of this authentic modern woman might be publicly recognised, and that she might be exalted as an inspiration and a friend for future generations of Australians and for many from beyond our shores.

Paul Gardiner, SJ

PART I

Background
and
Early Life

ONE

A HIGHLANDER
IN THE ANTIPODES

Alexander MacKillop (1812–1868)

On a summer's day in January 1838 the bounty ship *Brilliant* nosed in through the heads after many weeks at sea. As the vessel made its way slowly up the harbour, the passengers on the decks marvelled at the coves and the inlets and the headlands, and the low hills beyond. There was no Bridge, no Opera House, but it was Sydney, wonderful then as now.

Among those people gazing on the land of their adoption on that January day, dreaming of prosperity, was a young Scot, Alexander MacKillop. Twenty-six years of age on the morrow, he had already had an unusual career. In 1825, in his fourteenth year, he had gone to the Scots College in Rome to study to become a priest. According to family lore, he was a gifted student and a spirited debater, being "chosen for the Grand Act, Philosophy and Theology against all comers, and this in the days when the Pope presided and the foreign Ambassadors were present".[1] To cap this off, there is a story that a famous theologian once said to a friend: "MacKillop, I remember him well. He was the only man in Rome I was afraid of. Many's the night's sleep he took from me."

But after six years in Rome, Alexander had returned to Scotland "for health reasons". Eight months later he resumed his studies, at Blairs near Aberdeen, but left that seminary too after seventeen months. The Blairs register says (in Latin): "Here he studied Theology until the 8 August 1833 when he withdrew secretly [furtim] from the College without completing his course." The reason for his furtive departure has never been ascertained, although the family said he was annoyed at not being shown the consideration due to his Roman background, his seniority, and his health. His son told it thus in his memoir:

> From the old Folk at Blairs College Mary heard this story. After nine years in Rome my Dad found it cold in Scotland. He asked for a fire in his room and was refused. Now the young man who in Rome had been made much fancied himself not a little, no doubt when he found himself among the old Fossils of Blairs College went off in a huff to complain to the Bishop. Of course His Lordship advised immediate return to his College. This was too much! He returned to his home.

There are inaccuracies in this account written by an old man many years after he had first heard the tale—for example, his father was not in Rome for nine years—but there is a ring of truth about it all. There is something about the departure from Blairs, as there is about the vagueness of the ill health that obliged him to leave Rome, that is consistent with Alexander's later history. Little is known about his movements after he left Blairs, just that when he embarked for Australia on the *Brilliant* at the end of 1837 the ship's papers called him a teacher.

Soon after his arrival in Port Jackson in January 1838 he found employment with Campbells, importers and exporters, and did well. By the end of the next year he had moved south to the new settlement on Port Phillip, which was at the time not five years old. Still with Campbells, he immersed himself in the life of Melbourne's infant community, promoting cultural activities, setting up a library, and organising lectures. He was soon a member of the Board of Trustees and Treasurer of the Roman Catholic Church. In 1840 he had an address in Little Collins Street, and also owned some land between Merri Creek and Darebin Creek. In April 1841 he was described in the *Port Phillip Gazette* as engaged in commerce, and he was a member of a company formed to investigate coal deposits. There was every sign that he had made a successful start in his new world.

In April 1840 the typhoid-stricken ship *Glen Huntly* berthed in Port Phillip and its passengers were disembarked into quarantine. Among them was Mrs Catherine MacDonald, accompanied by her daughter Flora, whose age was given as twenty-two, and her son Donald, slightly younger. Another son had died on the voyage. There is no evidence that Alexander knew them in Scotland, but he was quick to offer help when they arrived in their new homeland. Within three months, on July 14, he had married Flora, probably in the small wooden chapel which stood near the site of the present church of St

Francis. Some time later the priest who had officiated at the wedding met the young wife, now expecting her first child.

"Flora", said Father Geoghegan, "I have a great present for you, and you must take great care of it." He explained that it was a relic of the Holy Cross, that he could not give it to her, but that she was to wear it until the child was born.[2]

In April 1841 Alexander had purchased a house in Brunswick Street, Fitzroy, and it was here that this child was born on 15 January 1842. In the adjacent pavement, within a stone's throw of St Patrick's Cathedral, a granite slab now commemorates the event: "On This Site MARY MacKILLOP Foundress Of The Sisters Of St Joseph Was Born On 15th January 1842."[3]

The MacKillops came from the Braes of Lochaber, the hills and mountains eighty miles north of Glasgow that have become famous in song and tradition. The Highlanders there risked a lot for the Stuart cause by supporting Bonnie Prince Charlie in his ill-fated campaign in 1745, and by helping him escape when there was a price on his head after the battle of Culloden. Lochaber's people have proudly retained the memory of these events, so when Donald MacKillop sat down to write a memoir his opening sentence had special significance: "My Father and Mother were both from the Highlands of Scotland, from the Braes of Lochaber."

The MacKillops were for centuries a sept (a clan giving support in peace and war) of the MacDonalds of Keppoch, which is just opposite Roybridge on the River Spean. These Highland Scots lived frugal lives on small holdings under unfair rules of tenure that barely allowed for subsistence, but their generosity and their hospitality were never in doubt. Gaelic traditions provided their spirit, their language, their music, and their humour. Memories of their past enabled them to bear their present poverty, and sustained them in hope for the future in this life and the next. They traced their faith back to the mid-fifth century, although it was not until a hundred years later that it struck roots deep in Lochaber. This was due to the influence of the great St Columba, who came in 563 to establish his famed monastery on the island of Iona. When his monks crossed to the mainland and made their way up the valleys, they planted the seeds of a faith that was to survive centuries of pressure.

Around the year 600 there was a missionary monk whose name is immortalised in *Cille Choirill* (Churchyard of St Coirell) in Brae Lochaber. The remains of the religious centre he established on an ancient site called *Tom Aingeal* may still be seen by anyone who cares to walk a mile or two from Roybridge. The MacKillop ancestors lived within sight of it. When Mary was there in 1873, she felt the finger of God in the history of her people. They once resided where she saw only a few ruined homesteads around the villages of Murlaggan, Achluachrach and Inverroy. She felt grateful that one of them crossed the world, became her father in a far country, and handed on to her the faith inherited through Columba and Coirell and generations of Lochaber Catholics.

On one of the tombstones in *Cille Choirill* there appears the name of a Duncan MacKillop, a tenant farmer at Murlaggan, whose descendants according to local tradition were brilliant but eccentric. It is most likely that Alexander was his grandson. Duncan's first wife was Margaret Beaton, from Achluachrach, and it seems that there were three children, John, Alexander and Angus. John married Helen McNab and had a family of seven, the first of whom was Alexander, Mary's father. The passenger list of the vessel on which they arrived in Australia with five of these children bore the information that John came from Lochaber in Inverness-shire, and that Helen came from Glenlyre in Perthshire, which can hardly be anything but Glenlyon— the register at Fort William says that the three youngest of the seven children were born there. When Alexander had arrived in Sydney a year before, his native place was given as Ardnasmurches in Argyllshire, which must be Ardnamurchan.

McNab was not a characteristic Lochaber name, but it appears in the local records in 1778. Some time before that, a Sarah McNab (Mór Liath, or grey-haired Sarah) had a reputation for holiness, and she has an honoured tomb in the chapel at *Cille Choirill*. The tradition is that she helped preserve the faith in the district by persuading the pastor not to leave when disheartened by an unresponsive flock. Alexander MacKillop was related through his mother, Helen McNab, to Father Duncan McNab, well known in Australian history for his work among Aboriginals. Duncan attended Alexander in his last hours.

Though John MacKillop left Scotland, many of the clan remain in Lochaber to this day. The only one of his children who did not migrate to Australia was Archibald. Mary took special trouble to visit this uncle, who had abandoned his faith, but although he received her kindly as his brother's daughter, he would not listen to any talk about religion, nor would he help her Institute. His brothers Duncan,

John, and Peter, and his sisters Margaret and Anne arrived in Australia with their parents in *The British King* early in 1839. Margaret and Peter are the ones who had most to do with their niece Mary.

Margaret was the first wife of Alexander Cameron, known as The King of Penola because of his vast holdings of land in the area. He was the founder of the town and in the early days its owner. To the MacKillops he was "Uncle Sandy". He and Margaret had ten children, and it was as governess to the younger ones among these that Mary went to Penola in 1860. Some time after Margaret died in 1863, Alexander took a second wife, Ellen Keogh, who bore him eight more children. He later moved to Melbourne, where he died in 1881 at the age of seventy-one. He had two uncles—half-brothers of his father and brothers of each other—Alexander ("Black Sandy") born in 1791, and Duncan, born in 1800 and hence not much older than his nephew. Duncan married Sarah Eliza Lee in 1835 and they had fourteen children. Mary MacKillop's godmother was a Sarah Cameron, which must be the same lady. Two years after Duncan died in 1860, Mary became governess in her household at Portland.

Mary met some Camerons in New Zealand. The one she called "Donald New Zealand", the first of the clan there, was Donald Angus, the son of The King's brother Ewen. His descendants have strong traditions about her visits and her reputation for holiness among them is firm. The older ones still tell a visitor that as children they were brought up to believe she was a saint. In a house where she stayed at Nokomai, in the south of the South Island, "Mother Mary's bed" was venerated for generations. Whenever there was illness there, the patient was put into this bed and recovered.

Other New Zealand Camerons are convinced that they are descended from Mary MacDonald, a sister of Mary's mother Flora. This lady married a Samuel Cameron, and their son Thomas Ross Cameron became a distinguished figure in New Zealand. Mary made contact with some of the family of this first cousin, and there are photographs extant showing that her sister Annie visited them in later years. Towards the end of her life Annie described this Mary thus: "my mother's half-sister, Mary MacDonald who went to America with her brother Sandy, and married a Cameron." This, together with the New Zealand Camerons' claim to relationship, confirms the suggestion that grandfather MacDonald had been married before he married Catherine Kennedy. Thomas Ross was a grandson of the first marriage and came via America.

Uncle Peter MacKillop, born in 1825, was the youngest brother of Alexander, but did not share the religious ideals of his niece Mary. He became a very wealthy man, having several properties in Victoria—at Merri Creek, then at Dunkeld near Hamilton and at Duck Ponds (now Lara) near Geelong. Afterwards he lived at St Kilda for some time, but spent the last ten years of his life in Queensland. When he died in 1901 the Melbourne *Argus* noted that he had left over £50,000. The Good Shepherd Sisters and the Little Sisters of the Poor were beneficiaries in the will, but there was no mention of the Sisters of St Joseph. Peter played a strange role in foreclosing on a mortgage on Alexander's home, but later provided hospitality for his brother's children when they needed it. Two of these, Margaret and Peter, died at his residence at Duck Ponds, and Alexander himself spent his last days at Hamilton. Uncle Peter married twice but had no offspring. His first wife, Julia Keogh, was the aunt of Ellen Keogh, the second wife of The King. She had a sister Mary who married Joseph L'Estrange, and Mary MacKillop's very first employment was as governess to their children. Though Peter MacKillop died in Queensland, he lies at rest in the St Kilda cemetery, Melbourne. In the same plot are his two wives and his niece Annie, Mary's younger sister.

Mary's uncle Duncan MacKillop lived in New South Wales and had nine children, of whom there are many living descendants. One grand-daughter became Mother General of the Sisters of Mercy. Duncan's sister, Mary's aunt Anne, comes briefly into the story as Mrs McPherson.

MacDonalds are prolific in Scotland and wherever the Scots have migrated. It was from the Cranachan branch of the Keppoch MacDonalds that Mary MacKillop was descended through her mother Flora MacDonald. They were Lochaber people, Keppoch being at the junction of the two rivers, the Roy and the Spean, and Cranachan being two or three miles up the Roy valley. Achluachrach, Alexander's native place, is about the same distance up the Spean from Keppoch. Loyalty was symbolised for the family by the fact that Flora bore the same name as the Jacobite heroine who at great risk had helped Charles Edward escape after Culloden in 1746. MacDonalds were loved and respected, and variously gifted as musicians, mathematicians, poets and athletes. Mary was impressed by those she met when she visited the valley: "Just imagine my going," she wrote in February 1874, "to a wild grand glen,—the home of five wonderful, eccentric Highlanders, all brothers and none married."

Two Donald MacDonalds—a grandfather and an uncle—were beloved of Mary MacKillop. The grandfather was in the habit of calling her *gnothach miadhail*, meaning "precious thing" in his native Gaelic. He taught her that language, and left her with a lifelong memory of a loving Highland Grandpa when she was tragically bereaved of him at the age of five. He had joined his family two years after their arrival in Australia. His son Donald married Eliza, already a MacDonald, being the daughter of "Long John", the whisky distiller. When Flora's daughters were beginning the school in Penola, this uncle Donald was manager of the *Royal Oak* hotel there.

Alexander MacKillop in Australia

In the three years he was in Australia before Mary was born, Alexander had accomplished much, certainly more than he could have hoped for in Scotland: prosperity, a family and a home, and the respect of his fellow citizens. His prospects looked promising but within a short time the picture changed disastrously. This seems to have been due to a combination of his character, his lack of business sense and the fact that there were a lot of smarter people around. More than once he allowed his idealism to have its head, and then became discouraged when things did not work out. The family's situation grew worse and worse, and this produced a sense of hopelessness. The most startling example of his style was his voyage to Scotland in 1851, leaving a growing family in Australia, in order to help a friend fulfil a dying wish to see the old country once more.

The catastrophe dated from the "Twelve Apostles" affair. A pioneer trader being pressed by a bank appealed for support around Melbourne. He managed to enlist eleven businessmen who made themselves "jointly and individually" liable for the sum of £10,000! The story is an extraordinary tale of dishonesty, treachery, opportunism and gullibility. Alexander MacKillop became one of this syndicate formed to rescue a man who did not need rescuing. Australian history of this period abounds in stories of disastrous bankruptcies, and in comparison with some other victims of dishonesty the "Apostles" were, according to one comment, "merely the victims of average petty larceny". The bank forced them to sell at a time when the market was poor and the purchasers later made huge profits by reselling. Alexander got caught up in this fraud and lost everything.

So in April 1842 he sold the house in which his daughter had been born in January. Two years later he was declared insolvent, but his letters to the newspapers indicate that he had not lost his spirit. It seems that he took up farming. He had suffered a setback, but he and Flora were still young; they had relatives and friends around them, and their new country had much to offer.

During these years Alexander was involved in political and religious debate. In very early Melbourne there had been much good will and cooperation between religious groups, but the Reverend John Dunmore Lang put an end to this by his campaign of no-popery during the Port Phillip election of 1843. Vicious sectarianism was firmly established when Irish mobs rallied to support his Catholic opponent, provoked by posters reminding Protestants that they were three to one in number and urging "down with the rabble and no surrender". Alexander MacKillop was in the thick of it. At first he expressed his views under the pseudonym *A Scottish Highlander*. But when his anonymity was exposed he lost his job with Campbells, and "Mr Highland MacKillop" became a byword for sectarian confrontation. *The Port Phillip Herald* of 1843 preserves proof that the brawling was rich in incident and lively in spirit. MacKillop, whose opinion of Lang's writings was that they were "a tissue of glaring falsehoods, infamous scandals, bigoted opinions, egregious calumnies, and seditious satires", certainly had a ready command of the language then current in political debate.

For his part, Lang gave in the same measure as he was given. He was convinced that the pope was the Man of Sin and that Catholicism was the great apostasy foretold in the Bible, "the great corruption of Scriptural Christianity and the fruitful source of irreligion and demoralisation". He was able to make the awful disclosure that his antagonist had been in a seminary: "Mr MacKillop is not only a Roman Catholic also, but was actually educated for the Romish priesthood, and is, therefore, what we should call in Scotland 'a stickit priest.'" The newspaper files of the period are full of this kind of thing, both in the correspondence and in the editorial comment.

Alexander had obviously not lost heart at this stage, nor had he ten years later, when he stood as a political candidate on a couple of occasions. His financial position could not have been all that bad, though it is clear from his policy speeches that he did not have enough money for effectual canvassing. The campaigns were again vigorous and acrimonious, but this time touched on real political issues, like

16

the provision of money for schools in remote areas, something that would not have escaped the notice of his eleven-year-old daughter Mary. She was old enough to be taking an interest also in the disputed matter of state support for religious schools, an issue about which she had decided views when defending the Josephite policy years later.

These incursions into political life in 1853 reveal features of Alexander's character that might escape the notice of those who see only an impetuous man who became dispirited when he was eventually unable to provide for his family. The reports of the political campaigning show that amidst all the heated arguments he had a dry sense of humour which prevented him from taking himself too seriously. In defeat he was not bitter, being quick to congratulate his opponents in a gentlemanly way.

This was in 1853, a year after Alexander returned from his trip to Scotland. The three eldest children, Mary, Margaret and John, were apparently attending a private school at this time. The explanation of this temporary prosperity may lie in the fact that the rich gold deposits discovered in Victoria had turned the whole economy upside down and had made that colony the focus of the Australian world. But things must have deteriorated, because in 1857 the family went to Sydney in the hope of finding something better. It was a fruitless venture, and they had to borrow money to return to Melbourne. In 1859 there again seemed to be light on the horizon. Alexander was appointed as "Clerk, Goldfields". This civil service job took him to Clunes, in the Ballarat area, where the first Victorian gold had been discovered in 1851. But again the family's hopes were dashed. The appointment had been made through John O'Shannassy, a member of the Cabinet who was soon to become Premier of Victoria. In his outspoken way Alexander publicly criticised O'Shannassy's land policy, and by August he found himself out of a job. About July 1862 he made what seems to have been his last effort to find a source of finance for his family. He went with his son John to New Zealand, where the prospects would have seemed attractive from across the Tasman. But he failed to strike gold there and returned to Victoria.

Finding his way to Portland where his daughters were teaching, he was joined by his wife and the younger children. The year 1864 began promisingly but his principles again brought disaster. Because the head teacher cheated in front of the children during an inspection, he demanded that Annie give up her job at a school where such a man was in charge. Relations with the parish priest cooled, and Alexander became a figure of derision in the town. He even took a boy Flannagan to court for hooting and jeering at him and his family.

The affairs of the family were clearly in crisis. As part of an attempted solution, Alexander went to live on Peter's property near Hamilton, a move which turned out to be a final separation from his family. Five months before he died he wrote a moving letter to his son Donald, who was evidently thinking of becoming a priest, about "the sacred state for which your poor father felt himself unqualified". It would fill him with joy to have a son a priest, he said, but "it would be a fearful thing to enter upon such a holy state" without a genuine call from God. He died at the age of fifty-six on 19 December 1868 with Flora at his side. Only two days previously Bishop Sheil had approved the Sisters of St Joseph in Adelaide, but Alexander probably never knew of this landmark in the history of his daughter's Institute.

In all that we know about Alexander MacKillop there is no evidence that alcohol was his problem. He certainly caused his family embarrassment and was not a good provider for their needs, and it would be easy to say that drink was the cause of it. The way the family spoke of him was vague enough—Mary always referred to him as "poor Papa"—and if there was a serious drink problem they did a good job in covering it up, even from the eyes of posterity. In a 1926 letter Annie made a reference to drinking: "I believe that he did speculate a lot, and he took too much spirits. He was a great favourite with other men." In its context this is an attempt to explain her father's insolvency—he speculated and he spent too much money on drink for himself and a host of parasites. But with reference to drink itself, how much is too much? The phrase can cover everything from taking any drink at all to being drunk and disorderly. What Annie says is no more than could be said, especially by a non-drinker, about many a habitually sober man who likes a whisky or two. At times, no doubt, he took more than he needed. But among all the abusive things said of him by his public antagonists, we can find no reference to drinking. The Reverend John Dunmore Lang would have been delighted to be able to call Alexander MacKillop "a drunken stickit priest", but he did not. Nor did anybody else.

The positive side of the story is that the education this intelligent man received in his youth was not wasted. He did not employ it as a priest, as intended, nor did it provide the foundation for a public career. But his talents and his training were brought to focus on his daughter Mary. She never attended any high-class school, yet her education was clearly of a superior quality. It can only be explained by the influence of her father, the "stickit priest".

In a monograph on Alexander there is a fanciful court scene where the jurors bring in a verdict of guilty on a man accused of having "generally conducted himself imprudently, improvidently and impetuously throughout his life". His defence had been simply: "I merely followed what I felt was, and was taught to be, Christ's teaching, admittedly with great zeal, but with genuine love for all men." "You are sentenced," the Judge says,

—to be reunited with your family and friends in eternity.

—to submit a bond to be of good behaviour until the Second Coming, specifically, to abstain from arguments with persons such as Plato, Aristotle, Aquinas, Henry VIII, Luther, Dunmore Lang, O'Shannassy, Flannagan, et al.[4]

Alexander may have considered himself a failure, and so may many another, but there could well be a very different verdict to pass on his life.

Footnotes

[1] From the memoir of Father Donald MacKillop S.J. (1853–1925), the seventh of Alexander's children.

[2] ibid.

[3] The house, Marino Cottage, no longer stands. It was about 15 metres back from the present frontage of 11 Brunswick Street, close to Victoria Parade.

[4] *In Search of Alexander MacKillop*, privately published in 1981 by Victor Feehan of Melbourne and Anne MacDonell of Spean Bridge, Inverness-shire, Scotland.

TWO

"A DANGEROUS PLACE FOR CATHOLICS"

Mary MacKillop's Australia

U ntil Captain Cook, Europeans had known the great southern
continent only through the desultory reports of adventurers
seeking to solve the mystery of the *Terra Australis Incognita* of
map-makers. When the First Fleet arrived in January 1788, convicts
and guards to the number of about a thousand had settled in the
vicinity of Sydney. The first free pioneers came in 1793, and by 1800
there were about five thousand people in all. Sydney expanded and
other foundations were made around the continent, while free settlers
and ex-convicts turned to the land to grow crops and raise sheep.
There was wealth in wool, and squatters followed the tracks of the
explorers into the vast interior where people were scarce and life was
tough. The western district of Victoria, and to some extent the
adjacent parts of South Australia, were exceptions to this pattern.
Settlement there was closer, and several seaports and service towns
sprang up within a short time. One of these towns was Penola.

Transport and communication were problems in those early years.
Small trading steamers plying up and down the coast had room for a
few passengers, with the constant threat of shipwreck, but for seventy
years transport meant Cobb & Co. Carrying people, goods, and mail,
Cobb's coaches went straight through the bush, on roads that were
simply deep ruts cut by heavy drays. The horses were strong, and
sometimes the only way to get through a bad place was at a gallop.
The driver yelled "Hold tight!". The passengers held tight and prayed.

Mary MacKillop once described a coach leaving Penola, with her
uncle Donald at the reins: "Thick smoke enveloped the travellers;
blazing trees added to their discomfort, crackling branches snapped
off and fell in their way. The horses reared and snorted; but the brave

old Highlander managed them, his familiar voice and steady hand encouraged them."

During the first twenty years of Mary's life as a Sister, travel was at its most primitive, although things improved with major rail projects in South Australia after 1875. The record of the distances she covered by coach, rail, and steamer is hard to believe. It took a toll on her health, which was never robust, but though the prospect sometimes daunted her she never shirked duty or a chance to be kind.

In the very earliest period of European Australia there was no call for education. But when the population became more mixed, schools were needed. At first these were private religious concerns supported by tax money, or Government orphanages. For Catholics, however, the scheme was unacceptable because they feared proselytism; so they made an effort to provide their own schools, and by 1833 they had about ten. But Archbishop Polding lamented in 1839 that "through the apathy of parents the street is the school frequented by very many children". For a while in the 1830s all the pupils came together for secular subjects, with separate religious instruction. This caused an outcry on the grounds that it infringed church authority over education. Polding was at first in favour of it; when he changed his mind, the Catholics were confused.

About this time the denominational system was introduced. Money for schools was given to all churches and where there were no church schools the Government set up its own. As this led to controversy, two boards were set up in 1848, one allocating funds to State schools and the other providing for religious schools. Local authorities still had control, but there was a growing movement in favour of treating all education as the business of one Government department. In South Australia this scheme lasted until 1851, elsewhere into the 1860s.

In 1866 Henry Parkes, the New South Wales Premier, set up a Council to control grants to schools. Its favouring of State schools was a clear sign of trouble for Catholics. In this third form of the denominational system, money was given for salaries and books, but management was in the hands of central boards. Conditions for grants became more exacting and the Catholics were gradually squeezed out. The story was the same everywhere. In Victoria the author of the Stephens Act of 1872 said:

> In a couple of generations, through the missionary influence of the State schools, a new body of State doctrine and theology will grow

up, and the cultured and intellectual Victorians of the future will directly worship in common at the shrines of one neutral-tinted deity, sanctioned by the State department.

The secularists knew what they were doing. One judge described the Stephens Act as "an endeavour to crush Catholicism under the heel of authority". In 1879, Parkes, introducing the bill which secularised education and withdrew State aid from Church schools, declared: "I hold in my hand what will be death to the calling of the priesthood of Rome". On the other side, Archbishop Vaughan became the spokesman for Catholic rights in education. In 1874 he warned against what he saw as a wave of infidelity threatening the country.

South Australia

The religious and ethnic composition of South Australia differed from that of the eastern colonies. Its pioneers were chiefly non-conformists who did not want religion to be a bar to civil liberty as it was in the United Kingdom. There were also some Germans who had come to escape the troubles of their homeland. By the time the colony was fifty years old, farming had replaced grazing on most of its arable land and it had become the granary of the Australian colonies. But it was dependent on the fertility of the soil and the regularity of the rains. The largest area with good rain, around Penola, was also the only settled area where grazing superseded farming. There were distressing periods in the 1860s and 1870s, but towards the end of the 1880s there was a decade of severe and unrelenting drought. This added destructive dust storms to the danger of bushfires as an extra menace.

The 1870s were years of almost continuous population movement, as settlers pushed out to the limits of the reliable rain and beyond. During the good years the land produced well; but when drought struck, it gave no returns at all. Many farmers were forced to abandon their holdings at great personal loss and to look for jobs in the city or on Government works. By comparison with the eastern colonies, South Australia was poor, because it relied principally on wheat and copper for its income. During the 1860s the world price of copper fell, while drought and red rust reduced wheat production, and the decade ended with a period of depression. One third of the people were now living in Adelaide, and many were out of work. The 1870s were a time of relative prosperity, with only one severe drought (that of 1876) and generally good wheat yields. But the drought years of the 1880s plunged the colony into another period of severe economic depression, well before the crash of the '90s and the depression in other colonies.

South Australia at first decided that all churches should be supported by the contributions of their members without any Government assistance. In the late 1840s limited aid was given, but in 1851 the Government withdrew all aid to religious bodies and a non-sectarian educational system was established. The Bible was to be read daily, but denominational religious teaching was forbidden.

The Catholics in South Australia, mostly Irish, comprised less than 15% of the population until well into the twentieth century. Their first bishop, Francis Murphy, came to Adelaide in 1844, eight years after its foundation. His diocese was far-flung and his flock of twelve hundred was mostly poor. He had few priests and little money, his buildings were small, and he had no source of permanent income. Then in 1851 the rush for gold in Victoria almost destroyed his mission. But he rejected aid because it entailed unacceptable conditions, and as he had no money he was unable to maintain any schools.

Murphy died in April 1858. He was succeeded by Geoghegan, Melbourne's pioneer priest, in November 1859. Such an interval may have been normal enough, but it was part of the remarkable statistic that during fifteen and a half years Adelaide had a resident Catholic bishop for little over five.[1] Absences abroad and two periods when the see was vacant help to explain why the diocese lurched from crisis to crisis with no evidence of a wise head or a strong hand in control. Geoghegan had been orphaned young and had been brought up in an anti-Catholic atmosphere. After study in Portugal, he worked as a priest in Ireland for eight years before going to Australia. He celebrated the first Mass in Melbourne at Pentecost 1839, and when Alexander MacKillop arrived later that year he welcomed him as a close associate.

Geoghegan had told the Select Committee on Education in Melbourne in 1852 that it was of paramount importance to foster children's religious faith. When he became bishop in Adelaide seven years later, he based his educational policy on this principle. On his arrival he was shocked by the lack of facilities for Catholic education. Though the Government was unfavourable and the Catholics were mostly labourers, he tackled the problem with an enthusiasm that inspired a vigorous response from his people. With only thirteen priests serving twenty-one churches, he announced the first independent school system in Australia. He proposed to set up a school, unaided, wherever there was a priest and people.

In spite of all difficulties Geoghegan opened nineteen schools in a little over two years and brought the number of churches up to forty-one. Though lack of money was a constant worry, the greatest problem was personnel. Nevertheless he did have some energetic priests, one of whom was Julian Woods at Penola. This parish consisted of some hundreds of Catholics scattered across a vast area in the south-east of the colony. Many of the children were too far away to attend any school, but Woods quickly learned the hazards of trying to run a school at a distance from a city or a large town. Early in 1862 the bishop went to Europe to look for priests and teachers, but he died two years later without seeing Adelaide again.

The third bishop (1866–1871) was Lawrence Bonaventure Sheil, another Irish Franciscan who came via Melbourne. After some years as a student and lecturer in Rome, and a period in Ireland, he was recruited for Melbourne by Bishop Goold late in 1852. He was put in charge of St Francis' Seminary (this later became St Patrick's) but in 1859 he resigned on account of ill health. His later lack of competence in money matters was foreshadowed by the sizable debt he left at the seminary without telling the bishop anything about it. Still, he did not fall out of favour. Goold put him in charge at Ballarat, and then recommended him as bishop of Adelaide. The weapons wielded in ecclesiastical battles in those days were usually accusations of being in debt and of drinking. Perhaps it was just another instance of this convention, but in attacking Dr Goold through the memory of Dr Sheil, Bishop Matthew Quinn made both allegations in a letter to Rome in 1873. After reflecting on Adelaide's huge debt, he took up the drink weapon:

> It would make you tremble to hear the way Dr Reynolds and the good priests of Adelaide speak of the two last Bishops of Adelaide Dr Geoghegan and Dr Sheil. They were both from the diocese of Melbourne and *known* to be addicted to drink when they were recommended to the H. See for appointment. His Eminence the Cardinal Prefect can easily see by whom they were recommended.

In any case, Sheil was appointed to Adelaide. Because the Church was too poor to pay teachers, much less to bring any from overseas, many children simply lacked instruction. It was a daunting problem, but there were two people in the colony, Julian Woods and Mary MacKillop, who had the will to set about providing a remedy. Woods proposed a body of teaching nuns, the Institute of St Joseph, as the solution of his problem in Penola, and when the bishop saw that the idea could be applied over a wider area he called him to Adelaide as Director of Education. Adelaide thus became the cradle of the Josephites, although Penola retains the honour of being their birthplace.

The new institute fitted easily into the local scene. Its members lived poorly like the people around them, suffering the same inconveniences, using the same means of transport. They were, as James Murtagh put it, "as much a part of the colonial scene as the drovers, shearers and bullock drivers".[2] They were prepared to go to the limits of settlement and to live in the most primitive conditions. Extremes of heat and cold, the constant shortage of water, the blinding dust storms of the drought years—such trials were regarded as a normal part of life. When the population shifted, the nuns simply moved to where the people were.

As the authorities in Rome had no idea what life in Australia could be like, Mary MacKillop composed a document to enlighten them in 1873. She began with her credentials: "It is an Australian who writes this, one brought up in the midst of many of the evils she tries to describe." In recommending her institute as a solution, she stressed an important fact: "What would seem much out of place in Europe is still the very reverse in Australia."

From South Australia the Institute spread to other colonies, first to Queensland and to Bathurst, then to Sydney and other parts of New South Wales, and to Victoria; they also went to New Zealand. Coming to the rescue after the various "free, secular and compulsory" education Acts of the 1870s and in 1880, they soon became a part of the Catholic education networks of Australasia. Because of the great simplicity of their lifestyle, they were the ideal answer when Government funds were no longer available. In each colony they went to the country districts and the poorer urban areas. Besides their main work in the schools, they undertook to help people in any kind of need. So they became as well known for their orphanages, their homes for old people, and their institutions known as Refuges and Providences, as for their schools.

When Mary MacKillop was a young lay teacher at Portland, the effects of a new secular liberalism were being felt in the world. Individualism was the vogue in political, economic and intellectual life. It had no theory about life or society, but was simply a spirit of freedom permeating the new society, an impulse to build a social order with equal opportunity for all, blended with a youthful spirit of nationalism and a materialism carried over from what Polding called the "gold mania years". From the basis of their secular faith, Australians worshipped material progress. When faced with the decision about national education, there were few who understood the real nature of the conflict or its implications.

The Catholic bishops, however, responded to the challenge. In their *Joint Pastoral* of 1879 they made the following statement which for a long time was cited as an example of intransigence, disloyalty and insulting exclusiveness:

> [The Church] knows that instruction is not education, and that a system of national training from which Christianity is banished is a system of practical paganism, which leads to corruption of morals and loss of faith, to national effeminacy and to national dishonour.

Archbishop Vaughan warned:

> We prize above all imaginable things, the Faith of our Fathers; that Faith is in peril in a great measure on account of the menacing condition of modern society; and cost what it may, it must be preserved and fostered in the hearts and intellects of the rising generation.

He saw the aim of his opponents as "the extinction of the Catholic religion, of the Catholic sacraments, and of the calling of the Catholic clergy". For a long time many thought that the Catholic stand was political blackmail or sheer perversity. But this was not some minor political skirmish—it was a battle between two conflicting views of the human race.

It is not hard to see why Vaughan gave Mary MacKillop a warm welcome to Sydney. Unlike many of the clergy, he understood her refusal to accept money from governments. He agreed that the Catholic faith was a gift of God not to be bartered for funds supplied by State officials. In her 1873 document for Rome, Mary alluded to the acquisitiveness of Australian society and the self-indulgence that militated against the welfare of the family. She spoke of the indifference of secular governments towards the Catholic poor, and described the problems of a Church which lacked the personnel to cope with the needs of its people. When she said that Australia was a dangerous place for Catholics she was speaking a truth that should have been clear to anyone with faith and half an eye to see what was going on. Her solution was no tentative plan. There was a group of women already in action, and she made it clear that she was seeking the blessing of the Church for a going concern, not for an idea.

Mary MacKillop was proud to be an Australian. In one sense, her life was an expression of her ambition for her country. She aimed to defend human dignity and human rights against the many public forces that were directed against them. Her vision was not restricted to one colony—it extended to the whole continent long before political unity had been achieved with the formation of the Commonwealth in 1901.

Footnotes

[1] Geoghegan was in Adelaide for about 26 months, from November 1859 until February 1862. His successor Sheil was there for 8 months after his arrival in August 1866, then absent for 20 months from April 1867 to December 1868. After 10 months (in October 1869) he left again for Europe for 17 months, until February 1871. He was then present in his diocese, a sick man, until his death on 1 March 1872. This reckoning takes no account of his visits to other parts of Australia, which were frequent. Reynolds was consecrated in November 1873. He was present in his diocese for the most part until he left for Europe in March 1879. He did not return for 27 months.

[2] James G. Murtagh, *Australia: The Catholic Chapter*, The Polding Press, Melbourne, 1969, p. 110.

THREE

"MY HOME WHEN
I HAD IT"

1842–1860

The child of Alexander MacKillop and Flora MacDonald born on 15 January 1842 was baptised Maria Ellen on February 28. The second name (a form of Helen, the saint of the finding of the Cross) was later treasured by the family as a portent.[1] Some Simeon or Anna (cf. Gospel of Luke 2:25) in St Francis' that day could have become memorable by uttering the name *Mary of the Cross*, but nobody has ever claimed that this happened.

Mary MacKillop was born close to the heart of modern Melbourne. Her father's future seemed secure, but she was scarcely three months old when he had to sell the house. This was not the end, but it was symbolic of what was to be the pattern for the future. They went first to Glenroy, and then moved in succession to other rural districts around Melbourne that are now suburban—Merri Creek, then Darebin Creek where Alexander received a gift of land from his father and set about farming. The second child, Maggie, was born there, as were the first two sons, John and Alick, and probably also Annie and Lexie. Later, when they moved further out to "The Plenty", farming seems to have remained their main source of income.

Merri Creek and Darebin Creek meant places like Glenroy, Campbellfield, and Somerton, while an address like the Plenty is even vaguer than the Darebin. All these names are covered by an area stretching some ten miles from west to east and up to about fifteen miles north of Melbourne. It appears that Alexander was reasonably successful on the land, as on two occasions while his address was the Plenty he was able to nominate himself as an employer of migrants. But as the years went on it became evident that he was not a good provider for his growing family. A sojourn in Sydney followed the

28

Plenty and Campbellfield periods, but, says Annie, "they soon returned to Melbourne where they had many trials and reverses— Mary being the eldest was always the little mother." They tried in turn Collingwood and Richmond (inner suburbs) but with no greater success. Though it would be wrong to say that they depended constantly on the good will of others, still, they were fortunate to have relatives and Highland friends around. Besides the grandparents on both sides, the Duncan Camerons, the Alexander Camerons, the Keoghs, and the L'Estranges were all ready to help.

Annie's and Donald's memoirs of these early years throw some light on Mary's character. Sisterly admiration nurturing the stories of a loving mother may account to some extent for what Annie has to say, but surely not entirely: "She was a very wise and beautiful child. People often stopped her nurse just to look at her, she was so like pictures of angels." She had grey eyes and auburn hair. "She had a wonderful memory," Annie says in another place, "and was always old for her years. One day when she was walking with her mother, Mary being then four years old, her mother complained of being tired, and Mary offered her arm to help her mother."

The tragic death of Grandfather MacDonald occurred on a day in April 1847 when Grandmother and Uncle Donald were visiting the MacKillops at Darebin. They had intended to return to the Plenty that night, but a thunderstorm held them indoors. The next day Grandfather was nowhere to be found. It seems that he had set out to meet them the previous evening, was caught in the storm, slipped down the steep banks of the Darebin Creek, and was drowned. Years later Annie lifted the veil a little: "It was while living there that Mary had her first great grief. She loved him very much and even last year reminded me with tears in her eyes of his birthday. M. Mary always remembered every incident of his loss with sorrow." Six months later she lost her little brother Alexander, aged eleven months, so that by the age of five she had had close experience of sorrow.

A childhood incident when she was staying with friends may have been the basis of some mysterious words Mary wrote when she was twenty-five. Donald gave this account of it:

> It was the custom of Mrs L'Estrange to go round at night to see that all was well—she would then kiss her little guest and retire. But one night a most beautiful Lady came, bent lovingly over the young girl and kissed her saying: "My child I will always be a mother to you!" I give this for what it is worth. I never got Mary's own version. My

mother most evidently thought the beautiful Lady was our Blessed Lady.

What Mary wrote in later years (addressing the Virgin Mary) was: "Ah, my Mother, think of the day when I knelt but a child to ask you to be my Mother, and I remember your gentle whisper when you said that you marked me as your child since my birth."

Not much is known about Mary's schooling. Annie says that when she was about eight she went to a private boarding school run by a Miss Kane, and while there made her first Communion at St Francis' Church. She had the experience of being wrongly blamed and punished by this Miss Kane—a Tartar, according to Annie—but accepted it and did not try to defend herself. The exercise turned out to be good preparation for later life. The three eldest children attended a private school during the Campbellfield period.

But whatever the quality of the schools, Mary always had her father at home to keep her up to standard. She developed a power to express herself that was quite remarkable. Her mature handwriting, her faultless spelling (the punctuation was that in fashion at the time), her ability to handle the most delicate and difficult subjects and to adapt her style to the status of the person addressed, her clear grasp of the teachings of her religion, her knowledge of Catholic history and traditions, not to mention her ability to speak the Scottish Gaelic—all these things added up to a well-educated woman. It is clear that Annie was also well taught, and the few letters we have of Maggie and John and Lexie tell the same story. The younger boys Donald and Peter were later taught by the Jesuits at Sevenhill. As young ladies the MacKillop girls were successful teachers, Mary being apparently outstanding. In addition, Annie was a good pianist and Mary too played in her youth. They showed every evidence of a good education, although, apart from music, they did not have what Mary was later to call "accomplishments"—foreign languages and the other fruits of higher study that they might have gathered at expensive private schools.

The young Mary appears in some of Annie's stories as something of the fighting Scot her father was. When she objected one day to the way a textbook handled Mary Queen of Scots on the grounds that it was not true, she was told she was a little bigot, though the teacher seems to have had some respect for her afterwards. On another occasion she came across the *Awful Disclosures of Maria Monk* while staying with some Protestant friends and it went into the fire. Yet another Annie story shows Mary handling a challenging situation at the age of eleven. When Donald was a baby, a nurse was supposed to be helping his mother cope with him and five other children, but one day Flora came in to find Mary dressing the baby and the nurse nowhere to be seen. "Where is the nurse?" she asked. "I sent her away," said Mary. Flora asked why. "Because she was drinking," said Mary. ("I think she put it more crudely," wrote Annie, who also pointed out, "Dressing a baby was much more complicated then, but it was all correctly done.")

Cutting across the lives of the MacKillop children at this time was their father's incredible absence abroad for seventeen months, during which Mary turned ten. Alexander had decided to accompany an old friend on his last trip home to Scotland. Not only did this mean that the family's breadwinner was away, but unknown to Flora the property at Darebin Creek was mortgaged to pay for the trip. Alexander apparently thought that his brother Peter, the mortgagee, had the same high ideals as himself, but it did not turn out that way. He was away beyond the term of the mortgage, and Peter foreclosed. This came as a great shock to Flora, who was trying to manage with her six young children. One can sense the depth of the family feelings in Annie's memory:

> He had not returned when the mortgage fell due, so his brother and his wife went out and took possession, though our mother easily borrowed the money from her friends the Bullens as soon as she and they knew of the mortgage. It was *not accepted*. Peter said he required the home for himself: it was conveniently situated for his wife, as her sister had also a home called "Somerset" on the Darebin! It was a very unhappy home for all, as our mother would not leave, and Aunt Julia always remained in her room, seeing no one but Mary, who brought her her food, etc.

Mary, aged ten, was thus in the thick of it, being the only one prepared to take meals up to Aunt Julia, one of the occupying powers! There is no record that she ever spoke unfavourably of Uncle Peter, but Annie said her sister's favourite uncle was Donald MacDonald because he never made much money, and that the reason she did not have so much time for her other uncles was because they thought too much about money. The plural seems a polite way of referring to Uncle Peter, who not only thought a lot about money but made a lot of it, and may unwittingly have taught a little girl of ten a lesson about love of possessions that went deep into her soul. The stalemate was solved by Uncle Donald MacDonald. He had a farm in the Plenty ranges and "he at once went to the Darebin and took his sister and her children to his place, and saw to all their wants".

What Uncle Peter did was legal, but it was hardly pious, and it certainly caused ill feeling. Annie wrote of it: "My mother's servant met Uncle P. one day when she was nursing the baby and cursed him and told him that he would *never* have a child. *He never had.*" We do not know if the curse was an effective one, but in later years Peter was consistently hospitable to members of his brother's family.

It is not clear when the family left the Plenty, but they were there for some years. Annie says that in all her memories of the Plenty Mary was there. After the father's return from Scotland their fortunes fluctuated, but the tide seemed to be going out. The goldfields fiasco and the New Zealand venture indicated this. So too did Alexander's attempt to find work in Sydney.

Annie's account of the return to Melbourne is quite moving, and shows what Mary meant by words that are really very strong ones: "My life as a child was one of sorrow, my home when I had it, a most unhappy one." The father went first, with the family to follow, that is, Flora, Mary, John, and Annie and Donald. It was close to the time of Peter's birth. There was no money, so they had to borrow from friends to pay the steerage fare in a ship. At Port Melbourne (at that time Sandridge) there was again no money, so Mary aged fifteen and John aged twelve had to walk the fifteen miles to Somerton to announce their arrival to the relatives and work out a way to bring the mother and the younger children to where they could find a roof over their heads.

During the various sojourns in country areas Mary learnt to handle horses skilfully and courageously. The tradition is that she could master the most spirited animal, and there are occasional glimpses of this expertise in her life as a Josephite. There is a vivid description in Donald's memoir of an early incident near Penola that could have proved fatal:

> Mary was a good horsewoman and when young fond of riding. The fate of Absolom was once nearly hers before she was twenty. We were going home from Sunday Mass, and Mary was riding Donkey, a brute very fond of bolting. He had bolted with strong men, and me, too, years afterwards. The honey suckle, a very useless tree, was very dense in the foliage region, if foliage the tangled mass may be termed. Now in those days the girls wore their hair in nets. Donkey tore away under

such a tree, and I saw Mary's net left hanging until retrieved by the station Blacks.

It seems to have been after Flora's attempt to run a boarding house in Collingwood, on their return from Sydney, that Mary took her first paid employment. The L'Estrange family, with whom she had stayed from time to time, needed a nursery governess and she got the job. All her earnings then and later went to her mother, and when John began to work he joined her in providing for the others. The employment with the L'Estranges possibly gave Mary some opportunity to study, because she spoke of her interrupted studies as if it were not this job but the next one that put an end to them. "I had never been able to study much, and had once to abandon the best opportunity I had of doing such, and follow another occupation very revolting to me, and thus help those I loved." Now her duties with the L'Estrange children were certainly not revolting. The reference is rather to the job with the stationers Sands and Kenny that she took up after that, apparently in her seventeenth year.

Though the work itself did not thrill her, it brought in more money, and it originated an association with people who became lifelong friends and gave her much needed support in later years. Besides the Sands and the Kenny families, there were the MacDougalls who helped her in England in 1873–74. They were part of the firm, and their name replaced Kenny in the later Sands and MacDougall. None of these people were Catholics.

At Sands and Kenny Mary was trusted with responsibility. She may not have liked the job, but she was getting experience which stood her in good stead when she later found herself with the duties of an administrator. One story told by Donald and Annie had clearly impressed the family. Donald's choice of words is sometimes fascinating:

> Mary took a situation under them to help keep the pot boiling. The consul for Belgium posed as an aristocrat of the first order. This man called once at Sands and McDougals [sic] and it happened to be Mary who had to show him round. Not long after this a Mr. Keogh gave an evening party and this Belgian was one of the guests. Mary was a guest also. Now this was too awful for the aristocrat. To have to acknowledge thus a factory girl! The ass showed himself a snob and Mary left the room. Mr. Keogh followed and found her crying in her own room. He prevailed upon her to return saying he would fix things up. He got back to the company first and quietly passed the word

round. When Mary returned she was made the centre of attraction, Queen of the evening in fact. The Belgian took the hint and soon departed.

You see my "Holy Sister" did not always kiss her Cross. Ah, well, she was young, in the full flush of her teens—from all accounts a very prepossessing and high-spirited girl, with a pedigree to be proud of, and the Belgian was very rude.

Mary's sister Maggie (1843–1872) would have been part of her earliest memories. There were only sixteen months between them, so she was possibly the one for whom the short form of the name Margarite was devised. Maggie was a family girl, loving peace and harmony, but having a mind of her own when the rights of others had to be defended. When Lexie seemed to be getting drawn into the Josephite net without being too sure about it all, Father Woods arrived at Duck Ponds to straighten out the problem. He expected opposition from Uncle Peter and Aunt Julia, but when Maggie "privately opened her batteries about Lexie" he found he had met his match.

Maggie shared in the early teaching activities of the MacKillop sisters, but rheumatic fever forced her to withdraw. She found hospitality with various relatives, chiefly Uncle Sandy Cameron in his grand house (a castle, some called it) in Melbourne, and Uncle Peter at Duck Ponds, where she eventually died on 13 December 1872. There was a graciousness about Maggie; she was an affectionate, compassionate daughter and sister. Writing to her mother when John died, she had good news too: "Papa wrote so nicely about poor John's death. Indeed, his letter (such a nice kind letter) did me good." She was a great one for relaying news of friends and family, weddings, and other grand events. We feel that, had she lived, she could have out-Annied Annie as a witness.

John MacKillop (1845–1867) was three years younger than Mary, but old enough to share the burden of the younger ones with her. He worked first at Melbourne's Swanston Street Railway Station. When he was seventeen, he went to New Zealand with his father looking for gold, and appears as a tradesman, a carpenter, and a builder, with ambitions to be an architect as well. Beautiful letters he wrote from New Zealand reveal a fine, strong, independent, loyal young man who took his religion seriously. Although New Zealand was not kind to Alexander, John managed to do better. He stayed on when his father returned, but he too ran into trouble, cheated and defrauded by his employer. He returned to Australia and earned himself a place in history by transforming an old stable at Penola into the first school of the Sisters of St Joseph.

John planned to go back to New Zealand but his mother had misgivings that he might give up his religion there. He enlisted Father Woods in his campaign to get her to change her attitude, and Maggie joined in on his side. He wished to help the family, but he chafed under any kind of dependence, and felt he could do it from "anywhere in the world rather than in Portland".

John did return to New Zealand and had some modest success there. Letters went back and forth across the Tasman, but he hoped in vain for one from his eldest sister. She had been such a good correspondent when he was in New Zealand before, but she was for some reason not writing now. When he realised that the silence was part of the process of becoming a nun, he found it "too hard" that she might never write to him again! But he had photographs, and found consolation "in being able now and then to look at Mary".

John was never to know of his sister's fame, but the sense of loss evident in these letters is a moving witness to the feelings of a younger brother, her companion on the long walk from Sandridge to Somerton. He died in Christchurch on 16 December 1867, as a result of a fall from a horse.

History records another brother of Mary's, Alexander, simply as "little Alick". But his sojourn of eleven months on earth in 1847 would have played a significant part in his sister's growth in faith. She was going on six when he died. When John died twenty years later, she referred as a matter of course to this other brother. It would be most natural that this little girl, who had been so affected by the death of her grandfather a few months previously that she recalled him with tears in her eyes years later, was deeply affected by Alick's death. Little girls of five get to know and love their baby brothers.

Anne Catherine (Annie, 1848–1929) was the last living link with MacKillop history. Those who knew their unmarried great-aunts half a century ago knew Annie's type. A grand old lady with a good, if inaccurate, memory, a fertile imagination, a ready tongue, a lively interest in what people were doing and had done and were likely to do, she lived her last days in the Josephite convent at Carlton in Melbourne. She carried herself with a dignity that was partly natural and partly (we may imagine) the effect of being Mother Mary's sister.

But Annie was her own woman, with her own views on everything, including her contribution to Josephite history. It is said that she claimed to be the foundress, because it was she and not Mary who had first gone to Penola at the end of 1865! She recalled the earlier years in memoirs composed on request, both before and after Mary's death, and in her evidence at the Canonical Process in 1928.[2] She also answered questions put to her by George O'Neill when he was preparing Mary's biography.

Annie seems to have spent much of her time as a child with relatives. She championed the cause of her younger brother Peter when she thought Mary's handling of his "vocation" was a little too demanding. He was, she insisted, trying to improve at his studies and in his behaviour, and "his childish faults ought not to be cast up at him". Annie taught the piano at Penola and later at a variety of other places. We do not know where exactly she lived for much of her long life, but she was a kind of abiding MacKillop presence, a point of reference for friends and relatives. The image of the dignified eighty-year-old tends to efface the image of the seventeen-year-old who with her even younger sister of fifteen did her best to test the patience and other virtues of the family's aspiring nun, tormenting her with ghosts, bishops, snakes, and whatever else was at hand.

This lively good humour of girlhood appeared in some of her letters to Mary during very serious times: "My dear old Molly," she began, "Please excuse the disrespectful beginning of this letter, but I wish you to forget your responsibilities for a while," and then she launched the idea of "pumping up a vocation" with a view to becoming Mother Mary's successor! More serious were the letters between the two sisters when their mother died in a shipwreck in 1886. They shared their sorrow, even as their hearts went out to their brother Donald, recently ordained a priest in Europe.

Annie used to recall in old age how she "stopped a few gaps" for the Josephites, especially when Mary's health began to fail. In Melbourne late in 1891 and early 1892, when it looked as if Mary were dying, she was there. She was called on also in 1902, to accompany Mary to New Zealand for the health cure during which she had the stroke that crippled her. Annie was with her also at the end; in fact she may have been the last one to whom Mary spoke. When she herself died twenty years later, her will became the channel through which some of Uncle Peter's money at last reached the Josephites. She left the Sisters "all of Uncle Peter's money in return for all (Mary's) kindness to me all my life, knowing that in that way I can make some return to the Sisters of St Joseph for all their kindness to me during the years I have lived with them." Annie is a symbol of the family's final reconciliation with Uncle Peter: she lies in a grave alongside his in the St Kilda Cemetery, Melbourne.

Alexandrina (1850–1882) was too long a name to carry through life, so "Lexie" she became. She taught with Mary and Annie in the early months at Penola, and joined Annie in testing Mary's forbearance. It is Lexie especially who lets us see just how well they all got on with Father Woods, and how they kept him in good spirits. She wrote to him when he was preparing to leave Penola for Adelaide, hoping that mops would be provided for his farewell appearance on the following Sunday. Reading of these happier days, we feel doubly sad about Julian Woods' refusal to have anything to do with Mary in his latter years. More contact with Annies and Lexies might have saved him a lot of trouble.

Lexie's religious vocation became a hot topic with the family, who felt that she was being pressured to join Mary's nuns. The difficult character of one of the pioneer group contributed to her eventual decision not to remain. In 1871 she joined the Sisters of the Good Shepherd at Abbotsford, in Melbourne, and was professed on 16 February 1874. Mary said: "Oh, thanks, a thousand thanks, to our dear good God that she is so happy. She is doubly my sister now."

Lexie was a gentle, delightful character, kind, selfless, generous, ever ready to help the aged, the needy, and the lost. In Penola she had brought true affection and healing, as well as the truths of the Faith, to the Aborigines and other poor folk of the district. The convent records speak of her wisdom and prudence, her amiability, and her untiring attention to some of the most hapless inmates at the Refuge. She was put in charge of the novices soon after her profession, but in 1882 her health declined and by the end of the year she was dying. Flora had come to dread December, as John, Alexander and Maggie had all died in that month. She and Annie hurried to Abbotsford, and were with Lexie when on the 30th of December she went "to join the others". Mary was in Sydney, quite ill, and when she wrote to Donald in Europe—"there are only three now left out of eight"—she told him that when she last saw Lexie most of the talk was about him.

"There never could be too many Donalds," Mary said once, recalling her grandfather Donald MacDonald. So there were two reasons why her brother Donald (1853–1925) had a special place in her heart: he was Donald, and he was a priest. Educated by the Jesuits at Sevenhill, he joined the order in 1872. After some years of study and teaching, he went to Europe in 1882, began his theological studies at Innsbruck, later went to St Beuno's in North Wales and was ordained in 1885. On his return to Australia he was assigned to work with the Aboriginal people in the north. His appreciation of their culture, and his dedication, led to his appointment as head of the Daly River Mission. His writings on anthropology and linguistics are considered to be of a high calibre. He was far ahead of his time, trying to reconcile Aboriginal beliefs and habits with Christianity. But lack of interest down south, and the severe economic depression of 1892–93, led to grave difficulties. The bishops spoke good will but nothing came of it.

Alexander's son can be seen in Donald's statements criticising official policy and the meanness and lack of foresight of governments who turned a deaf ear to pleas for the Aboriginals. Such statements made him unpopular, as they were less fashionable then than they are now, but they have won posthumous praise for a man sensitive to the dignity of every human being.

In 1897 poor health forced Donald to withdraw from the mission, and for some time it seemed that he would not survive long. He wrote to Mary shortly before her death: "If you do go to God soon, I shall be disappointed if you do not manage to come to me, cure me and send me back to some more years of work." She apparently took heed, as he was able to work in parishes in Adelaide and Melbourne until his death sixteen years later.

The youngest of the MacKillops, Peter (1857–1878), never lacked patrons ready to offer advice. He was a normal boy who suffered as the others did from the family's economic troubles. When Flora decided to leave the boarding house at Portland, she sent Peter to school with the Jesuits at Sevenhill. Things went smoothly for a couple of years, but unpayable bills made her decide that his schooling would have to finish there and then. Then, when it was discovered that someone had erred in sending the bills, Peter went back to Sevenhill. He was said to be clever but inclined to be idle, as many of his companions would have been, but he afterwards improved. Annie too took up his defence against the helpful suggestions of Mary and Donald, and insisted that he was really trying.

Peter's eighteenth year, 1875, was one of crisis. A threat of heart disease raised doubts about his future, as the illness was becoming more complicated and he was having fits. He told Mary he wanted to get away from Sevenhill and go to work. In due course he announced his engagement, but it was not long before he was once more very ill. At first he was nursed in Adelaide by his mother and Annie, and then he was moved to Uncle Peter's at Duck Ponds. When he died, a few months short of twenty-one years, Flora and Mary and Annie were at his side. He left a little poem for his family, tender and full of faith.

Mary once spoke of her home as "a most unhappy one". There is nothing in the evidence to let us know whether this was because of a constant lack of money, or because of quarrels and bitterness, or for some other reason. Though there are no clear signs of disharmony or rancour, what the children say is sufficient to assure us that Flora needed a touch of heroism to cope. Her husband's domineering righteousness, alternating with his fits of depression in an atmosphere of constant financial uncertainty, seems to have been the main cause of the trouble. Though Mary did not condemn anybody, she did remark to her mother when her father died, "I am sure that you cannot regard Papa's death as a trial."

Flora's own view of herself was expressed in a letter to Donald after Lexie's death: "I consider myself one of the truly blessed mothers, being the instrument in God's hands of rearing all my children, and that under great difficulties for God's glory." For her part, Mary regarded her mother's lessons as a wonderful example to her. When her mother was troubled about her becoming a religious Sister, she had reminded her:

> You ever taught me to look up to and depend on Divine Providence in every trouble and when you saw me dull or unhappy you always had the same sweet reminder for me. Ah, do not now forget what you were the first to teach me.

Footnotes

1. Flora had worn a relic of the Cross during her pregnancy. The register has "Maria Ellen". Donald wrote: "So Mary was baptized Maria Helena. The Cross again." He remarks that when it was proposed to add the name Helen his mother "could not understand. It was not a family name." Yet it was the name of the paternal grandmother. She was always called Nelly, and many did not realise that this was a form of Helen, or that Ellison and the Scottish form Eilidh were also Helen.

2. The investigation of Mary MacKillop's life, initiated in Sydney in 1926 with a view to her canonisation as a saint, was called the Ordinary Process, or simply the Process. Since it was conducted according to the norms of Church law ("Canon Law") it is also sometimes referred to as the Canonical Process.

FOUR

TWO YEARS IN
THE BUSH

Governess at Penola 1860–1862

In 1860, when she was eighteen, Mary MacKillop left her native Melbourne for Penola in South Australia. Her arrival in that little town gave a direction to her life that she could not have foreseen. Her mind was firmly set on helping the poor and the distressed, but her main concern for the moment was to provide bread and butter for her younger brothers and sisters. The youngest was only three, so it looked as if she would be at it for some years yet. In the meantime her health had been causing concern and she was advised to get away from the job at the stationers. Just at that time her Aunt Margaret and Uncle Alexander Cameron at Penola were looking for a governess for their children, and in asking Mary they were offering a guaranteed income with the benefit of country air.

The Camerons had come to the district sixteen years previously. Searching one day for grazing country, Alexander saw the smoke of a camp fire in the distance and went over. At first he could find nobody, then he caught sight of an Aborigine up a tree. Convincing him he was a friend, he asked where he could find grassy country for his sheep and cattle. The man took him to a lagoon and it was there that Penola Station was established. This incident became a legend, and the Aborigines were always treated with the greatest respect by the Camerons.

Conditions were not what Alexander had known in Scotland, but before long he was a successful grazier on the fifty-eight square miles on which he had secured a lease. Red gums and stringy-bark were everywhere as was wattle, ti-tree and low scrub. There was no snow, and not too much water. Stone fences were not known, roads were hard to find, and bridges did not exist. There was no town anywhere in the vicinity. Once settled, Alexander and his uncle Black Sandy decided to build an inn. They called it *The Royal Oak*, as the oak was part of the Cameron escutcheon; the vaunting of the Royal may have had something to do with the nickname "King" by which Alexander came to be known. Late in 1848 the *Oak* was granted a licence, but there can be little doubt that it was operating well before that. There was nowhere else for miles around where a man could find a drink, so this "public house of notorious repute" attracted many a thirsty traveller and teamster. A clientele of colourful personalities used to pass the night camped nearby at the junction of the bullock tracks and horse paths on Limestone Ridge.

This was the start of Penola, at first a private township. In 1852 it consisted of one hotel, one store, one blacksmith's shop, and about four other wooden-slab buildings. Alexander had built a big house for his family by the lagoon, the haunt of many black swans. It was of stringy-bark, with stone chimneys, and by 1859 it had fifteen rooms— as well it might, because by the next year there were ten children. The parents were concerned not only about living space and the material well-being of these children, but also about their education. That is how cousin Mary came into the household.

Not much is known about her life as a governess, but Annie has left a few details. There was a girl called Nancy Bruce, whose father, an immigrant, milked the cows and did odd jobs about the place, and whose mother, an Aborigine, spent much of her time "gone bush" with her tribe. Neither parent gave the child the care she needed. Mary undertook what Annie described as the most distasteful task of combing the lice out of her hair and nursing her sores. At the same time she taught her the catechism and gave her what other lessons she could manage. She did this also for the other children on the farm.

Mary's arrival in the district brought her into contact with the parish priest, Father Julian Woods, and the name Penola will always be the background of the story of the historic enterprise these two people undertook together. Long afterwards she told Archbishop Kelly of Sydney:

> Circumstances have overshadowed the part played by Father Woods in the inception and early growth of our Institute. Nearly all was due to him, as will appear from our correspondence, which I have preserved. He may never be overlooked in the history of what God has done by our Sisters.

This English priest was among the most notable personalities in nineteenth century Australia. It would be a gross distortion of the truth to allow him to appear as some kind of stubborn madman because of the circumstances that occasioned his alienation from the Institute he founded, and not as the highly gifted, devoted, and good man he was.

Julian Woods was born in London in 1832 of a Catholic father and an Anglican mother into an unusually gifted family. In his adolescent years he began to take his Catholic religion seriously. At the age of eighteen he entered the Passionist Order, but some months after profession he was advised to leave on account of chronic ill health. After a period of uncertainty around London, and some study and teaching with the Marists in France (he was technically a novice) he again found himself undecided about his future. Invited to Australia by the Bishop of Hobart, he arrived in Tasmania early in 1855. But the work assigned to him was uncongenial, and before long he had crossed to the mainland, unsettled and uncertain about his future.

It seems that at times he intended to return to England and that at other times he intended to marry, but a chance meeting with the Bishop of Adelaide persuaded him to go on with the idea of becoming a priest. After some months of study with the Austrian Jesuits at Sevenhill, he was ordained for Adelaide in January 1857. After a few weeks in the cathedral parish in Adelaide, he was appointed to Penola. His flock was scattered over some 22,000 square miles of country, half desert and half taken up as sheep and cattle runs. Apart from a few wealthy farmers like the Camerons, they were isolated battlers—shepherds for the most part and miners—trying to eke out an existence in very primitive conditions. "There are no houses," wrote Julian, "bark huts, slab huts, log huts and weather-boarded huts—but no houses." At the start his friend Father Tappeiner had given him some good advice: keep a good horse, "take care that you do not break down before your bones are hard enough", and say the Divine Office.[1]

There were three towns in the parish: Penola, Mount Gambier, and the port of Robe, although in that context a town was little more than a hotel, a blacksmith's forge, a couple of stores, and some scattered houses. Penola itself was more pretentious, being a centre of contact with both Adelaide and Melbourne, on the road from the sea to the goldfields. A disused shop known as Anderson's Store functioned as both church and presbytery when the priest was in town. But for much of the time he was on the move miles away visiting his parish. Travelling was difficult and often dangerous. In summer the heat was intense and the mosquitoes a menace, water was mostly scarce, and when it did come it turned the dry creek-beds into dangerous torrents. There is one story of a wedding that had to be celebrated with the bridal party on one side of a flooded river and the priest on the other, because there was no way anybody could cross it.

Woods' constant travelling about this untamed country offered him great opportunities for the scientific observation on which he was so keen. On the road from Penola to Naracoorte there is a big gumtree labelled *Father Woods' Tree*, because the tradition is that his friends used to put a table and chair out under it so that he could work on his books and his specimens undisturbed by children and other noise. He was interested in the earth and the sea, animal, vegetable, and mineral, present and past. It may surprise many to learn that he and the poet Adam Lindsay Gordon, often his companion on the road, used to keep each other entertained by reciting poetry in English, Latin, Greek and French. As the horse-breaker and the priest waited one wild night for a storm to abate, crouched cold and hungry under a tree, Gordon entertained Julian by reciting long passages from various authors on the subject of storms, including the one from *King Lear*: "Things that love night love not such nights as these."

But primarily Julian Woods was priest and pastor. One of his most pressing problems was the lack of education in the outback, where religious instruction suffered the same fate as the rest of it. Parents had a hard enough time surviving, so education was a luxury they hardly dreamt of. They were often familiar with only the most basic truths of their religion, and some showed little enthusiasm about seeing that their children were any more enlightened. The problem preoccupied the priest during his long periods in the saddle, but no solution came to mind. From time to time, however, he recalled some nuns he had seen in France. They did not have grand convents or elaborate schools, but lived uncomplicated lives in country areas teaching the catechism and simple skills to peasant girls. In later years he spoke of the impression made on him by these women, not highly educated "nor, probably, very refined". He said they inspired him with the idea of the Sisters of St Joseph. Australia was certainly very different from France, but he allowed himself to dream. Could something like that be done here? It seemed totally impractical; but if God willed it, nobody could call it impossible. Meanwhile there was no harm in dreaming.

It was in Father Woods' fourth year at Penola that the governess came to live with the Camerons. Her new surroundings were not what she had been used to—here there were far more kangaroos and emus than people. She settled into her work and took her place in the life of the small community. It was not long before she met the pastor. He became her spiritual confidant and heard of her desire to live a religious life in the service of the poor. He believed it was divine providence that brought her problem to his attention just when he was grappling with the challenge of providing education in his parish. He began to see that a single solution could possibly provide for both. Mary later wrote: "I heard the Pastor from the Altar speak of the neglected state of the children of his parish—and I had to go and offer myself to aid him as far as the nature of my other duties would permit." But for the time being all they could do was discuss, think, and pray, hoping for the day when they might open a Catholic school in Penola. The Camerons had given land for a church, and the priest had hopes that when the time came they would not only give land for a school but build the school as well.

Mary's desire to be a religious went back a long way. It has been said that she was on the point of joining the Sisters of Mercy when Father Woods intervened and diverted her into the Sisters of St Joseph. He seemed to believe it himself in his later years, as he included it in his memoir in which his recall of the past was not only embittered (he does not mention her name once) but was as inaccurate as his predictions of the future nearly always were: "She had been a governess in the district where I was, and was about to enter the convent of Mercy in Melbourne but on my unfolding my designs to her she readily consented to join the undertaking and give her life to the work." Annie mentions the same thing: "Fr W. wished M. to be the first of them, but she had promised the Bishop of Melbourne (Dr Goold) that she would join the Sisters of Mercy at Nicholson Street. However she agreed at last when Fr W. promised to make it right with Dr Goold; (which he did *not* do)."

How Annie could have known this is not clear. We have no evidence that Mary ever told her; on the contrary, all evidence from Mary contradicts it. Annie mentions that Dr Goold was Mary's confessor. It is possible that Mary went to confession to him, but he would hardly have told Annie what transpired. When Annie gave her evidence in 1928, she was just on eighty, and she was talking about what happened when she was ten.

Those who speculated about Mary's future possibly reasoned this way: here is a girl obviously bent on being a nun, or at least acting as if she ought to be. The Sisters of Mercy up there in Fitzroy are good nuns, and we cannot see too many others about; so Miss MacKillop intends to join them. The story goes hand in hand with another—that she was educated by the Sisters of Mercy in Fitzroy. No evidence has ever been found in the school records or elsewhere to support such a statement. The nuns came in 1857, and it is hard to see how Mary could have fitted in any time with them between her job with the L'Estrange family and her employment with Sands and Kenny by the time she was sixteen.

Annie seemed to think that Archbishop Goold was never friendly to Mary and that his disappointment in her Mercy vocation was the reason. Mary had problems enough with bishops, but Dr Goold was never anything but friendly, even if at one point he was cautious about the Institute. It has been said that Mary was afraid to meet him because she had failed him in the matter of her vocation. She certainly did have misgivings about meeting him in Rome in 1874, and she told her mother so. But she also mentioned the reason, and it had nothing to do with the vocation question. It was not Melbourne 1858 that was worrying her—it was Adelaide 1871. Dr Goold had been the patron, as it were, of Dr Sheil, and Dr Sheil had seen fit to excommunicate Sister Mary. Sister Mary was therefore not too sure what sort of reception she would get from Dr Goold. In fact she need not have worried, as he proved very friendly towards her.

It is easy to say that Mary MacKillop intended to join the Sisters of Mercy. The idea even has a touch of the dramatic about it—it is a kind of prologue to the entrance of Father Woods to set things right. Woods himself seems to have come to believe it, but his fame as founder of the Josephites is assured without this theory, and his contribution to that work as Mary's director is not based on it either. As for Goold, there is no evidence that Mary did anything more than let him know she was inclined to the religious life; we can surmise that he had replied with the obvious remark that the Sisters of Mercy were there waiting for her. It is possible that he had promised himself that she would join them and began to speak as if it were she who had made the promise. Feeling awkward about it, she felt obliged to tell him what she was doing. That is all speculation, certainly, but it is better than the myth that Mary MacKillop intended to join the Sisters of Mercy until Father Woods came along.

She never intended any such thing. She had no doubt about her call to be a religious, but she could not see any order that would offer what she felt called to embrace. Her famous *Kangaroo* letter to Bishop Sheil in 1871 should settle the issue:

> I saw so much of the evils attending a merely secular course of education, that all my desires seemed to centre in a wish to devote myself to poor children, and the afflicted poor in some very poor Order. My confessor thought at one time I would have to go to France ere I could meet with what I desired.

Footnote

[1] A set of prayers (mostly psalms) and readings set down as the official prayer of the Catholic Church. Anyone can use this book, but it is a duty (*officium*, hence office) of priests and religious to do so.

FIVE

PORTLAND SWEET AND SOUR

Governess and Teacher 1862–1865

Mary stayed with the Camerons at Penola for about two years. In April 1862 she returned to Melbourne, intending apparently to remain there. However, by June she was on her way to Portland in western Victoria, where she was to remain for three and a half years. A busy port from which much of the colony's produce was exported, Portland was not a small place by Australian standards in those days. It was not so far from Penola across the border, and because of their distance from their capitals the two towns felt a kind of fellowship. Father Woods sometimes came over, but his main contact with Mary was by letter.

Mary's first job was with Eliza Lee Cameron, whose tenuous claim to the title "Aunt" was based on the fact that her late husband had been the uncle of Aunt Margaret's husband. She needed somebody to help with the education of the younger children. It was no sinecure, as the young ladies were not used to discipline and decorum. Woods must have been referring to some concrete problem when he wrote: "A spirit of insubordination is like a disease for which we must compassionate the sufferer and try to make them correct it by gentle means."

There was a church and a priest in Portland, and Mary soon had the job of sacristan. One night she spent an unplanned vigil of prayer when she was locked in the church by mistake. She made many friends in the town, including some who later became Josephites. Mary Finn, to whom she stood as godmother, remained a lifelong friend, and her daughter (who became a Loreto nun and lived to be 100) never lost touch with the Josephites, retaining vivid memories of Mother Mary until she died in 1982. When she had apologised for not joining the Josephites, Mary told her, "But, dear, you must go where the Lord calls you."

In Penola, Aunt Margaret was critically ill, and it was expected that the coming marriage of her daughter Margaret would further break up the family. Shortly after the Camerons' 1862 Christmas party Father Woods wrote of "the prospect that the same party will never meet again in the same manner to have another". What he did not know was that the younger Margaret would die a few months after her mother. The bereaved Alexander moved out of the district some months later, so that when Mary MacKillop returned to the town in 1866 to open a school her Cameron relatives were gone.

In 1861 Woods had established a Catholic school in Penola, although there was no actual school building. School was wherever the teacher was, and fees were charged. What he and Mary envisaged was a school where no fees would be demanded. Despite his warning that he was unlikely to be there forever, Mary suggested early in 1863 that she might be available to teach in such a school. The project must have been discussed when Woods visited Portland shortly before that, since he wrote about it on his return to Penola as if it were a familiar topic.

But the Penola teaching post was in fact not yet available, and in any case the pastor preferred to wait until some stability was guaranteed. The income that would come from school fees would be poor and would have to be supplemented by fees from boarders. Woods was also unhappy about a plan of Mary's to unite the family around her in Penola. While he had the greatest admiration for her mother, he feared that her father could cause trouble if he were included in any arrangements. He was wary of "anyone who was likely to interfere" with his control, adding more specifically: "I dread very much the presence of your father, to break up your little home again if you made one. I think you should make it understood that he is not to come."

But the Penola scheme was temporarily set aside when Mary had the chance to become a teacher in the Denominational School in Portland. She had to sit for an examination first, and although she had little opportunity for study she was successful. This was October 1863.

Mary could satisfy her duty towards her parents while living what Woods called "a very perfect and pious life" under the guidance of the priest at Portland. He possibly looked on the deferred Penola plan as an opportunity to begin her dedicated life, but forty years later she herself wrote:

> Miss M—was acquiring in the Portland school the experience and practical knowledge which fitted her for the work she was designed for; though, at that time, the idea of it was not very clearly defined in her mind, or in his who was to aid her in carrying it into execution.

Alluding again to the damage that could result from her father's indiscretion, Woods advised Mary not to consider purchasing a family home at Portland. In October she had been residing at Fitzroy Cottage, a four-roomed rented house on the cliff-top, but at the end of the year she rented *Bay View House*, a fine building belonging to one of the pioneer Henty brothers.[1] The rental and the furnishing contributed to the "Portland debts" that were to be a worry for some years. But early in 1864 the family at last appreciated having a home of their own in a happy atmosphere where there was plenty of homemade music. Maggie spoke of it to Father Woods:

> Oh! it is so pleasant to have Papa with us. He is so nice, kind and good to us all. I do not remember ever being so happy . . . I would not ask for more happiness in this world than to see Papa, Ma and all my dear brothers and sisters happy and comfortable. I trust in God that we will be able to go on smoothly and keep down our little debts.

It was a financially risky venture that struck terror into the heart of Mrs MacKillop, but the family was together. The idea was to use the building for a boarding and day school—the *Bay View House Seminary for Young Ladies*. Maggie was to see to the teaching, and Flora would look after the house. Mary would help when free from her own school duties. Annie was soon to join her on the staff at the school, so it looked as if the family's financial position was being stabilised. This new hope is reflected in a vivacity both in Maggie's letters and in Annie's later memoirs. "We were all very happy for a while at Bay View House," Annie tells us, "until Pa and Ma disagreed."

Apart from her work of teaching and management, Mary led a quiet and retiring life. "One great happiness I enjoy," she wrote in October 1864, "is, I have charge of the Altar and the Lamp, and being able to go into the chapel at any time, where the Blessed Sacrament always is, is a precious favour indeed." Father Woods kept up a constant stream of advice about prayer and detachment—"let not a particle of earthly consideration taint any one of your motives"—but we read in Mechtilde's *History of the Institute* that in spite of Mary's efforts she "had many difficulties to overcome, and suffered much through the attention paid to her by a gentleman of wealth and position who desired to wed the virtuous maiden."

An honoured guest at Bay View House was a "Holy Man", an old Portuguese named Rodriguez, called by the children "The Black Doctor" or "The Japanese Doctor". Donald remembered him as "evidently genteel, always wore black clothes and a silk hat— both very much the worse for wear." They were not quite sure who he was: "Whether he had a diploma or not, I do not know. He used to prescribe in a quiet way for the poor, and was very poor himself." His name was to be dramatically recalled in the convent at Franklin Street on the morning in 1871 when Mary found herself excommunicated. Donald continued:

> When the awful day *did* come and as Mary MacKillop she was ordered by the Bishop in full pontificals to return to the world from which she came and to take her sin with her, Mary dazed and weeping was departing, when another—she was a Portland girl—said to her "Why so troubled. Don't you remember what old Rodriguez told you at Portland." "Good God, Anne, what put that into your head now," said Mary.

What old Rodriguez had said was that he saw Mary "at the head of a long line of Virgins who wore a peculiar dress, that she would be excommunicated, but that the Pope and Rome would right her again. This was a few years before the Sisters started."

It soon became clear that things were not going to be easy at Portland. Woods' reminders about the value of adversity may have come in the normal course of spiritual direction, but in the correspondence (of which we usually have only one side) he makes numerous tantalising references to problems and disappointments of which the details elude us. One story at least shows that the troubles were not all of Mary's making. When she asked her grandfather MacKillop to help pay for the piano on which Maggie and Annie and the boarders learnt to play, he had generously met the whole cost. Somehow or other her father saw the money as a present to himself, and spent it.

But there was worse to come, and in a sense it was an answer to prayer. Mary was beginning to hope that the time might not be far off when she could unload the burden of being the family provider. The others should soon be able to take her place and allow her to turn to the religious life. Her proposal did not please either pastor or people at Portland, as they did not want to lose her. In view of the fine work she was doing among them, they wondered how she could imagine that God would want her to do something else. "I was too much loved there," she reflected later. But she coped by asking her friends and the children to pray for nine days for an intention she did not specify, but which was that she might be able to leave Portland.

The memory of it was still green when she told Monsignor Kirby about it in Rome eight years later. She also wrote to the nuns from Rome, asking them to organise nine days of prayer, as it was through such a *novena* at that time of the year long ago "that the ties which bound me to the world were broken". She can hardly have been referring to anything but the Cusack affair. When the inspector was due, Mr Cusack, the head of the school, juggled the rolls so that Mary and Annie saw their pupils transferred to his class, while they were given the ones who were normally his. Annie told the story:

> Mary took great pains with the girls and had their books in beautiful order, and my little infant school were also bright. I was proud of them. We were getting on famously, when, *shortly* before the Inspector was expected, Mr Cusack, the head Master, took for himself the classes we had taken such pains with and gave us the backward ones he had had. Mary felt it dreadfully and our father was furious when he heard of it. I was taken home. Mary stayed till the end of the year, when she left for Penola.

Then, to cap it off, Cusack performed some startling feat of cheating by showing answers to the children on a board held up behind the inspector's back. It was impossible to keep the matter quiet in the MacKillop household, especially with twelve-year-old Donald an interested and talkative witness. Alexander exploded with indignation. He protested to the pastor, demanding that something be done about having such a man as Cusack in charge of children. He refused to allow Annie to continue as a teacher at the school—though there is no evidence that he tried to get Mary to withdraw. Not only did the family lose Annie's salary, but they became the centre of a storm which really should have centred around Mr Cusack.

We do not have the full details, but it seems that Mary was blamed for the whole business. It was no light matter: "For four months this storm raged—and I stood alone." She saw it as the answer to the novena prayers: "In one short week after the novena the storm burst." It certainly detached her from popularity and from Portland: "God permitted a very bitter enemy to rise up against me, who said such things of me that all I cared most for, turned against me." What exactly was being said about her we do not know, nor is it certain who the very bitter enemy was.[2] It is likely that it was Mr Cusack himself, and that he interpreted his dismissal as an act of vengeance on Mary's part.

The novena had solved one problem, but the family still had to be maintained. Gentlemen boarders were taken at Bay View House, and the girls transferred to Fitzroy Cottage, but these changes had not stabilised the family's affairs. Father Woods thought it was time for Mary to begin the school at Penola, as the Misses Johnson had retired from teaching there. But he could see that if Mary were to go Flora would scarcely be able to manage a domestic situation that included Alexander. "You cannot deny that your father is an unfortunate manager and might embarrass your position very much," he told her. He proposed a plan and promised to help with the debts and the boys' education, but, as Annie recalled, he "did not pay".

The plan was this: Flora should remain in Portland with the two boys, Donald and Peter (who would later go to the College at Sevenhill); Alexander should go to his brother Peter's place near Hamilton (fifty miles to the north); John should continue to look for work in South Australia (where he soon found it); Maggie (whose health was causing serious concern) should go to Duck Ponds to Uncle Peter's; and the three other girls (Lexie only after much hesitation) should go to teach in Penola. Annie went before the year 1865 was out, in answer to an appeal from Woods for someone to "stop the gap". "Send Annie up," he had written to Mary in October, "but the how and the when I must leave you to settle with your uncle." A month later he wrote: "I consider Annie's presence here no more than a makeshift because the school cannot be properly conducted until you come up yourself." When he treated this period in his memoir he could not bring himself to mention Mary's name. She is always "the teacher" or one of "the first assistants God sent me". "The school at Penola", he says, "was founded according to a plan; and I obtained the cooperation of a teacher who was then in charge of a Government school in Victoria." One might be forgiven for wondering what he is talking about! He does attempt to explain his vagueness, so startling in view of all we know of the pre-Penola planning: "I would best consult the interests of all by avoiding much detail about these early beginnings—at least all that has reference to the young persons by whom I was assisted."

So in January 1866 Mary and Lexie set out by coach for Penola, to join their sister Annie as teachers in a Catholic school. Mary knew the significance of leaving her mother on this occasion, as it was the beginning of the fulfilment of her dream of devoting her life to God in the service of his poor and neglected ones. The details were vague, for as yet there was no religious congregation in existence—in fact not even the school existed—just the plans and hopes of a priest and a young woman.

Footnotes

[1] Mary was delighted when the Loreto Sisters leased it in 1884 and bought it in 1894. They built around it for the needs of the boarders and day pupils of the Loreto Convent Secondary School. In recent years the nuns have moved out and the property is part of a Christian Community College.

[2] Sister M. Rosalie later wrote: "Years after, Mother was in Sydney and whilst waiting for a boat at Circular Quay, saw the schoolmaster. He was old, crippled and in rags; at once Mother recognized him and offered help." Rosalie seems to be saying that Mary was helping an old enemy, not just an old acquaintance.

PART II

Origins of the Sisters of St Joseph

SIX

A STABLE IN PENOLA

Josephite Origins 1866

When Annie MacKillop arrived in Penola late in 1865 to hold the fort, there was no school building and she had no house, so the church had to serve as a classroom. The Misses Johnson had held school in their own home, with fees to be paid. But now all children would be welcome and money would be accepted only from those who could afford it.

Uncle Donald was at this time the licensee of the *Royal Oak*, so Annie had somewhere to stay when she arrived. When Mary and Lexie joined her in the new year they rented a small house called *Winella Cottage*. In an untechnical sense *Winella* was the first Josephite convent, as it was there that Mary, Blanche Amsinck, and Lexie later donned simple black dresses as a sign of their dedication, and Bishop Sheil addressed Mary as "Sister Mary".

For a time Lexie seemed to be content to be part of the scheme, but she always had her doubts. It cannot be said that Annie ever seriously considered joining. These two young ladies—Annie was seventeen and Lexie was fifteen—made sure that life at *Winella* offered Mary more than an atmosphere of devotion. They kept things lively with practical jokes, some of which were directed at Mary's habit of spending long periods in prayer. In a letter to Father Woods in September 1866, Annie described one of Mary's "nonsensical fancies" consisting of some sort of vision of a bishop using his crook to dip her as one would a sheep. It is unlikely that Annie fabricated the story—Woods could so easily check it—and it would have been quite out of character for Mary to make it up in the first place. The bishop dipping the sheep does seem to be a good allegory of what happened in Adelaide in 1871. But Annie certainly did not regard the vision or prophetic dream or whatever it was as too sacred to burlesque, as one of her next escapades was to dress up as a bishop with a sheet for cope and a broom for crozier. He was looking for a lost sheep, and Mary at her prayers was the one he found. He prodded her with his crook and washed her with water dashed from the broom. Speaking of this clowning sixty years later, Annie mentioned more than once that it was impossible to make Mary irritable or angry.[1]

At first two of the small rooms of their residence were used as classrooms in addition to the church, but before long something more spacious became available. This was an old stable belonging to the owner of *Winella*, and he let the MacKillops have it for a nominal rental. Their brother John volunteered to transform it into a school building. He removed the stalls, put in lining and flooring, and fitted a new door. When the Josephites came to look back at their origins, the link with Christ's birth in a stable was not lost. The block on which it stood is now a public garden named *Mother Mary McKillop Memorial Park*, with a commemorative plaque.

The fact that John found a job had helped to convince Mary the previous August that she could now leave the family's finances in his hands. She knew he would be as generous as she had been in devoting his wages to them, whereas there was little prospect that she would be able to contribute anything herself once the Penola school began. In fact, the money that came in at Penola was scarcely enough to keep the sisters alive. Annie said later that they often lived on bread and treacle. But when John died as the result of an accident in New Zealand at the end of the following year, the spectre of family debts loomed once more.

Because Mary was now living in Penola, she had more contact with Father Woods. Little of their correspondence from the earlier part of 1866 is extant, so we have no direct evidence of their planning at this stage. But when Mary appeared in a plain black dress on the Feast of St Joseph, March 19, she set people talking. On March 20 a report in the *Border Watch* said that the school had thirty-three pupils, and that it was doing very well. Now that he had a permanent teaching staff, Woods was able to turn his attention to getting a better school building. Mary was led to hope it would be completed before Christmas, but it was ready only after Easter.

Adelaide had been four years with no resident bishop when Dr Sheil was appointed in January 1866, and it was another nine months before he was installed. When Woods was in Melbourne for Sheil's consecration in August, he was pressed by Bishop Goold to stay and begin his experiment there. He might have been tempted to accept the offer if he had taken notice of the new Vicar General of Adelaide, who greeted the project of the school institute with "deluges of cold water". But the bishop was favourable. Moreover, Woods was now his secretary, which meant that he would be in close contact with the authority controlling the destiny of his institute. Within a month he was writing to announce news that was even more significant: the bishop had made him Director of Education, Chairman of the Board, and Inspector of Schools. He would be leaving Penola for good after Christmas, but in the meantime he had been authorised to proceed with the school building there.

Blanche Amsinck, an English lady with a rather aristocratic style, was invited by Father Woods in Melbourne to learn Mary's method of teaching and then to take over at Mount Gambier. She joined the MacKillop sisters at Penola around the end of October, and Woods himself arrived about a week later. He now had about him the nucleus of his institute. On November 21 Mary and Lexie and Blanche discarded their secular garments and dressed as religious postulants. Woods gave them a short rule and addressed them as "Sister". Mary was surprised that the dream was being so quickly realised, and wrote to her mother: "Your loving heart will, I fear, be inclined to grieve at this perhaps earlier separation than you expected, but ah! do not indulge the feeling, for does not God honour us all?"

On January 30 Mary wrote to Rose Cunningham expressing the hope that they might soon have the happiness of welcoming her to their Institute. Rose arrived on March 23, after Woods had left, but she did not settle in very smoothly. "It was as much as I could do," Mary wrote, "on more than one occasion to prevail on her to wait patiently instead of running away to Hamilton." But Rose persevered despite her misgivings.

Until the move to Adelaide there were two schools to be staffed, Penola itself and Mount Gambier about thirty miles to the south. Various combinations of the few available teachers were tried, but the need to assign Lexie and Blanche to different places (because of Lexie's problems at Mount Gambier) posed a problem. Woods did not want Mary to go to Mount Gambier, and he did not want to leave anybody on her own there; they had to make sure there was somebody to play the organ at Penola, and in time both Lexie and Annie became unavailable as staff members. However, there was a new postulant,

Julia Fitzgerald. Blanche hesitated for a time, but she settled down and remained with the group. Towards the end of April they moved out of *Winella* to a cottage they called *McElroy's*. School was conducted in the church as well as the stable.

Mary's letters to her mother at this time are full of gratitude, especially for the lessons about God's will that she was putting into practice in becoming a Sister: "One child who loved you above all others in this world left you only when convinced that it was His Will to do so." Flora was fearful about the prospect of religious vocations in the family, probably because of Papa's history, but Mary reminded her that they would be the fruit of ideals implanted by herself.

The case of Lexie was coming to a head. She was doubtful and hesitant, and her relatives said quite plainly that she was being pressed. They thought she was too young to decide, and they were angry because they saw her being drawn into what they considered a harebrained scheme of Father Woods. The priest had heard their views for himself when he was over for the bishop's consecration, but he had to face an even more devastating attack when he returned to Melbourne early in March. What they were saying about Lexie was in a veiled way being directed at Mary too, though her maturer age prevented them from saying she was too young. There was among them no sense of pride, nor even a hint of approval of what she was doing. They thought "it was cheek of her" to be wanting to establish a new religious order when there were already so many. The centre of the opposition was Duck Ponds and Uncle Peter. He was ably assisted by Aunt Julia, with their house guest Maggie playing a strong supporting role. Mary had written to this uncle for help with the Portland debts, but she was disappointed in any hopes of relief from that direction. Woods relayed Peter's explanation of why he could not contribute anything, namely, that he was not well off. There might have been something in this claim, but it leaves us wondering all the same. Peter had Papa and Maggie on his hands and that was good of him, and he was helping with Donald's clothing. But by his standards the debts were really trifling, and the thought persists that because he did not approve of the whole Woods enterprise he was not going to do anything to ease any burden. He was not so badly off that he was not prepared to have Lexie on his hands if she could be persuaded to leave Penola.

Flora was also becoming restive, writing Mary a letter (an unkind one, Mary thought) blaming her for her influence on Annie and

requiring Lexie's immediate return to Duck Ponds. A letter came also
from Julia which Mary said certainly did not deserve an answer. Uncle
Donald and Aunt Eliza were quite annoyed with it. Unfortunately for
history, this letter does not seem to have survived, but it obviously
summed up in a manner that was not ladylike what they thought at
Duck Ponds about Mary's vocation and the proposed institute. Eliza
and Donald were Mary's only consolation. She told Woods that Eliza
was amused at the sudden interest Julia was taking "in our welfare",
and that "poor Uncle is really pained and doesn't know what has come
over some of them." Woods heard the Duck Ponds' views for himself
when he walked into the electric atmosphere there. The storm of
words that broke included thunderbolts aimed at his own character:
"They regard me as an imaginative enthusiast not overblessed with
candour and sincerity." They told him plainly that they mistrusted
him and did not think he was dealing candidly with them. In effect,
they objected that he was bullying Lexie.

The relatives were not without a case, and it need not have been
based on worldliness alone. Behind it all was the figure of Papa, Peter's
elder brother, the "stickit priest", who had gone off to Rome before
he was fourteen. His subsequent lack of stability would naturally have
been associated in their minds with this youthful experience. When
Lexie was first caught up in the Penola scheme she was little over
fifteen years old. She was really only going to help out, as far as we
can judge, and she hesitated about that. But with the family breaking
up she hardly had anywhere else to go. She found herself being swept
along in the current of vocation enthusiasm that seems to have been
taken for granted by Father Woods and to some extent by Mary. Their
view was that membership of the new Institute was a good thing, but
they were vulnerable when they concluded that therefore God was
calling Lexie to it.

Woods had a powerful personality and was very persuasive. He had
no time for distinctions where spiritual principles were concerned,
and any good young person he came across was regarded as a likely
candidate for his Institute. What the MacKillop relatives were saying
was that all this did not add up to the conclusion that Lexie's place
was with the Sisters of St Joseph. They maintained that she wanted
to get away, at least for a time, and we can guess that what she wanted
to get away from was not only Blanche, but the Institute itself and the
domineering presence of Father Woods. But the priest seemed unable
to envisage that this could be possible. From his point of view all the

pressure was coming from the Duck Ponds people. He never admitted the possibility that they could be right about what Lexie wanted.

As later events showed, Lexie did not lack goodness or generosity of a high order. When she was a few years older, and was perfectly free to go back and become a Josephite, she did not do so, and in spite of Woods' forebodings this did not have disastrous consequences. She joined the Good Shepherd Sisters, and, although she was pursued by his prophecies of doom, she persevered and died with a reputation for holiness. Her congregation, but not the Josephites, shared the riches Uncle Peter could not take with him.

After a final farewell at Penola on February 10, Woods joined his bishop in Melbourne, and then travelled with him to Adelaide in early April. His letters to Mary at the time spoke glowingly of the simplicity and humility of the new Institute, and assured her that Dr Goold liked the school plan and thought she was "very fit for it". But back in Adelaide he found his prayers for tribulation fully answered. The bishop, his one sure support, was on the point of departing for Europe for the best part of two years. Then not only was his Institute ridiculed by the clergy and feared as a potential scandal, but there was opposition to his plan for reorganising the Catholic schools. He was even attacked in the newspapers. It is not always clear whether it was his new system of education or the idea of a sisterhood that was causing the trouble. People were asking, "What can you expect from colonial girls without any knowledge of a religious life and no one to train them?" In fact the Sisters became so identified with the new system that opposition to one meant opposition to the other. But the bishop supported both; he was enthusiastic about the Sisters, and he gave their founder full power to act in the field of education despite the doubts of his Vicar General.

The new Director of Education was not at all impressed by what he found: no real planning on a diocesan level, poor organisation, schools below standard and ill equipped, and teachers who were untrained, incompetent and unsuitable. The steps he took to remedy these deficiencies, beginning with the dismissal of teachers and the closure of schools, made him very unpopular. This antagonism grew to such proportions that when the bishop returned he found a situation he could not handle.

Probably because of the needs created by his dismissal of so many teachers, Woods told Mary early in May 1867 that she was to prepare to come to Adelaide. This meant that some practical matters had to be settled quickly: the habit and headdress of the Sisters, class timetables, and studies. Mary went to Mount Gambier to consult her companions about these matters, and to encourage Rose, who had not been having an easy time. The companionship of Blanche nearly had the same effect on her as it did on Lexie.

At the end of May, the founder sent Mary the Rule he had written for the Institute, commenting, "Of course it can be altered and modified as we see how it works, but it must never be spoken of as my work". The bishop was to approve this Rule shortly after his return in the December of the following year, but when Mary took it to Rome in 1873 the officials of the Holy See found much to criticise in it. The Roman expert to whom it was entrusted was of the opinion that it was confused and in some parts hardly made sense. He thought so poorly of it that the revision he produced was in effect a new document. Meanwhile, however, it guided the Institute.

There is a phrase, innocent enough at first sight, used by Woods in May 1867 that may hold a clue to the puzzle of his increasingly strange behaviour:

I have been overworking and rather indiscreet in doing without food, and I find myself failing. Pray that I may persevere in my present mode of life. *This is a secret to you alone.*

What he meant by his mode of life is not clear, but it does not sound prudent. If he were just feeling unwell there was hardly any need to hold Mary to such secrecy. His health had never been robust, and it was especially inclined to crack under strain, but his bouts of ill health at Penola seem to have been ordinary enough. With hindsight it may be possible to see in these early months in Adelaide the beginning of a breakdown that touched both body and mind, but especially the mind whenever it concerned itself with spiritual affairs or with the Institute. He was doing far too much, and trying to do even more, taking on responsibility for every detail of the life of the nuns and even for what took place in their schoolrooms, as well as for the organisation of education in the diocese in the teeth of strong opposition. All of this, in addition to his demanding journalistic activities, he was trying to handle without the support of close friends, and with a diminishing number of friends of any sort among the clergy. He was putting himself under an unnatural strain, and the consequences became evident in the course of the next three or four years. It is a striking fact that when in later years he had become a *persona non grata* in every diocese in Australia and was no longer involved in spiritual direction, his letters to his friend William Archer are urbane, witty, balanced, and interesting, betraying no trace of mental strain.[2] Even before that, there is a notable contrast between the sober judgment he exercised in his scientific publications and the increasingly bizarre imprudence of his handling of spiritual problems.

There was never any secret about the fact that there were MacKillop family debts, and on May 14 Mary reassured her mother about them. What she had to say indicates how relatively trifling they really were. Uncle Peter could have wiped them out by a light stroke of his pen. Father Woods was well aware of them, but not long before Mary left for Adelaide he wrote her a somewhat harsh letter reminding her of the importance of prudence in money matters. It reads strangely, coming from a man who was later to disclaim any connection with that virtue, and who had reassured everybody at Portland that Mary could leave with a good conscience because *he* would see to the debts! It is a trial to him, he says, that there are still family debts just as he is about to move her to Adelaide. She is to study her expenses each day lest she should compromise so high a cause as theirs by imprudence. The letter is a mixture of abstract wisdom and gross insensitivity. It reveals a man of high ideals who is beginning to betray signs that he has not enough time for quiet reflection.

The lifestyle which both Julian Woods and Mary MacKillop envisaged for the Institute is evident in what they wrote to each other as they prepared for the move to Adelaide. He pointed out that nothing but essentials, and those of the poorest kind, should be brought from Penola. For her part she warned him that the convent should be particularly simple; it was to be neat and clean, but there were to be no carpets or nice curtains. He was able to give these reassurances about the cottage being prepared in Grote Street by Miss Ellen McMullen, who was probably renting it. This young lady ran a school in Adelaide, and when she was asked to help prepare a house for the new Sisters, she not only offered her help but arranged to join them. As Sister Josephine she became a stalwart of the early Institute and a veteran of the wars in Queensland.

Finally, on 22 June 1867, Mary left Penola for Adelaide. She was driven by Uncle Donald to Mount Gambier, where she was joined by Rose, and then on to Port Macdonnell where they embarked on the vessel *Penola*. The first two Sisters of St Joseph arrived at Port

Adelaide on the vigil of St John the Baptist, a special patron of Mary
and of the Institute.

Footnotes

[1]   Annie's letter has also a colourful account of a ghost: "We went for a picnic last
Saturday out to the new Cemetery, but we didn't know for what the place we
were playing in was intended. Harry Roden died last Sunday and was buried in
the very place that we were playing in so we hadn't our picnic too soon. He left
all his money to Mrs Lye and one shilling to his wife, so they say that it is troubling
his mind and that his ghost appears between the Chapel gate and the lane, so
don't you think that he wants to get to the Church now that it is too late. Old
Wilson, Laidlaw and a good many others have seen him. Some say that he appears
as a kangaroo, others as himself in his burial clothes.

     "Mrs Mooney suspects that she was the ghost herself, for she had on a light
dress on Monday, and she was going home by your fence with Katie in her arms
and a light shawl round both of them, when she heard someone coming behind,
and so she went in close between the fence and the bushes till the man passed.
She thinks it was old Wilson. He says that it disappeared suddenly (I suppose
when she hid herself) but that he knew Harry's ugly face."

     A postscript says: "Mrs Mooney was not the ghost for some people in the
Temperance Hall dressed up an emu and sent it after Mr Wilson." Life in Penola
was not dull.

[2]   Anne V. Player, R.S.J. (ed.), *The Archer Letters*, Sisters of St Joseph, North
Goulburn, 1983.

SEVEN

A DREAM
COME TRUE

The Institute in Adelaide 1867–1869

When Mary and Rose arrived in Adelaide on Sunday, 23 June 1867, Father Woods took them first to Bishop's House where they put on the black habits ready for them. They then went to Miss McMullen's *Pelham Cottage* for prayers and an instruction. The habits were exchanged after a few months for the brown ones which became known far and wide as the garb of the Josephites.

When classes began on 2 July in St Francis Xavier's Hall, it was evident that Adelaide's welcome was cautious. There were only sixty children in attendance, more than half being former pupils of Miss McMullen. But as the school settled down other parents must have been pleased with what they saw, as six months later the enrolment was two hundred. Yet all was not well. Opposition—much of it from the clergy—now took the form of criticism and ridicule. One object of mockery was the way the children were marched home through the streets after school. Woods actually proposed to include this practice in the Rule of the Institute.

The Sisters' principles were quickly put to the test. They were told that one distinguished pupil would attend if he were treated with particular care, separate from the other pupils. His grandfather was Governor Daly and his father was a member of the Catholic Board of Education, but in spite of this the nuns refused to agree to these conditions. They were happy to teach him, but without special arrangements. Mary commented years later: "The Dalys were annoyed at first, but in the end admitted that the Sisters were right. The principle then struggled for has always been maintained, but often in the face of much opposition from well-meaning but mistaken friends."

On 15 August 1867 Mary made her first religious vows (or profession) as Sister Mary of the Cross in the little oratory at Grote Street. On the same day two postulants received the habit, Josephine McMullen and Clare Wright. On September 8 a Miss Fitzgerald became Sister John Baptist, and on November 21 another Miss Fitzgerald (Julia, from county Kerry in Ireland) became Sister Francis, and Margaret MacDonald became Sister Teresa. Blanche Amsinck, who was a late arrival after continuing to teach at Mount Gambier, received the habit on December 8 as Sister Francis Xavier. The register of the Institute shows ten names by the end of 1867.

Writing to her mother on August 21 Mary spoke of her new title. Accepting suffering as the will of God, and joining it with the Cross on which Jesus Christ suffered and died, had long been part of her life. Now she was more deeply conscious that she was called to share this Cross. The list of her troubles—the injustices, misunderstandings, and slanders she suffered—is long and at times hard to believe. In addition, her life seemed to have more than the normal share of the physical pain, annoyance, disappointment, and disturbance that is the lot of human beings. Mechtilde later wrote: "Under the trials of government, poverty, debt and persecution, she was always uncomplaining, even-tempered, and approachable."

Mary was a sufferer, but not a sad sufferer, and she was certainly not a confused sufferer. She was always serene. The Cross had value only because it enabled her to achieve the union with Jesus Christ that she desired more than anything on earth. She saw it as "a sweet and dear instrument in the hands of a great and good Father in making His children all that such a Father has a right to expect His chosen children to be." There was never anything morbid about her thinking, and she never got into psychological tangles by saying she was glad when things went wrong. It would be hard to say the same of Father Woods, who talked like this constantly. Mary MacKillop became aware early that it is hard to move in the spiritual life without making mistakes. This is especially true of those who are cultivating a love of the Cross. She reminded Father Woods more than once that it is not a good thing to allow others to think badly of you unjustly (so providing you with a cross) when it means that those others are unduly disturbed because of what they believe about you. True humility, she said, demands that you set their minds at rest by speaking out the truth. It is perverse to refrain from this lest you be deprived of a Cross.

Though Woods was full of reassurance, the joy of Mary's religious profession was clouded by the shadow of the family debts in Portland. "Father Woods will see that those dreadful debts are paid," she told her mother, "not yet, for he cannot, but sooner than I could by remaining in the world and earning money for that purpose alone." It is not easy to determine just how great the debts were. Whenever details are available the sums are all in two digits and the total never seems to be much over £100.[1] The debts were dreadful because they were there, not because they were enormous. Mary certainly did not think she acted unreasonably when she left for Penola in 1866 to begin the school: "At last I began to think that my obligations to my family were nearly fulfilled, that others could now take the place I had held, and that I could freely turn to God alone."

The critical state of the family budget was due to the failure of the Portland venture (itself partly due to the ill health of Maggie and Lexie) and also to the presence of Papa, whose ideals always brought danger to any enterprise involving finance. The piano money incident and his demand that Annie resign as a protest against Mr Cusack are instances. It seems also that he wasted money on cronies in the local hostelry. Mary did not think she was exaggerating when she wrote her famous sentence to Monsignor Kirby in 1873: "When I was little more than 16 years of age, the principal care of a very large family fell upon me, and from that until I was 25 I felt its burden yearly more and more." Nor could anybody seriously challenge her statement that: "(God) gave me a most keen sense of *duty*, and in the discharge of what appeared to be *my duty*."

Woods made the strangest of remarks to Flora on 8 October 1869: "Of course I did not understand much about the state of affairs in Penola after I left but I am sure that she would not have cleared off the debts by remaining there as she was only getting deeper and deeper into debt the longer she remained." Yet it was his school, and one would imagine that he would have taken more interest in how his teachers were managing to survive. He should have known that even bread and treacle cost money. Flora mentioned no names, but she could have been referring to Mary when she said "there must have been gross mismanagement when there was such a debt incurred". But what these Penola debts could have had to do with her we do not know. We can hardly imagine Woods and Mary sending her the bills for the upkeep of the young ladies teaching in their free school for the poor.

Mary was ready enough to admit that she was not a financial genius. She may have wondered whether the term could have been used of her patron St Joseph, and whether the accusation of imprudence could not have been made against St Francis of Assisi. She had not been rewarded with monetary success for nine years of sustained dedication to the interests of six younger brothers and sisters, while a thriftless father stood by helplessly. Now she was entering on the unchartered waters of teaching poor children for the love of God and not asking a penny from their parents. Was she imprudent, or was she trusting in divine providence?

These early experiences alerted Mary to the need for guidance in the path on which she was entering. Spiritual ideals can sometimes seem to clash with the demands of justice. Father Woods comforted Flora when she was in low spirits by telling her: "Don't trouble about the world. God will always take care of you and wishes you to think of Him alone. Ask him to detach you from the world." She may well have replied, "Yes, but what about the creditors? Will they appreciate my detachment?" Another consolation he offered her was: "I agree with you perfectly in thinking that you are not long for this world but that is no sad news to anyone." Again, except perhaps to the creditors! In fact Flora lived another seventeen years, and her problems were not solved by the early demise predicted by Woods. Her debts were relieved by help from two family sources: a legacy to Mary from her aunt Anne McPherson (Papa's sister), and some money that grandfather MacKillop had left to charity. Uncle Peter and others were administering this money left by John MacKillop, and when at length they decided they could with a clear conscience let Flora have some of it as charity, she wryly assured Father Woods that "they needed have no scruple regarding it".

The increase in numbers provided problems as well as opportunities for the Sisters of St Joseph. The Grote Street place was too small, so they moved to three cottages at the corner of West Terrace and Franklin Street. When these cottages were vacated for the Dominican Sisters, the Josephites spent a short period in Gouger Street and then moved to a sizable building called *Franklin Cottage* in Franklin Street, near Grey Street. The square enclosed by Grote Street, West Terrace, Franklin Street and Grey Street was to see most of the dramatic events of early Josephite history. In 1869 a "poor school" was built next to *Franklin Cottage*, consisting of two storeys, the lower one for the classrooms and the upper one for the Sisters.

Mary did not like this idea of a "poor school" for non-payers. She wanted all schools to be open to everybody, but here she had to bow to the wishes of her superiors.

By October 1867 the first country school had been opened at Yankalilla, about forty miles south of Adelaide. When Mary left for Brisbane in December 1869 seventy-two Sisters were conducting twenty-one schools around Adelaide and in country districts, as well as caring for the orphanage and similar centres of care for those in need. They practised the poverty they professed. One community, for example, had no lighting and had to eat raw cabbage because there was no fuel to make a fire to cook it.

When three nuns who had been postulants in 1869 were questioned in 1926 about Mary MacKillop, it was her kindness that emerged as their most vivid memory of her. She was thoughtful about the needs and feelings of others, gentle and humble when she had to admonish anybody, and full of respect, compassion, and love towards everybody. As well as this kindness, they spoke of her inner peace and her trust in divine providence. All three mentioned also that because of her personal love of Jesus Christ she saw to it that priests were treated with great respect and that the chapel always had pride of place in her convents. She was never known to criticise a priest, or to allow anybody else to do so. She went out of her way to help one if he was in trouble—on one occasion it was a man who had shown hostility to her in the past. As for the convent chapels, although she insisted that the rest of the house should be simple and austere—no carpets, no pretty curtains—the chapel and the altar were always adorned as nicely as resources allowed.

From the beginning of the Institute the chief arena of the Josephites' charity was the classroom, but Mary saw to it that it was not confined there. She led the way in visiting the sick and people in prison, offering help and consolation to anybody in trouble or sorrow, irrespective of religion. At first there was some embarrassment on the part of people who had never met a nun before, but when they experienced the warmth of her personality they accepted and admired her.

By mid-1868 she had undertaken the care of an orphanage, a Refuge, and a Providence. The orphanage already existed, but in mid-1868 when the girls' section was relocated in Franklin Street the Sisters were given charge of it. The Providence (so called because the nuns relied on God's providence for its support) cared for neglected children, girls in danger, and the aged poor. It began in a little cottage, expanded to a shop with residence attached, then moved to a house opposite the convent and eventually to one on West Terrace.

The Refuge was a home for women off the streets or coming out of gaol with nowhere to go. This work too had been in existence, under the care of two lay matrons, before the Josephites took it over. Support came from laundry work and the contributions of generous people. One Sister, Bernardine, who spent her life at this work was described thus:

> She had an influence over them that no one else had. Her good humour and tact in dealing with them would settle their disputes without an angry word. She spent the long space of 48 years in working for the poor stray ones of the flock of our Lord.

The number of people the Sisters were caring for increased so rapidly that they had to go out and beg in the streets, in the shops, and from door to door. They collected insults as well as food and money, and one of them said that the work was so trying "that it was only for the love of God that it could be undertaken". But it had its funny side too. One day a young Sister arrived home from an expedition with an empty sack. It appears that the bones she had begged had attracted the attention of several big dogs, and rather than be eaten herself, she explained, she had fed them her load, bone by bone.

A fourth type of institution was the Solitude, at St John's near Kapunda. It was established to take care of the aged, the incurably ill, and "respectable people given to intemperate habits". Mechtilde's *History* says these people paid fees and were "waited on by young girls, who had, in one way or another, made a false step, and wished to place themselves under the care of the Sisters". These young ladies had a little Rule of Life and were called Magdalens. The Solitude moved to Glenelg and later to Norwood before it was eventually closed in 1877.

In July 1867, at about the time Mary and Rose were moving to Adelaide, Bishop Sheil presented his report in Rome. He made no mention of the Josephites, and there was no specific reference to them in a letter he sent his diocese from Ireland praising the new system of education. But in letters to Father Woods he was very enthusiastic about the nuns. He was delighted with the way things were going, and confident that sufficient funds would be found. Although he had been disappointed in his efforts to bring Sisters of Mercy to Adelaide, he was still "determined to get a first rate teaching order for the respectable females". He managed to find a community of seven

Dominican nuns to take charge of the education of the well-to-do, thus recognizing the role which the Sisters of St Joseph saw as their own—educators of the less respectable. Since no provision had been made for the Dominican group, Mary gave them the cottages which had been the Josephite convent for more than a year and moved her own Sisters to a house in Gouger Street not far away.[2]

At a First Communion ceremony on 8 December 1868, soon after his return to Adelaide, Bishop Sheil spoke in glowing terms of the Josephites. On the 14th he visited their convent. On the 17th he went over the Rule with Woods and Mary and, after making a few minor changes, gave it his written approval. This caused them great joy, but there were outsiders who thought the expansion was too hasty, that some candidates were unsuitable, and that many were not properly prepared for the work they were called upon to do.

Almost exactly a year after Mary received the news of the death of her brother John in New Zealand, her father died in Hamilton. It is indicative of the pain and sorrow he had unwittingly inflicted on his poor wife that Mary had no qualms about remarking to Flora: "I am sure that you cannot regard Papa's death as a trial." Her letter was full of faith, compassion, and love, blending references to heaven and earth. She was always realistic, with deep emotions, but with a faith too strong to allow sentimentality. She had written the previous year: "Though I do feel for his lonely state, I hope that much good may be derived from it." Now she recalled that John and little Alick would have been awaiting him: "What comfort and joy for you in the thought that you have two children in Heaven."

At this time Father Woods hoped that the Passionist order would come to Adelaide, and that he could rejoin them. When he applied he was told he could be readmitted if he returned to England to do so. Nothing was done about a foundation in Adelaide, and there the matter rested.

At a meeting of the Council of Education on March 9 the bishop expressed his satisfaction at the high standards being achieved by the nuns. Having been generous with his praise at the Refuge the previous day, he was doing much to counteract the opposition. However, in addition to many of the clergy, there were other Catholics who were critical, and in the latter part of March such people found strange support from outsiders who had no love for the Church. A young convert from Anglicanism had been admitted to the sisterhood, and when she left soon afterwards claims were made that the nuns had tried to detain her forcibly. The newspapers took it up, and enemies of the Church seemed happy to find confirmation of their worst prejudices against popery. Shortly afterwards, on April 3, Woods was shocked to be told that there could be no more begging. He thought at first that the measure was the result of the unfavourable publicity, but when he saw the bishop he was presented with a list of complaints from the clergy against himself. Some of the priests had even threatened to leave the diocese. The ban on begging made things awkward, as the Sisters were caring for many needy people, young and old, who depended on what could be collected here and there from sympathetic people. It was in fact lifted, as Sister Mary was out begging later that year and sent other Sisters to do so.

A synod of bishops was held in Melbourne in April 1869, in preparation for the Vatican Council. Woods was there with Sheil, and said later that he had never had to work so hard in his life. Though he made a request to address the synod about his new Institute, it is not known whether he did so. But he told Mary that "all the bishops have expressed the greatest sympathy with your work". Goold in particular was very encouraging, and asked for four nuns to establish a Providence in Melbourne. James Quinn of Brisbane was also interested, but said that he was not in a position to pay any travel expenses. With Sheil's consent, Woods promised to send some Sisters who would beg their way to Brisbane, but nothing was done about it at the time.

Sheil left again for Europe on 13 October 1869 to attend the Vatican Council. It was only ten months since he had returned after an absence of nearly twenty months, and this time he would be away for a year and a half. His Vicar General, John Smyth, died in the middle of the following year and left the government of the diocese even more uncertain. On October 18, when the bishops made a stopover in Western Australia, Quinn wrote to Woods reminding him of his promise to send nuns to Queensland. Sheil added a note at the end of this letter: "See to this as soon as possible—take Sister Mary and begin the good work." As a result, preparations immediately began in Adelaide. It is not clear why the foundation had been postponed so long. Whatever the cause of the delay, Mary was not happy about it.

Decisions had to be made about who would go to Queensland, and who would be in charge in Adelaide during Mary's absence. Up till now, her place had been taken by Bernard whenever she was absent.

Woods seems to have proposed Francis Xavier as *locum tenens*, though Mary suggested instead that Clare be appointed and that Ignatius be superior of the main convent. On his return from Sevenhill at the end of November he announced that Clare was to go with Mary and the others. Meanwhile there would be no Guardian in Adelaide, but Ignatius would be in charge of the main house. The proposal that Angela be one of the Brisbane group was countered by the surprising information that Sheil had forbidden the transfer of Ignatius and Angela outside his diocese until he returned from Rome. On 8 December 1869 Mary and Clare made perpetual vows, and then with Teresa, Francis de Sales, and Augustine, they set out on the first leg of their long journey, taking with them a young woman, Mary Joseph, who was to cause much anxiety during the course of the next twelve months.

Reflecting on this period thirty years later, Mary had very positive and sympathetic things to say about the founder. They could easily have been overlooked after the intervening years of turbulence in his relationship with the Institute, but she did not forget them. Recalling in her *Life* of Woods that he founded an Institute of Brothers as well as the Sisters, she made it clear in her own gentle way that he was overworked, and that he was burdened with much trouble, care and anxiety. The forces around him were gathering the strength that was to burst on the Institute like a tornado. She saw him as too innocent, too much of the dove and too little of the serpent, too slow to think evil and to recognise the presence of hypocrites and impostors.

This was very gracious language as far as Woods was concerned, but in defending him she used some strong words about others. Who were the hypocrites with a fair appearance of piety? Who were the impostors who took advantage of his charity? The events had such an impact on the Institute and on her personally that she could hardly have forgotten any detail. No names are mentioned, but it was common knowledge that there were Sisters who had set out to deceive the founder and had succeeded beyond what could have seemed possible. Everybody knew who they were—Angela and Ignatius. Angela's later confession to systematic deception made it clear that hypocrite and impostor were exactly the right words.[3]

It is not clear when it all began. Letters between Woods and Mary in 1868 and 1869 are not plentiful, as they were both living in Adelaide. Thus from about mid-May to mid-October 1869 we have none of his letters, and there are over the longer period (1868–69) less of Mary's preserved than of his. But by May it is already evident that Ignatius and Angela have laid claim to a special place in his thinking. It is possible that there was some poltergeist-type activity in Adelaide, like that which occurred later in Brisbane, but there was so much deliberate staging of phenomena that it would be impossible to be sure. What can only be called gullibility is revealed in what Woods was writing about their visions and preternatural experiences.[4] From October onwards and through 1870 it is only too obvious that he was grossly deceived.

Simply reading the letters gives one a feeling that things are not right. There is a lot of talk about feelings, strange thoughts, temptations, graces, crosses, but few specific references. Whenever Mary suggested that all was not well she was told that she was "under temptation", a state permitted by God to purify her soul and make her humble, and that was that. She did her best, and even adopted the temptation language to describe what was occurring in her mind, but it would still not go away: "My temptations are only hushed, or deadened, for they are not quite dead." By January 1869 Woods had developed the habit of expressing a deep conviction about his own misspent life, frivolity, conceit, overbearing pride, intense self-love, abysmal misery, radical wickedness, and total unworthiness to be directing the Sisters. At the same time he had become firmly convinced that his Institute was under the special protection of the Blessed Virgin. "She will never suffer me to let it go wrong," he wrote, and "she would not allow such mistakes to happen either to you or to me." He assured Mary that she therefore had no grounds for anxiety. But he more than once told her that he was upset at the high opinion she had of him. He need not have worried, as she reassured him with a startlingly frank revelation in November 1869: "Oh, if I could dare to tell you the thoughts that sometimes come into my mind, you would soon be undeceived."

He relied on the Virgin Mary, with a total distrust of human means. His rejection of "human motives and principles of action" in fact meant that he had no use for traditional Christian wisdom or for ordinary prudence. He was unworthy and unsuited, but he was the chosen one with the special protection of heaven. Sister Mary did not wish to deny that the Blessed Mother was looking after Father Woods, but she had reservations about the effect of this on his guidance of the Institute: "I could not always feel sure that everything was done by you which might be. I really do believe that there are some things done which we should not do." But attempts to get him to change his tack were fruitless. He was unworthy, he always insisted, but the Josephites needed him. He spoke of the time when he would be separated from them, presumably when God had found somebody safe to take his place. His distrust of the Jesuits was explicit, and he later regarded Mary's reliance on them as a further sign of her loss of the Josephite spirit.

The letters between the two over the last weeks before she departed for Brisbane might lead one to exclaim in desperation: "What on earth are they talking about?" When it is known that the founder was controlling the Institute on the principles that have just been described, Mary's dilemma becomes clear. She was torn between respect for one to whom she owed obedience and before whom she felt her thoughts should be an open book, and on the other hand the nagging thought that his methods were doing harm to the Institute. She told him this as openly as she could, but he retained the view that she was suffering a temptation, as though it were indigestion or a headache. What she had to say was never taken seriously—it was to be put out of mind as coming from the enemy of human salvation.

There cannot be much doubt about the general picture. However, it is more difficult to disentangle Mary's thoughts about Angela and Ignatius personally. These Sisters were not the whole problem, but they were at the centre of it. It has been said that she distrusted them as fakes almost from the start, and that Woods sent her to Brisbane to get her out of the way. But the documents do not support this. For a start, it was Bishop Sheil who specified her as one of the Queensland pioneers, and besides, her letters of this period show a high regard for Ignatius and Angela. She suggests that during her absence Ignatius be put in charge of Franklin Street, and adds some personal praise. About Angela there is nothing but good in her letters. The problem is partly solved if it is remembered that she had to make a choice. Either she obeyed her director and tried to see her doubts as temptations, or the whole structure of authority and obedience in the Institute could collapse for her. She could not willingly regard Angela and Ignatius with suspicion if she were bound not to allow her uneasy thoughts about them to become convictions. So she may have felt obliged to go out of her way to concentrate on the positive qualities of these Sisters.

Two things she wrote late in 1869 pinpoint the cause of her anxiety, although no names were mentioned. She did not really have any sure way of testing the visions, but she did have a sure test of a Sister's faithfulness to her calling: "If the spirit that leads them is purely of God, it will never prevent them discharging their duties, and when they do fail, the fault will be their own." Then, along with the good qualities of Ignatius, she mentioned "her peculiar kind of life which renders her, in so many ways, unfit for the duties of the Schools", a surprising thing to have to say of a member of a teaching order. She thought that the priest at Port Adelaide had a valid point when he complained of nuns who found active duties distasteful and irksome. She even referred to the danger of "listless apathy".

Mary's concern was about a far more important question than making a judgment on the two visionaries. They could well have been impostors, but she might not have lost too much sleep over that. But what was at stake was the fate of the Institute if their style of thinking became the normal state of mind of the nuns. Woods had once referred to "S.Ignatius, whom God has so specially called to inactivity that she might suffer for others." This would not have seemed to Mary a likely call for a Sister of St Joseph in good health and the prime of life. It is not likely, either, that she was very impressed when Woods told her (speaking of the reaction of Ignatius to the ban on begging): "I never saw her so radiant with joy as she was when the news came." A more realistic Josephite reaction would have been to accept the setback but to be more concerned about how to feed hungry people in the Refuge and the Providence that night and the next day.

Though not a central figure, Sister Rose was thrown right off balance by what was going on. Mary suggested that exact observance and fidelity in the classroom were the antidotes to the exotic spiritual ambitions she was cultivating. The situation was complicated by the fact that at this time Woods was planning another institute, the Dolorist Sisters. The Josephites knew about it, because he was on the lookout among them for likely candidates for his new venture. It was affecting their thinking and confused them. They were also being disturbed by his habit of prophesying the future.[5] Mary took it up with him: "If not a positive fault it at least seems a dangerous and insidious imperfection."

She had something real to worry about—a threat to the Institute, not in Ignatius and Angela, but in the founder himself. She was by no means happy with her own spiritual performance, nor with the way she was doing her job as Guardian, but God's love kept her going: "There are times when the thought of God's immense love and patient mercy come before me with a force that I cannot describe." Some months later she made the comment: "Well, the angels must wonder at it all."

Footnotes

[1] Some idea of the value of money may be gathered from the fact that Bishop Sheil was given an offering of £250 when he visited Penola for the First Communion day in 1868.

[2] A similar concern was shown by Mother Mary when the Sisters of Mercy came to Adelaide. "There is room and work enough for all," she said, "and I can now help some poorer country places."

[3] George O'Neill S.J., writing a quarter of a century after Mother Mary wrote the *Life*, thought it discreet to use the pseudonyms Abra and Isaura for these two Sisters. Known in Sydney as Mrs Gertrude Abbott, Ignatius lived for several years after O'Neill's books were published. She was more of a psychological puzzle than Angela. Mechtilde held the view that she seemed to have had experiences of some kind or other, and that Angela was imitating her.

[4] One sample from January 1869 should suffice: "Sister Angela has been visited again in a very trying manner. Sister Clare heard her moaning last night and found a great log of wood lying across her neck and it was an hour before they could restore her to consciousness. I saw the log of wood and didn't know whence the devil could have brought it. There were two this time, one like a serpent and another like an ape. Sister Ignatius saw one but he was like a cat. He fled away from holy water but stood in the doorway gibing Sister A., abusing me and S. Ignatius and spitting at Sister Clare."

[5] A good sample of his prophesying is to be found in a letter of 12 March 1870, when he issued a list of the precise dates of the deaths of Teresa, himself, Mary, Ignatius, and Angela. Mary he gave as 8 September 1891 (it was 8 August 1909), and Ignatius as 16 January 1898 (it was 12 May 1934).

EIGHT

BRISBANE
NIGHTMARE

A Thorny Mission 1870–1871

Mary's year in Queensland, 1870, was a troubled time. Her letters not only tell the story of the trials and achievements of the Institute, but give a remarkable insight into her personal spiritual growth during that year.

As she and her five companions passed through Melbourne they lodged with the Good Shepherd Sisters, who assured them that Josephites would always be welcome. Other nuns were also kind, but with a certain reserve. But at least one Melburnian was overjoyed at the visit. Mary's old teacher Miss Kane ("a wreck of what she was") cried tears of joy to know she had not been forgotten.

Mary got the impression that many of her Catholic relations and acquaintances in Melbourne were ashamed of being thought religious. It was her Protestant friends who brought a ray of sunshine, her former employer Mrs MacDougall busying herself "to collect for the Poor School from amongst her friends". On the whole, however, her native city was a disappointment: "I heard so much that was distressing in Melbourne—my heart seemed almost wrung at times. Poor Mamma thinks me unfeeling and many reproaches from old friends have been made." Yet throughout it all she felt a powerful sense of the presence of God. She left with "many a bitter pain" and yet with a mysterious inner peace: "I have never felt more calmly in sorrow than I did this week."

They collected money privately for their fares, being forbidden to beg publicly, and set sail. In Sydney they divided. Some stayed with the Good Samaritans; the others went to the home of Mrs Eliza Lee Cameron, whose children Mary had tutored at Portland. Mary wrote to her mother about one of her former charges: "Sarah could not be nicer than she is." At Hunters Hill the Marist Fathers from the Pacific missions were very heartening in their praise of the Institute, and planted in Mary's mind the idea of a Sydney novitiate. The meeting with the Benedictine Sisters at Subiaco was indirectly the beginning of a precious contact for Father Woods, providing him with a haven of peace when he needed it in the years to come. Mary was very impressed by these nuns, and was much encouraged by the lady in charge: "I felt so humbled when I heard so holy and dignified a Religious speak as she did to us, that I could not help reminding her of the immense distance between us."

Mary was always sensitive to the kindness of nuns with whom she stayed, and was quick to praise their spirit. But in the case of these Benedictines it was more than their friendliness that she remembered. In the light of their own experience, they thought it well to speak to her of her title, Mary of the Cross, and to warn her that the way of God's service is never smooth: "In proportion to the greatness of the work to which God has called us, so would he send trials and heavy afflictions to prove it." Mary relayed it to Flora: "My title, the happy one given to me at my Profession, implies a life of Crosses and afflictions."

A postulant joined them in Sydney, and having begged their fares the seven set off for Brisbane on December 28. Arriving on the last day of 1869, they were taken by Dr Cani, the Vicar General, to the convent of the Sisters of Mercy, *All Hallows*. After three weeks they moved to a "nice little house" in South Brisbane and set to work teaching. Later they moved into an old disused hotel. With Mary there was Clare, Augustine, Francis de Sales, Teresa (a novice), Gertrude (the postulant), and the strange girl Mary Joseph. They were soon to be joined by Joseph and the Carolan sisters, Josephine and Collette.

The enormous diocese of Brisbane—it embraced the whole of Queensland—had been established under Bishop James Quinn in 1859. His style is reflected in the large volume of correspondence in the Roman archives involving priests, nuns and laity who disagreed with him. Some of his letters contain accusations about unauthorised departures, while many of theirs are filled with countercomplaints about the intolerable conditions of life in the diocese. The bishop was absent during the whole of Mary's time in Queensland in 1870–71, but the Vicar General obviously had instructions about how to deal with her. The nuns were allowed little contact with other clergy, and they did not receive much encouragement from Cani. He appointed himself their confessor, excluding all others. Yet he rarely gave them an opportunity for that sacrament or even for Mass, and never provided the devotional ceremony of Benediction or a spiritual instruction. Mary's letters to Woods speak of his reserve: "He seems to take no interest in us in any way, has never asked me a question about our meditation or choir duties, and has not once been in any of our schools, excepting once." His absence—"humiliating neglect"—caused unhappiness, and his presence brought little consolation.

The situation was too extreme to be ignored, yet Mary saw in it the hand of God, and urged her Sisters to think of it that way. "Dr Cani is so good," she wrote, "but he is not the director to help our poor sisters much, but then he is the one God has given us and that is everything." Apropos of his habit of silencing her when she tried to explain anything to him, she said, "If I were a Saint or even a little humble I would *at once believe* that he is right, but I am neither. It would be hypocrisy to say I do, but from my heart I wish I could." There was more to it than a lack of helpfulness. There was an extra element—the person she looked to for guidance and encouragement was the very one repulsing her.

She spoke very delicately of her anguish: "Sometimes he has puzzled me. I was once tempted not to believe something he told me, and that thought gave me pain; but it passed away, and I only looked at his intention which I knew to be good." She tried to excuse everything, which she was able to do with the help of faith, but she could not deny that the situation was difficult. Cani often neglected to answer questions, even if submitted in writing. He caused delays by avoiding the Sisters for weeks at a time. The Rule was given little consideration. No authority within the Institute was recognised—the bishop's authority, exercised by the Vicar General, controlled everything.

The seeds of the crisis that developed on the bishop's return were thus present from the beginning in Brisbane. If Cani were not acting under instructions from Quinn, his behaviour would be quite incomprehensible. Mary once said she thought he was afraid of the bishop, finding this the only way to explain what was going on. Certainly Cani's later kindness to her nuns when he was a free agent as Bishop of Rockhampton revealed a different man altogether. But in 1870 he was far from cooperative.[1]

The principal subject of contention was the Government grant for education. At that time, the grant went to Catholic as well as Anglican schools, but there were conditions entailed: standard curricula and textbooks, and restrictions on religious instruction. It was the policy of the Brisbane diocese to accept the grants and the limitations that went with them.[2] The Josephites were told that they were to accept the money and would have to function under the General Board of Education, like the Catholic schools already operating in Queensland.

Mary refused. The Josephite Rule did not allow the grant, and Mary was deeply convinced of the principles on which this refusal was based. Woods wrote in support of the stand she was taking, but she was not the one who needed persuading. It was part of the Rule she had vowed to live by, and she was not prepared to ignore it because of pressure. When Cani, expecting that she would accept the grant, found she would not, he became quite exasperated and accused her of being self-willed and obstinate in holding out against learned and enlightened superiors. When Woods told her to tell Cani that the bishop had promised that the Rule should not be interfered with, she replied: "I told him that I could not understand how the bishop in his conversation with you in Melbourne had not clearly seen the spirit of our Institute in this matter. As soon as I said that, Dr Cani did not insist so much." Her view was that both he and the bishop knew about it but hoped she would not have the courage to oppose them when they ignored it.

In her letter to the Sisters on the topic she insisted that they were to rely on God for the necessary means to do this work, whereas the world trusts in false maxims and human means. She would not allow the world, for all its friendly talk, to control the handing on of the Catholic tradition. Making a distinction between the respect the nuns should have for those who opposed them, and their own right not to conform when duty forbad it, she warned that clinging to duty could possibly have unpleasant consequences. They could be told to leave Queensland and not be provided with means to do so.

In the meantime Cani had orders to follow. Why, he asked, should these nuns not follow the wise decision of the bishop rather than selfishly cling to their own Rule which came from a simple priest and had no validity outside Adelaide? When he heard that the Board might shortly accept no further registrations, he asked Mary again to submit in deference to the bishop. She stood firm, writing "with indescribable pain" on March 27:

My position as Guardian of our Holy Rule enforces this and in the presence of God I must say what the voice of conscience and duty dictate. It *is impossible* for us to become in any way connected with Government and be true to the spirit as well as the letter of our Rule.
For the time being the matter seems to have been dropped, perhaps because it was too late to do anything about it.

She took the matter very seriously indeed. She was protecting the freedom of the Sisters to be faithful to a principle they had vowed to live by, and at the same time she was witnessing to the value of her faith. She refused to be casual about the word of God; she considered it a disaster to be allowed to live as if that word had never been uttered, or to regard it as just one of the interesting things that might be studied.

Cani considered her letter rather offensive, and said he would have to send it to the bishop. What the bishop thought of it we do not know, but on his return he tried for a long time to bully the nuns into conforming. It became an open contest about authority, which was implicitly what it was from the start. Was there to be recognition of any independent authority residing in the Institute, or, in spite of the Rule, was the bishop to be the ultimate authority for everything, even the content of the vows?

In spite of Cani's lack of enthusiasm for their principles, the Josephites were conducting three schools in Brisbane within three months of their arrival. It is well to bear this daily toil in mind when reading of the history of the time. The more spectacular problems, the tensions, and the conflicts tend to be in the news, whereas the daily toil of the nuns can be forgotten. Mary's letters certainly deal with problems, but they also contain much about the individual Sisters and their dedication. As well as being responsible for the whole mission, she herself taught in the schools and helped in the house with the rest. She gave instructions to the First Communion children, and washed their feet in imitation of Christ washing the feet of his disciples—a scene that left a lasting impression on those who saw it. The Sisters were forbidden to beg, so they had to rely on alms. They lived very simply and suffered real need. Cani did, however, organise collections for their support later in the year, and he sent them some money himself from time to time.

Repeated requests for permission to establish a Refuge for needy people were ignored, but the nuns did their best to help the stream of women and children who came to the door of their poor convent. In some cases they painfully sought to gather the money necessary for steamship tickets, and sent the people on to Melbourne or Adelaide. The priest in Gympie, ninety miles to the north, asked them to open a school there, but Cani refused his approval. By July, however, they had opened one in Maryborough, forty-five miles further north, following a suggestion of Cani himself. But he would not allow Mary to travel up with the Sisters to see them settled.

The Josephites became well known around Brisbane for their schools and their work with the needy, and for encouraging people to go to the public devotions each night in May. This popularity was all very good, but it had its drawbacks. Before long they had 300 pupils in their three Brisbane schools, many children living near them having transferred from the Sisters of Mercy. These Sisters pointed out that the bishop would be upset if they lost the Government grant because of diminished numbers. Mary handled the situation by expressing admiration for the spirit of the Sisters of Mercy, and leading the Sisters of St Joseph in visiting the families involved to persuade them that the children should return to the Mercy school. By October the Mercies were directing vocations to the Josephites.

The reception of these candidates meant that the Josephites could expand their work, but Cani's control over admissions made things difficult. He allowed the postulant from Sydney to receive the habit, but would not do the same for candidates from Queensland. The two Carolans wondered if they were ever going to receive the habit. Mary insisted that delay was contrary to the Rule, but it made no difference. Three were sent to Adelaide, deemed suitable by the Sisters but not by Dr Cani.

Mary saw the contradictions in the situation. She asked Woods what she should do if she felt it her duty to visit Maryborough, and if Cani refused to approve the journey as he had when the group first went there. She warned that the Rule would be much interfered with in Queensland, and asked him to give every possible help to the one who would be in charge after she had left. She said it was impossible to express the difficulties of the place—yet this was long before the bishop came back! She had no doubt there would be more trouble when he did. The forestalling of such trouble was one of the reasons she went to Rome. She thought that if the Rule had Roman status it would be respected, but James Quinn and his brother Matthew were to teach her to widen her expectation of what is possible in this world.

No Paraclete in Adelaide

Mary kept hoping that Woods would come and confront Cani. But events in Adelaide made this impossible. Besides, he said the bishop had forbidden him to go to Brisbane until further notice. It looks as if Quinn was constraining Sheil in Rome.

The story of 1870 in Adelaide is that of the tide going out for Woods. His confidence that God was with him made it impossible for him to read the signs around him or to hearken to the warnings from Brisbane. He was interpreting disaster as victory, and what proved to be studied deception on the part of two nuns, he saw as the fruit of special divine favour. He was getting deeper into debt, he had been overworking for three years, and it was becoming evident that his health, mental as well as physical, was seriously affected. He narrated the most bizarre experiences, conversations with the Blessed Virgin, Satanic visitations.[3] He repeated what had been revealed to him about the fate of the departed (because these included priests, the news did not enhance his popularity with the clergy), and he kept up a stream of predictions about the future and the destinies of those around him.

Early in the year he made a begging tour of his old mission territory around Penola. But the season had been a bad one, money was very tight, and instead of being able to contribute towards helping others, more and more people were themselves asking for help. So in spite of his appeal the debts grew. Yet in April, without money and without permission, he announced additions to the convent, since not to do so would have been a lack of trust in God. The priests regarded him as a deluded fanatic. Many of his prophecies and visions had become public knowledge, provoking derision among his colleagues.

In April two events occurred which had serious consequences for the Josephites. The first was at Kapunda. The Sisters had evidence that one of the priests there, Father Keating, was guilty of scandalous conduct and they informed Father Woods. He in turn called in Father Smyth, the Vicar General, and as a result Keating was sent away. This turned his fellow Franciscan, Charles Horan, into a mortal enemy of Woods and of the Sisters.

The second event took place in the Franklin Street convent. On April 11, the Monday of Holy Week, the sacramental hosts disappeared from the tabernacle in the chapel. At first Woods suspected Keating, who had just been recalled to the cathedral. But when bloodstains appeared on the altar cloth the following day, he was convinced that the events were miraculous. He also attributed a sudden outbreak of fires in the convent to the devil. The clergy was convinced that the nuns themselves were responsible for everything, and raised doubts about the accusations against Keating as well. Smyth said he would have to write to Rome on the matter, hinting at the possible dissolution of the Institute. But Woods maintained that Christ had withdrawn himself, and foretold that the glorious return of the Sacrament would prove him right. The board of enquiry called the whole thing nonsense and fanaticism, attributing it to Sister Angela.

Angela eventually confirmed this verdict by a public confession that the whole series of episodes was a deliberate fraud. But Woods saw it as a sign of divine favour, an attitude he maintained even in the face of Angela's admission of deceit. Mary wrote of Angela and Ignatius to Monsigner Kirby in 1875: "All that I used to think or say about them was treated as a temptation by our poor Father, and even now that she confesses everything and that we have so many proofs she is sincere, he will *not believe*." There is scarcely a letter of Woods in 1870 which does not mention these Sisters, always fulsomely— "two such saints would sanctify any community".

On June 2, after some saccharine remarks about Angela, he told Mary: "I don't think it would pain her if she knew your temptations about her except on your account." This refers to the fact that from Brisbane Mary suspected that there was something false about the whole Adelaide scene. In this she was fully justified, as Angela's confession proved. But Woods' enthusiasm matched his lack of judgment. The sentimental nonsense he wrote is embarrassing to read.[4]

He relayed the messages of the visionaries with joy. Thus, on the death of a young Sister: "Two persons worthy of credit say her soul went to heaven, and one saw her bless all the religious as she went." His sending of Angela to Queensland for a few weeks was in his mind the greatest favour he could do the Sisters there: "I have never met a more obedient religious. Even the powers of nature seem to feel this. You must not be concerned about Angela." But towards the end of the year when pressures were mounting against him from every side, he wrote that Ignatius and Angela were not much help.

These two seem at times to have been in collusion, at other times in competition. Their groans and sufferings are graphically described by Woods, who had become an easy prey to their schemes. Both are declared to have the stigmata. Beds are set on fire, there are other conflagrations in the convent, blows are struck on head and shoulder, sleep is interrupted by boiling grease causing scalds, the bell of the Wesleyan chapel is broken in answer to the prayer of Ignatius—the list could go on.

Woods' own strange experiences, though often distressful, delighted him no less. He told Mary once: "I have been suffering a great deal lately but about things you will not feel much compassion for." She had made it clear that she was not happy about what was going on in Adelaide: "My want of faith in some things you tell me is a bitter cross to me, but ah, my Father, I do not wonder at the weakness of my faith." At other times she expressed her fears in terms of traditional Catholic thinking.

She was always respectful in the way she said things, but she said them: if he looked more to the guidance to be found in the wisdom of the Church he would be "more prudent and more simply distrustful in some things". But wisdom fell on deaf ears. His stock response was that she was under temptation. Yet as he could observe Rose becoming "more fanciful, extravagant, and imaginative" he had to admit that she was "simply mad". This may have been the closest he ever came to admitting the need for prudence, but he put the idea out of his head as a temptation.

Woods was becoming more and more isolated. One priest told him plainly that he was being led by a spirit other than the Spirit of God, and that he was being imposed on. Rose's fate was hardly calculated to pacify Horan and the rest of them, or to allay their suspicions about the Institute. The strength of the opposition was evident when they applied for the Government grant for the Hectorville school without consulting the Director of Education. The Vicar General, however, loyally held to the bishop's policy.

As support from the clergy lapsed, the debts grew. It was a bad season on the land, so there were many extra calls on charity as well as the normal demands from all sides. But in June Woods announced that he had a heavenly assurance that he would never want for money, and prepared to go further into debt by building additions to the convent.

Then Father Smyth died unexpectedly and left Woods without any support at all. From Sydney Polding put Patrick Russell in charge until the absent bishop could make other arrangements. Russell was close to the Dominicans, and not at all friendly to the Josephites. He did not object when within a month the priests held a meeting at which they voted to accept the grant.

The enquiry scheduled by Smyth into the disappearance of the sacramental hosts was belatedly begun by Russell in August. The report he sent to Rome indicated that Angela was responsible for the outrage, and traced it all to indiscreet selection of novices for the sisterhood. The nuns were openly insulted by some of the clergy, and at times were refused the sacraments for weeks on end. Woods was hopefully awaiting the one person who could take things in hand, Bishop Sheil. The bishop's letters early in 1870 were full of enthusiasm for the Sisters and did not betray any anxiety about debts. A petulant message to his Vicar General, however, revealed signs of the ill health and lack of balance that were to be evident on his return. When he did eventually arrive in February 1871, he seemed to know nothing about the serious dissensions that plagued his diocese.

Thus the key to the drama of 1871 in Adelaide was the year 1870, the year of Sister Mary's absence in Brisbane. The fact that the bishop was also absent made the year a crucial one for the Institute, for he alone, perhaps, could have eased the tension. The roots of the trouble were:

— the preoccupation of Father Woods and some Sisters with preternatural phenomena, visions, inspirations, prophecies, miracles, and diabolical visitations;
— the growth of substantial debts because of the works of the Institute and of the diocese;
— the alienation of some of the clergy from Father Woods and the Sisters;
— the implacable opposition of Father Charles Horan.

Sister Mary's Reactions in Brisbane

Even before leaving Adelaide, Mary had expressed concern at the nuns' interest in visions and such matters. From faraway Brisbane she felt helpless as the situation deteriorated, and thought that if Woods came up as planned she should first return to Adelaide. But he told her that he and Ignatius had decided that it was not God's will that she should return at that time. Moreover, he deemed it best not to pass on to the Sisters a circular she had written in her concern about dissension in the convent in Adelaide.

Anybody reading her letters can see that she was quite outspoken with Woods on the need to be prudent about the alleged wonders. She even blamed herself at times for not speaking out more insistently. However, she did it so politely that he always missed the point. Or perhaps nothing on earth would have made him pause. With regard to his advice to the nuns, he was confident that "to make me, the representative of God in their regard, also a dupe to lead them astray would be what our sweet loving Mother *could not* do or see done".

Mary remonstrated that while she did not doubt the Blessed Virgin's love, she thought that "slight mistakes had been made"; and she suggested: "Whilst I think your way of acting or thinking in many things is good, I keep thinking that there is yet a more perfect way." She was hoping that if he set more value on sound spiritual traditions, he might be able to avoid the "slight mistakes".

But his reaction was always the same: she was clearly wanting in confidence in the Almighty and in the Virgin Mary, who could not possibly allow Father Woods to go astray. Any doubt about his style was considered a temptation, so the more she returned to the topic ("If I speak the plain truth I must say that I believe something to be wrong") the more evident it was to him that she was under temptation. She was in a no-win situation. He took no account of her authority as Guardian, and it never seemed to occur to him that she had a duty to be concerned about what was happening to the nuns. Sealing off his mind from any possibility of self-doubt—"God always spares me the pain of doubt"—he urged her to do the same.

It looks as if by December Ignatius had guessed that Mary was on the track of the deception being practised by Angela and herself.[5] Mary in fact suspected, correctly, that Ignatius was reading her letters to Woods and then narrating to him (as if from the Blessed Virgin) the "temptations" she was undergoing in Brisbane. In any case, Ignatius was anxious that Mary should not allow her mind to be occupied by thoughts about what had been happening in Adelaide. Even if the visionaries' activities were delusions, she said, there was much to be grateful for, because they were the means of giving God great glory! The Sister Guardian should not think about the subject, for that would be doing the devil's work.

The ranks in Adelaide were evidently closed, and from her distant station Mary could do little about it. Even her reference to Woods' farcical prophecy of Father Roach's death by accident may have been aimed at getting him to admit a mistake. The closest he came to this was to say that he sometimes did not rightly interpret God's revelations. Thus when Roach was still hale and hearty after the deadline, he granted that he had got the date wrong, but the prophecy still stood. The list of failed prophecies is long: Peter MacKillop would become a priest and a bishop—he died as a young layman of twenty; Lexie would not persevere in the Good Shepherd Sisters—she died as a nun with a reputation for holiness; "the time will come when the Dolorist Fathers will be the principal directors of the Sisters and will watch over their Institute"—the Dolorist Fathers not only did not direct the Josephites, they never came into existence; "Dr Quinn would not be long Bishop of Brisbane and will never interfere much with you"—he lived long enough to be a terrible thorn in the side of the Institute for ten years. In spite of the most obvious failure Woods would became his usual confident self a few days later.

However, it was not the prophecies that worried Mary so much, nor even Woods' ordinary imprudence. What disturbed her was the weird and bizarre behaviour he encouraged as the norm for all who aspired to sanctity—as though it were directly inspired by the Holy Spirit. Worse still, he was acting in accordance with maxims and directives issued by the Blessed Virgin and relayed to him by Angela and Ignatius. When Mary suggested that he consult his own director about this chain of command, he dismissed the idea out of hand: "To think for one moment of letting another guide the Institute would be betraying my trust."

In reply to Mary's reminder that prudence was one of the cardinal virtues, he said, "Prudent I will never be." This was not just a prediction, it was a declaration of policy. Oblivious of the harm he was doing, he remarked that it was a wonder to him that he had done so little harm. He was not likely to be impressed by Mary's request: "I hope I am wrong in these strange thoughts, but I must ask you to enquire into them." Nor was he going to be affected by a reminder that his "sweet Mother" has a Son, this Son has a Church, and this Church has advice to offer about handling the dangers of the spiritual life. Mary asked him if he was sure he had sufficiently consulted "those works provided by the care of the Church to guard her servants in the dangerous paths of a highly spiritual life". He insisted it was she who had the problem. As he would be unhappy to hear she had a headache, so he was unhappy that she was suffering these doubts. But apart from this, she should be reassured that it was not causing him any suffering to hear about it. Her heart was in the right place and

Flora MacDonald MacKillop, Mary's mother.

Unless otherwise indicated, all the photographs
are from the Archives of the Sisters of
St. Joseph, and used with
their kind permission.

Alexander MacKillop, Mary's father.

*Probable site of the MacKillop family home in the late 1850's,
Richmond, Victoria.*

Mary's mother, Flora, and brother Peter, the youngest MacKillop.

*Margaret (Maggie) MacKillop, second oldest of the MacKillop children,
just sixteen months younger than Mary.*

Anne Catherine (Annie) MacKillop, the third daughter and only one to survive Mary.

Alexandrina (Lexie) MacKillop, the youngest daughter, who died at age thirty-two, as a Sister of the Good Shepherd.

Donald MacKillop, a priest of the Society of Jesus and the only brother to survive Mary.

what was in her mind was irrelevant to him.

The most vivid instance of Mary's dilemma was the case of Mary Joseph. This strange young woman had been rescued from a relative of dubious habits and was looked after by the nuns in Adelaide. One of Woods' inspirations told him she would be a wonderful saint, and he sent her to Queensland with Mary. When the bad reports started to come in, he sent up reassuring prophecies that she would die young and would perform miracles both before and after death. In fact she was a tremendous scourge. She was foul-mouthed, violent, malicious, cunning, and at times quite mad. She could be dangerous and unmanageable, so someone had to stay with her the whole time.

Mary was faced with two facts: Mary Joseph was insane, and Father Director, declaring that this mad girl was destined to be a great saint, had issued orders that she be retained in the Brisbane community. In June she pleaded: "I am sure that you can plainly see that I think her quite insane and that I long for her to be removed from here, and in this, I but faintly echo the wishes of all the Sisters." Cani was much too hard-headed to be of much help. Mary said of him: "There is no use in my speaking to my Confessor here about it, for he will say that her madness is too evident to be doubted." He was not at all open to the idea that the girl was an instrument in God's hands to do much good by exercising the nuns in virtue. At one point Mary Joseph seemed more normal, but the change was short-lived, and Mary had to beg Woods' permission to take her away to Adelaide with her as she had promised the others.

There is hardly a letter of Mary's during this year that does not mention Mary Joseph's excesses. Yet Woods from the other side of the continent continued to insist that the girl was a saint in the making. At first he forbad Mary to call in any assistance. But as the months went by he allowed her to do so, adding a rebuke: "I fear (a little, just a little) that sometimes you look too humanly at things and people and their motives and conduct." Yet he was admitting that Rose, close at hand in Adelaide, was quite mad.

The Mary Joseph episode was a severe trial of Mary's loyalty to Woods, typical of what was happening generally. Accepting his authority, she wanted her obedience to be complete and internal as well as external. But she had to admit: "I am so sorry when I am unable to see everything as you do—that is, when my mind is tempted against the implicit confidence which I ought to have in the slightest thing you, as my spiritual Father, tell me." She could hardly accept that he was deluded, yet she could not share his views, much as she wished she could. Her growing spiritual maturity, evident in these 1870 letters, is something she seems to have been aware of herself:

> It seems to me now that our good God gave me great graces for the position to which He called me . . . There is some strange, almost wonderful change in me for which I cannot account.

Yet it was a most distressing situation for her. There was a tension between her duty to correct others with regard to obedience and her doubts about her own superior. This led her to wish she were no longer the Sister Guardian.

As "the exponent of the will of God", Woods did not seem to envisage the possibility that God, who had chosen him to establish the Institute, might also want him to listen to advice from others or hearken to the wisdom of the Church. The intervention of others he explicitly excluded and the directives of the Church never seemed to influence him at any period in his priestly life. Appeals to prudence appeared as a temptation to presumptuous self-reliance, to be set aside in favour of the folly of total confidence in the goodness of a God who can never fail those who trust him. He could not see the dangers of allowing himself to be led "by the spirit" before first ascertaining that the spirit was from God.

In spite of all this, towards the end of 1870, he wrote Mary some words that are among the finest he ever penned. It is doubtful if he knew just how true they were:

> God designs all this especially to teach you the Will of God, the Will of God. No one seems to me to be brought so near to the perfect knowledge and submission to the Will of God as you are. God wants you to glorify that Will in a way that is seldom given to creatures to do.

In some of her Brisbane letters Mary mentioned peculiar happenings in the convent, like those attributed to poltergeists. It is clear that something strange went on, but she treated it all in a matter-of-fact way, attaching little significance to it. When the Sisters had some terrifying experiences of noises like thunder and violent shaking, she wrote: "The noises, screams and pattering of bare feet was something dreadful to those who heard them. As for me, I did not hear either the pattering or scream but I did the rest." The disturbing spirit seemed to appear to a young lad in the form of a savage dog, then to cause noises and screams at night, and some days later to appear in the form of Mary herself. It has been suggested that the old hotel which had become their convent had a reputation as a haunted house, and that this was the reason why it had been so long unoccupied before the Sisters came.

In early June 1870 Mary broke a long silence to write to her mother. She had prepared her for the silence in September 1869, revealing a blend of natural affection and readiness to sacrifice all to God. In May, realising that she had written to various people her mother knew, she feared that when her mother heard this she would be terribly offended. So she wrote her a letter full of affectionate gratitude:

> Often, indeed I was tempted to think that no one ever had a mother like I had. And when I would tell my Sisters who had been my teacher, they would turn with joy to give thanks to God for His goodness to me and them.

As the year 1870 drew to a close, the time was approaching for Mary to return to Adelaide. The Sisters in Maryborough were overworked, but Cani had made the admission of new candidates practically impossible. Only after protracted delays did he consent to two postulants receiving the habit. December was a busy time for the nuns, with the final examinations, the closure of the school year, a flood in Maryborough, and the need to collect money for the journey. They had to borrow five pounds from the landlord to make up the fares, and when Dr Cani heard of this he promised to settle it.

The travellers arrived in Melbourne for St Joseph's day, March 19. The main group proceeded to Adelaide, while Mary went through Portland and Penola. Father Woods told her: "I believe you will come into a nest of crosses." His words could be said to be a rare example of under-prophesying.

Footnotes

[1] "A semi-lunatic and an unmitigated tyrant", was how Father Andrew Horan, a nephew of Bishop Quinn, described Cani to Kirby in March 1882. This may have been special pleading to prevent him from being appointed to a bishopric, as Kirby was an influential force in Rome. But Cani was made a bishop in 1882. When he died in 1898, Cardinal Moran referred to him as a most pious and humble man who had lived and died in poverty.

[2] Mary was not critical of other nuns. She told her Sisters in her letter of March 27: "There is no reason why other Catholic teachers, or even Religious Communities, may not have their schools under Government where the bishop wishes it. Not for one moment do we think there is, but when it is against our Rule and its spirit there is every reason in our case."

[3] Here is one example: "In a very short time I was rudely awoke by a devil—the

one which usually assaults me and whom I believe to be a fallen spirit of a very high order. He was like a hideous dog but walking erect with like-human limbs. He had a drawn sword of a very wide blade in his hand, a kind of sharp heavy scimitar. He gave me a blow on the left leg above the foot and nearly severed it. I began to bleed as you may imagine and soon I was in a pool of blood. The bed and everything was saturated and I felt myself dying . . . My guardian Angel removed everything from the bed that was saturated with blood and placed other things perfectly similar there. I am sure these blood-stained things will be found again some day." Letter of 21 June 1870.

4   "The beautiful way in which she called upon her Mother through it all was a lesson of love to Mary not easily forgotten. 'My *own, own* Mother,' she would moan out in the midst of her anguish in the most thrilling accents of plaintive love. 'Anything for Thee, yes, anything.' Oh, how I envy her love she has for Mary; but to love like her requires a heart as pure and simple."

5   Ignatius sent Mary some startling stuff, e.g.: "I suddenly saw your soul—the temptations and defects were strikingly visible, and each one seemed painted in different colours. My dear Sister, the appearance I will never forget. You would think Nature with all its strength could not exist under such a conflict. For days after I could not bear to hear your name mentioned, much less, my Sister, to write to you. I saw as if in a mirror, every thought you had about me, but you must not think they disturbed or pained me."

PART III

First Adelaide

Crisis 1871

NINE

"A TERRIBLE MISTAKE"

The Excommunication Episode 1871

B ishop Sheil returned to Adelaide on 2 February 1871, after an absence of nearly seventeen months. Poor health was his reason for returning so long after the Vatican Council had broken up. At the time there were 127 Josephites in his diocese, running 34 schools. They had been expecting that he would present their Rule for approval in Rome, but he did not do this.

On the day after his return Sheil received a written complaint against the Josephites signed by about half of his priests. It seemed to come as an unpleasant surprise, as he retired to bed for the next three days. There were real problems to be resolved between the clergy and the nuns, but what was submitted in this document went far beyond these. It alleged that the nuns were incompetent teachers, that they disregarded priests (apart from Woods), and made no provision for boys. If something were not done about the situation, the diocese could find itself burdened with a large body of ignorant and useless women. Government grants were not mentioned, and there was nothing about the visions. According to Tappeiner, some of the signatories had not even read the document—they were simply exasperated by Woods' high-handedness.

The bishop was upset, but he gave no sign that he was dissatisfied with the nuns. He was happy to bless their convent extensions on March 19, and he implicitly approved of them in his Lenten pastoral letter when he said he was satisfied with the way the schools were being run. Woods had been hoping the bishop would help to unravel his alarming financial tangle, but the signs told him he had fallen from favour. He said later that he should have resigned there and then.

Meanwhile, in reply to Russell's report to Rome on the

disappearance of the Sacrament from the convent chapel, Cardinal Barnabò said that the whole matter should be submitted to the bishop. He asked the bishop himself what he was going to do about the dangerous tendencies indicated by stories of visions and wonders. In reply, the bishop sent a long letter claiming that Russell's report was inspired by partisan spirit and by jealousy of Woods. He described the great advances made in the diocesan system of education, and the indispensable role of the Sisters. In a strong and emotional attack on Russell, he explained that he had granted him a year's leave, alleging health reasons but clearly meaning to get rid of him altogether. The Archdeacon had acted irresponsibly, he said, neglecting his work and loading the diocese with debt to the point of bankruptcy. The reply from Rome defended Russell and did not accept the bishop's facile diagnosis of the troubles among the Sisters. Sheil did not reply to this or to subsequent letters from Rome.

The author of the text of the complaint against the nuns was Charles Horan. The bishop had brought this fellow Franciscan from Ireland on his return to Adelaide in 1868, and had given him the prize mission of the diocese, Kapunda. When Keating was expelled from the diocese in April 1870, the Administrator (Smyth) considered that Horan should also have been dismissed, but because of Sheil's regard for him he hesitated to take further action. Now Horan filled the office of Vicar General in all but name, being the constant companion and adviser of the bishop. It was no secret that he was determined to destroy Woods through the Sisters in revenge for the expulsion of Keating.

Woods continued to make decisions affecting the nuns, without taking Mary's views into account and apparently without even consulting her. This did not worry him, but his debts did. He had spent a lot of money on his magazine The Chaplet, on the needs of the Sisters and of his Brothers, on extensions to the convent, and on the institutions which had suffered distress in the confusion following the death of Father Smyth. Now the banks wanted their money. The bishop was sympathetic, but declined either to regard any of the debts as a diocesan responsibility or to help to pay them. He was obviously not worried about money, as he ordered a collection for a stone fence around the cathedral and the hall and announced his intention of starting a seminary. Early in August Woods left Adelaide to visit Bathurst, as Matthew Quinn had asked for some nuns and Sheil had agreed to send some.

Mary had arrived back in Adelaide in late April 1871. As she passed through Victoria she heard startling stories about visions and other extraordinary happenings in Adelaide. These lost nothing in the telling, and they may have coloured Bishop Goold's thinking. Whatever the reason, he declined to receive her personally, and although sympathetic with her Sisters he forbad them to beg in Melbourne except from their friends. Mary visited Maggie, who was very unwell at Uncle Peter's at Duck Ponds, and next called in at Portland where the MacKillop family was in the process of being broken up once more. Lexie was about to become a Good Shepherd nun, and Annie was going to Melbourne to look for a job. Flora was preparing to go to Duck Ponds to look after Maggie. The two boys were at school at Sevenhill.

As Mary moved closer to Adelaide, via Penola, she heard more of the gossip that was circulating and saw the ridicule to which the nuns were subjected by some of the clergy. When she reached Adelaide the bishop was in Victoria. On his return, she was in Port Augusta establishing the Sisters there. On her way she had visited those she could reach while the steamer was in port at Wallaroo, and their problems made her decide to visit them again as soon as she could. In fact, apart from a short stay in Adelaide in June, she was to spend the next few months in that area.

As the bishop's health deteriorated he came more strongly under Horan's influence. In July the two of them were in Victoria again, where the clergy regaled them with the "strange and scandalous things" that Mary herself had heard. Yet Sheil showed no displeasure with the Sisters until the end of August, when something happened which made him send a terse letter to Woods and caused Mary to send out signals that there was trouble ahead. Horan announced that a message had come from Rome telling the bishop that his letter was not satisfactory and that he should see to the Sisters. But it was the outbreak of visions and other extraordinary happenings that worried Rome, and these were not the things brought up locally against the Sisters. What was brought up was the old charge of incompetence.

On September 1 (just when his health of mind and body had taken a notable turn for the worse, according to the Commission of 1872) the bishop visited the nuns at Franklin Street and was displeased to find some of them idle. In fact he had met some invalids, but he decided to divide all the Josephites into choir and lay Sisters. This alerted them that there was some kind of crisis in the air, and they warned Mary that she should return from Kadina. She came back on the 6th, and went the next day with Teresa to see the bishop. He complained of the number of useless nuns at Franklin Street, and said he did not like the "methodistical" custom of so much singing in the schools. He intended to raise standards and to introduce new subjects, including music, and proposed to have the Sisters examined in order to send away those unfitted for teaching. The convent whose additions he had blessed for the Josephites in March, was to be taken over by the Dominicans. Mary always defended his right to dispose of the convent in this way, and neither she nor Teresa expressed displeasure at giving it up. Finally, he told Mary to go up to Kadina and bring Ursula back to Adelaide, as Father Kennedy was unhappy with her. Having just left Father Kennedy, who seemed quite satisfied with Ursula, Mary was surprised, but she prepared to go.

It was clear that a number of important issues were being raised, and in spite of the bishop's irritation Mary felt she had to mention them. What was to be done with the invalids who used to be cared for at Franklin Street? He replied that each house would look after its own sick. All the houses would in future be separate, and there would be no such things as common retreats. The bishop himself would take charge of the town house, with Mary as its head. When she hesitated about sending away the nuns declared unfit for teaching, he said that any who did not accept his alterations of the Rule would be dispensed from their vows. He told her that all this would be put into effect towards the end of the year, but after she left for Kadina that evening the Sisters were informed that they were not to go to the schools the next day, as the bishop wished to have them examined.

It became clear, when Mary arrived at Kadina and found Father Kennedy indignant that his name had been used against Sister Ursula, that the whole story about Ursula was a ruse to get Mary out of the way while the changes were being effected.

On board the steamer *Kangaroo* on her return journey a few days later, Mary composed a clear and firm letter to the bishop. Taking care to express her respect for his authority and her dependence on him, she declared that he had every right to change the Rule, just as he had approved it in the first place. She outlined the development of her own religious vocation, and concluded that should the Rule be changed in the manner he had indicated, she would choose not to remain in the Institute but to look for some opportunity to live the Rule elsewhere. After sending the letter she showed a copy to Tappeiner and sent a copy to Kennedy; both men approved of its contents. In his Commission evidence in 1872 Tappeiner analysed the situation:

> The bishop has power to dispense from vows, and if he does, the Sisters are free to enter any new institute he might found and make new vows, but they are not bound to this by their present vows. These bind only to the Rule under which they were made. Though the bishop can change the Rule he has approved, he cannot alter a vow already made and direct it to an end other than the one intended by the person who made the vow.

To Mary this was all perfectly obvious. She said, "My first duty was to God and to the Rule which for His sake I had vowed to follow no matter what obstacles might be thrown in its way."

But the bishop and those around him were not willing to reason about it or to attend to distinctions. For them it was a case of "the bishop knows best", and anything but complete cooperation was disobedience. When Sheil received Mary's letter he went and reproached her bitterly for it. All she could do was repeat that she did not deny his right to alter the Rule, but that if he did so she felt obliged in conscience to choose the alternative he offered and leave the sisterhood. This was the last contact she had with him before the fateful September 22.

Meanwhile, on September 8 while Mary was at Kadina, Horan and another priest came to the convent twice, to test the fitness of the nuns to teach, and to take an inventory of what they had there. Some changes were also made in their appointments, with no reference to Mary or to the local superior. The examining was confined to Sisters brought in from the orphanage and the Providence, together with some young ones engaged in teaching infants, those doing the housework of the convent, and some invalids. The manner of questioning was so distressing that it aroused Teresa's indignation. She told Horan that no man should behave that way, let alone a priest.

On Tuesday September 12 the bishop left for Port Augusta, where he remained until the 20th. Though Mary was aware that there was bitter feeling against her, she knew also that older priests like Reynolds supported her. As the pressure mounted, she thought it might be possible for the Sisters to continue to live according to their vows elsewhere. She spent the morning of Thursday September 21 at the Hall school. A telegram from Woods asking for nuns for Bathurst was an additional reason why she wanted to speak with the bishop. In the afternoon she went to the house in King William Street which had just been rented in place of the convent the Josephites had been told to vacate. There she heard she had been ordered to Bagot's Gap, fifty miles away. In the early evening she went to Norwood to consult Tappeiner, who told her that she could not leave before the status of the new Rule had been clarified. He advised her to insist on seeing the bishop before she went away, reassuring her that if the Rule were changed the Sisters would be bound to the new one only if they were dispensed from their vows and took new ones to live the new Rule. Then she went home to Franklin Street.

The bishop also had had a busy day. He had gone first to the convent with Horan. He dismissed Ursula (though he had previously examined her and declared himself well satisfied), and told Teresa she was to take charge of the Hall school, as Sister Mary no longer had any authority. The Sisters from the Providence, the orphanage, and the convent were to be assembled the next morning. He then visited the orphanage, proposed the new Rule, and dismissed a Sister who was unwilling to accept it. In the afternoon he visited the Hall school with Horan and outlined his plan to divide the Institute into choir and lay Sisters, to dismiss the postulants, and to put every convent under the control of the local priest. He pointed out that the nuns had not taken a vow to obey Father Woods, whereupon Monica said that they *had* taken a vow to obey the existing rules. He replied that those who would not accept the change would be dispensed, but he dismissed as a female whim a request for a copy of the new Rule. Finally, he announced that Sister Mary was to go to Bagot's Gap. This message was taken to her at the house in King William Street.

Horan had been busy too. After accompanying the bishop on his various visits during the day he returned to the convent about 7 o'clock. He played down the changes in the Rule, and said Mary was to go, not to Bagot's Gap, but to the equally distant St John's. He was examining more Sisters when she returned about 8 o'clock. Hearing that he had denied that the Rule was to be altered, and being unable to reconcile this with the bishop's actions that afternoon, she decided to ask to see the bishop. When Horan had finished his examining, he told her in the presence of Teresa that she was to go to St John's by the first train in the morning. After the Ursula experience it was obvious that this was simply a means of getting her out of the way. It was admitted later by her opponents, and explicitly stated by Horan. Her duty as superior was simply not considered.

Mary replied that she particularly wished to see the bishop before she went. Besides the problem about the Rule, there was the telegram asking for Sisters for Bathurst. Horan said he did not think the bishop would see her, but he would relay her message. Mary said it was her duty to know about the proposed changes, because if they were serious ones she could not in conscience consent to them. No copy of the new Rule was available (probably because there was none) but Father Nowlan later gave the Commission a document in which it was clearly set down that there was to be a division into lay and choir Sisters, no superior, no principal house, no place of teacher training (not even a novitiate), groups of two and three were to be subject to the local priest, with the bishop over all. In the judgment of the Commission these changes were not minor matters but touched the essentials of the Institute.

When questioned, Horan had to agree that the intention was to introduce two grades among the Sisters, and to change the form of government so that each convent would be under the control of the local priest. When Mary suggested that the changes be delayed until the founder came back, she was met with the indignant accusation that the Sisters seemed to think Father Woods was their bishop. When she asked why a Chapter of Sisters was not called, she was told that the bishop was their Chapter. When Horan pressed for a direct answer on the matter of going to St John's, she replied, "Father, how can I under those rules?" Her later comment was: "I feared refusing to go and yet dared not give my Sisters cause to think I accepted the new Rule."

Horan left, saying that the bishop would see her the next morning. After he had gone, many of the Sisters asked Mary insistently about the new Rule. Though she saw the issue clearly, she did not impose her view on others. She told them to seek only to know God's will and to carry it out, and not to be influenced by the actions of others, even her own. Each one should read her act of profession and decide for herself.

When Horan returned to the convent about 10.30 p.m., Mary had gone to bed, tired and unwell. Teresa received him and was told that unless Sister Mary complied with the bishop's wishes she would be excommunicated. She took the message to Mary, who replied that she could not but act as she had done. The reply was relayed to Horan, Teresa adding that not only Mary but all the Sisters in the convent were unwilling to accept a new Rule. The priest went back and told the bishop that she refused to go. Mary wrote that same night to Sister Francis Xavier at Kapunda telling of the penalty for not complying with the bishop's plan for a new Rule. Her main concern was that the Sisters should not act proudly, and that while they might feel obliged to refuse to cooperate in the proposed changes they should do this humbly.

Sister Ignatius McCarthy told the 1872 Commission that she heard Horan asking Mary if he should tell the bishop that she refused to go to St John's, and that the reply had been: "No, but tell him I wish to see him before I go." The consistent evidence of Mary, Teresa and Ignatius referred to Horan's promise that the bishop would see Mary the following morning as she had asked. It is clear that Horan was in control. It was he who brought the bishop's message to Mary and it was he who took back an account of what is supposed to have transpired between them.

The nuns were stunned by the turn of events. Convinced that Mary had already been excommunicated, they imagined that the same fate awaited them for having the same attitude. In their confusion they did not attend the cathedral Mass in the morning as usual. Around 8 o'clock the bishop walked the short distance from his residence to the convent, accompanied by four priests. The nuns were first asked why they had not been at Mass that morning. On giving the reason, they were told that as usual they had misunderstood. Father Horan had not said Sister Mary was excommunicated, but that she would be if she did not comply with the bishop's wishes. Teresa begged pardon for having misunderstood. The bishop then ordered Mary to be summoned. He was told that she was not well and was only then getting up. Meanwhile the nuns from the other houses had come to the convent. When Mary entered the room she knelt for the bishop's blessing, but he refused it.

They then moved to the chapel, where the bishop, complete with mitre and crozier, said he had to excommunicate Sister Mary because of her disobedience and rebellion. Teresa thereupon knelt beside Mary, but returned to her place when ordered to do so. The sentence was then pronounced by the bishop, together with some remarks on spiritual pride and the wickedness of the world that Mary MacKillop had brought into the convent with her. He said that anyone who communicated with her would suffer the same penalty. He was acting in total disregard for all the formalities required by law. This is how Mary felt:

I really felt like one in a dream. I seemed not to realize the presence of the Bishop and priests; I know I did not see them; but I felt, oh, such a love for their office, a love, a sort of reverence for the very sentence which I then knew was being in full force passed upon me. I do not know how to describe the feeling, but I was intensely happy and felt nearer to God than I had ever felt before. The sensation of the calm beautiful presence of God I shall never forget.

When she rose to leave the chapel, the feelings of some of her companions overflowed. Paula "shrieked like one possessed", deaf to all entreaties to desist. She had to be taken to the dormitory and did not return to the chapel. Before leaving the house Mary got her to promise to be quiet, and warned the others not to tell people what had happened. They all returned to the chapel, where Horan read out the names of those who were to be lay Sisters. The first four declined and were dispensed, but when more said they could not follow the new Rule and wished to be dispensed, the bishop said they should remain as long as he thought fit, threatening to excommunicate anyone who left without his permission. Some were granted dispensations, others refused. He sent the postulants home.

An inventory was taken of everything in the convent. The altar furnishings had already been moved to the new house, and he ordered that these and some candlesticks (a gift to the nuns) be brought back at once. He took the key of the tabernacle, and shortly afterwards one of the priests removed the Blessed Sacrament. The Sisters left that evening or the next day.

Teresa was put in charge but was soon replaced by Monica. Granting that the bishop had the right to change the Rule, she said she could not in conscience follow a new one. When she was told that there had been no change, she replied that much had already been done contrary to the Rule. She wrote for a dispensation for herself and some others, and this was granted a few days later.

On September 29, when Matthew Quinn had telegraphed to ask what was going on, Sheil told him:

Their Superioress General I have expelled and excommunicated because she excited the Sisters to rebel against my authority. Many of the Sisters challenge my power to alter or modify their rule which derived all its force solely from my approbation.

No proof was ever provided for the first accusation either by the bishop or by Horan when he repeated it at the Commission. As to the second, far from denying the bishop's power to change the Rule, Mary had repeatedly acknowledged it. But she maintained that because of the serious changes to be introduced in the Rule each nun could choose whether to leave the Institute or to take vows to live the new Rule. This alternative was not only a natural right but had been offered her by the bishop.

Mary was at no stage questioned that morning, nor was any specific reason given for the censure imposed. Tappeiner said that apart from the Horan faction everybody considered the sentence to be invalid, because there was no fault in the first place and the whole thing had been in contempt of all legal procedure. Mary told her mother the same thing in a simpler way: "The holiest and best priests say I have only done my duty, and that our poor, dear old Bishop has made a terrible mistake." Bishop Goold commented from Melbourne, "Poor Dr Sheil, he must labour under mental disease."

Did Sister Mary in fact disobey the bishop's command to go to St John's? Horan, the only one who said that she had, raised the issue of obedience on the night of the 21st, and Mary explained her position once again. She granted the bishop's right to change the Rule, but "as I had not only vowed to observe the original Rule but had also been fully prepared for the greatest struggle in its defence, I really could not follow any other."

Horan's account was contradicted by Mary and Teresa, the two who conversed with him, and by Ignatius who overheard the conclusion of the discussion. At the enquiry none of the other priests claimed that it was a clear case of disobedience. The most Father Murphy would say was that it was either evasion or refusal. The Commission's report said that Horan had falsified, or at least exaggerated, all that regarded the Sisters. Mary herself strongly denied disobedience: "I dare say that the way in which my not going to Bagot's Gap was represented to Father Hughes quite justified him in thinking I had been disobedient, but never mind, God cannot be deceived." On October 30 she wrote even more strongly:

> I now know *for certain* that Father Horan *denies* the substance of the conversation we had the night before I was excommunicated. It was with a keen pang of sorrow and shame that I heard from the Kapunda Sisters that he had positively denied the conversation we had, and made it out to them that I had simply refused to obey the bishop about going to Bagot's Gap. Father, it is hard to think a priest *could* tell a lie and in such grave matter.

Soon afterwards the bishop went to Horan's parish, Kapunda, whence he sent a message to Bathurst that there were no nuns available for anywhere, informing Woods at the same time that he was to take no action in the matter, and that he was moreover welcome to remain longer in Sydney. The Sisters were disappointed, as they had been pinning their hopes on the founder's return. It made them suspect collusion between the bishops to keep him out of the way. Father Nevin was appointed pastor of North Adelaide in his place, and also replaced his *locum tenens* Tappeiner as confessor to the Sisters. Sheil returned to Adelaide on October 3 and expelled Teresa from the Institute for her contemptuous conduct on the morning of September 22. He also directed that the priests were to see all correspondence to and from the Sisters.

Realising that if she did not go quickly the Sisters would not obey the order to refrain from contact with her, Mary went at once with Mechtilde to the Woods' residence nearby (Mechtilde's home) without telling the others where she was going. She stayed there for almost two weeks, but not before Mr Woods gave her a solemn assurance "not to write one word against the Bishop or priests as long as we are under his roof". When the *Irish Harp* announced on September 30, without comment, that she had been excommunicated, Mary thought at first that Woods was responsible, but soon found that he was not. Still, she left the house the next day and went to stay with some Protestant friends. This was to avoid the extra scandal that would have ensued if she were staying with Catholics when the whole thing became public knowledge. The Jesuits had made it clear that they did not regard the censure as valid, and quietly gave her Communion. At times they allowed her to stay overnight in the church at Norwood or in a room over the sacristy.

To Mary's dismay the *Irish Harp* of October 7 carried an article by J. D. Woods justifying the Sisters' stand and criticising the action of the bishop. This made her want to flee Adelaide altogether. She told her mother:

> That vindicates me, but oh at a terrible cost. It was written without
> my sanction and against my express wish. It is too painful. I am glad
> they did not know more to put in it . . . The dear old Bishop has made
> a terrible mistake. Be careful how you speak of any of these matters.

The bishop wrote to the priest at Kadina and told him that for grave reasons Ignatius, the visionary, was to be dispensed. But when she came to Adelaide and begged pardon, he said she had not offended in any way. However, he was not obliged to explain his actions, and in fact gave her no idea what the grave reasons were. Angela, whose admission of guilt had been well publicised by the nuns' enemies, was also expelled. Thus within four weeks of September 22 all the town Sisters except those at the orphanage and the Providence were either dispensed or expelled. The country schools were able to work on in relative peace, but there was an atmosphere of uncertainty and insecurity everywhere.

The rent could no longer be found for the house in King William Street, so the nuns moved to one provided rent-free by a Jew, Mr Solomon. Their living together was presented as a sign of rebellion. They were attacked publicly from the pulpit, and were given a bad time in confession, being told that it was pride and presumption to think they knew better than the bishop. They were not prepared to attend Mass at the cathedral for fear of being denied Communion, so they walked daily to the church at Norwood. Some were working to support themselves and the Refuge, which was continuing as a much needed work. They suffered hunger too, but Mary's pleas to friends in Victoria met with a poor response.

Mary was dismayed at the continuing scandal and division in the Church in Adelaide, and her letters at the time return constantly to the theme that God in his mysterious way would bring good out of this great evil. She recommended charity and humility to the Sisters, whatever their difficulties and trials. In the furious debate in the press the bishop's party blamed her for everything, and the confusion was made worse when the bishop denied that he wished to change the Rule.

Some priests supported Mary, but this very friendship was a burden because she feared it might bring the displeasure of the bishop on those who offered it. One of the few things that moved her to indignation in these trying months was the persecution of Father Bongaerts for defending the nuns. She was deeply moved that he could not perform an act of kindness, even of justice, without wicked minds putting evil constructions on it. "May God forgive them," she said, "This is a cruel, wicked world."

These events could not, of course, escape the attention of Mrs MacKillop. Her reaction was to write to the bishop "under the impression that only notorious sinners could be excommunicated" wanting to know what was happening to her daughter, as "the great sin of her life, in my opinion, has been the leaving me and putting herself under your Lordship's protection." Mary told her some things to ease her mind, but warned her not to allow them to go further and cause ill feeling against the bishop. She undertook to send her Uncle Peter some details to pacify the astounded relatives, provided he promised to tell nobody else. She kept up her correspondence with Father Woods and with various Sisters. Plans were even afoot to send a group of those who had been dispensed to Queensland.

Her letters were calm, with no suggestion of despair or panic. In her view, the trouble was something allowed by God in a great work, and it was a privilege for one as unworthy as herself to suffer for her Lord. Hence, "I must at least try not to abuse God's love by speaking ill of—or making known the faults of—His servants." She was very gentle with these servants of God whom many would have seen as her enemies, speaking of them as the instruments of divine providence which would draw good out of evil.

What she felt keenly was not her own predicament, but the scandal that threatened the name of the bishop: "It is far harder to have to think ill of others than to be the one thought ill of." She was concerned to let Father Woods know how the nuns were suffering, but she shielded the bishop as far as possible from any blame: he has been misled, he is confused and perplexed, he sometimes contradicts what he has said a moment before. True, some of the priests have not been sincere, but "I am not in the least troubled about these Fathers *and bear them no ill will*. It is not to make you think ill of them that I speak but because I think you ought to know these things."

She was perfectly disposed to forgive everybody who had injured her. Even towards the few priests whose conduct she could not explain she bore no ill will, although she was pained by their cold hard spirit. Faced with a plain lie, she says, "I have been able to find excuse for everything but that, not for my own sake, but for the sake of the sacred character of him who could say what was not true." As she tries to excuse or mitigate a lie, she is realistic enough to say she does not trust the author of it. She is not happy about all this, for "Bishops and Priests have an awful power—and terrible in the sight of God must it be if that be abused."

Bishop Sheil did not have long to live. There is much that is not clear about his last days, although the 1872 Commission's report spoke of a longstanding illness, and Polding had earlier referred to his "long and distressing illness". Addiction to drink is mentioned by Reynolds and Fitzgibbon, though the latter says nothing of illness. The terms of reference of the Commission at first included his drinking, but when he died this was dropped. Hughes said he had been unwell since returning from Europe, while Reynolds claimed on the authority of the doctor that from May onwards he was suffering from mental aberrations. According to Tappeiner, he had been so weakened in the head for two years that he could in no way exercise his office. His conversation was sufficiently clear as long as it was about ordinary topics, but when anything important came up his mind instantly became confused and he agreed with anything proposed. His memory had been so weakened that after a few minutes he forgot what he had just said and proposed the opposite. The picture is vivid:

> Father Horan was his constant guide and companion and, what is worse, he kept the bishop who was like a little boy, in a torpid state, bringing him some brandy mixed with water because of his ill health and stomach weakness. But this made his stomach, as well as his mind, weaker and is thought to have accelerated death.[1]

There was already common talk of the bishop being unwell in December 1871, and by early February his condition had clearly become serious. Although he had surprisingly consented to a collection for the Refuge, there was as yet no sign of a change of attitude towards the Josephites. Yet everybody could see that he could not live much longer. When in mid-February he did seem to be aware that death was near, he showed for the first time that he realised he had been deceived by those he had trusted. One observer quoted him as saying: "I am dying with a broken heart. Those whom I trusted contracted bad habits. At times I acted at their suggestions—I'm sorry. That is why I am so unhappy."

Disillusioned at last with Horan, he said to him: "You are that Father who does all the great things." The irony was not lost, and Horan left the room immediately. The bishop then began to show a special regard for Reynolds.

On February 23, when it was clear that there was no longer any hope of his recovery, Sheil received the sacrament of anointing at the insistence of the priests now around him. At the same time, Father Hughes was told to lift the censure on Sister Mary. He met her as she was travelling south towards Willunga, and absolved her in the church at Morphett Vale. There was no formal request on her part, no penance imposed, no retraction demanded, and no preconditions laid down. This amounted to an admission that the censure had not been valid. Mary told her mother that the bishop had admitted he had acted unjustly towards many of the priests as well as towards herself and the Institute, and that he intended to make amends. She learnt this from Hughes, who later told the Commission of the bishop's wish to restore the Institute with her as superior.

The dying bishop resisted attempts to have him designate Horan as Administrator on his death. He chose Reynolds instead, but the fact that he did not do this in writing proved a source of friction in the months to come. When he finally died on 1 March 1872, some priests and others appealed to Polding to heal the divisions in the diocese, with the result that Reynolds' appointment was confirmed. Believing that it was Sheil's dying wish to undo as much as possible of the harm done to the Sisters, Reynolds soon authorised the restoration of the habit to almost all those who desired it. The first group, Mary and ten others, received their habits back at Norwood on March 19.

Only days after this, a new storm burst about the Sisters. On Palm Sunday, March 24, firstly at Kapunda and then in the cathedral, Horan delivered a "funeral oration" in honour of the late bishop. It was really a vicious attack on Reynolds and the Josephites, whom he called "women who, for ignorance and fanaticism have never, so far as my knowledge of ecclesiastical history goes, had a parallel in the Church of God". Their readmission after dismissal was presented as an insult to Sheil's memory.

When the sermon was published, it created an even wider gulf between the Horan party and the rest of the clergy. Finding himself suspended by Reynolds, Horan went to Sydney but got nowhere with Polding. He then appealed to Rome. His two grounds of complaint were the reinstatement of the Sisters and the patronage given to the *Irish Harp*, a journal condemned by the bishop. No mention was made of the bishop's change of mind before his death or of his lifting of the excommunication.

In addition to being attacked by Horan, the Sisters were scurrilously libelled in *The Protestant Advocate* in early April. They were recruited, according to two letters it published, from the girls at the Refuge, and when the bishop found that three of them were about to become mothers he disbanded the Institute. They were guilty, too, of blasphemy, sacrilege, arson, drunkenness, thieving, prostitution and attempted murder. Reynolds was accused of conniving in these evils. He and Mr Woods (brother of Father Woods and father of Mechtilde) sued the publisher, Mr Lewis. The nuns were unable to appear on the streets because of the verbal abuse they attracted.

The defendant at first offered to settle out of court, but either because he changed his mind or because his proposed apology was unsatisfactory, the case came to trial before Judge Wearing on June 5 and 6. Mechtilde said in her *History* that the judge was very much impressed by Mary's modest, straightforward, unhesitating manner. The defendant produced no evidence, but simply repeated the libels, adding the allegation that it was "generally known that there was every species of immorality and wickedness among them, and that sin and crime alone reigned triumphant". The writer of the letters was sitting prominently in the court, but as he was not called to give evidence it seemed that he had none to give, and the defendant knew it.

The jury found Lewis guilty of publishing a false, malicious and defamatory libel on the nuns, and of publishing a similar libel on Reynolds. Reminding him that "the charges are of such a character that you could not have published accusations of a more serious nature", the judge sentenced him to a fine and six months imprisonment on the first charge, and bound him over on a surety to present himself for judgment on the second. The good name of the Sisters was vindicated.[2]

Footnotes

[1] From the report on the Adelaide diocese sent by Tappeiner to his Superior General, Father Beckx, on 30 October 1872. Beckx was startled by some of the things in it, especially about the character and behaviour of Horan, and hesitated to forward it to the Holy See. But he did so because it had been commissioned.

[2] The letters were written by a Mr James McLaughlin, who, in spite of the verdict of the court and the fate of the publisher, repeated the accusations in two letters to Rome later in the year. Religion had not suffered one iota, he informed Cardinal Barnabò, and all his charges against the nuns (apart from the pregnancies) were as true as the Gospel.

TEN

THE POOR BISHOP IS DEAD

Re-establishing the Institute 1872

During these troubled months of 1871 Father Woods was in New South Wales and Queensland. When he arrived in Sydney in mid-August he embarked on an energetic programme of missions, retreats, and sermons, interspersed with bouts of illness, in the far-flung dioceses of Sydney, Bathurst and Brisbane. The bishops had agreed to keep him busy, and Archbishop Polding saw to it that he did not return to Adelaide.

He was taken on a tour of the Bathurst diocese to see the places where the Josephites would be working. He preached with effect in Bathurst, Orange, Dubbo, Wellington, Gulgong, Sofala, Keane's Swamp and Mudgee. This constant moving about was the reason why it was the second week of October before he knew what had happened in Adelaide in the period leading up to September 22. When he could see that things were serious, he sent some general advice, making light of the difficulties, and telling the nuns not to worry because they would be welcome at Bathurst in any case. He suggested that Mary should try to speak to the bishop, and wrote at the same time to the bishop asking him to deal with the nuns directly and not through intermediaries. Mary replied that the bishop was "not one who would admit that a woman has a right to differ from him in opinion".

In the meantime it was she who had to make the decisions about practical problems. What was to be done about the dispensed Sisters? Should they return to their families, or remain together and try to preserve some unity? Where were they to live? How were they to manage economically? The founder's instructions about Sisters for Bathurst and Queensland were an added complication.

The message that he was to remain away from Adelaide was

reinforced when his parish was given to another priest. He made contact with the Marists at Hunters Hill, where Father Joly, who had been a friend in his Marist days in France, proved a kindly host. He also stayed with the Benedictine nuns at Subiaco from time to time, helping as a chaplain. Polding sent him there to recover when his health broke down badly at the end of October. Unable to eat or sleep, he wrote to Sheil lamenting his hard lot and wondering what he could have done to deserve such treatment. He believed it was all the work of evil advisers. It was not too late, he pleaded, for their work to be undone.

His letters were strong but respectful, expressed in noble English prose. He was clearly upset, but there were no signs of mental disorder. When ten letters went unanswered he began to suspect that somebody was tampering with the bishop's mail. So he sent one in late November "by a sure hand" begging for an answer.

When he spoke to Polding about the Adelaide debts the Archbishop organised a meeting with the bishops of Bathurst and Maitland. They were kind and reassuring, and proposed that Woods stay in Sydney while they dealt with Sheil. Late in November he resumed his travels, this time to the Shoalhaven, eighty miles south of Sydney. Then, as Polding had made it clear that he was not to return to South Australia, he seems to have offered his services to the Bishop of Bathurst. On his side, Quinn was anxious to attract the Institute west of the mountains, so he was particularly kind in listening to the troubled priest. He reassured him that the Josephites would always find a staunch friend in Bathurst.

Before leaving for Brisbane in the new year Woods wrote to Mary to tell her that Bathurst wanted six Sisters at once, and that another two should be sent to Queensland. On his own arrival in Queensland he was his indefatigable self as priest and scientist in Brisbane, Maryborough, Gympie, Ipswich and elsewhere. He was on the move so much that when a letter from Sheil ordering him back to Adelaide was delivered a couple of months after it was written, the bishop was dead. At that point Polding summoned him back to Sydney.

Meanwhile Mary had sent six Sisters, three for Bathurst and three for Brisbane, but Woods had brought them all to Brisbane and told her to send over another eight. He said that if Adelaide did not want them they should go elsewhere, speaking of the need for "complete justice". He did not specify what exactly he meant by this phrase, but he was certainly taking the nuns away from Adelaide. It did not seem to Mary to be very just that the priests who had at personal risk sought to help the nuns should be the ones who in the name of justice would find themselves without teachers in their schools. Woods said he had twenty postulants ready to fill any gaps, ignoring Mary's need to consult with those in charge in Adelaide. He eventually agreed that she could consult Reynolds, but insisted that the Sisters be sent. His plans had to be suspended because the libel case was coming up, and also because Rome had ordered an enquiry into Adelaide's affairs.

There is much evidence from this period of Woods' revelations concerning the living, the dead, God's intentions, and the future. He repeated freely any prophecy that came into his head. The Marists were puzzled, especially Father Joly, who asked, "Illness or the devil? I don't know, but I rather believe that it is illness." He wondered about two candidates Woods had in tow for some new women's institute, "Were they privileged souls or really cracked?". The priest at Camden, finding "both them and Father Woods a great joke", said he was mad and denounced him to the Bishop of Bathurst. This throws light on the growing disagreement between Woods and Mary concerning the visionary Josephites. It came to a head when he wrote to Ignatius deploring the harshness with which Angela had been treated. Angela's admission of guilt had been valuable ammunition for Horan in his attacks on the nuns, and Reynolds thought it better not to readmit her, asking Mary to make sure that letters between her and the Sisters were supervised. Woods told Ignatius that these measures were unjust. He explained the whole situation to Mary by declaring that God had gratified Angela's thirst for humility. Mary told him that by writing to Ignatius and not to herself, he had given the impression that she was acting against his will. "I do beg," she wrote, "that the Sisters may not be allowed to think that I am acting against your wishes."

Mary's view was that Angela had been deceitful and had led others to deceive their superiors. She reminded Woods that she had disagreed from the start with his wish to appoint Angela and Ignatius as consultors. Neither of them had the true spirit of the Institute, and for her part she was weary of the whole vision business: "Much more mystery will I hope be spared me, for I have neither health of mind or body to bear it." Woods then admitted that they were not meant for the Institute, and told Mary to do what she saw as her duty.

Mary could see the gap widening between herself and the founder when he wrote on April 16: "I dread the friendship of some more than the enmity of others. Friends have done you more harm than enemies have done to Sister Mary Angela." She remarked in reply: "I thought if you knew all you would not have that opinion." Her letters at this time express quite strongly her misgivings at the conduct of Ignatius and Angela. Of Angela she asked, "Could it be God's spirit that could make her disobedient and untruthful?" Pained that Ignatius was a threat to the Institute by encouraging deception towards her superior, she wondered: "Where will the unity of our Institute or its spirit of obedience be?" Worse still, these two had had the constant support of the founder. A powerful piece of writing from Mary's pen some years later, telling how the drama of Ignatius and Angela developed, does not conceal the important role he had played in it: "They murmured against the decision of their Superiors, and Father Woods took their view of the case." The spiritual ideas of these Sisters had not met with the approbation of the episcopal Commission, but Woods continued to encourage them.

If they had chosen to submit to moderate restraint, to be satisfied with the ordinary confessor appointed for the nuns, and in some cases perhaps to accept contradictions, they might well have settled down. The chief restraint was that they were not to write to each other or to two other Sisters to whom they were very much attached. But Woods sought to win them more freedom and wished Angela to resume her habit. He was annoyed when this was not done and said that it would then be better for them to leave altogether. Mary had agreed that that certainly would be better if they did not intend to obey their superiors. They did in fact leave, taken away by Woods, not dismissed, and dispensations were sent after them to prevent a too glaring violation of the vows.

Writing to Woods late in April 1872, Mary pointed out that their differences were not just due to the influence of her Adelaide friends. She was aware that painful experiences had changed her: "Sister Mary is lost in the Sister Guardian, for the duties of the latter require what the former could never do." The problem could be traced to Woods' view that trust in human considerations was a lack of simplicity. His habitual disregard for the Church's traditions in the matter of visions and revelations had done much harm and would do more. But he was not disturbed: "I have not been wrong in one single thing." On this occasion a head-on collision was avoided, as he covered all problems by professing eternal affection, and simply ignored issues like Angela's deceit.

The Episcopal Commission

Cardinal Barnabò in Rome was aware that all was not well in Adelaide. A long memorandum from a group of Catholics, and various newspaper excerpts, determined him to order an enquiry. His letter to Sheil is actually dated on the day before the bishop's death. At the same time letters were sent to other bishops, informing them that Dr Murphy of Hobart and Dr Quinn of Bathurst were commissioned to conduct an enquiry. Because of Sheil's death no immediate action was taken, but early in April the cardinal indicated that it should proceed. He gave the Commissioners faculties to take the measures they thought immediately necessary, and he would take further action in the light of their findings. They moved quickly and arrived in Adelaide at the end of May 1872.

The Commission's terms of reference were: the affairs of the Sisters of St Joseph and the bishop's action against them; the alleged misuse of funds in the diocese; the activities of the priests Horan and Nowlan; and the alleged drunkenness of the bishop. As the bishop was now dead, the last item was dropped. When the enquiry opened on June 1, emphasis had shifted from the excommunication episode to the discord in the diocese. Two reports were sent to Rome, on June 17 and July 10, with summaries of some of the evidence—included were Mary's written submission to the Commission and her *Kangaroo* letter to the bishop. There were also summaries of two reports, one prepared by Mary and the other by Monica and Teresa. None of this material deals with the founder's style of spiritual direction or his preoccupation with unusual phenomena. Yet we know that many questions were asked about these things.

The first two to be questioned were Mary and Teresa, both closely involved in the critical events. Mary was asked about the various matters that had been a cause of controversy in the diocese: about the training of the Sisters, the nature of their novitiate and their competence as teachers; about the visionaries; about the means of sustenance of the Institute; about the change of attitude in Dr Sheil.

When Horan's turn came he said he was the one who prepared the petition against the Sisters. Sister Mary, he claimed, simply refused twice to go to Bagot's Gap, and was excommunicated because she incited the others to rebel against the bishop's authority. He offered no evidence to support the latter accusation. He made much of Angela's admission of guilt in the Blessed Sacrament episode and claimed that the change in the bishop was caused by a letter from Rome about the visionaries. This emphasis on the visionaries was clearly aimed at discrediting Woods, the one responsible for advising them. Together with what Mary and Tappeiner had to say, this would have provided grounds for the measures later taken against the founder. Tappeiner subsequently supplemented his evidence with a long report on the diocese which he was asked by Rome to prepare. Although he spoke of Woods as an excellent and zealous priest, what he had to say about his imprudence was very damning.

After an adjournment during the libel case the Commission interrogated a number of other priests—Hughes, William Kennedy, Nowlan, and Tappeiner—and then Monica, Paula, and Ignatius McCarthy, the latter two being close witnesses of the events of September 21–22. It is not clear whether Woods was questioned personally or not. It would seem strange if he were not, as he had come to Adelaide for the occasion. The evidence from him forwarded to Rome (his written submission only) treated of the foundation of the Institute, the aid promised but not forthcoming, the growing opposition of the clergy, the petition against the Sisters, the bishop's subsequent defence of the schools, his inertia in the face of growing debts, and his change of attitude after Woods had been sent to New South Wales. "Certain Fathers of the Franciscan Order" had opposed Woods because he had been instrumental in the dismissal of some priests of that Order for drunkenness and immorality (his use of the plural does not correspond to what is known from other sources). He attributed the opposition of the clergy to their anger at the refusal of the Government grant and to their low opinion of the teaching ability of the nuns. The debts were due to the lack of the collaboration he was entitled to expect in his work for the schools and various charitable institutions.

On Sunday June 23 Bishop Quinn announced in the cathedral that the enquiry had been carried out and that information had been forwarded to Rome. In a reference to the libel case, he said that the Sisters were quite innocent of the charges made against them. Speaking ten days later in reply to an address of thanks made on behalf of the laity by Dr Gunson, he exhorted everybody to charity, stressing that in the Adelaide situation breach of charity was the greatest crime. The bishop took advantage of his presence in Adelaide to finalise plans for the delayed foundation in Bathurst, with the result that on July 16 three Sisters arrived there.

The Commission's report exonerated Mary and the other nuns, and declared that the blame for everything lay with Horan, who exploited his influence on the failing bishop to take revenge for the expulsion of his colleague Keating. It stressed, too, that the bishop had changed his attitude before he died. There was no evidence that money had been mishandled, though there was unfortunately a considerable amount owed by the diocese at Sheil's death. This debt was incurred in building churches and schools, in bringing priests and religious from Europe, and in other religious and educational expenditure. No mention is made of debts incurred by Woods, nor is it stated whether his debts are included in the £11,000 mentioned as owed by the diocese.

The Commissioners recommended that a good bishop be appointed as soon as possible, preferably an outsider not involved in the local factions. They concurred in Reynolds' decision not to readmit the two visionary nuns, and recommended that Horan and two others be recalled to their monasteries. In October Tappeiner was still urging the removal of Horan, "the leader and soul of the clique", a source of scandal and discord. There was no mention of any decisions taken about Woods, though it is clear from other evidence that he was advised to leave Adelaide until the appointment of the new bishop. Tappeiner replaced him as director of the Sisters.

For years Mary had suffered anguish because she could not agree with the founder's procedure in some important matters. Now she wrote to warn him: "The way I was questioned about spiritual things, I fear dear Father that your treatment of the Sisters may be censured for its want of prudence." In addition to his encouragement of visions and revelations, she was never happy with Woods' practice of sending untrained teachers into the schools and of shifting nuns frequently from place to place, and she was uneasy about the lack of consideration he showed towards local pastors by failing to consult them. She urged him to accept his dismissal, but it was not easy: "This was a terrible task to me and caused me much suffering which nothing but the thought that God required it of me could have supported me under." It would soon be seen, she said, whether the Institute could stand on its own feet, since the Sisters would now have to look only to their Rule without his presence. For his part, though deeply hurt, he sought to make light of the decision. He told her that as he visited convents for the last time he had found the nuns quite cheery despite his impending departure. Early in August he left Adelaide, never to return, but (as Mary wrote in her *Life*) "to struggle on through many weary trials, and not a few years, for the end was not yet."

From Robe and Penola he travelled slowly across western Victoria to Melbourne, where he visited Lexie at Abbotsford and went to see Maggie, who was dying at Duck Ponds. Then he proceeded north, and spent October, November and December working in the Maitland and Bathurst dioceses. At Christmas he was with the Sisters at Bathurst. Early in 1873 he was in Brisbane, and then moved north 1200 miles along the coast to Maryborough, Mackay and Townsville, to supervise foundations there. He returned to Brisbane early in March. The single extant letter from Mary in these months was probably not posted, but she wrote frequently. This can be deduced from his comments, which also indicate something of the contents of her letters. These reached him in lots of as many as eight.

In Adelaide the chief event during the rest of 1872 was the acquisition of the Kensington property. One of the first concerns of Father Reynolds was the readmission of the Sisters to the habit and the provision of a central residence for them. When a suitable property was eventually found not far from the Norwood church, it became the official Mother House. The nuns took possession on 29 August 1872, and to meet the costs Sister Mary began a begging campaign.

Preparations for Rome

It was clear that somebody had to go to Rome to have the Rule approved there without delay, as there were bishops who were planning to win approval for their own version of it. As the months went by, the matter became more urgent. "Depend upon it," wrote Woods in January 1873, "we shall have trouble again if something is not done before long." He was convinced that Mary was the person to go: "I don't see how this can be done without your going to Rome. It will be done better by you than by anyone else." Both Reynolds and Tappeiner could also see there was good reason to act quickly, so it was decided that she should leave at once.

She was to carry two letters from Reynolds, one presenting her to Cardinal Barnabò, the other recommending her to the care of Dr Kirby, Rector of the Irish College. These letters leave no doubt that it was the Administrator's decision that she should go. Woods later fell into the habit of saying it was her own decision, and that he knew nothing about it. Mary herself assured the Sisters just before she left,

"It was our dear Father Director who first proposed that I should go, and the Administrator in virtue of the authority which he possesses is sending me." Reynolds wrote to Kirby: "I have resolved to send her to the fountainhead of all authority," and to Barnabò: "I determined to send her to your Eminence's paternal care."

On learning in Brisbane that Mary had gone without seeing him, Woods wrote a pained letter to Monica: "I have had a good many trials about the Institute but this was the worst." He clearly felt he was the proprietor of the Institute, and resented anybody else having a say in any decision concerning it. He attached no weight to Mary's duty of obedience to lawful superiors, people who had moreover been in Adelaide with her during the troubles and had supported her at personal risk. He saw no significance in the fact that he had been replaced as director by legitimate authority. He seemed to forget that he had been the one who first suggested that Mary go to Rome, and spoke as though she was "alone" when he was not about.

Even so, the most startling thing about this letter is that Woods makes no mention of Reynolds' attempt to arrange for him to meet Mary. A message had been sent directing him to come at once to Adelaide to see her. If he could not come in time, he was to send a telegram so that she could delay her departure for another month. Instead of obeying this instruction by either returning to Adelaide or sending a telegram, he replied that the Episcopal Commission had forbidden him to return to Adelaide, as if a short visit and not prolonged residence were what the bishops had ruled out, and as if Reynolds, his superior, were not aware of what they had meant. Though thus citing the Commission's ban in defence of his own failure to comply with the Administrator's request, he deeply resented the directive of the same Commission, reinforced by the Administrator, that he be supplanted as director of the Institute, and took no account of it. He added that there was no pressing hurry about Mary's journey, an assertion which did not tally with his earlier concern about the attempts of some bishops to have their own version of the Rule approved in Rome. Though expected in Adelaide, he wrote repeating his wish to meet Mary in Sydney about the end of May. His letter arrived after she had left.

His next known letter to Mary, from Mackay in north Queensland, is dated 28 July 1873. It is much more serene, but it reveals his confused ideas about what obedience meant. He is no more embarrassed about ignoring Reynolds' directive to go to the Northern

Territory than he is repentant about disobeying the summons to come to Adelaide to see Mary before she left. He had decided, on what authority we cannot guess, that he would do more good working at missions and extending the schools in Queensland than by doing what he was told to do. He failed to see that Mary's sense of obedience gave her no choice. She had not found it easy at all to disappoint him—"I am crushed with sorrow," she said, but she tried to bring him to see that orders were to be obeyed.

Six years after these events Woods was spreading the story around Queensland that Mary had gone to Rome without his knowledge and consent, that he had not wished her to go, and that he had no part in urging it. In her astonishment Mary made doubly sure that she had not misinterpreted some rumour (she had not—"Dr Quinn has several times told me the same thing") and then penned a long letter of protest asking Woods to bring his grievances to her directly or to her superiors, but not to talk that way to the Sisters.

Before making this protest to Woods himself, she had felt she owed it to the Sisters to let them know what exactly had transpired before she left for Rome. She told how the founder first suggested and then insisted on her going, and how the Adelaide authorities eventually decided to send her. She described how the elaborate plans to allow her to meet him before she left had ended in frustration. Her memory is quite specific: Woods was told by his superior to come to Adelaide at once, or to telegraph if he were held up. If such a message came, her departure would be delayed until after his arrival. No return telegram came, so they expected him in Adelaide on the next boat. But the boat did not bring the Father himself, only a letter in which he told Mary to cross half a continent to see him in Sydney, and go to Europe later.

PART IV

European
Journey
1873–1874

ELEVEN

AN AUSTRALIAN
IN ROME

On 28 March 1873 Mary MacKillop left Adelaide in a coastal steamer headed for Albany, Western Australia, where she was to join the mail-steamer *Bangalore* bound for Europe. To make her departure unobtrusive she travelled as Mrs MacDonald, and because the political and social turmoil in Italy made it dangerous to appear in a religious habit she wore secular dress.

During the wait at Albany, Alexander Cameron of Penola chanced to stroll past the cottage where Mary was staying and was much surprised to see her. His wife Margaret had died about a year after Mary left their home, and in the course of time he had remarried. He was now on his way to Europe with his second wife, Ellen Keogh. Mary must have known this, as she had a letter for him from Father Reynolds asking him to give her whatever help he could. Writing to her mother about Ellen's kindness during the voyage, she told her it was clear that the relatives had no idea how the nuns had suffered from hunger in the crisis of 1871: "I did feel more than words can tell and Ellen has now heard all." After a stop in Ceylon, the *Bangalore* made its way to Bombay, where the passengers joined the SS. *Golconda*, bound for Aden and Suez. From Suez they took the train to Alexandria, where they boarded the SS. *Simla*. Mary disembarked at Brindisi on May 9, and was accompanied by the Camerons in the train as far as Foggia. There she left them to go on her way via Caserta to Rome.

It was 9.30 p.m. on Sunday, 11 May 1873, when she arrived in Rome and found a room in the *Anglo American* Hotel. The daughter of Alexander MacKillop was thus lodged for her first night in Rome in the via delle Quattro Fontane, just opposite the Scots College where he had been a student forty years before. She has left no record of her thoughts on that evening, but when she was shown over the

125

building later she noted that "the Church was the same one in which poor Papa had so often been". In recalling some memories of her father to Monsignor Kirby, she revealed her deep sense of gratitude that he had taught her "so much of the teachings of our holy Faith".

On Monday, May 12, she set about the business for which she had come so far. Her first visit was to the principal church of the Jesuits, the *Gesù*. There she found Father Lambert, an Englishman who proved to be a helpful friend. He arranged for her to meet a Swiss colleague who in the course of her sojourn in Rome was to give her guidance that proved invaluable for the rest of her life. This was Anton Anderledy, at the time Assistant to the Jesuit General Superior and later to succeed him in that office.

From the *Gesù* Mary went to the Irish College, where she met Monsignor Tobias Kirby, the Rector, and gave him her letter of introduction from Reynolds. He found lodgings for her in a nearby convent, the *Monastero della Compassione*, where the nuns treated her kindly but as only one of them was able to manage a little English communication was difficult. The building is now a student residence under the Dominican Fathers, and the memory of Mary MacKillop's sojourn is retained with pride.

On Tuesday she visited St Peter's with great emotion. "I could not *see* much that day," she told her mother, "but I *felt* a great deal." On Wednesday she visited Kirby again and discussed with him the documents she had brought from Australia. A meeting with Cardinal Barnabò, Prefect of the Congregation for the Propagation of the Faith (which dealt with Australian Church affairs) was arranged for Thursday. The old man, nearly blind, received her kindly and suggested that she present a formal petition for approval of the Rule, although he thought it would hardly be considered until the views of the future bishop were known. He arranged for her to meet Cardinal Bilio, Prefect of the Congregation of Rites, who was to present the Adelaide questions at a meeting a few days later.

That same afternoon she met Father Anderledy for the first time. Her name would have already been well known to him, as information about Adelaide had been sent to the Holy See through the Jesuits. She noted in her diary: "Saw Father Anderledy, like him more and more each time, he is so holy and charitable." She saw him twenty-six times in ten weeks, and her letters make frequent mention of his helpfulness.

It is remarkable that this man, who did not encourage Jesuits to spend time on the spiritual direction of women (because he thought they were already well supplied) should have given so much of his time to Mary MacKillop. She was especially anxious to clarify her ideas about authority, a sphere in which Woods was really nothing but a menace, and she availed herself freely of Anderledy's experience. When we observe the sureness with which she exercised her own authority in later years, and the respect, courage and intelligence with which she related to the authority of bishops, we are led to wonder who it was that helped her to understand so well the issues involved. It certainly was not Father Woods. The cloying nature of some of his spirituality, his imprudence with the visionaries, and the unsoundness of his views on obedience, would have found a powerful antidote in the advice of a man born and reared to toughness in the remote Alpine village of Berisal, a priest widely recognised as a reliable spiritual guide and a no-nonsense director. On her return Woods was well aware that she had been under powerful Jesuit influence, and he did not hesitate to repeat an earlier expression of his disapproval: "I thought your friends had done you more harm than your enemies."

Describing her first meeting with Cardinal Bilio at *S. Carlo ai Catinari* on Friday May 16, Mary told her mother that he was kind and paternal, laying aside all ceremony and making her feel at home. It was a reassuring meeting, as the cardinal upheld the contested parts of the Rule, but it was probably also on this occasion that Mary was told that Woods would have to be replaced permanently as spiritual director.

She was meanwhile preparing a number of documents for the Roman authorities. The first was a formal request for approval of the Rule. She gave two reasons for this: the good the Institute hoped to do, particularly for poor children; and the dangers that arose when people considered a Rule without Roman approval as of little account. With the text she sent a note acknowledging the faults of the nuns and expressing forbearance towards the Institute's enemies. It was the inexperience of the Sisters, she said, that led to ill feeling among young and inexperienced priests, "who suffered even more than any of us did".

With her request she included her *Observations*. These began with a short history of the Institute and went on to stress the need to share the lifestyle of the poor and the importance of providing schools which did not demand payment. To safeguard these ideals, she begged that the prescription of the Rule "never to acquire property or to have convents or lands of their own" be upheld. Other matters she called attention to were central government, the refusal of all government aid, and the exclusion of the teaching of instrumental music.

Attached to the text of the Rule there was a note in Latin about its weaknesses, its lack of clarity on some points, and the obvious need for modifications. The Holy See had had in its hands for some time (by favour of Tappeiner) a brief *Outline of the Institute* which emphasised the rule on poverty and the importance of central government. A few months later Mary made a written submission on the latter topic, "to let those who can have any voice in defending our views, know them as much as possible".

It is clear that in all the matter she presented Mary was seeking approbation of the Rule. Her documents became relevant some years later when Woods referred his differences with her to her alleged attempts to have the Rule changed in Rome, in particular the section on poverty. On the contrary, she was so concerned about preserving it that she wrote a very strong plea for the original form of poverty, and had it printed and distributed to people she considered influential.

A long letter she wrote to Kirby on Ascension Day, May 22, is a revealing example of Mary's openness with him. Beginning with her upbringing and the sense of God's watchful presence that she had from early childhood, she gave him an insight into her mind and heart unsurpassed by anything else she put on paper. The keynote is the will of God, which she called "a dear book which I am never tired of reading".[1] Her principal concern in life, she said, was to seek that will always and to carry it out, and in comparison no sacrifice seemed worthy of the name. The letter contains only passing references to the excommunication. These speak of the interior peace she experienced on that occasion, and express more concern for the bishop than about the injustice she suffered.

On May 19 the cardinals met to consider the affairs of the diocese of Adelaide. Bilio presented a record of the events that led up to the 1871 troubles, based mainly on the two reports of the Commission, on Reynolds' letter, and on the long review of the diocese prepared by Tappeiner. The substantial agreement of these documents led the cardinals to recommend that the Josephite Rule should be examined, that Woods should be removed as director, that Horan and Henderson should be ordered to quit Adelaide within thirty days, and that the Pope should name Reynolds as Bishop of Adelaide.

The decisions were approved by Pope Pius IX on May 25. Mary's joy at hearing the name of the new bishop was understandable, unclouded by any suspicion of what was to occur in Adelaide in ten years time. Like Woods, Reynolds had very little formal ecclesiastical training. Unlike Woods, however, he was not a man of distinguished intelligence, nor was he noted for his scholarly energy. He had the reputation of being a good and zealous priest, but in the course of time it became evident that neither his natural gifts nor his training met the demands of his office. Mary MacKillop was to suffer the full impact of the incompetence of this good and dedicated man.

Pentecost Sunday, June 1, was according to Mary's diary "a day never to be forgotten, a day worth years of suffering". She had her first audience with the Pope, with Barnabò and Kirby there to introduce her. Because there were severe measures against religious in Italy at the time, it could be dangerous to move about in the religious habit. But for this audience she wore her habit, and was able to report home: "Our loved habit has at last been blessed by the Pope." There was deep feeling in what she wrote to her mother:

> What he said, and how he said it when he knew that I was the *Excommunicated one*, are things too sacred to be spoken of—but he let me see that the Pope had a Father's heart, and when he laid his loved hands upon my head I felt more than I will attempt to say.

On May 29 the Rule was sent to Father Raymund Bianchi, Procurator General of the Dominicans. He was asked to suggest any emendations he thought advisable, and to say whether a preliminary decree of approval (*Decretum Laudis*) might be granted to the Institute. Three weeks later Mary went with Kirby to *Santa Maria sopra Minerva* to speak with him. Bianchi let her know he was not impressed by the objections of the bishops, but he did not think the form of poverty set down in the Rule would be permitted. Thus the Holy See, through the agency of this official, declared its mind early on the two aspects of the Rule that were to be "signs of contradiction" on Mary's return to Australia—central government and the ownership of property. The former was ignored by several bishops, and because of the latter the founder was embittered for the rest of his life.

Bianchi also said that the Rule would have to be rewritten. An amendment here and there would not meet the case. He would have given Mary, in milder terms probably, the substance of what he wrote later in devastating language in a report accompanying his revision of the Rule. It is unlikely that Woods ever read this report, but his reaction to the mauling his text suffered could hardly have been more unfortunate if he had.

One element in the Rule that puzzled Bianchi was that nuns went in twos and threes into remote areas, in primitive conditions, and without any income. At Kirby's suggestion, Anderledy wrote a note to explain why this kind of life was necessary for anybody trying to provide education for the children of the Australian outback. As for income, he said, if they waited until they were sure of revenue they would never get any school started. In any case, the divine providence they relied on had so far never failed them.

Some people have been puzzled by the secrecy surrounding Mary MacKillop's departure for Rome and her negotiations there. It has to be remembered that what the nuns called their troubles were the product of deep and vicious feelings. Both laity and clergy were involved. It would be wrong to imagine that the death of the bishop had calmed the stormy waters. The infamous Horan sermon was evidence that this was not so. Another sign was the solid financial support given by sympathisers to the "malcontents", the priests who had fallen out of official favour on Sheil's death. It would not have been at all surprising if these people had used the occasion of her departure to stir up trouble by abusing the Administrator and condemning the Institute. Reynolds told Kirby that some were hoping that a new bishop would get rid of central government or even disband the Institute.

In writing from Rome, Mary kept news about her activities in a low key. As Kirby had asked specifically that certain things be not noised abroad, she was torn between a desire to tell her mother what was happening, and fear that the news might come to the wrong ears. She knew that not everybody would be pleased that the Holy See was supporting her. Nobody had greater respect for the priesthood and for the authority of bishops than Mary MacKillop, but experience was teaching her not to be naive in her expectations of how even the best human beings might react when their own interests are involved. A phrase in one of her letters about not letting the bishops know too much caught the critical eye of Archbishop Kelly, Judge at the Canonical Process in 1926. In fact what she had said was just what her advisers in Rome had told her to say, and they had good reasons for telling her to say it. But her caution did not mean that she tried to prevent the bishops from making their views known in Rome. On the contrary, she wrote in her diary that she "went to see Mon. Kirby to ask him to tell the Cardinal the views of Dr Matthew Quinn". She had received a letter from Quinn the day before and was anxious that the cardinal should be aware of his wishes. At the same time she saw nothing wrong with a prudent reserve with those who were not her superiors.

She wrote regularly to Reynolds, Tappeiner and Woods, though the latter received his mail only after a long delay or not at all. Strangely, too, she wrote many letters to Kirby, though he lived just around the corner. She told him she felt she could express herself more candidly on paper than by word of mouth: "When writing I feel alone with God, and as He knows all things, am not kept back by my fear of what He may think." She wrote also to the nuns in Adelaide, Queensland and Bathurst, as well as to individual Sisters and to her mother and various friends. Her letters to the Josephites often contained what she called "little sermons" on kindness and unselfishness, and on the beauty of their vocation.

Quinn wrote to Kirby regularly from Bathurst, feeding him news and comments and making no secret of his opposition to central government. He never left any doubt about the matter in Mary's mind either, but she kept hoping that when the Holy See issued directives he would accept them. The full Bathurst story will be told in due course, but two remarks may be made here. The first is that the bishop knew perfectly well that the Rule was based on central government. His later encouragement of the myth that it was not is hard to understand, because he had told Kirby early in 1873 that one of the first things wrong with the rules was "that they are under one general superior, . . . and the superioress in my opinion ought to be induced to change it". The second thing is that at this stage Quinn spoke in a very positive way about Mary and the Institute. From her behaviour during the troubles he had come to believe she was a holy person. In fact it was what he had seen in Adelaide that induced him to ask the nuns into his diocese.

Mary's Roman diary and letters have lots of references to meetings and discussions, and there is plenty also about churches, novenas, Masses, pilgrimages to the catacombs and the tombs of the saints, and visits to convents and monasteries. But there is nothing about museums or art galleries, and scarcely a reference to the relics of momentous secular history surrounding her. She could hardly have failed to see the Colosseum from where she lived, but she saw it as the place "where so many thousand martyrs shed their blood and were destroyed by wild beasts". When "the cruel tyrant Nero" rated a mention, it was because of the martyrs who were victims of his cruel tyranny.

She did mention her difficulties with the Italian postal system, but her only references to the historic events going on around her amounted to concern about what was being done to injure religion and the papacy, such as the sequestration of the Quirinal Palace and a similar threat to the *Gesù*. However, her letters are full of human interest, lively bits of colour, and little stories about people. Thus, at her first papal audience:

> There were such a lot of people—ladies and gentlemen in full dress. *Of course* the dress peculiar to the Pontifical Court, *ladies in black*, no bonnets, but black lace veils thrown over their heads and shoulder and dresses high fitting, not low as is usually understood by full dress.

Another day she was delighted to meet "a mitred Abbot digging away in the field" at Tre Fontane, a little out of Rome, and extracted from him (as she did from other monks and nuns she met) a promise to pray for the Josephites.

Mary herself prayed a lot in Rome, in her favourite churches and elsewhere, opening her mind to God and imploring him to let her know his will. She was often in St Agatha's, adjacent to Kirby's residence and quite close to her own lodgings. But she was most frequently at the *Gesù*, where she often attended Mass in the rooms of St Ignatius and at his altar in the church. His tomb was a special place for her, not only because she had always esteemed the Jesuits, but also because her brother Donald had recently become one. After the *Gesù*, the church she visited most was one situated at the western end of the via del Quirinale, just opposite the palace. Once she had discovered it, she was an almost daily visitor and spent many hours there. It was part of a convent of enclosed nuns who paid special honour to Christ in the Eucharist, but when Kaiser William II came to visit Rome fifteen years later it was demolished to allow him a better view from his palace window. The site is now a public garden.

At first Mary's health in Rome was good, but as the summer heat grew more severe, the diary has more frequent references to illness and tiredness. When she says she was too sick to get up for Mass, she was certainly not well. When she did not go out all day, or "had to come home ill, very ill", we may be sure that she was speaking the plain truth. Early in July she wrote to Kirby about the matter. In view of her chronic health problem, for which the doctors could not do much, one can read between the lines a discreet hint that it is more than the Roman weather that is troubling her. Two weeks later she was unable to eat, and the nuns at the *Monastero* became anxious. So the authorities told her she should leave Rome, Barnabò assuring her that the interests of the Institute would be in safe hands.

At first it seemed that she would be going home immediately, but it was decided that she should remain until the end of the month and then to go to London. Besides hoping to beg her fare back to Australia, she wished to visit schools, obtain educational materials, and possibly gather postulants. She was also hoping for promises of priests for Adelaide. Dr Grant, the Rector of the Scots College, offered to assist if she decided to visit Scotland as well as England.

On July 24 she had a second audience with the Pope, "but this time in a quiet and homely way. The Holy Father came into the room in which we were, and walked round it, first talking to one and then to another, with a cheerful merry word to each." She could not say all she wanted to say because her interpreter Kirby was absent because of illness, but some of those present did what they could to help. July 31, the feast of St Ignatius, was her last day in Rome. She was busy with liturgy and devotion, but she made time to visit her chief benefactors to thank them and to say goodbye. She saw Kirby at the Irish College, Bianchi at the Minerva, Lambert and Anderledy at the *Gesù*, and Barnabò at the Propaganda.

This visit to Barnabò was memorable. When she had met him at a convent a few days before, he had made some joking remarks about the excommunication which had reduced her to tears. This time he was "like a kind old Father in the way he spoke". His Italian was so soft and gentle that she understood almost every word. He made up for his playful remarks by saying many kind and encouraging things, and by telling her not to mind the past and never to let it trouble her. He had already written to Reynolds telling him that she had completed her mission, and promising that the Institute would be approved in due time. His letter finished with an assurance that "her behaviour in Rome confirmed the very favourable account you gave of her".

"He had all his Council about him at the time," Mary wrote of this farewell, "and I was able to kneel down and kiss the hand of his chief secretary." As this secretary, Archbishop Simeoni, had taken a kindly interest in the Institute, she was pleased at the strong rumour that he would succeed Barnabò, but when the old man died seven months later he was succeeded by Franchi, not Simeoni. However, a new pope in 1878 moved Franchi up to be Secretary of State, and Simeoni changed over from that office to the one Franchi had been occupying at Propaganda.

On August 1 Mary was up for early Mass at the *Gesù*, and caught the 7 o'clock train to Loreto.

Footnote

1   The decree issued by the Holy See on 13 June 1992 declaring that Mary MacKillop's life was one of heroic virtue—a milestone on the road to canonisation—begins with a quotation from this letter to Kirby: "To me the will of God is a dear book which I am never tired of reading, which has always some new charm for me. I cannot tell you what a beautiful thing the will of God seems to me."

TWELVE

TO THE

HIGHLANDS

Mary visits England and Scotland 1873–1874

After a wearying journey from Rome, Mary arrived in Loreto on Friday evening, August 1.[1] Although she was pleased to observe the simple devotion of the people at the Sanctuary of the Holy House there, she found herself unable to share what they seemed to be feeling. But she attended Mass often and prayed much for her loved ones at home.

After two days in Loreto she left for London, though she had only enough money to get as far as Munich. She had the usual adventures of a foreigner travelling alone, like the supper she took in the corner of a noisy waiting room at Bologna during a three-hour wait in the early hours of the morning. In Munich she put Anderledy's recommendations to good use in finding a friendly convent and making a realistic friend in the Reverend Baron Obercamp. Of the Baron she wrote: "As if God had inspired him he asked me if I had enough money for my journey. The truth was that I had not."

At Koblenz she was warmly welcomed by the Franciscan Sisters who were to be her hosts for almost a week. There were some prospective postulants she wanted to see, and she took a great interest in the schools. She was impressed by the practice of an early daily Mass for the children and delighted by their sweet soft singing. She asked them to pray for the children in Australia and promised that her Australians would in turn pray for them. This was a common feature of her visits to schools—to ask for prayers and to promise prayers from Australia.

She set off for England on August 12, but through a mix-up of trains in Belgium she found herself in Brussels instead of Ostend. Her Roman letters came in handy with the Brussels Jesuits, who were impressed not only by the signature of such an important man as Anderledy, but also by the seal of the Society of Jesus that accompanied it. She eventually arrived at Ostend too late for the crossing, so she had to stay overnight. In the end she was happy about the mistake, as the earlier Ostend train was first class only, and she was spared the costly surcharge.

As the ferry approached Dover the next morning after an unsteady crossing, she felt an impatience to see the White Cliffs, although she had not felt any such desire to see other sights. This daughter of the Highlands MacKillop wrote: "If I felt that for England's cliffs, what, you may imagine, must I not wish to see if I go near Scotland."

There was a minor contretemps on her arrival in London. As the MacDougalls were away they had arranged for Mr Sands, a partner in the firm, to meet her. But he waited at one station while she arrived at another. She had a letter of introduction to a lady in London, however, so she took a cab to her house and with her help found lodgings in South Street, not far from the Jesuit church.

London seemed lonely and dreary, and Mary felt herself out of place and afraid. She even felt a strange fear of presenting her letter to the Jesuits, addressed "Fr Christie or . . .". Though this particular priest was marked absent, he had in fact just come back from Ireland that morning. Mary then saw the hand of God in her delay at Ostend, for if she had arrived in London as she had planned she might not have been directed to such a valued friend and director as Christie turned out to be.

On August 15 the MacDougalls sent a telegram saying that they would return the next day, and that in the meantime Mary was to go to their house in Clapham Park and make herself at home. The servants had been well instructed, and Mary was overwhelmed. At first she was inclined to feel concerned at the luxury, but then she simply had a good laugh at the incongruity of finding herself in "a grand high bed" in such a place. She stayed on about a week after the MacDougalls returned. Although they were so kind, she was not really at ease in such surroundings, especially as she was some distance from a church. When Mr MacDougall had to go to Australia, she was relieved to be able to return without offence to the cheap and convenient lodgings in South Street. But the MacDougalls continued to be helpful in her search for the school supplies. She may have had her head in heaven and felt it a weakness to be interested in the White Cliffs of Dover, but she had a sharp eye for the earthly details that concerned the work of the Institute.

Father Christie strongly advised her to join his group on a national pilgrimage to Paray-le-Monial, to commemorate the bicentenary of the apparitions there.[2] The group was part of a big contingent of pilgrims (including some of the high nobility) from England, Ireland and Scotland, which excited widespread interest, some puzzlement, and even some bitter opposition. On September 2, after Mass at 4.30 a.m., they took the train to Newhaven, then the ferry to Dieppe. Mary was very tired by the time they reached Paris late that night. Next morning she was not well at all. She found the day a struggle and was very ill on arrival at Paray late that night.

The next day was "a never to be forgotten one". She managed to keep up with the pilgrimage, yet she chided herself that she was tepid when she should have been fervent. She loved the convent gardens, and was delighted to be able to get "as a precious relic, *one leaf* from the tree under which our Divine Spouse told many things to Blessed Margaret Mary". She spent all the second night in the chapel of the apparition, hearing Mass several times before leaving in the bitter cold for the station at 4 a.m. She prayed for all those dear to her, and in particular that she would not have to return to Australia without some document to protect the Institute. She had been very impressed by the unity in faith and the friendly spirit of the pilgrims, "Peers and peasants, Lords and Ladies mixed with their servants as fellow Catholics."

Friday saw the group back in Paris, where Mary spent two days visiting places of religious interest. She lacked the touristic spirit, and was disappointed to find herself in the palace of Versailles when she was expecting to be taken to the tombs of some martyrs. She suffered bouts of sadness too, possibly because of the memory of her father who had long ago told her about what now surrounded her. A consoling angel appeared appropriately in the person of a priest from Scotland, "the Highlands too!"

The Guardian of the Sisters of St Joseph of the Sacred Heart had now gone out of her way to honour at Loreto the house which Joseph shared with Jesus and Mary, and also Paray-le-Monial, memorable for the Apparitions of the Sacred Heart of the Son of God. She had a great sense of the meaning of a name, and never saw patronage as a mere formality. Praying in each of these places she felt she had a right, in fact a duty, to recommend to God the interests of the Institute and of each of her Sisters.

The party returned to London on September 9 after a rough passage via Dieppe and Newhaven. The next day Mary noted: "Took medicine last night, felt better in the morning and able to go to Mass." It seems that it was not seasickness that bothered her, any more than in Rome it had been the heat alone, but something more like the periodic indisposition that was to trouble her so much in the years to come. Her letters from Britain mention when she feels better, which is an indication that her health was not good during these months.

A visit to Scotland had been in the air for some time. She had an emotional link with this land ("you know how my heart ever clinged to anything connected with Grandpapa and what he loved") and she was interested in relatives there, but she did not feel that this alone would justify a visit. She would think of going only if Scotland held some promise of providing postulants for the Institute and priests for Adelaide, or if she might expect Scottish friends to offer financial and spiritual support. She carried a letter of introduction to the Bishop of Glasgow, and imagining that her business could be dealt with by correspondence, she gave it to Father Christie, to be forwarded to the bishop with one of her own. She hoped that Father Coll McDonald, her mother's cousin, would act as intermediary, thus dispensing her from any need to go to Scotland in person. But Christie told her that she should go, and she was urged to go also by Monsignor Capel, who had been one of the Paray pilgrims and had subsequently organised hospitality for her and arranged various contacts. She had been diffident about meeting Capel in London because he was such a busy man, "so much so that many have thought he had not the time for such as me".

Mary was clearly not bounding along confidently as the competent woman of affairs. Rather, she was hesitant and lonely, and it was only the conviction that God required it of her that gave her the courage to keep going in the most unpromising situations. Mrs Laura Vaughan, a friend she met through Father Christie, had been invited to visit Lady Gordon in Scotland, but she would go only if Mary went with her. So they set out on October 15. It was the feast of St Teresa, a fact that greatly heartened Mary—"dear St Teresa," she said, "that day she got fresh strength for me."[3]

Monsignor Capel had recommended her to the Sisters of the Holy Child in Liverpool, and on arrival there she saw a good omen in the name of the lady in charge—Teresa. She stayed there a week and spent much time visiting the schools. These visits really amounted to inspections, since she wanted to take a professional look at how things were done. She saw the orphanage, the Poor School, the Training School, the Pupil Teachers' Night Class, the Day Boarding School, the Industrial School, and "more schools, St Joseph's in particular".

After Liverpool she went to Preston, where she waited for four hours in the dead of night for the train to Scotland on which Mrs Vaughan was already a passenger. A gentleman and his daughter, both invalids, urged her to spend the time of waiting at their home. When she assured them that she would be happy to remain at the station and get on with her letters, they made sure she had "a nice fire" and alerted the policeman on duty to keep a watchful eye on her.

When she and Mrs Vaughan got to Glasgow, they called on the Archbishop, who took the trouble to plan their onward journey for them. Next day they set off for Greenock, where they took a steamer for Oban, and after another overnight stay they went on by steamer until a rowing boat met them off the coast near Drimnin. This boat was manned by four Highlanders who to Mary's delight were speaking "the Gaelic". As the men rowed on, discussing their passengers, they decided that one was "a Sassenach", but as they puzzled over the other they went very red when they realised that she could follow what they were saying.

Lady Gordon had a truly Highland welcome awaiting the first religious in that part since the times of persecution. Mary was pleased to find that the house had its own private oratory, and when she met the local priest she discovered that he had been a companion of her father in the seminary. Not only that, but Alexander had himself been a guest in that very house. "How wonderful," she wrote home, "that without knowing it I should come to the very part where they were all so well known."

In one story told by her hostess, Mary could easily recognise the character of the father she had known and loved. On his return from Rome, said Lady Gordon, Alexander would not allow her to serve Mass while he, a cleric in minor orders, was present. Mary stayed at Drimnin for two weeks, during one of which, confined to her room by illness, she was nursed by her hostess with "the most tender care". When she was up and about again, various errands of charity were organised for her, such as a visit to the isle of Mull to see Father McNab's sister.

Encountering the past in people with memories of her father was to be a frequent experience for Mary MacKillop during her visit to

Scotland, and she was very moved by it. The sense of discovering her roots was surprisingly strong. As we read her accounts of these weeks we become aware of the depth of her feelings. There was never any doubt about her readiness to sacrifice everything for the love of God, but this did not mean that there was nothing to sacrifice. Her conscious ties with the MacDonalds were stronger than those with the MacKillops, perhaps because of her memories of the MacDonald grandfather she had known until her sixth year.

It is moving to read even now what she wrote to her mother after visiting MacDonald cousins in Cranachan: "The moment I saw John Cranachan in Church it was more than I could bear unmoved." She shared with her mother the feelings she experienced in a country which was, after all, not her own but her mother's: "Won't it cheer you my own dear Mamma to know that your child sees the parts you have known and loved, and meets so many who have known and loved you." Lady Gordon had a Jesuit grandson, and Mary hoped to cheer Flora by relaying the message that "she says you must be a happy Mother to have so many of yours in the service of God".

When eventually Mary left Drimnin House she went to Fort William, in the shadow of Ben Nevis, to "one of the oldest Highland Mansions of the country" that belonged to "a clan always true to the faith". This was the home of cousin Donald Peter MacDonald (the son of the "Long John" who named a distillery after himself), his wife Jessie Carmichael, and their seven children. Mary spent two weeks "quietly" in this household. Among the children was a young son, not quite three, who later became Archbishop of St Andrew's and Edinburgh.

After Fort William she moved into the heart of her ancestral country, the Braes of Lochaber. She reported that Father McDougall was delighted to be able to help, and that he "has announced to the people that he will go amongst them with me collecting for our cause". She began a begging tour in the Braes in the last week of November. The pastors escorted her on visits to their people, and passed her on from one to the other. From Keppoch she wrote to her mother about the kindness of one of her dear friends of long ago, who "bids me ask you if you remember the days you spent at Achluachrach and if so you will remember a lot".

Though the people were for the most part poor, they gave what they could. She recognised the effects of persecution in the poverty around her, and in the sight of a number of deserted old homesteads which had once been the happy and hospitable residences of Catholic families. Recalling the history of this region—her region—which she had absorbed in her childhood, she was both saddened and uplifted. There was no joy in the thought of "the former occupants either dead or forced to leave, in poverty", but reflecting on the historical process by which she, the daughter of former occupants, came to be born an Australian, and came to profess the values on which her Institute was founded, she concluded triumphantly: "So, thank God, in Scotland, as well as in many other places, the true faith has been preferred to all the wealth in the world."

From the Braes she returned to Fort William, where illness delayed her again for a few days before she could start for Fort Augustus. She was overjoyed to meet on the canal steamer the priest who had consoled her in her loneliness at Versailles. This was the pastor of Nairn, Father Forbes. He paid her expenses and handed her over to her relative, Dean MacDonald of Fort Augustus, with whom she then stayed for three days. The story was the same everywhere—helpful priests and kindly welcomes in convents. But at Stratherrick, the next stop, she struck "the best and nicest priest" she had met since leaving Rome. This man, Father Bissett, gave her soul "the help and encouragement it sometimes so sadly needed".

Leaving with regret, she moved on to Inverness where two of her previous hosts had prepared the way for a warm welcome. Of this she remarked: "It was so nice to find myself inside a convent and away from the incessant chatter of the world." Then after enjoying Father Forbes' hospitality at Nairn she moved on to Aberdeen, spending on the way an unscheduled night in the railway station at Keith. A gentleman there called the stationmaster and the guard to order when he found she had been misled about her train and had to spend the night in the waiting room; he did not desist until she was made comfortable and her ticket was guaranteed valid for the next day. At Aberdeen she stayed in a Franciscan convent, met Bishop MacDonald and others, and had a chance to see a large orphanage.

The bishop at Edinburgh, another old friend of her father, received her kindly and had great praise for the way her Sisters struggled to educate the poor. He encouraged her in the main points of the Rule; because of painful experience he commended strongly the prohibition on teaching music. She stayed with Mrs Carmichael (the mother of Mrs MacDonald of Fort William), "an old lady of seventy, who was a near relative and in such deep affliction that it pleased all parties that

I should do so." Her sojourn in Edinburgh, originally planned for a week or ten days, extended to a full month, probably because her begging had been unsuccessful. As usual she visited as many schools as she could, and had special praise for those conducted by the Ursulines. She also admired the great work of the Little Sisters of the Poor.

During this time a visit to her Uncle Archibald in Alloa confirmed Mary's fears that he had given up the Catholic faith. This brother of her father was "a mixture of Uncle Peter and Grandpapa with very much of Uncle's manner". He was kind to her personally, but "so much against our religion" that he would give no support to her work or listen to her attempts to help him back to his religion. She told the Sisters that he had "brought up a fine family in miserable darkness", and asked them to "pray for the grace of repentance for this unhappy father and his family". There is a glimmer of hope in the diary for January 22, when Archie's son took the trouble to meet her at Liverpool: "Met by William, my cousin, at the station. His wife, a pretty young creature, received me with much affection." An Australian grandson of Uncle Archie became a Catholic in 1966.

Disappointed that promised help was not forthcoming, Mary left for Glasgow on January 17. Although not well, she visited as many schools and orphanages there as she could. She received much kindness from the nuns, and was especially encouraged by the head nun at the Franciscan convent where she stayed. This "woman of much sense and experience" told her how blessed the Josephites were in being unrestrained by Government. Recalling her struggle against accepting Government funds for the schools, Mary told her Sisters: "She spoke so touchingly of the miseries of Religious, arising from the control of Government, and confirmed me more than ever in all my past ideas on the subject."

Moving south once more she came to Preston, where Monsignor Capel's sister, Sister Gabrielle, awaited her. The Sisters of the Holy Child Jesus impressed their visitor both by the warmth of their hospitality and by the style of their schools. Citing the excellence of these Preston schools, Mary urged her own Sisters to be faithful to their timetable and to be careful about order and cleanliness. Blending realism with encouragement, she reminded them of the importance of observing regulations about school work, a thing she had often heard stressed by experienced teachers.

Her long news-letters to Australia abound in colour and warmth and detail. The attractive humanity that shines through them goes some way towards explaining how she was personally so dear to the nuns and to her many friends. There is evidence aplenty that she was a single-minded nun engaged in God's business, but it was clearly not her Catholic faith that attracted the goodly number of Protestants with whom she formed warm and lasting friendships.

Her letters and diary during her voyage to the north reveal much about her thoughts and affections. She was always quick to recognise God's hand in coincidences and kindnesses that helped her on her way. From time to time she amused herself by wondering what her Sisters would think if they saw her. She encouraged them to be faithful and selfless, devoted to the poor, and above all kind and united. She taught her best lessons simply by telling of the kindness of the Sisters she stayed with, and describing what it was like to be a stranger. She had generous praise for some nuns in Paris who wore no distinctive dress and mixed much in the world: "It is their vocation and God blesses it, but it is not ours. Their Superioress General is a wonderful woman."

Her letters are full of brief and vivid pen-pictures of various friends, such as Lady Gordon, Lady Georgiana Fullerton and Mrs Carmichael. She had a ready eye for striking or amusing incidents, like her visit to the wild, grand glen, the home of five eccentric Highlanders of Cranachan. She was amused at attempts to guess her age, especially when people placed her at seventy (she was thirty-one), or called her "that funny-looking old lady" or "that old lady dressed in black". She described a Protestant friend calmly lighting his cigar with an anti-Catholic tract given to him in her presence by a bigoted clergyman.

There was the fussy Italian railwayman who looked after her during a three-hour wait for a train, and the German who picked up her fallen rosary and was delighted to speak English because his sister's governess had been English. There were priests who reminded her of the ones she knew in Australia.

There were embarrassing episodes, too, such as the time at Munich when neither she nor the head nun could speak a word of the other's language; and even less happy moments, as when she was afraid some drunken louts would come into her train compartment on one occasion. There were also some quaint stories, retold for what they were worth, like the tale of the bishop who stole the stone from the House of Loreto and was pursued by heaven until he replaced it.

Her difficulties are not fully revealed in the letters—to her mother she hardly speaks of them—but the diary sets them down as facts. She does not pretend that she is superhuman or that everything is smooth in her path. She refers to severe sick headaches, extreme tiredness, a heavy heart, and loneliness. "A sad night, cried myself to sleep," says one entry, "was so weary of the struggle, and felt so utterly alone." Unable to say her ordinary prayers, she offered her weary heart to God "with the wish that He would do His will". The note "No Mass" (she could not go even on her birthday) signals that the trouble was nothing trivial. Old Mrs Carmichael, who had evidently learnt something during her seventy years, gave her brandy, the remedy her doctors prescribed for what seems to have been the same condition. At all events, after Mrs Carmichael's prescription the result was: "Became better."

The physical elements in this poor health would have been reinforced by worries about her mission, the mixed success of her begging, the unpleasantness of cold refusals, uncertainty about Roman approval of the Institute, separation from those she loved, and concern about what was happening in Australia. Anxiety about travel arrangements, changing trains, long waits, the tedium of the travel itself, uncertainty about accommodation, are things even a person in good health can find something of an ordeal.

Kindness and generosity touched Mary in a way she never forgot. She took care to keep in touch by letter with the various priests who had helped her during the "sweet string of Providential events" in Scotland. On the other hand she was sensitive also to the coldness of some she approached for assistance. She did not take it as a personal affront, but could not help reflecting that it was the rich, not the poor, who refused her: "No welcome for the beggar from the rich ones of Edinburgh." She was more concerned about their deafness to the teachings of their religion than about being rejected. But it would be wrong to say that people with money never helped her. The McDougalls, Mrs Vaughan, Lady Gordon, and a number of people she met through them, became not only friends but also good benefactors.

It was January 26 when she finally returned to London to be welcomed by Mrs Vaughan at 23 Chapel Street, where she was to reside for most of the time before she left for Rome on March 14. Her health continued to give trouble, and Mrs Vaughan's kindness did not prevent an occasional sense of loneliness and frustration. But she kept going. She wrote a short article on the Institute, appealing for subjects to share the work and asking for prayers and financial aid. The Sisters, she said, were devoted to a work "opposed to the worldly tone of the present age", trusting only in God. Mrs Vaughan had enlisted the help of various people, including the Duchess of Norfolk and the Marchioness of Lothian, and their interest encouraged others to join them.

Her original contacts had led to others, such as Monsignor Howard and Dr Vaughan. The former became a cardinal later on, and was on the committee that recommended the confirmation of the Institute in 1888. He now promised to do what he could to help her, and told her to "ask Dr Vaughan to try and hasten matters when he went to Rome". Vaughan, just appointed Coadjutor to Sydney, became one of her strongest supporters. She was cheered by the many letters waiting for her in London, and was glad to hear from Kirby that she could await the decree if she wished.

The letters from Australia brought good tidings but also some warnings. She was saddened by the absence of any sign of life from Father Woods. Reynolds (who had not yet heard of his appointment as bishop) cheered her with news about the nuns. Tappeiner took up the theme of music, prompted by the threat of the Bishop of Bathurst. Apologising for writing to one who hardly needed convincing, he used some incisive language to make his point. If the nuns get a taste for accomplishments, he said, "they will soon lose their interest in the dirty, ragged little girls and boys," and then, "the poor, poor children, what will become of them?" Families of the children they were called to teach could not afford a piano or a violin.

The mail from Queensland did not bring good news. Adelaide history was being repeated there. The founder was making constant changes, sending untrained novices to teach far from the central house. Mary called this "a new evil threatening our work in Queensland, an evil which I hoped would not again be permitted". She alerted Kirby to the danger, pointing out that although Woods had the best of motives it was not in the best interests of the Institute to allow his policy to continue. As a countermeasure, it was important to urge the Holy See to allow only one novitiate for the first seven years.

In view of the Roman disapproval of the rule forbidding ownership of property, Mary's next initiative in London was to compose a defence of this rule, conscious that she was presenting a case, not making a demand: "Having given this explanation as far as I was able, the rest I leave to God." She was cautious, almost diffident, about this pamphlet. She consulted her confessor beforehand and submitted it to him when it was done, "though more inclined to burn it". He told her to have it printed. Even then she wrote to Kirby: "I think that perhaps I did wrong in printing the accompanying statement, that at least I might have waited until I had asked you about it." She sent him six copies for people in Rome, "but only on the condition that you approve, otherwise burn them".

Mary told Kirby that in spite of her repugnance to publicity she felt that God wished her to take this action: "I have found it easier to do disagreeable things if they seem necessary in the line of my duty." She was hoping that it might influence Bianchi. Kirby reassured her about it, and said the text was good. Years later she wrote on a copy that is still preserved: "Written and printed 22 years ago at a time of threatened danger to the Institute. We must all try to keep to the spirit of the work which should be the same now as then."

After a beautiful opening prayer, the pamphlet states the author's credentials: "It is an Australian who writes this, one brought up in the midst of many of the evils she tries to describe." Pointing out that what would seem out of place in Europe was the very reverse in most parts of her native country, she hopes that what she has to say may help those in authority to understand the Institute's situation better. Its avowed aim is the education of the poor. This cannot be carried out unless the nuns are disposed to accept nothing for their work, expect no particular living conditions, and rely only on charity. She paints a picture of the wonderful fruits of such dedication. To safeguard it, the Sisters "shrink with positive terror from the idea of possessing property of their own" and hope that they will be allowed to retain the original form of the rule. "Need the poor writer of this," she pleads, "ask the holy and learned ones to whose judgment she commits it, if it be not the teaching of our dear Lord Himself, which the Sisters humbly seek to imitate."

Then follows a defence of the additional works of the Institute, such as home visitation, which are seen as helping the primary work. On the other hand the teaching of instrumental music does not harmonise with a mission to the poor, and its exclusion is defended. Mary seems to have sensed the need to make this point to her European readers—certainly her compatriots a century later are puzzled by it all. But what she was talking about was the absurdity of the idea of a musical instrument in the homes of "the dirty ragged little girls and boys" whose families were barely managing to survive.

Mary was helped in the preparation of this pamphlet by Lady Georgiana Fullerton, a noted English novelist to whom she had been introduced by Father Christie. This lady not only undertook to revise this and other texts she wrote, but in doing so conceived a lasting admiration for the Sisters of St Joseph and became one of Mary's trusted friends. A year later she wrote a fine article for *The Messenger*, speaking not only about the works of the Institute but also of what went on in the soul of the foundress.

On November 18 Mary had sent Kirby another document, on the need for central government. She had composed it in Rome but had not submitted it, apparently because central government had strong support there from the beginning. Now, probably because of what Matthew Quinn was trying to do, she decided to present her views on the subject once more.

The document begins with an oblique reference to the bishop: "Should anyone say there should not be a General Superior, the Sisters humbly reply that upon this point they are unanimous in imploring the Holy See to strengthen and confirm their dear Rule." The preservation of the original intention of the Rule—the education of poor children in Australian conditions—is seen to be tied in closely with the unity of the Institute, a unity that cannot be achieved without a General Superior. If the Sisters were subject to the bishop alone, they would "dread the many inroads that would be made both on its spirit and letter" by those having only local interests at heart. A General Superior "is bound to preserve the Rule", and would be "as solicitous for all as for one". Far from interfering with episcopal authority, her task would be to uphold it. She would be as anxious for the rights of a bishop as for those of the nuns, consulting him on matters that affected his diocese. Only if he wished something contrary to the Rule could there be any difficulty. The reason why she would in that case be on her guard, is that the nuns have the duty to follow their conscience, and "they cannot expect to do this but by fidelity to their Rule". In 1873 this seemed an abstract question, but within two years it was a flesh and blood issue at Bathurst.

The news from Rome was not good. The Italian government was making things very difficult for religious, and this could mean delay in obtaining approval for the Rule. Kirby reported in November that nuns were "the special objects of the hatred of the enemies of religion", the Jesuits were thrown out of all their houses, the

Franciscans from most of theirs, and the Dominicans expelled from the Minerva. Mary's reaction to the delay was: "I esteem it an honour for our Institute to share a little in this way with the far greater troubles of our loved Church and her suffering servants." But Christmas brought better news. Bianchi had reduced the rules "to a truly religious form according to the spirit of the Church", cutting out "unecclesiastical and irrelevant phrases". It was likely that this new composition would meet the approval of the Holy See.

Bishop Reynolds was urging the needs of his diocese with both Mary and Monsignor Kirby. A few days after his consecration he wrote to the latter about Adelaide's debts and its need for priests. Even at this early stage he was preoccupied with the debt. He was never a good temporal administrator, and in time his concern about the debt contributed to the loss of equilibrium that was so evident from 1883 onwards. But even more significantly, there is also detectable in this early letter something of the wordy, gossipy, even catty, style that became characteristic of him when he disapproved of somebody. At this point his disapprobation extended to the Bishop of Melbourne, Dr Goold, and to that prelate's candidate for the See of Ballarat, Father James Moore. The dialectical method Reynolds brought to bear on the question of this episcopal appointment is to be seen in any issue in which he imagined he had adversaries.

His case against Moore begins with hearsay repeated across half the face of the earth: "His character for sobriety is often called in question by his confrères in Victoria." It is then strengthened by the piling up of guilt by association or heredity or suggestion, for not only was Moore's brother a noted drunkard and more besides, but "other priests relatives of his have given scandal in like manner" and "a sister of his was imprisoned for arson". The culmination is an emphatic prophecy of doom: "His appointment to the episcopacy would be a *calamity* to the Church in Australia." In one short anacoluthon Reynolds is able to blast not only Moore and his patron Goold, but also his own two predecessors in the See of Adelaide, Geoghegan and Sheil:

> The Bishop of Melbourne who not satisfied with the two whom he had been the means of foisting on Adelaide, would fain send another of the same stamp upon us in the person of Fr James Moore.

Writing to Mary, Reynolds mentioned the debt, but only to say how humiliated he was to have to submit a balance sheet at meetings called to discuss it. He did not suggest that Mary was in any way to blame, only his predecessors. He hinted at coming trouble in Bathurst, "but it will all end in the progress of the good work".

Tappeiner appreciated Mary's long accounts of what she was doing, and kept her informed in turn about home affairs. He had good news about Adelaide, and about the dedication of the nuns. He hoped she had seen Polding's newly appointed coadjutor, which in fact she had. He sounded warnings about Matthew Quinn, with whom he had had conversations. He saw him as the reverse of Polding, whose view was that "as long as the Sisters remain poor and humble, and mind the poor, they will do great things, but as soon as they aspire to higher things they are lost!".

It was, however, one of Woods' letters, written at the end of August, that gave Mary most food for thought. It opened with news about his work and his difficulties about going to the Northern Territory as desired by Reynolds, his superior. But it was when he came to the differences between Mary and himself that he touched the heart of the matter: "In the beginning of the institute you were guided by me and I see no reason why you should ever take any other guide in the conduct of it." Mary had written of her distress in having to differ from his views, and this reply made her realise how firmly he was set in those views. He was maintaining that she was unfaithful when she followed other spiritual guides instead of adhering to the will of God as interpreted to her by the Father Founder.

Matthew Quinn was always honest in speaking his mind to Mary about the parts of the Rule he did not like. In September 1873 he declared his "very strong convictions on this matter", and said that since the Rule was in the hands of the proper authorities "we should only pray to God that the Holy Spirit may guide those authorities to carry out His holy Will". In his mind, however, the expression "to carry out the divine will" meant to do what the Bishop of Bathurst wanted. He never gave Mary any reason to believe that if the Holy See continued to maintain central government he was prepared to accept it. She had warning enough, but for a long time she clung to the hope that if Rome approved of central government so would Bishop Quinn.

Thus, whilst still in Europe, Mary had due warning of two issues that later developed into major problems. Firstly, the trouble with Woods was foreshadowed in his 1873 letters. Secondly, the trouble with Matthew Quinn was there too in embryo in 1873, though she could hardly have expected it to be as heavily fraught with consequences as it turned out to be. On both issues Tappeiner was a shrewd judge. In January 1874 he said about Woods: "I thought— perhaps his task is finished"; and about Quinn: "Perhaps it will come to schisms in Bathurst yet."

With regard to Reynolds, in 1873 Mary could have had no long-range warning that central government would become an issue with him too, or that he would become so bitter. Yet something of his potential is indicated in his 1873 letters.

Footnotes

[1]   The religious devotion at this small Italian town (on the Adriatic, just south of Ancona) centres around the house in which Jesus Christ lived at Nazareth with Joseph and Mary. The authenticity of the physical house at Loreto, now enclosed in a mighty church, is a matter for discussion; but the basis of the devotion is sound Christian faith in the true humanity of the Son of God and the sacredness of the family.

[2]   This French town is north-east of Lyons. Between 1673 and 1675 a nun in the Visitation convent there, Margaret Mary Alacoque, claimed to have had several apparitions of Jesus Christ. He called attention to his heart, she said, as a symbol of his great love for mankind, and charged her to promote this devotion. She was mocked as deluded, but after the meticulous investigations that are customary when the Church is confronted with alleged wonders, it was announced that she was trustworthy. She was declared a saint in 1920. Devotion to the Sacred Heart of Jesus does not profess a new doctrine. It calls attention to the "divine love in a human heart" revealed in the Gospels and so often neglected by Christians.

[3]   Teresa of Avila, sixteenth century mystic and energetic woman of affairs, foundress of the reformed Carmelites.

THIRTEEN

ROMAN CEMENT

Second Visit to Rome 1874

A constant question in Mary's mind towards the end of 1873 was, "When do I go back to Australia?". Her heart was set on returning as soon as possible, but when could she consider her mission completed? Her main purpose was to secure protection for the Institute, and she was told at Christmas that she could come for this as soon as she liked. But she also hoped to recruit priests for Adelaide and gather postulants for the Institute—challenges to which a visit to Ireland might provide answers.

Her decision was influenced by the situation in Rome, by her own lack of funds, and by the hope of finding postulants in England and Ireland. The plan was to leave at once for Rome, then to return to London and to depart for Australia in July. This would give her friends in London time to collect money for fares. On Saturday March 14 she set off early for Paris via Calais, with a first-class train ticket quietly procured by Mr McDougall. After a day in Paris she started for Rome via Turin and Florence. Arriving late on March 17, she went to her *Monastero* "so tired, and glad after a visit to our dear Lord and cup of tea, to get into bed".

When she was in Rome eight months previously she had been promised the decree of approval, and Kirby had advised her to wait and take it back home with her. Then the delays led him to suggest that it would be better to return to Australia as soon as convenient. Although Christmas brought the news that the revised Rule was ready, there was further delay when Cardinal Barnabò died on February 24. It was just a week before Mary's return to Rome that he was succeeded by Cardinal Franchi.

It soon became clear that the decree was not going to be granted.

Official approval would not be given to a Rule which was in fact untried, and the promise had probably been made before it was evident that the text would have to be rewritten. Mary told Kirby that she was quite confident about the issues of central government and music, but she was honest about the objections from Bathurst: "You may wonder then that I should now ask you if it be possible to represent the Bishop's wishes more urgently to those in authority at Rome." With regard to how Bianchi would react to her plea for the no-property rule, she wrote: "I am in no way anxious should he still maintain his opinion after having the substance of the remarks made in the little pamphlet I sent you, explained to him." She wished the authorities to be fully informed of her opponent's views as well as her own, and she was prepared to accept their decision.

But she knew that Australia was a long way from Rome, and that protection was therefore all the more necessary. The very first batch of mail she got in London convinced her more than ever that she needed to return to Australia with some official backing for the single novitiate. She saw it as an important factor in preserving the unity of the Institute, since a separate novitiate in each diocese would be a weakness that could be exploited by opponents. In accordance with the original Rule, provinces had been established in Brisbane and Bathurst, with a novitiate in each. The Bathurst Quinn had promised that novices would be permitted to complete their training before being sent out to the schools, but alarming news from Brisbane indicated that his brother was not exercising the same care. Mary was keen to have a single novitiate, but if several were retained she was anxious that at least the rule about spending adequate time in them should be strictly enforced. This would prevent a repetition of what happened in Adelaide when young Sisters were sent to distant schools without proper training.

During these weeks in Rome her health continued to give her trouble. She noted in her diary, like any other fact, that she often felt ill and tired. On March 30 she was forced to miss a papal audience. On Easter Sunday, six days later, she wrote: "Felt more united to God's Will but oh, so sad. When invited to recreation in the evening, it was too much—I cried and the poor Sisters were so sorry." The delays, anxieties, uncertainties, and loneliness sharpened by the fact that she and the *Monastero* nuns had no common language, would all seem to have contributed to her breaking down in this way. The diary for the next day says: "Bodily health bad, but mental distress worse

152

than all." Yet when writing to her mother and Annie she put a good face on it all, and spoke about how kind everybody was to her.

The contents of a letter from Tappeiner at this time would not have relieved her distress. He had news of the death of a young nun, Sister Anne, but that was not a thing to worry Sister Mary—it was "one more Sister in heaven". What did worry her was what he had to say about Bathurst and the even more serious news about Woods in the north. At Bathurst there was great pressure to teach music, but authority was the basic problem. "The very kindness of the Bishop may be the greatest temptation," he said, urging her to make sure that something was decided in Rome.

With regard to Woods, Tappeiner reported that on medical advice he had not gone to the Northern Territory as his bishop wished, but had gone to Tasmania instead. He had been replaced as director of the Sisters by Tappeiner himself. When Reynolds reminded the nuns that all letters coming into the diocese or going out were to be seen by the Sister in charge, he was taking precautions against Woods, whom Tappeiner did not find "open or candid". The acting Guardian opened a letter one day to find Woods asking one of the Sisters to join him in one of his new ventures, "telling her to come, her vows would be up, no one could keep her then and such like". He had written to Sister Editha:

> I do not think it is advisable, that you should remain longer in your present doubtful and unsatisfactory state. I always thought that Sister Mary ruled your mind and had mentioned the subject to Father Tappeiner that he would not have been in any doubt.

Here Tappeiner interrupts his narrative with a protest: "I know nothing at all that he ever mentioned anything of this to me—I had no line from him when this arrived." When giving Editha the address of the former visionary Ignatius, so that she could go to Sydney and join her group, Woods had added, "I think it better that you should not say anything to Rev. Mother or the Bishop for the present." Startling as that was, Tappeiner says there is worse to follow. He had a letter from Woods saying he had told Editha to consult him [Fr T.] and Sister Calasanctius! His astonishment is reflected in his syntax:

> This is really very hard. He tells her, you ruled her mind, I do not understand him, not see things as he sees them, not a word about consulting, Sister Calasanctius' name not even mentioned, and to me he writes that he told her to consult with us! Really I think the poor Fr must be under some great delusion!

A letter from Woods himself was the cause of further concern to Mary, as it manifested less than the respect which she thought was due to Bishop Reynolds. A serious problem was developing, so she wrote to the bishop, with an enclosed letter for Woods, in an attempt at reconciliation. Apologising for bringing the matter up, she concluded her appeal: "You will feel a Father's pity, and with a Father's love pick the best means of gradually setting him right." Unfortunately Reynolds did not have the qualities that were called for in such a delicate situation, a fact that is amply illustrated not only in his relationship with Woods, but in his treatment of numerous other priests who crossed him.

Even at this early stage, many of the Adelaide clergy disliked Reynolds. Some years later a group of them sent a very strong expression of their disapproval to Rome. Allowing for the exaggerations that are characteristic of such statements, it is nonetheless possible to recognise in their picture of the bishop the distraught man of later years. Dean Fitzgibbon wrote some very strong letters about people in his time and now took up his pen against Reynolds. Some time later he was warned by his friend Father Maher that his letter had been returned to the bishop for comment! Maher adds an analysis of the situation: "For my own part unless I hear things from another source I could not take his word. Look out my friend the Bp is to write to Rome to defend himself and he won't spare you!"

This warning made Fitzgibbon reach for his pen again, to write Rome a letter containing the nouns malice, jealousy, vanity, and laughing-stock, and the adjectives ignorant, ambitious, and vindictive. It is to be hoped that this too was not sent back to the bishop for his comments. Signing off, the dean indicated that he could say much more about the bishop's defective education ("he hardly knows his catechism") and about the way he managed to become Administrator in the last days of Dr Sheil. Meanwhile the bishop had concluded his counterblast to Fitzgibbon's earlier attack with the declaration, "I will most gladly give him his exeat, notwithstanding the very great want of priests in this diocese."

In Easter week Mary met another member of the Australian hierarchy in Rome. This was Dr Goold of Melbourne. He had just acquired the title of Archbishop, as two new dioceses had been formed in Victoria. He was not liked at all by Reynolds, nor by the Quinns, nor by their cousin Murray in Maitland. He had resented the attempts of these prelates to dictate the decisions about the division of his diocese and to exclude priests not of their style from the new sees. He was now feeling pleased and relieved that Rome had taken no notice of them. Father Moore, against whom Reynolds had written so venomously, was with him.

Mary had been a little apprehensive about meeting Goold and was relieved to be able to write to Annie: "He was quite bright and warm in his manner, not in the least cold or formal." What had worried her was the 1871 trouble, not because of what she had suffered, but because of Dr Sheil: "Those who knew him in his bright days must painfully associate me with his dark and sadder ones." She saw Dr Goold again a week before she left Rome.

On April 9 she was received by Archbishop Simeoni, the secretary at Propaganda, and by Monsignor Rinaldini, who spoke good English. She stressed the Institute's need for protection, but hated to appear to be asserting its rights against the rights of any bishop. "I am as anxious," she said, "for the rights of the Bishops as for our own, ours could be nothing and should be nothing without them." She was simply asking for a statement about the rights of an institute which she was prepared to defend against unjust pressure from anywhere.

It was beginning to look as if she might have to return to Australia without the official approval that she had come so far to seek. This is reflected in her diary: "Much tempted at times to anxiety. Everything looking so uncertain," and "struggled on midst many conflicting thoughts". On April 15 she learnt that the documents were finally available. In the meantime she was visiting the Passionist headquarters trying to arrange for a foundation in Adelaide that would not only bring priests to the diocese, but would hold out some hope of having Father Woods return if he could rejoin that order.

At last, on Saturday April 18, two documents composed by Bianchi were given to Kirby for Mary. The first contained a number of comments on the original Rule, and the second the long-awaited revised Rule. On Sunday Kirby explained the details of the new Rule to her. She received the texts on Tuesday April 21. Bianchi had also written an assessment (*votum*), but this was not given to her. It was his official response to the request to examine the Rule. After a brief historical introduction he said that he found it "so imperfect, obscure, confused, and in some places so lacking in sense" that it was impossible to provide a remedy by changes and corrections. It needed to be rewritten. He had therefore prepared a text more suited to the spirit of the Institute and better conformed to the normal practice of the Church. The nuns should try it out and say what they think about it, so that their suggestions might be considered when in due course they apply for formal approbation of the Institute.

Bianchi's comments on the original Rule consisted of seventeen paragraphs and several concluding remarks. There is much detail in the old Rule, he said, that should be decided by General Chapter or by superiors. The only major change he made was in the rule about the ownership of property. His words, "This cannot be approved", were to become the rock on which the founder's already listing interest in the Institute was finally wrecked. Most of the other comments touched on details of daily living. The one novitiate is mentioned, and attention is called to the fact that while the Sisters should respect bishops and priests, their vow of obedience relates to their religious superior. There was a warning that those in remote areas should not be without priestly ministry for too long. Finally, he suggested that when they apply for the Decree of Approbation, they should submit statistical and geographical information about the works of the Institute. Letters from interested bishops were also to be made available.

The new Rule begins with an outline of the Institute, and then has three parts: entry to the Institute, its activities, and its administration. It insists on the General Superior who, with her four Councillors, is elected at the Chapter. The novitiate is to be spent at the Mother House. The need for a proper formation is stressed. Novices should not be engaged in other work; it is preferable also that the newly professed remain for a year or two at the Mother House to complete their formation. In some important sentences of Chapter VI the role of the local bishop is spelt out, as well as the limits of his authority over the nuns:

> A diocesan bishop cannot change the Constitutions nor can he abrogate or lessen the authority they give to Superiors in matters concerning appointments, visitations, the holding of Chapters and other such matters. The bishop in whose diocese the Mother House is located has no authority or jurisdiction over houses or Sisters outside his diocese.

Only the Holy See can remove the Superior General from office or accept her resignation. Only the Holy See can permit the transfer of the Mother House to another diocese, the setting up of a second novitiate, the establishment of provinces, and the separation of houses from the Institute. The bishop may dispense from first vows, but only the Holy See can dispense from perpetual vows. Most of these matters became contentious issues in the years that followed, for when bishops ignored these Constitutions, Mother Mary felt bound to point out that they were issued by the Holy See, with an instruction that changes were to be made only by the Holy See.

The Superior General must be at least thirty-five years of age. After election for two terms (twelve years) she cannot be re-elected without an interval unless the Holy See grants a dispensation. Minutes of her election should be sent to Rome. If a major difficulty arises at a Chapter, it can be resolved by the presiding bishop, but the Holy See should be informed at once. The music issue was confined to a directive that the Sisters should not play the organ in church, nor sing in the church except when instructing their pupils.

The Constitutions were accompanied by two letters from Cardinal Franchi, dated 21 April 1874, one for Bishop Reynolds and one for Sister Mary. The bishop was told of Mary's admirable docility in accepting the decision that the original Rule could not be approved. The new Rule was to be tried under his direction, but it was made clear that only the Holy See could make decisions about any changes thought advisable by anybody. In his letter to Mary, the cardinal said that the Rule should be shown to the bishop and then with his approval put into practice. After the experience of some years it should be returned to Rome for approval, together with any proposed changes.

These letters are important. They show that the Holy See was taking a sympathetic interest in the Institute and had reaffirmed and reinforced its central government. While Mary had received no formal Decree, she was going home with a document headed *Constitutions*, together with two letters signed by the Cardinal Prefect of the Congregation for the Propagation of the Faith and the secretary, Archbishop Simeoni,[1] to the effect that desirable changes were to be suggested to the same Congregation for approval. This precluded the introduction of changes even by the General Chapter, and likewise by outsiders, even prelates.

In view of all this, it is surprising to find that Kirby could write to Reynolds in July 1884 (ten years later): "in fact the 'Constitutions' which she took with her from Rome were no Constitutions at all". Kirby's mind had been soured against Mary by what he had been reading for years in letters from the bishops of Adelaide, Bathurst and Brisbane. It is really astonishing to find Kirby saying that after

Bianchi had put the rules into a decent form, "the new form of the Rules was given to her with a verbal recommendation of some of the officials in Propaganda to take them with her to Adelaide and try how they should work for a few years." Kirby's memory must have failed very badly in ten years to allow him to write as the climax of his piece of misinformation: "Her rules as she took them from Rome had not an atom of Papal or Propaganda authority." Reynolds' mind was confused enough by this time without this extra piece of mischief-making falsehood coming from what seemed to be a knowledgeable source.

Mary had documents endorsed by the highest authority at Propaganda, not a mere verbal recommendation of some of its officials, to make it clear that in fact she had achieved in 1874 what she had set out to do. The Constitutions could not have made it clearer that the Institute was not under the bishop in each diocese but under a single General Superior. They supported a single novitiate, and excluded provinces without prior Roman approval. Ownership of property was the one major issue about which the Holy See insisted on a ruling opposed to her desires, and having made a strong plea against it she was content to see the decision as the will of God.

She saw it as an act of affection, loyalty, and obedience towards the See of Peter (as the Rule directed) to accept her instructions with respect and to strive to carry them out faithfully. If she had told her Sisters that the Holy See had rejected their old Rule but that the new one she brought home "had not an atom of Papal or Propaganda authority", what would we think of her intelligence, let alone her obedience?

The new Rule did not, however, resolve the concrete problems which remained. What of the bishops who objected to an institute which was not diocesan? What of novitiates and provinces already established in accord with the original Rule? What of postulants and novices accepted under the original Rule? On her last day in Rome, April 24, Mary wrote to Kirby begging him to bring these difficulties to the notice of the Holy See. She was hoping for some statement which might help to bring about the desired unification of the novitiates.

Her last days in Rome were devoted to completing various items of business, and to making farewell visits to the various priests who had assisted her. She went to the German College (the modern

Collegio Bellarmino) and the Passionist headquarters, as well as to Dr Chatard at the American College, Dr Grant at the Scots College, Father Bianchi at the Minerva, Father Mullooly O.P. at San Clemente, Father Lambert S.J., and others. A conspicuous absentee during her 1874 visit to Rome was Father Anderledy. He had gone to Fiesole with his Father General when the Jesuits were expelled from the *Gesù* in October 1873.

On Monday April 20 Mary attended a Papal Audience, at which Kirby had arranged for a blessing signed by the Pope to be given to her—a portrait and blessing still to be seen at North Sydney. Unhappy about the absence of a specific mention of the founder, she asked Kirby to present a petition for "some mark of our Holy Father's Benediction upon him too—something we could treasure with the other". It was concern for Father Woods too that led her to visit the Passionists on the day before her departure, to explain the Adelaide situation and speak of his hopes. His feelings were again in her thoughts when later on she suggested that he might be invited to help with the modifications in the Rule with which it was hoped to placate Dr Quinn.

On Tuesday April 21 she met Cardinal Franchi for the first time. "The Cardinal extremely kind," she wrote, "promised to be our Protector." On the same day she received the photographs of Cardinal Barnabò which she had asked for so that the Sisters could see the man who had shown such kindly interest in them. As she left for Florence on April 24 Kirby gave her a letter of introduction to Cardinal Cullen of Dublin, and asked two priests from the Irish College to see her off at the station. She wrote back a special word of thanks for this escort, as the two were able to handle some boorish railway officials who became troublesome.

Footnote
[1] When the bishops in synod in Australia voted against the Josephites' central government in 1885, it was Simeoni who as Cardinal Prefect himself ordered the deletion of that particular decree, and three years later it was he who signed the approbation of the Institute. Thus Mary had had a powerful friend in Rome throughout all the troubled intervening years.

FOURTEEN

ENGLISH FRIENDS
AND IRISH RECRUITS

24 April–25 December 1874: Rome to Home

Mary spent the weekend in Florence making contact with people she wished to see. Father Anderledy had been in Fiesole nearby since shortly after they last met, and she went up there to see him on Sunday to resume their Roman conversations. She also wished to enquire about some Irish Jesuits for Adelaide. Much of her energy was devoted over these months to this task of recruiting clergy for Bishop Reynolds, though eventually to no avail.

On Monday April 27 she left for Reggio, where she stayed overnight in a community full of joy over a Sister who had been cured by Our Lady of Lourdes. Ill health was still causing Mary herself some concern and the next morning she saw a doctor. After her usual school visitation she set off for Turin, where she was delighted to find herself lodged just opposite a church dedicated to St Teresa. But to her dismay she discovered that she had left a small parcel at Reggio. It contained some gifts from the Pope for the Adelaide bazaar. It was so special that she had kept it apart from her main luggage, and then had left it behind! This oversight kept her in Turin for over a week.

During this delay she wrote to Monsignor Kirby about the reason for having only one novitiate and one training school. The need for uniform spiritual training "seems too evident for me to doubt the wishes of the Propaganda in its regard", she told him. Of the need for a firm foundation for the Institute's educational system she said: "Our whole strength in this system lies in our unity, and in the careful training of the members to it." As there was a limited number of nuns capable of taking charge of the training, high standards could not be expected if the trainees were spread over a number of centres. She recalled a cause of the Institute's early troubles: "Thus the system was planned, and partly acted upon, but we divided too soon, and the training was not properly kept up." This letter was a blend of delicate care not to blame others and a strong expression of conviction about how to guarantee the future. Any inconvenience involved should be borne for the general good. She knew quite well that there could be objections from Bathurst and Brisbane, but she hoped that wisdom and a little patience would solve any problems.

It was not her idea that the restriction to one training centre should be a permanent arrangement, but she was convinced that time was needed for the maturing process. Meanwhile, though she was faithful to principles, she was flexible and realistic in applying them. She was prepared to allow the present novices to continue where they were, while new candidates would use the novitiate in the Mother House. When the matter was referred to Bianchi, he agreed that the phasing out could be gradual. Mary could also see that it could be inconvenient to bring everybody together for final profession, so she suggested that this practice might be recommended but not insisted on.

In Turin she was able to visit the Cottolengo, "a grand institution supported entirely by alms". She called on various convents, and also visited the Archbishop, who was very cheerful and gave her two sets of rosary beads from the Holy Land. With the aid of the influential Count D'Aglie, the affair of the parcel lost in Reggio came to a happy ending on May 6 and she was able to leave the next day.

Bishop Reynolds had urged her to go to Lyons in the hope of getting aid for Adelaide from the Society for the Propagation of the Faith. She felt discouraged and was tempted not to go, but the bishop's wishes prevailed. She was received with genuine affection in a very nice convent in Fourvières to which the Jesuits had sent her. She spoke a number of times with Father Henri Ramière, the apostle of the Sacred Heart who had organised the Apostleship of Prayer into a worldwide devotion. He would have found a kindred spirit in Sister Mary. Living near her lodgings and speaking English well, he undertook to do what he could to fulfil her bishop's wishes. He had already learnt much about Adelaide from Woods and the Jesuits, and was brought up to date by Mary. During her week in Lyons she continued to inspect schools, according to her custom, and was a frequent visitor to the Shrine. In one convent she was delighted to meet another Sister Mary of the Cross, "an old Religious of St Joseph, who had a nice Providence".

On May 15 she left for Paray-le-Monial, armed with a letter from

Father Ramière asking that she be permitted to stay at the convent of the Visitation. In the event she was disappointed in this hope because of language difficulties—they thought that by quiet repose she meant a retreat, and "they could not understand how I would manage with French books only". So she stayed nearby for her few days of prayer and tranquillity. She was glad to rest from outward activity "without feeling that I am neglecting any less agreeable duty to which I should attend". People observing Mary MacKillop's busy life would have failed to understand her spirit if they had thought of her as a "woman of action". She certainly was a very active woman, but only because she saw it as God's will that she should be so. Activity was the "less agreeable duty" which took her away from the contemplation that was her natural bent.

After three days in Paray she left with a document of affiliation to the Visitation Convent for her Josephites (an unofficial bond of friendship), and arrived in Paris on the morning of May 19. She was delighted with the convent of Notre Dame in the Rue de Sèvres, where she found the simplicity and charity of the nuns charming to witness. This always gave her great joy, and she never failed to commend it to her Sisters. Her main concern was to recruit priests, but her hopes were disappointed. She could not help making a few reflections to Kirby on the number of priests in Europe "waiting for a settlement of Church affairs which may yet be some years off", while there was such a crying need for them elsewhere: "I have this matter so much at heart that I am sure you will in charity bear with me." She went to Bordeaux to see an old family friend, Annie Curcier, who had been generous to her on her arrival in Europe, and who had recently lost her husband. Apart from this visit Mary was in Paris until the 31st, when she left for London.

At this time her plan was still to leave for Australia on July 20, after a visit to Dublin. But soon after her arrival in London on June 1 she decided that she would not leave until September. She was busy writing letters to the Sisters about her movements, about the religious she had stayed with, the schools she had visited in Lyons, Paray, Paris and Bordeaux, and about her hopes for the Institute. She was full of encouragement: "The good Religious I meet often talk of you all, and many look upon our mission with a kind of holy envy, but admit that they would not have courage for its privations." She wrote to her mother on June 2 about the happy outcome of her main business, saying she was "fairly bewildered at the mystery of the whole".

Her mail brought a letter from Tappeiner confirming that Matthew Quinn was coming to Europe with a mind as firm as ever about the Josephite Rule. "If you have time yet," he wrote, "you may break a lance with him." There were some very good postulants, he told her, and "the greater part of the Sisters are really very good and there is no difficulty of any importance". But there was startling news about Angela. She had made a full and open admission that she had carried out systematic deception in her career as a visionary: "She openly declares that she wilfully deceived Father Woods, that she did do all the extraordinary things attributed to the devil." This would have come as no surprise to Mary, but she was taken aback to hear that "Father Woods still thinks as before concerning her. After all this he writes to our Bishop that he hopes time will clear up this mystery, he does not believe yet that he was deceived."

Tappeiner apologised if this news was painful, but he thought Mary should know. His words about this latest strange aspect of the founder's character are gentle: "He is a good man and pleasing God, doing so much good. It is the extreme goodness of his heart that carries away his head."

On June 8 Mary arrived in Dublin where she was received kindly by Cardinal Cullen. This was the first of three visits (of one month, two months, and two weeks) she was to pay to Ireland. She found lodgings in Gardiner Street, near a convent of the Sisters of Charity. She set about visiting schools, asking questions and seeking advice about her problems in Australia. She expressed to Kirby a mixture of fear of what was going on in the world and of extraordinary confidence in the power of God to support her in her work for his cause. Her conviction about the role of the Institute in providing education for the poor grew always deeper. She had the comfort of finding postulants, though of course this meant that additional funds would have to be begged for their fares to Australia. As she left for London early in July the cardinal encouraged her to return to recruit more young women as Josephites. He told her too that Matthew Quinn was coming. The need to organise the postulants, the hope of finding priests for Adelaide, and the desire to see Dr Quinn, led her to conclude that July 20 would be too early to leave for home.

Having decided to stay until September, she wrote to Kirby asking for written authorisation to ask around for priests. She did this because Cullen had told her that the bishop should make his wishes known in some proper form, and the Jesuits too had suggested that they would like a few lines from Reynolds. Mary remarked that "more than my word in such things is necessary", and Kirby sent her a formal statement. There seemed little hope of finding Passionists, but the prospects were better with the Jesuits. Two might be available, but those in charge hoped that at least part of their fare would be found by the Adelaide diocese, that is, by Sister Mary begging from her friends in England.

She returned to London and set about it. Lady Georgiana Fullerton helped her again, this time by writing an inspiring article on the Institute to stir up some practical interest. Mary's begging activities extended also to seeking books for a spiritual library suggested by Tappeiner. Among those she approached was Woods' old friend Oakeley. She was also busy ordering school supplies to take home with her.

By August 6 she was again in Dublin, having visited the Bishop of Southwark and gone to see Monica's sister at Princethorpe Priory. This stay of two months in Ireland was to take her on a journey around the southern part of the island, gathering postulants and support, and visiting the families of her Irish Sisters. She had stayed with the Sisters of Mercy in her last week in London, and that order continued to be hospitable in Dublin. Because of a retreat at Baggot Street, they arranged for her to stay in Lower Gloucester Street where "they playfully say I shall be a Sister of Mercy before I leave them". The same remark was made in another place where she wore a Mercy habit while her own was being washed. The kindness of the Sisters of Mercy followed her as she moved about the country and she wrote of it in words of high praise.

As she set out south on August 11, a cheering show of support came from Reynolds in the form of some money to help her bring out postulants. She went to Wexford first, then Waterford, where she had one of the adventures which later became part of Josephite lore. The nuns she went to thought her letters were fakes! The bishop too proved to be difficult—"he seemed very angry about my business at first"—but he mellowed when he heard of her setback at the convent, and developed into a staunch supporter. In Waterford, then in Dungarvan and Cappoquin, Mary did all she could to visit relatives of nuns and priests in Australia. A nice little detail came from Dungarvan: "I have ever so many little tokens of love for those of you who have namesakes there, but must keep you waiting for them." Besides these tokens, the nuns had four postulants for her too.

Mary spread her net wide for candidates and for supporters. The Abbot of Melleray Abbey gave her a diploma to associate the Josephites with all the good works of the monks. Then by way of Limerick, Ennis, Gort and Loughrea, she made her way back to Dublin, intending to go to London with the postulants for a retreat. By the time she reached Dublin she had eight postulants and there were others making enquiries.

The Bishop of Bathurst had already arrived in Dublin, and Mary met him on September 7 at the Baggot Street Convent where she was a guest. When the Josephites had first gone to Bathurst in July 1872, no conditions were imposed by the bishop in relation to their Rule. In June 1873, however, he wrote to Mary from Australia candidly stating his objection to the idea of a General Superior as well as to the ban on music. He wrote about the same time to Kirby, in high praise of Mary and the Sisters, but asking that his objections be noted in Rome.

Writing from Suez on his way to Europe, Quinn returned to the topic. Aware that the Holy See had given a sympathetic reception to the parts of the Rule he objected to, he said he would have to provide otherwise for his diocese. This bore out Tappeiner's view that he would set up his own Institute if the Rule did not suit him. In Mary's eyes what was at stake was the dedication to the poor which she saw as essential to her Institute. She had a firm conviction about her vocation to serve the poor, and she had been assured in Rome that the path she had taken was a secure one.

She esteemed other orders and was generous with her praise, rejoicing that there was such variety in the Church. But this very variety made her all the more concerned to protect the spirit of the Josephites. She thought various groups should cooperate, not compete with each other or take over each other's work. She had union and harmony very much at heart: "Oh if the Church everywhere were only more united."

Moderns who wonder what all the fuss was about when Quinn wanted the Josephites to teach the piano, should bear in mind what life was like in 19th century Australia. The social conditions of the time are hard to grasp in an Australia where the poorest home has its television set, and probably each child has a transistor radio; where the sight of stereo sets, electric guitars and musical gear of all sorts, as well as computers and electronic games, is commonplace in ordinary homes. In Mary MacKillop's time a piano or a violin in the home was a sign of affluence. She had no aversion to music (in fact she loved it, and was enthusiastic about teaching singing in the schools) but she guarded jealously the claims of the poor on the Josephites.

Governments in Australia were promoting a secularist system of education, and her answer was another system, for which she saw unity of training and approach as essential. This insistence on unity was remarkable at a time when Australia was a group of colonies a quarter of a century away from becoming a single commonwealth. Her work was not only for Bathurst, or for Adelaide, or for Queensland. It was "for the Poor of all Australia, and for my own part after the strictest self examination, I really feel that I dare not face my God in judgment were I to fail in *trying* at least to secure for the Institute that peculiar training which is necessary for such a work." Her view was not a whim, it was a conviction, calm and deep: "If in Australia we want to battle, as battle we must for our children and their salvation, we must, to succeed, be united. The one spirit must pervade all."

The meeting with Quinn on September 7 was a hurried one because he was on the point of starting for London. But he made it clear that he was annoyed at the attitude of the Roman authorities towards the Rule. As well as his objection to central government and to the ban on teaching music, he was upset that novices from Bathurst would be taken to Adelaide out of his personal sphere of influence. Mary described him to Kirby that evening as "disappointed", "annoyed", "sore", and "jealous of his rights as a Bishop". Her letter was tranquil, but she wondered what should be done if the bishop simply took over in Bathurst. She begged Kirby to put this question to Franchi, who had promised to protect the Institute: what should she do if Quinn decides it is "his duty to go his way as he says and leave us to ours (that means separating the Sisters from the Mother House)"?

The question showed that Mary had no delusions about what might happen at Bathurst. What did happen was not something she stumbled into blindly. It was something she foresaw and tried her best to forestall. To make it clearer that the rights of bishops were not being violated, she thought some limitations could be placed on the authority of the Superior General. Thus it might be agreed that nuns would be removed from a diocese only if there were prior agreement with the bishop (in the case of disagreement only after an appeal to Rome), that they would not be admitted or dismissed without the consent of the bishop, and even that a separate novitiate might continue to function in Bathurst, provided that the Sister in charge were appointed by the Institute. "With these two clauses inserted," she said, "I do not think any reasonable Bishop can object to the Generalate." But with regard to what was to be taught and how it was done, she maintained that it was up to the General Chapter to decide. She was even prepared to see the Chapter, with Rome's approval, modifying the stance on music. But her conviction about the need for unity was unshaken: "I cannot sufficiently explain though I so strangely, and so strongly feel it."

Mary's second meeting with Quinn took place shortly after his return to Dublin on September 12. His attitude had hardened, if anything. He had decided to form his own institute and to train his own Sisters according to the needs of his diocese. Those who had come from Adelaide might return if they wished. The Roman authorities, especially Bianchi, would hardly have been sympathetic to his view that "anything so unsuited to Australia as nuns formed on these rules can scarcely be conceived". Quinn sent this account of the meeting to Kirby:

> When I remarked to Sister Mary that the original conception regarding the Sisters of St Joseph had been *essentially* changed, that consequently I could have nothing to say to them, she burst out crying and said she knew they (the rules) were; that the change was made against her will.

Dr Quinn never gave any sign that he was in the least interested in the poverty issue—the only part of the Rule that *was* changed, and changed certainly against Mary's will. It is therefore hard to guess how he was able to say that the original conception was essentially changed. The Sisters of St Joseph had never taught music, and central government was enshrined in the original Rule, so it would seem to be more accurate to say that he objected because it was *not* changed. If there were tears, we can only guess too at the quantity and the cause of them. It was an upsetting experience, after all, for a young woman, faced with the powerful and persuasive personality of a bishop in full flight, having to disagree with his analysis of the situation and to refuse to cooperate with his proposed dismemberment of the religious Institute for which she was responsible.

The two must have met again shortly after Quinn had written this letter, for on September 24 he wrote again to Kirby saying that he and Sister Mary had "come to a perfect and cordial understanding". The principal terms of this were that (if the Chapter agreed) the

Sisters would teach instrumental music, and that "external matters" like changing nuns from one place to another, and especially from one diocese to another, would be left to the bishop. If the Chapter did not agree, he said, "her community will take their way, and my community will take mine."

There was in fact no document signed by the two parties as a memorial of their "perfect and cordial understanding", and it is very unlikely indeed that Mary would have agreed with the bishop's account of what was said. What he meant by "my community" is not clear. If it included the professed Sisters who had come from Adelaide to Bathurst, there is no way imaginable that Mary would have agreed to let them "go his way". They were already bound to "go her way", that is, keep their vow and obey their superior. If she had been prepared to let them forget this vow there would have been no Bathurst crisis. The bishop seemed to be presuming that that is what they would all do. The whole point was that Mary could never agree that it was right. But if he was referring to his Irish postulants and other unprofessed Sisters who wished to remain with him, that was quite legal. Mary had no radical objection to it.

Kirby's reply to a letter of Mary's sent with this one of Quinn's was an exhortation not to conjure up new difficulties, and to trust in God that all would work out for the best. He was very encouraging, but he did not seem to grasp the nature of the threat that Quinn represented for the Institute. He cited the story of the holy women concerned about the big stone blocking the entrance to the sepulchre of Jesus Christ—"It was no longer there!". But difficulties did not need to be conjured up. They were there in the person of a determined bishop who was not going to be dislodged by an angel, like the stone. Kirby reassured her, however: "You have already received your instructions and the Propaganda has written to your Bishop." Fidelity to these instructions cost her abuse from many sources, including Kirby.

Early in October Mary spent a busy week in London. She had to organise a journey to Australia without knowing how many would be in the party. She also had to arrange to transport the school supplies she had collected, and the books gathered for the library. Returning to Dublin on October 12, she saw to the details of the retreat for her postulants. Aware of the importance of what was happening, she had asked Kirby to obtain the blessing of the Pope for herself and her group.

Writing to Franchi at this time, Mary referred again to Quinn's difficulties: "I grieve to find that the good Bishop of Bathurst is not pleased at the way things have been decided about our Rule." She said that she had asked him to be patient until after the Chapter: "I hope that he will see that his interests will not be forgotten, nor his rights as a Bishop interfered with." With regard to his insistence on a novitiate at Bathurst, she knew now that he wished to form the candidates according to his own mind, and in spite of her earlier acquiescence she was not now in favour of it: "Without unity in training, spirit, and method of teaching our schools can never succeed." In the same letter she again expressed her regret that the Holy See could not see its way to approving the no-property clause of the original Rule: "I am sorry that we are allowed to possess property," she said, "and until that is *finally* decided will pray that, if it be God's Will, *that* may yet be altered for us." The cardinal's reply did not touch on the property question, but it reassured her about the novitiate.

By the date of departure there were twenty-five people in the party. As well as the sixteen Josephites (Mary and fifteen postulants—all from Ireland), there were three Dominican nuns for Adelaide, three Good Shepherd nuns for Melbourne, two priests sent by Dr Quinn, and one student for Adelaide. Mary remarked sadly to Kirby: "There are no priests for poor Adelaide." The Dominicans were coming from Cabra to provide a much needed infusion of spirit for a group which had fallen on hard times.

When the party moved to London on October 28 in preparation for departure on the 31st, Mary found a letter awaiting her from Tappeiner. Quite a lot of mail seems to have gone astray, and he knew he was taking a chance with this letter, but since it was a cheery one it was a good thing it reached her. No special problems have cropped up, he said, but the Sisters are missing her, some are becoming impatient, and they are all anxious to know what exactly she had achieved in Rome. There have been many applications to join the Institute, and there will be more when it has some form of approval from Rome. He recalled the drama at Franklin Street: "The snare is broken too by the mercy of God—the enemies meant harm and have done much good. That is the way of God to bring good out of evil." This letter from Tappeiner was mentioned by Mary in her farewell letter to Kirby on October 30. She also told him of her letter of thanks to Franchi, in which (she said): "I tried to write *round* as you said to Cardinal Franchi, but succeeded very imperfectly."

Some of Mary's luggage—which had grown massive with the

books, school supplies, and other materials she had been collecting—
had been misplaced on the way to the ship. Mr Sands came to her
help in this small crisis and recovered the missing articles. On
October 31 Bishop Quinn kindly saw the party on board the *St Osyth*
at the South West India Dock, London. Fifty years later one of the
postulants, Patricia Campbell, recalled a detail of the voyage—an
arrangement which Mary thought "hardly rubrical" but which pleased
everybody: "One of the priests brought the Blessed Sacrament in a
leather case to Mother's cabin and we kept a light before It."

At last, after seventy-four days at sea, the *St Osyth* entered Port
Phillip heads and made its way up the bay towards Melbourne early
on Christmas morning 1874. When it berthed at Sandringham the
first person to come on board and greet the travellers was Mrs
MacKillop. After the welcoming excitement had died down she
accompanied the three Good Shepherd Sisters to their new home at
Abbotsford, where Lexie was now in charge of the novices. When
they appeared unannounced, the nuns thought it was a practical joke,
"that they were secular young ladies dressed up to give them a Xmas
morning surprise".

The rest of the party was delayed in Melbourne, and it was not
until the morning of 4 January 1875 that they reached Adelaide.
Bishop Reynolds was at the city railway station to welcome them, full
of apologies that nobody had been at the Port. He took them in cabs
to the Dominican Convent in Franklin Street (the former Josephite
Mother House, scene of the drama of September 1871) and after
lunch Mary left with her group for Kensington. Nearly a hundred
nuns were waiting there to welcome her back after an absence of
twenty-one months.

PART V

Troubles for the

Renewed

Institute

FIFTEEN

A SECOND
SPRING

The First General Chapter, March 1875

O n her return to Adelaide in January 1875, Mary set about preparing for the General Chapter. In a letter to the Sisters she outlined what was to be done to select delegates from Adelaide, Bathurst and Brisbane. She made it clear that this was not just any meeting of Sisters. Like a leitmotiv running through her text was the fact that it was a Chapter being held in obedience to the highest authority, and that she had been given detailed instructions by Cardinal Franchi about how to organise it. In no less than nine references to her authority for what she was doing, she stressed that she was acting "according to the instructions of the Propaganda and the rules laid down for us", and made it plain that the Institute was following "an obedience now strictly enforced by the decisions of the Propaganda".

Father Woods was a conspicuous absentee from the scene. He had left Adelaide in August 1872, after a visit for the Episcopal Commission, and never set foot in that city again. Effectively, however, he had left at the end of July 1871. The Commission had recommended that he should no longer be director of the Sisters, and Mary was told the same thing in Rome. Touching on this delicate matter in her circular letter, she said it was uncertain whether the founder would attend the Chapter as there were some "sad things" preventing it, but he would write in any case and be there in spirit.

Although expressed cautiously and kindly, this was a clear warning that all was not well. Woods was unenthusiastic and edgy in two letters he wrote to Mary early in February. He began by telling her— surely a prophetic touch—that he had become ill on the very day he learned of her return to Australia. Then in words that seem at first to express personal concern for her "after weary journeys and many trials", he betrayed a total lack of sensitivity by describing her achievement as "so much distraction". He had no realistic sense of the huge task that faced her as she grappled with the problems of organising the Chapter and supervising the renewed Institute. "Take a good rest," he said, "and give repose to both body and soul." Then came a clear sign of trouble: "I did not write to you because I did not think I could be of any help to you and I was sure, as I fear now, that my letters would only give you pain." It had been "a heavier cross than usual", he said, to receive a letter from the bishop telling him that Rome had confirmed his dismissal and that he "should be allowed to have no communication with any of the Sisters except through the proper channel".

But there was another important issue, namely the battering his Rule had taken in Rome. Three times in two paragraphs of a second circular Mary stated explicitly that Roman approbation of the Rule as it stood was out of the question. Coming to the no-property rule in particular, she said: "In one dear point a decided change has been made." Pointing out that the original idea "met with a most decided disapprobation", she outlined the reasons for the change, stressing the danger to unity and even survival under the old rule. The Roman people had illustrated their point by reference to the disastrous experience of how the thing had worked in Adelaide in September 1871.

After dealing with some other matters, Mary made a point that was calculated to put the Sisters on their guard. She reminded them that the fact that an idea is inspired by God does not guarantee that it will not be mixed up with one's peculiar ideas. We cannot be sure that what looks good is really so. But when we submit our difficulty to the Holy See, we may be sure that we are safe in following its guidance in the matter. There is no specific mention of the founder, but the message touches his frame of mind and anticipates the attitude he was later to adopt openly. It is true that she cited in the very next paragraph some words of his which seemed to indicate acceptance: "I shall thankfully and cheerfully accept what has been decided for us, and am sure all the Sisters will unite with me in thinking ourselves happy and privileged to submit our judgments." She soon came to learn that in fact he was not in the least degree inclined to accept the decision.

There was warning enough in his reaction to her suggestion that he should help the Sisters. His language was polite, but the pique is evident: "It is kindest and best of me in your present circumstances not in any way to interfere with the Institute of St Joseph." By "present circumstances" he was referring to the Josephites' intention to obey the Holy See by holding a Chapter concerning their new Constitutions. His non-interference took the form of refusing to come to it, refusing to write to it even at the request of the bishop, and indicating that he did not wish to write to Mary again or to hear from her.

The Bishop of Bathurst was still abroad. Mary could have had no doubts about his attitude after what passed between them in Dublin. Even as early as eighteen months before that he had written: "There is no need of many reasons on these points. My mind is finally made up on them." He had made it clear from the start that he would not tolerate central government in his diocese. He knew quite well that the old Rule contained this provision, otherwise he would not have constantly stated his objection to it. Before Mary ever arrived in Rome, Quinn told Kirby he had read the Rule carefully. Although he thought it good on the whole, he objected "that they are under a general superioress". This should be changed, he said, and the bishop of each diocese should be the superior. The fact that no crisis had arisen in Bathurst earlier was due to the small numbers in the early days, and to the shortness of the interval between the foundation there and Mary's departure for Europe. The bishop left for Europe before she returned, and her Vicar did not call much attention to her authority in the meantime.

James Quinn in Brisbane shared the views of his brother. He was grateful to have nuns working in schools and caring for the poor in his enormous diocese, but he was no more disposed than Matthew to accept central government. The difference in early 1875 was that, whereas Matthew was still in Europe, James was resident in his diocese. Mary was hoping that both would change their attitude when they saw that Rome was behind all that was being done, and so she took care, when informing the Bishop of Brisbane of the Chapter, to stress the role of the Holy See. She could hardly have made it clearer when she wrote him a paragraph containing four references to that authority, concluding: "Cardinal Franchi has taken our Institute under his kind protection and, in writing, instructed me to put into practice the regulations made for us in Rome." But Quinn's reaction was not sympathetic. He was not at all disposed to allow matters to develop as Rome had directed. Instead, he began a campaign to break all contact between the Josephites in his diocese and their superior in Adelaide. He spoke of central government as a new idea brought back by Mary from Rome, although she had written:

> I know, my Lord, and have for some time known that you do not like the Central Government of our Institute, but please let me remind you that it *always* was a fixed point in our Rule. Now that it has met with approbation and been taken under the protection of the Propaganda, we gratefully cling to it more than ever.

James Quinn never respected the truth stated explicitly in this letter. Only by consistently ignoring it could he appeal to the difference between the old Rule and the new as the justification for what he proposed to do. There *was* a point on which the new Rule was different, namely the ownership of property. But it was Father Woods, not the bishops, who cared about that. The bishops were concerned only about authority, and in the new Rule the Holy See left authority where it had been from the beginning, in the hands of a Superior General.

Quinn said that what he was doing was "pending the instructions of the Holy See", as though it were not explicit instructions of the Holy See that Mary was obeying. She had been told that, until a new decision came from Rome, she was obliged to maintain the status quo, not the policy of someone wanting something different. If a bishop wished for changes he could submit them for Rome's decision, but he could not justly put them into practice in the meantime. Quinn certainly had changes to suggest—he thought the bishop should be in full charge in each diocese (or in his absence a priest appointed by him), and he wanted the duties of the nuns to be whatever the bishop decided. He was, of course, perfectly entitled to make these suggestions, but instead of submitting them to the Holy See as indicated by Franchi he acted as if his wishes were already law.

Mary found it hard to understand how a bishop would not harmonise his actions with the instructions of higher authority. In any case, she saw only one course open to her, namely to do what Franchi told her to do and to entrust the final outcome to God. She pleaded with Quinn to be patient, assuring him of her confidence that her Sisters would be able to work in harmony with him while at the same time observing the directives of the Holy See. But he had made up his mind and there was really no prospect that he would change it.

After receiving Mary's letter, Quinn wrote to Sister Clare, who was in charge of the Josephites in his diocese:

> We hereby relieve you, till further orders, of your Office as Superior
> of the Convent of St Joseph, South Brisbane, and also as Head
> Superior of the Institute of the Sisters of Saint Joseph in this Diocese.

He was clearly assuming full authority over the Josephites in Queensland. To reinforce his point, he kept referring to the Chapter as "a meeting of the Adelaide Sisters". He repeated twice in a letter a week later that Clare was going to Adelaide because he was sending her, not because she was summoned by her superiors. The whole Rule needed to be revised, he said, but "the formation of such a Rule is hardly woman's work, and I cannot venture to hope that your Meeting of Sisters will accomplish it".

This reference to the formation of the Rule as something yet to be achieved is puzzling. It seems to indicate that he was unaware that it had already been done in Rome by Bianchi, a very competent man who held high office in his order and in the Church. It is just possible that there was some failure in communication here, in spite of Mary's repeated efforts to let Quinn know that Franchi had given her the Rule with instructions about what to do when she got home. But it would have made little difference in any case, as on April 13 (by which time he certainly had read the new Rule) he told Mary she was to cease to exercise any authority over the Sisters in Queensland and to break off communication with them. His explicit statement that he had read the proposed Rule seems to be contradicted by his claim on May 29: "You have shown me no document from Rome nor have I seen any complete copy of the Rule." The very fact that he and his brother objected to the central government of the old Rule proves that they knew about it.

The implication of Quinn's remark about a document from Rome is that central government was a novelty brought back by Sister Mary, and it is hard to avoid the conclusion that he hoped to create confusion. He wanted the nuns to be under his authority and no other, so he said they *were* under his authority and no other. But Mary had a perfectly clear mind on the issue and never allowed her Sisters to be bluffed about the Rule. At all events, Clare went to the Chapter. Dr J. Quinn sent his good wishes, phrased as though the Chapter had nothing to do with the Brisbane Josephites.

So, with Father Woods abstaining in Tasmania and Bishop Quinn threatening in Queensland, the First General Chapter of the Sisters of St Joseph of the Sacred Heart opened on 19 March 1875, the Friday before Palm Sunday. The minutes say that the Sisters met "as his Eminence the Cardinal Prefect of Propaganda had desired". Bishop Reynolds presided and Father Tappeiner assisted as theologian. The Constitutions were accepted after being read and explained point by point, and Sister Mary was unanimously elected Mother General.

The Chapter saw nothing of Woods, but it heard some words he had written in a private letter to Mary, to the effect that he accepted what the Holy See had done but regretted the change to the Rule on poverty. Mary in fact shared this regret, but for the founder it was the prelude to a lifelong bitterness, in spite of his fair words. Significantly, the *Letter on Obedience* of Ignatius Loyola was taken up by the Chapter and received among the laws of the Congregation. Mary MacKillop had learned well from her Jesuit advisers the lessons inculcated in that epistle, and her conviction of its importance had influenced the Chapter's decision.

Everything at the Chapter had gone smoothly according to the Roman instructions, and it finished on Holy Thursday, March 25. Then after an eight-day retreat the nuns renewed their profession according to the new Constitutions. Mary reported to Kirby that the relationship of the Bishop of Adelaide to the Josephites was excellent. He was kindness itself, and "most warmly supported all the wishes of the Propaganda at the Chapter".

It was not the same story with the Quinns. James in Brisbane was the immediate threat, since Matthew of Bathurst was still in Europe. However, they held identical views, and each was to apply pressure on the Josephites to withdraw from obedience to their Mother General. It was not long before James justified Mary's fear that he was "determined to oppose us in every way". She described how he forbade the Sister in charge in Brisbane to return if she accepted the Chapter. He ordered the nuns there to break off all connection with Adelaide, and "not to write either to her or to me and said that any letters from us were to be forwarded to him". Quinn made this clear to Reynolds when the two met in Sydney shortly after Easter. Reynolds was hoping that he might convert his confrère to a more favourable attitude, but Quinn had no intention of changing his mind.

Writing on March 2 to Cani, his agent in Rome, Quinn expressed his views on Mother Mary, "this sentimental young lady who is now only 32 years of age", rather than on the legality of what he intended to do. He saw something sinister in the phrase "where these wishes are just", which Mary had used in speaking of her readiness to fulfil the bishops' desires. Citing it as "a sample of the spirit of Sister Mary of the Cross", he did not seem to think it possible for a bishop to wish for something, as an end or as a means, that could be considered unjust. Subsequent events in his own diocese and in that of his brother were to illustrate only too clearly that it was possible for a zealous bishop to wish to use means that were by no means just in order to achieve a good end.

At this point there appears a factor that was destined to play an important part in the story. James Quinn was aware of the disgruntled attitude of Julian Woods and he decided to utilise him in his efforts to break the Queensland Sisters away from the Constitutions. It must be remembered that Woods was very popular with the nuns and wielded a strong personal influence over many of them. This was due to his uncommon gifts of personality, his eloquence, and his patent goodness—characteristics which he did not lose when Rome removed him from the office of director. So now Quinn, in addition to forbidding his Josephites any contact with their Superior General, was encouraging false views among them about what had happened between the Institute and its Father Founder.

Woods' declaration of "non-interference" has already been noted. Mary begged him, in fact if not in so many words, to contribute what he could to the Institute within the limits of proper authority. Instead, he said it was best for him "not in any way to interfere with the Institute of St Joseph". His fine words submitting to the Holy See were indeed read to the Chapter, but they were an extract from a private letter and he never repeated them publicly. He certainly never put them into practice. Instead, he made a mysterious reference to "fighting this battle out to the victory". He spoke of "saving the Chapter", meaning that the Chapter should reject the Rule given by the authorities in Rome and restore the one they had judged quite unacceptable.

In spite of Woods' assurances that "I am in no way changed in your regard and you are just as dear to me as ever", Mary could have had nothing but a sinking heart as she read:

> We should be putting ourselves out of the plain track indicated by
> God's holy Will as evident in present circumstances if we did not just
> let events go their own way according to the light God gives us.

She could not grasp how such a holy man could be unaware that God's "plain track" is indicated in the decisions of those in authority.

"Present circumstances" for her included a plain and detailed directive from the Holy See. She would have been puzzled to see the principle "to let things go their own way" as a form of obedience. His actual words were: "Let us both go on in our own way and do what we can to serve God."

"I fear you will make havoc," he wrote two months after the Chapter, "and I ask myself if even then I shall be justified in stepping out of my neutrality to save the wreck." He never gave a sign that he was prepared to do what he could for the Institute in cheerful obedience to his superiors in the Church.

Such was Woods' frame of mind when he was drawn into the stratagem of James Quinn, who was telling the nuns in Brisbane that their founder had been treated shabbily. Mary wrote to Kirby deploring this untruth, and warning that "some mischief is on foot". The Sisters, she said, were being told that she was responsible for the destruction of the Institute, and she told him plainly that "poor Father Woods was not interdicted the positive direction of the Sisters any too soon".

Mary was not happy to have to write these things, but it was important that the people in Rome be enlightened about what was going on, especially as Matthew Quinn was there with letters from his brother encouraging him to do what he could to win their ear. He was to get together with Cani, who was there too with orders from James about how to handle the Josephite problem, having been told: "Our Sisters, as you are aware, are now under diocesan authority and so shall they remain." This news would have greatly surprised his Eminence Cardinal Franchi.

It is clear that it was Kirby's influential position in Rome that induced Mary to meet the danger by writing to him in detail on these delicate matters. She explained that if Woods had not been checked, evils and scandals would most certainly have followed. She gave two instances to support this view. The first concerned the chief Adelaide visionary, Angela, who had revealed publicly that the whole structure of mysticism and wonders was a fake built on systematic deception. She declared in a witnessed document that she had deceived Sister Mary as frequently as she could, and that she had deceived Father Woods in almost every way. But Woods was so deeply committed to the visionaries that he always treated attempts to tell him the truth as temptations. He did not believe Angela's confession.

The second thing Mary wanted Kirby to know about was Woods'

plan to found other religious institutes. She had thought at first that there might have been something in this initiative, but her confidence was destroyed by the course of deception carried on by his favoured souls. In particular, she had learnt from experience to dread the influence Sister Ignatius had over him. There is a good sample of this woman's style in a letter she wrote late in 1870, in reply to Mary's doubts in Brisbane about what was going on in Adelaide: "What a cruel cruel wretch our enemy is to dare fill a soul with such mean thoughts... I am sure our sweet Mother will not let you entertain so cruel and unjust a suspicion." The suspicion was that Ignatius was seeing Mary's letters to Woods, which in fact was true. He was showing her some, and she and Angela were opening others.

The "course of deception" to which Mary alluded was one in which Woods himself participated. While she was away in Europe he had made efforts to draw some Josephites away to form the nucleus of a new religious institute he was proposing. Paradoxically telling one of them that "the time has come when you are to show your fidelity to our Blessed Lord", he outlined his plan for her to leave the congregation to which she was vowed and come to Sydney. Mary commented: "There is a painful want of straightforwardness in Fr Woods' conduct which is a mystery to me in one so holy."

SIXTEEN

THE FOUNDER
ALIENATED

How did it come about that the founder was absent from the first General Chapter of the Josephites? And how was it that shortly afterwards he could be manipulated by the Bishop of Brisbane against the interests of the Institute which he had done so much to nurture and encourage?

Speaking of these matters in her *Life of the Rev. J. E. T. Woods*, Mother Mary mentioned that the danger of being arrested for debt was the reason he gave for his absence. But when the debts story first surfaced it was not regarded as one of the "sad things" preventing his participation. Whether or not the debts stopped him going to the Chapter, they certainly did not stop him writing to it. But he would not even do that, and Mary had to make the most of some words he had written to her in a private letter.

From August 1872 Woods had been on the move from one popular mission to another, far from Adelaide. He had wanted Mary to cross the continent to see him before going to Rome in 1873, and he was very upset when she did not do so. He reproached her for making the wrong choice when she had to choose thus between his advice and that of other mentors. The fact is that he was no longer director of the Institute, and she had gone to Rome when she did because she was told to go by legitimate authority. Woods resented being replaced as director and he was chagrined at what happened while she was in Rome.

His bitterness over Rome's treatment of his Rule is obvious in his letters. He was convinced that he was God's "chosen instrument to guide the Sisters", and the rejection of his text was equivalent to upsetting the order of divine providence. Years later he spoke of "the wayward spirit of novelty" that inspired a change God would not bless. The officials of the Holy See would have been startled to hear their action described in that way.

The focus of Woods' opposition was the new rule about property. Mary was just as attached to the old one as he was, but when it was rejected the reactions of the two could not have been more different. She wrote a pamphlet pleading for the old rule, but when this was unsuccessful she accepted the decision. Woods never accepted it, and left no doubt about his feelings:

> It has been almost a death blow to me to see the poverty and simplicity of the Institute of St Joseph destroyed and that without my being able to say a word in its defence. I can never get used to that and it makes me sick with sorrow whenever I think of it.

He saw the change as a source of great evils: "The little seed now sown in the Institute will soon bear its fruit." In a circular sent to the Bathurst Josephites not long before his death, he commented on the evil fruit of this seed:

> And I ask you also to bear in mind what struggles our holy rule has come through, and what opposition it has had. But I think the time will come when the wayward spirit of novelty will depart from these experiments and all St Joseph's children will be brought back together again and be what they were in the beginning.

The opposition he is talking about is the work of the Holy See, aided and abetted by Mother Mary. His resentment, coupled with his imagination, had led him to believe that she was the cause of all the trouble. When in 1879 he was spreading it around that it was she who had brought about the change in the rule on poverty, she protested:

> I must remind you of the charges the Sisters had to bring against me in excuse for their own disobedience: 1st, I had gone to Rome against Father Director's wishes; 2nd, that while there I had got him removed from the direction of the Institute; 3rd, that I had got the Rule with regard to Poverty purposely changed.
>
> You must know, dear Father, that I could deny each and every charge, and bring forward your own letter in proof of my truth. . . I have a letter of yours in answer to one in which I had told you how opposed Rome was to our being without convent property, and in which you acknowledged having received the pamphlet I had printed defending as well as I could our views—this defence you even praised in your letter. How then could it be said that I had asked to have it changed?

This is probably the strongest passage to be found in any of Mary MacKillop's writings. Woods took it all personally and refused (though always courteously) to allow her to visit him in his last years.

Two years before his death he wrote: "I must ask you to bear in mind that I utterly decline to renew any relations with your Institute." In his last letter some months later he said: "I do not think it necessary to enter into any explanation so as to make this unpleasant matter more painful than it is." The unpleasant matter was that he would not speak to her because thirteen years previously she had obeyed the Holy See rather than comply with the wishes of a director who had been relieved of his office. In fact, she did manage to see him before he died.

He was convinced that he had been betrayed: "What you have done has been most trying to me and has caused me very much bitter humiliation and suffering." Her trouble, in his view, was that she had begun to take advice from others, especially the Jesuits. Though not denying her good intentions, he pointed the finger:

> I also think that since you took the management of the Sisterhood of
> S. Joseph into your hands it has been very disastrous to that which is
> so dear to me and God has not blessed it.

The Jesuits had helped him to prepare for ordination, and he had been their guest from time to time at Sevenhill. But they had very little influence on his spirituality, and he resented their influence on Mary MacKillop. He insisted that he admired them, but their mental culture and their "elaborate and peculiar" spiritual training counted against them as directors of the Sisters of St Joseph. He regarded it as a disaster that their style had superseded his in the guidance of the Sisters:

> I always thought that the result of too exclusive a direction by the
> Fathers of the Society would be a change in the spirit of the Institute
> and would eventually turn it aside from that for which I originally
> designed it.

Here is a man conscious of vocation and destiny. The glory of God demanded that things be left as Father Woods designed them. No other created will, whether of the officials of the Holy See or of the Jesuits, should have been allowed to intervene.

What then was the difference between the thinking of the Jesuits and that of Father Woods? It had to do mainly with spiritual judgment. The Jesuit tradition in this difficult field is based mainly on the guidance given by their founder, Ignatius Loyola, in the rules for making spiritual judgments which he proposed as suitable for the second stage of his Spiritual Exercises. These rules are the result of the personal experience of their author, and of his reflection on the experience of Christians over many centuries. The fourth one warns that the matter is subtle:

> It is a mark of the evil spirit to assume the appearance of an angel of light. He begins by suggesting thoughts that are suited to a devout soul, and ends by suggesting his own.

Woods was certainly aware of the evil spirit, but he never seems to have suspected that the attack on a good man like himself would be of this subtle nature. He was taken up with spectacular phenomena such as physical attacks on his person and seemed pleased to be a distinguished target. Mary once suggested that he might consult his own spiritual director about his guidance of the nuns, because "the spiritual life is one of deep deep danger to those who follow it and those who are guides in it, and it is hard to move without making some mistake". But Woods was not worried by the danger of making mistakes, and readily ascribed to the enemy any hesitation on the part of his nuns to follow his advice. He did not imagine that a person with good intentions could be misled:

> I believe that I am the chosen instrument to guide the Sisters and God will give me all necessary lights and graces. To think for one moment of letting another guide the Institute would be betraying my trust.

Mary's suggestion that his spiritual discernment might be sharpened by outside advice (possibly from a Jesuit) was seen as superfluous and dangerous in the light of God's special care of his chosen instrument, Father Woods.

This attitude had calamitous consequences in 1870–71, and led to Woods' dismissal as director. Given his ideas on the virtue of prudence, this was not a surprising outcome. When Mary had suggested that he did not "seem to take those precautions which *prudence* suggests, to guard against danger", he wrote this extraordinary explanation:

> I know you are right in this. I have no prudence. I cannot be trusted in spiritual matters. The wonder is, of course, that I have done so little harm in this way. But, seeing how much our Blessed Mother has protected me, and watched my actions, I never have any fear.
>
> If I were a saint and had great spiritual light and knowledge, I would take precautions, make provisions and divide and dissect and plan and arrange, well then I would not pass over anything without turning it inside out and looking at the cause of everything . . . If, my dear Sister Mary, I go wrong, it will be my own sheer ignorance.

The last sentence, no doubt intended as an expression of humility, is one of the best prophecies ever uttered by this man much given to prophecy. He regarded the spiritual training of Jesuits as an undesirable influence on the Josephites. No names are mentioned, but Jesuits are presumably among those who encourage people to take precautions, make provisions, divide, dissect, plan, arrange, not pass over anything without turning it inside out, and look at the cause of everything. The list suggests a gentle parody of the sixth of the Ignatian rules on discernment, where a person who has been tempted is advised to review the course of the temptation, considering how the series of good thoughts was subtly diverted into an evil conclusion.

Not only refined spiritual wisdom but even common sense seemed to play no role in Woods' approach to spiritual direction. He was confident that he had all the lights he needed to secure the welfare of the Institute. The cast of his very active mind was never affected by systematic spiritual or theological training. It followed that even the most ungifted Jesuit, with some knowledge of Christian traditions, and a little practical expertise, would have been better equipped than this gifted but untrained man to help people face what Mary called the deep, deep danger of the spiritual life.

Julian Woods' genius was many-sided, his goodness and gentleness undeniable, his power to inspire widely acknowledged, but his education in the sacred sciences was sporadic and his reading was eclectic. His only opportunities for methodical study of theology and spirituality were his year as a Passionist novice in England, interrupted by ill health, and then some months as a student. A few years later he spent an even shorter period as a novice with the Marists in France. The fact that a breakdown in health caused him to leave each of these congregations in turn seems to indicate that an orderly regime of studies under supervision did not suit him. He certainly did not lack the energy or the will to work—his output in natural science alone, achieved alongside prodigious missionary activity, is astounding. He had read much, but in the theological field it was restricted to what he found congenial and unlikely to disturb his confidence.

To those who might observe that a lack of disciplined systematic training impaired the efficiency of splendid gifts, Woods might just as well have replied that, granted God's care of him, it was no loss at all. But two facts are indisputable: firstly, that he had an astonishing disregard for what many serious and holy people have regarded as important guideposts to spiritual sanity; and secondly, that his attitude did in fact sow disaster around him. At the same time, two achievements can never be denied him: his work as a missionary preacher was extensive and fruitful, and he was a religious founder, notably of the Institute of St Joseph.

In her letters from Queensland in 1870 Mary revealed a conflict between respect for Woods as priest, founder and friend, and the growing suspicion that his spiritual judgment was unreliable. Five years later we find the same respect, but her suspicion had grown into conviction. Having now a clear duty to protect the nuns from his imprudence, she warned them gently in her circular letter on the new Rule:

> We know and fondly believe that God inspired the idea of the Institute . . . But it does not follow that one's own peculiar ideas do not become mixed up with what is purely God's in the way of carrying a thing out.

The influence of long discussions with her Jesuit advisers at home and abroad is visible here. She was clearly recalling the last of the Ignatian discernment rules:

> A spiritual person must cautiously distinguish the actual time of consolation from the period which follows it. In this second period the soul frequently forms resolutions which are not granted directly by God our Lord. They may come from our own reasoning, . . . or they may come from the good or evil spirit.

This was a different world from the world of Father Woods, and he took it amiss that those who moved freely in it were influencing the spirituality of his Sisters.

It is obvious that Mary was following the counsels on obedience given by the founder of the Jesuits when she submitted her pamphlet pleading for the old rule on poverty. The most obvious demand of obedience is that a command be carried out (in all cases where there is no sin) but the ideal goes beyond that. It proposes that not only the will but the judgment be conformed to that of authority. Loyola wished that this principle "were as well understood and put into practice by men as it is acceptable to God", because when a person broods on unwise or undesirable aspects of what he has to do he is going to lose his earnestness, and his performance is going to be half-hearted. That is not to say that it is wrong to represent difficulties or other points of view—indeed, there is sometimes an obligation to do so. But once the final decision is made, the person under the authority of a leader not only carries out directives but cultivates a frame of mind that harmonises with them, thereby making his performance more effective. As far as effectiveness is concerned, a comparison with a sporting team's acceptance of its captain's decisions can make the point clear.

Mary MacKillop's obedience followed these principles, but it is hard to find evidence that Julian Woods accepted them or even understood them. There is certainly no evidence that he practised them, and even the element of carrying out orders is not conspicuous in his life. His missionary activity in the various colonies was not the result of being sent but of being invited, with his own eager cooperation. When he would not return to Adelaide in 1877, though his bishop wished him to do so, he explained: "I believe I am doing the most perfect thing and my strict duty in acting as I am doing." He was sure he could do more good where he was than by going back to his diocese. Rebuking Mary for bringing the bishop's message to him, he warned her against "the perilous path of interfering between a bishop and priest. Let the Bishop be his own mouthpiece."

This is not the place to analyse the record of Woods' own obedience, but it is important to see how different his view of this virtue was from the one that Mary MacKillop had made her own. He was a good man, and from all we know of him he would not knowingly have done what was wrong. We can only conclude then that he understood the matter wrongly, in fulfilment of his own prophecy: "If I go wrong, it will be my own sheer ignorance." Mary had not learnt obedience from him, and he resented those who had taught it to her.

The breakdown of their friendship was not due to a difference about the ownership of property. Rather, it was the consequence of their disparate views on obedience and on the process by which the will of God is discerned. They were both seeking to do the will of God. Mary believed that the way to it was through lawful authority, whereas Woods had the notion that it was revealed sufficiently in regard to the Institute when God chose him to be its founder. In his view, obedience meant that his nuns were to carry out all his directives and outsiders of whatever office or rank were to cooperate. The hierarchical nature of the Church did not play a significant part in his thinking. It was his own charismatic gifts that mattered, and even the highest authority ruling in an opposite sense could not shake his conviction that the will of God for the Institute was always to be found in the decisions of the founder.

In June 1875 Woods told Mary that he had seen the influence of the Jesuits in her letters to him, and said in plain words that these friends of hers had done her more harm than her enemies. It is not always clear whether he meant that their thinking was undesirable in itself, or simply that in practice they ignored the faith dimension. His words at times could be interpreted as referring only to some individuals, but there can be no doubt that he blamed them for Mary's failure. It is easy to see, moreover, at what points they would have brought their influence to bear on her. It would have been through their advice on spiritual discernment and obedience; that is, they schooled her in techniques of finding and doing the will of God. To Father Woods the will of God had been made known in a way that made further seeking superfluous, and there was no need of methods which relied on human powers.

While she was in Europe Mary had consulted a number of Jesuits in Rome, in London, and elsewhere, but the one who gave her most time was Anton Anderledy. It cannot be doubted that the advice of this distinguished man had a formative effect on her mind. Surmising an influential future for her, he could hardly have neglected to counsel her on the nature of authority, its limits, and its exercise. Woods was right when he discerned from the other side of the world that what she had learnt from him about the religious life had been supplemented by other doctrine.

As time went on he became more upset. There was little logic or reason in his words, but Mary had to try to make sense of what he was writing. She tried to get him to overcome his despondency and help the Sisters in ways that were acceptable to authority. But he thought after a different pattern and interpreted everything very personally. He never seems to have adverted to *what* she was saying—he always spoke of the effect it was having on him, in expressions like "feeling deeply", "not causing pain", "not interfering", "saving embarrassment", "raking up old misunderstandings".

"I don't want explanations while facts are as they are," he told her, "and it is useless carrying on a painful, nay distressing correspondence." In spite of his remarkable talents he seemed to have no sense of juridical realities.

He habitually called on sentimental expressions to rescue him, when what the situation demanded was wisdom, prudence and an accommodating humility. When he said he trusted that all would turn out well, he meant that his desires would be fulfilled, and that his original Rule would be restored, not that he would be helped to conform his will to authority and work in harmony with it. When he told Mary, "I constantly pray our sweet Mother to guide you aright", and expressed the noble sentiment, "I am fully confident that your sweet resignation to the Will of God must lead you right in the end", he did not mean that he was praying that she would carry out the instructions of the Holy See, but that, misguided and mistaken as she was, she would come around at last to his way of thinking. When he wrote: "For the rest I won't interfere until God will open one of our eyes," he meant until Mary should come to see things as he saw them, not that his own spiritual vision could possibly improve.

Mary's attempts to improve things only made them worse. Woods' replies became sharper, even at times waspish, and he went so far as to accuse her of what he himself was so plainly guilty of, that is, a "lively sensitiveness about anything said to oppose your ways of thinking and acting". When she tried to persuade him to return to Adelaide, where he could have done much to encourage the Josephites without stepping beyond the limits imposed on him, her meaning was cleverly and unfairly twisted, so that it was *she* who ended up being accused of acting against the bishop's wishes.

In her *Life of the Rev. J. E. T. Woods*, written in 1903, Mother Mary devoted only a few sentences to these events. They are remarkably discreet:

Those who could or would befriend Father Woods were being withdrawn by death, or absence, or other circumstances.

At the end of 1874, Sister M. returned, bringing a revised rule for the acceptance of the Sisters with letters to the Bishop, from Cardinal Franchi (successor of Cardinal Barnabò) on the subject.

A meeting of the Sisters, known as the General Chapter, was appointed to be held on 19th of March 1875. To this, Father Woods was invited, the Bishop and Father Tappeiner being also present.

Tasmania was not a place where much money could be made, no rich gold fields working there—and he had not been able to send the necessary sum. Therefore, glad as he would have been to meet once more those whom he loved so much, and whom he had so longed to see, he must forego that pleasure.

Later on, he met Sister M. in Penola, and afterwards in other places, but the majority of the Sisters he never saw again.

Being unable to attend the Chapter he sent a letter, in which he regretted the change made with regard to Poverty; but at the same time expressed his perfect submission to the decision of Rome, and his wish that all should prove their fidelity to the Holy See, by obeying it. The first rule of the Sisters had forbidden them to own any property. Therefore, when the misunderstanding came they were ordered to quit the house they occupied in Adelaide, and were left homeless, no one objecting. To protect them from such dangers in future, the words "The Institute may possess money, lands, and income" were inserted in the new Constitutions. This was the matter referred to in the letter of Father Woods.

Dr Reynolds signified his willingness to accept the services of Father Woods on condition that the latter should have no authority in the management of the convent; but this he declined, and continued his work in Tasmania, where he was much beloved.

Mary did not claim that the *Life* was a scientific history of the times. She presented it merely as a labour of love, an unpretending sketch of a gifted and holy man with whom she had been closely associated. It is possible to recognise in it an outline of what happened in 1875, but so much is left unsaid that as a source it is useful only as a confirmation of what is already known.

She says that Woods' friends were being withdrawn from him "by death, or absence or other circumstances". The last two words are as close as she comes to saying that there was a breach between the founder and the Institute because he disapproved of what the Holy See had done. She touches on the General Chapter, being careful to note that it was held at the direction of Cardinal Franchi, but the founder's absence is handled with great discretion. There is a vague reference to the debts, but his objection to the Roman decision is not mentioned. Just as she had given prominence at the Chapter to the words of "perfect submission to Rome" which he had written in a private letter, so she gives them prominence in the *Life*, though their source is not indicated in her text.

The fact that he never put these fine sentiments into practice is passed over in silence. The closest she comes to it is to mention his regret about the change in the property rule. She devotes some lines to an explanation of one of the Holy See's reasons for this change, but there is not a word about the antagonism that Woods sustained for the rest of his life. His refusal to return to his diocese is mentioned very gently, and with the remark that he was much beloved in Tasmania she resumes the account of his missionary activities.

But first there is the pathos and the kindly reticence of the words dictated by this great-souled woman in her last years as a record of the estrangement of the beloved founder who by then had long since departed the vale of tears in which the tragedy had been enacted:

Later on he met Sister M. in Penola, and afterwards in other places, but the majority of the Sisters he never saw again.

Sunt lacrimae rerum.

There is much in this story about the limitations of a gifted man and his alienation from Mary MacKillop and the Institute they founded. It is fitting therefore that as a counterbalance there should be included the last two paragraphs of the *Life* she composed to honour his memory. They are a moving climax to a story that leaves the reader in no doubt that the author was one who knew Julian Tenison Woods well and loved him dearly:

> How appropriate is the last resting place of the gentle, learned priest and naturalist! Crowned with the Cross, beneath the statue of the "Sweet Mother" whom he had so tenderly loved,—a little child in the next grave,—Australia's gifted son Deniehy at his feet,—the "Silver-tongued" Dalley close by,—typifying all that during life had most delighted him—Devotion, innocence and intellect!
>
> There, on the hill side, overlooking the Pacific, which far below washes the rocky cemetery, and murmurs a perpetual requiem in its own soul-stirring music, the mortal remains of Father J.E.Tenison Woods await the Resurrection.
>
> May he rest in peace. Amen.

It is recorded history that Mary MacKillop responded to the demands of divine love and sacrificed the friendship of this man, Julian Tenison Woods, in order to be faithful to her conscience and fulfil the will of God.

SEVENTEEN

THE BATHURST STORY

1872–1876

J ames and Matthew Quinn, sons of a well-to-do Kildare family, both studied in Rome at the Irish College when the Rector was Paul Cullen.[1] James returned to Dublin to found St Laurence O'Toole's school, and Matthew worked in India before joining him there and succeeding him as head. James was made Bishop of Brisbane in 1859; Matthew followed him to Australia as Bishop of Bathurst six years later.

Both Quinns created problems for the Josephites, but things came to a head more quickly with Matthew. When he arrived in Bathurst, he was challenged by a territory extending 500 miles west to the border of South Australia. To meet his people he had to face long journeys over roads that existed mainly in the imagination, in weather that was often very unfriendly. It was not going to be easy to organise a system of education, but his brother's approach to a similar problem in Queensland induced him to ask for some Josephites. When peace was re-established in Adelaide, he pressed his request, and shortly afterwards was able to welcome the first Sisters to Bathurst.

These pioneers—Teresa, Mary Joseph, and Hyacinth—arrived on 16 July 1872, accompanied by a young woman who later became a Sister. They were conducted to Perthville, five or six miles to the south of the town. Because it was on the Charlotte Vale Road, this place has always been known as the Vale, and it is still the central house of the Bathurst Sisters of St Joseph. There was no real convent for the first few months, not even a small cottage—just the comfortless little vestry of a country church, with the walls unplastered and the slabs in some places an inch or more apart. The bishop immediately took in hand the construction of a residence and novitiate, determined that his nuns should have adequate training.

It does not seem that Dr Quinn's disagreements with the Rule had been sounded before this foundation was made. Although nobody could have been more pleased than the Sister Guardian about the proper training of postulants and novices, nevertheless warnings of the future could have been discerned in the manner in which this was achieved. It was the bishop who determined that the new convent was to be built, and it was he who decided that it was to be the central house, commenting that the Sisters would thus always be under his own immediate supervision.

At all events, a neat little building was finished by November, and postulants had begun to appear. After six months there were sixty children at the school, and before long other schools were opened at Wattle Flat and Trunkey Creek, little towns about twenty-five miles to the south and to the north. The nuns knew that the Rule had always been based on central government and they were not surprised when this was reinforced by Rome. But in the mind of the bishop they were never going to be anything but a diocesan body, totally under his control.

On her way to Queensland at the end of April 1875, Mary paid a short visit to Bathurst, and on her return in mid-August she called in again, this time for a visit that was to assume sinister significance in the mind of the absent bishop. The priest in charge, Father McAuliffe, who was also the Sisters' director, insisted on bringing them all to the Vale so that the professed could renew their vows, the novices could be professed and the postulants could receive the habit. Mary allowed the professed to renew their vows "as they had no intention of deviating" from their profession, but she refused to allow anything to be done about the novices or the postulants until the bishop came back. When he did come back and disapproved of what had been done, Father McAuliffe asked Mary to support him in his pretence that he had had nothing to do with it.

After the vow ceremony Mary departed for Adelaide, and the Bathurst nuns went on with their work. But their peace was rudely disturbed when Dr Quinn returned just before Christmas 1875 with a group of Irish postulants. He assembled everybody and made the position clear. He would give them a few minutes to decide either for the Rule as originally drawn up (which he said he was upholding) or for the new Constitutions. He was thus already propagating the false view that the old Rule was diocesan. Those who chose "to continue to follow the primitive Rule" would remain at the Vale, while the others would be sent to the outlying convents. The professed Sisters (including Teresa, the superior) and six of the novices chose to remain with the Constitutions. One temporary professed chose the bishop, and one with life-vows, Hyacinth, was more amenable to his ideas than the others. Teresa's health was failing fast—she was in fact dying—and this made it more necessary than ever for Mary to hurry from Adelaide to support her companions.

She set out on 11 January 1876, but when she reached Melbourne she heard that Teresa had already died. She continued on to Bathurst, anxious to see the bishop and discuss the problem created by his action. She wrote to him on her way up: "Please let us settle the matter in peace. It grieves me to the heart to have the least shade of contention with anyone, above all with a Bishop of our Holy Church." She did not suspect that it would prove easier to see him than to see her Sisters, yet when she arrived she was told she was not to go to the Vale but to the convent of the Sisters of Mercy. A Mother General was being forbidden to visit one of her own houses.

Towards the end of January Mary received a reassurance from Hyacinth: "Do not doubt that I would ever waver." She replied with a message for those not professed:

I do not want to influence them in any way. Tell them so. If they adhere to the Mother House as you say, let them candidly tell the Bishop so, but let there be no insincerity or double dealing either with him or with me.

A few days later the one who would never waver sent her this:

My dear Mother Mary,

I wish to acquaint you that I have entirely placed myself under the authority and care of the Bishop of Bathurst.

I have taken this step for the glory of God and the salvation of my own soul.

Begging a share in your pious prayers, . . .

The thing that really worried Mary about it all was the casual way Hyacinth's vows were being treated, and for years afterwards she was concerned that no dispensation was ever sought. There can be little doubt that Hyacinth had a clear conscience, having been assured by the bishop that there was no reason for concern. She was obviously still a Sister of St Joseph, and there was no need to be legalistic about the change. But her note (which reads as if the bishop had a hand in it) was in fact announcing that she was walking out of the Institute to join a new one which had some local and historical continuity, but no juridical identity, with the one to whose superiors she was bound by vows.

On her return to Sydney Mary wanted to set the record straight with Dr Quinn on a number of points. By making much of the fact that she had once "travelled alone and at night", he had suggested to Rome that she was irresponsible. She wrote to him to defuse this charge, explaining what had happened—it was "nothing that had not been done before", as the Sisters of Mercy too had had to travel by the night coach. This particular journey was undertaken at the time when she was forbidden to go to her convent at the Vale but could manage to get to outlying places where the nuns were in great distress. They were affected by the tension with the bishop, some were quite ill and had no doctor in attendance, and there were debts they saw no prospect of paying. Mary did not like the night travelling but when there was no alternative it had to be faced.

As to going alone, it was very simple: "I had to travel alone to Wattle Flat, but was that my fault? No Sisters were left to go with me, and I was not allowed to go to the Vale to see if any would come with me." She could not leave the "exiled" Sisters unsupported, and it was not as though she were doing all this furtively. Quinn's own Vicar General told her she had to do it that way, and in fact he arranged it for her, making the booking and telling the coachman where to pick her up. She also explained to the bishop the truth behind another of his dark references: "The 'public house' at which we stayed was the one to which our Sisters had always had to go when thus travelling, a quiet respectable Hotel, kept by good Catholics." Summing it all up she asked, "Now my Lord did I really do anything so out of the way in any of these things?"

The pettiness of all "these things" contrasted with the fatherly manner Quinn normally adopted towards the Sisters. There can be no doubt that he was a zealous pastor of his flock, but he was lobbying in Rome by means of misrepresentation. Mary was upset to realise that he was using unfair tactics, and told Kirby she could not think "that all things done towards us lately in Bathurst were either just or kind".

Another matter that was vexing Mary was the gossip being spread around that Sister Mary Joseph, Teresa's successor as superior, was harsh and unfit to have authority. This would pave the way for Hyacinth to move in more easily, and since she was more open to Quinn's ideas it was hoped that she would eventually be able to draw the others away with her. She was working behind the scenes to support the bishop by creating the impression that any nuns who left Bathurst would be unwelcome in Adelaide. Some told Mary she had informed them "that you would not receive them even in Adelaide, and if she were in their place, she would remain with the Bishop". One pleaded: "Send for us as soon as you can, for I can plainly see what Sister Hyacinth intends doing." Mary told the bishop that so far from being harsh, Mary Joseph was loved by all as a kind and considerate friend, and that many Sisters had written to say that she had their entire confidence. One had said: "We would have died in this lonely place but for the very great kindness of Sister M. Joseph."

Mary also took up with the bishop his anger about her August visit. She had presumed that Dr McAuliffe would explain his own initiative in the affair, but when this priest became aware of the bishop's reaction he had instead taken steps to cover his tracks by trying to get her to connive at his silence. The Sisters knew what was happening and insisted that the bishop be informed about everything. Another authority (probably the Archbishop of Sydney) also told Mary she was bound to see that this was done. So she told the bishop that his Vicar General had urged her to the visit and had insisted that she see all her nuns, even ordering them to come in to the Vale to meet her: "I did not suppose that he was doing anything for which he was not ready to account to you. I did not believe it possible that he would allow you to remain under the impression that I had acted in any way without his full knowledge and consent." McAuliffe had made frantic efforts to keep the thing quiet, but Mary told him she could not be a party to this kind of deception: "I did not believe that you had sanctioned anything which you were not prepared to uphold." But she begged the bishop not to be hard on him—a plea she was to repeat on future occasions when she had to tell a truth that could get an ecclesiastic into trouble.

When the bishop accused Mary of breaking her word in conducting the August profession, she told him that if she had wished to break her word the novices would have been professed also, and the postulants would have received the habit. In fact she had not given her word to refrain from any of the things she did. What was said in the Dublin conversations is known only from what the two parties later reported about them, and the versions differed about what she promised. It is inconceivable that she would ever have agreed to anything contrary to the Constitutions in order to placate an angry bishop or to avoid offending a cajoling one. If she had been that kind of woman Mary MacKillop would have saved herself a great deal of vexation over the years. It is hard to see how Bishop Quinn ever came to think she promised to allow her Sisters, vowed to live in the Institute entrusted to her care, to remain unsupported and undefended while he was attempting to separate them from it. The fact that she was worried that there would be trouble makes it clear that she had *not* agreed to allow them to be treated as though they were not bound to the Institute.

Novices and postulants were in a different position, and Mary did nothing to confuse their status with that of the professed. That is why she refused to allow the novices to be professed or the postulants to receive the habit during her August visit. But she could not make commitments for free individuals to remain in Bathurst if they did not choose to do so. When novices insisted that they did not wish to stay if the bishop simply took over, what was she to do? What of those who wrote to her saying that they had regarded her as their mother and that she was now abandoning them? She blamed herself for not making particular reference to such cases in the Dublin talks, and for neglecting to state explicitly that the freedom of the postulants had to be respected. But this, surely, should have been taken for granted in any agreement between honourable people.

Did Mother Mary act improperly in not leaving the Sisters in Bathurst longer? And did she have the right to withdraw them at all? With regard to the first question, there is no doubt that to make the transition less disturbing she was anxious to delay the withdrawal. She was prepared even to let Hyacinth stay on to train the postulants if her Council approved. But the Council did not approve—they sent a "decided and unanimous refusal".

With regard to the withdrawal itself, the bishop hoped that his "appeal to Rome" would paralyse Mary into inaction. She was most respectful of Roman authority, but she was not one to be frightened into silence by the mere mention of the name Rome. She had been there, she knew the people allegedly being appealed to, and she remembered what they had told her to do. Talk of an appeal did not give her reason to withdraw support from nuns entrusted to her care. What Rome had already laid down, not what the bishop wished it to say in the future, was to remain in force while any appeal was being considered.

The only appeal that had been made to Rome at this stage was a private message from Quinn to Kirby to lobby for him.[2] He was perfectly entitled to do that, but it was pressing the point a bit far to call this an "appeal to Rome" in the hope that it would freeze a Superior General. Even if a regular appeal had been lodged, it could not inactivate her authority, and any changes it might lead to could have no automatic effect on the status of Sisters already under vows. In no way could the nuns simply be told they had been transferred to the jurisdiction of the Bishop of Bathurst as their Superior General.

Mary had advisers to reassure her about her decision. She explained the position respectfully to the bishop, referring to theologians and to an authority (probably Vaughan) who told her that what she was proposing was not only licit but in fact obligatory. The members of her Council in Adelaide were given the same advice. What they were hearing from Bathurst was so disturbing that they not only approved the decision about ultimate withdrawal, but rejected the proposal to allow some Sisters to remain for a time. Among the several telegrams sent, one from Tappeiner read: "You cannot consistently leave any let all return all unanimous Hyacinth must obey until Rome dispense." The Council was not prepared to allow the Sisters to be exposed to harassment and to hearing their Institute and their superiors ridiculed by the clergy. Mary pointed out to the bishop that "neither they nor I could be justified in leaving our poor Sisters in positions where their dearest ideas of duty were constantly talked against". It might have been possible to leave some in Bathurst for the time being if they had been treated with respect and tolerance, but the evidence indicated that this was not the case and was not likely to be. When Mary reflected on her Council's verdict, she wondered why she had not been quicker to see things in the same light.

One of the things that aggravated Quinn was the idea that his diocese was being controlled from Adelaide. He does not appear to have grasped the fact that although the Mother House was in Adelaide the Institute was just as independent of Reynolds as it was of himself. Mary spoke of this to Kirby: "Fancy Dr Matthew saying to the Sisters in a sermon that he would not support the reign of Dr Reynolds and Mother Mary." Quinn put it this way: "So four nuns in another diocese can upset mine and close my schools." His schools were no doubt upset to some extent, but the reason was that he himself was upsetting the members of a religious congregation by refusing to allow them to live by their rules. As he was also failing to protect them from constant discourtesy, their superiors decided it was wrong to leave them exposed to this treatment.

Never at any stage of this affair did any acrimony appear in Mary's statements or comments. She was committed to doing her duty to the Institute, but she was no less concerned about the bishop's feelings. Her attitude is summed up in the letter she sent him from Sydney on 11 February 1876. She did not speak of his failure to be just to the Sisters, but of her own failure to save him trouble:

> I think your Lordship will soon see that as we could not work together as before, it was better to part at once. I have completely failed in my effort to save you from additional care and annoyance, and at the same time to do my duty to the trust reposed in me by my Sisters.

Quinn had made some ungracious remarks to her in a letter two days previously, when the withdrawal had been decided:

> These Sisters cost this diocese a considerable sum, and if this sum had been advanced by the people I should resist their going, but fortunately it was advanced by myself and by Dr McAuliffe who I make no doubt will forgive his share of the debt as I certainly do mine.
> I have before now given my time and money in the interest of Adelaide and I am glad to do so again.

The snide suggestion that he had all along been pouring out money in the interests of Adelaide was hardly justified. The Sisters had been working for him for three and a half years for nothing, living very poorly and mostly in very primitive conditions, and they were not taking the Vale convent with them. But Mary interpreted the letter generously: "Your charity and kindness dictated a letter to me which has made me grieve more than ever at not being able to meet your wishes more. Its kind tone touched me to the heart." Her only comment about expenses was: "Forgive me, my Lord, when I say that I cannot see how our Sisters cost so much especially to Dr McAuliffe."

The subsequent Bathurst traditions about these events were derived from the bishop's view of the matter. For this reason Mary's name was for a long time not held in unchallenged veneration in that region. Expressions such as "when Mother Mary made her raid on us" were neither a fair summary of the history nor calculated to inspire admiration for Mother Mary. Woods made his contribution also, as one Sister indicated in later years: "Father would speak so sorrowfully of Mother Mary's failings." The myth that Bathurst was faithful to the old Rule made Mary look like some kind of traitor who had abandoned the founder and the true spirit of the Institute to follow innovations. Worse still, she was accused by Cani to Franchi of misrepresenting the facts to induce Rome to make the changes she wanted. Quinn said in so many words that she had gone "with the direct object of getting the Rule changed".

The grossness of this last remark is startling. One might wonder if the man had ever read the old Rule at all, except that we have his own word for it that he had, and we know very well how he repeatedly stated his objection to the idea of central government that it contained. In drawing up the rules of his diocesan congregation he went through the new (Roman) Constitutions with Woods and substituted diocesan authority for every reference to central government. In addition, the two of them went through the *old* Rule, excised every reference to central authority, substituted diocesan, and then appended the adjusted text to the Bathurst Rule as an *Explanation of the Rule.*[3]

Quinn was entitled to issue whatever rules he wanted for his new congregation, but he should not have continued to encourage the tradition that the original Rule was diocesan and he should not have allowed the printing of Sheil's name and the date 1868 under the mutilated version as though it were the original text. There still exists a copy of this version with all the changes carefully noted in Mother Mary's handwriting. She had found it hard to believe her eyes when she read "+L. B. Sheil, Bishop of Adelaide, December 17, 1868" at the bottom of the diocesanised text fabricated a decade later than that date. She said simply: "This has deceived many into the belief that it is the same as the original Rule." Sheil's name was removed on protest from later printings, but the text remained and was treated as though it were the old Rule. In such manner are myths sustained, and in this case it was a myth very damaging to Mary MacKillop's name in Bathurst.[4] The worst she would say about these matters was that they were disagreeable truths.

With regard to Mary's purpose in going to Rome, it certainly was not to get the Rule changed. She looked on the Rule as a sacred trust, and hoped to have it approved. Whoever gave Bishop Quinn the impression that her goal was to induce the Roman authorities (by misrepresenting the facts, it was said) to alter the Rule, did a service neither to truth nor to peace.

While acting as agent for Quinn in Rome, Cani made a number of submissions to Franchi on 20 August 1875. Number five was: "By representations not corresponding to the facts she obtained in Rome, and had approved in Chapter, serious changes in the rules of the Institute. These changes are not suited to dioceses other than Adelaide and do great harm to religion." If Franchi wanted representations not corresponding to the facts he had only to read Cani's other submissions:

1. Dr Quinn accepted the Sisters of St Joseph in his diocese because the purpose of the Institute and the essence of their Rule is that they are subject to and dependent on the local bishop.

[It was precisely the fact that the Rule did *not* say this that Quinn (whom Cani was representing) had always objected to.]

2. Not satisfied with this alone, the bishop made an agreement with the superior of the Sisters in Adelaide, to the effect that the houses in Bathurst would not be governed or directed by the superiors in Adelaide.

[The history of Mary's troubles shows that she would *never* have agreed to this. It was her sustained refusal to do so that Quinn found so objectionable.]

3. In spite of the fact that the bishop had got a novitiate built for the Sisters in Bathurst, she managed to effect changes in the rules of the Institute, changes very harmful to the diocese of Bathurst; and she wishes to take all the novices to Adelaide.

[The officials of the Holy See could remember for themselves who took the initiative in changing the Rule. It was certainly not Sister Mary. And the changes had nothing to do with introducing central government; that was there already, and the bishop knew this as well as Mary did; otherwise the two of them could not have discussed the problem it involved.]

The suggestion that somehow Mary brought the Roman officials to a point of view fraught with ill consequence scarcely reflects creditably on the intelligence or the memory of the members of the Sacred Congregation for the Propagation of the Faith. It was hardly a subtle move on Cani's part to submit such a statement to the very man who had given her the new Constitutions.

Cani was but a visitor to Rome. It was Kirby who was the principal Roman agent of the Irish bishops in Australia. Throughout this whole business he never put the Quinns right about Mary and her visit to Rome. He had been her trusted confidant at that time and he knew exactly what her state of mind was, what the old Rule said, and how the new Constitutions had come into being. He was now hearing from Australia that the old Rule was diocesan, and that Mary had come to

Rome with the direct object of getting it changed. Not only did he not correct this falsehood, but he became an agent of its dissemination. He put it in writing a number of times. There is a note in the Roman archives, dated 28 January 1876, in which he states that the old Rule was diocesan until Bianchi changed it, with Sister Mary practically standing over him while he did it.

Kirby could have acted as a peacemaker, knowing what he did, but he seems to have preferred to lend support to whatever the bishops were saying or doing. Thus he told Matthew Quinn that he had laid before the authorities of Propaganda in writing "the articles of agreement entered into by Your Lordship and Sister Mary in Dublin". There were no written "articles of agreement" between Bishop Quinn and Sister Mary. Any agreement they reached was verbal. What Kirby meant was that he had written down a version of what Quinn had told him had been agreed to, and submitted that to Propaganda under the title "articles of agreement". He might have been warned, by the inaccuracy of Quinn's account of Mary's activities in Rome, that his report of the Dublin conversations and of her involvement in the Bathurst events could be similarly flawed.

On 18 April 1876 the bishop sent Kirby a letter in which, after a slighting reference to Mary (now, 1876, the Mother General) as "merely the first to present herself" to Woods' Institute, and the statement (which could not have been true) that he had taken the Sisters "under the distinct understanding come to with Father Julian Woods and Sister Mary that these Sisters should be guided by me as their superior", he went on:

> My appeal to the Propaganda stands still as firm as ever it did on the first day.

[On that first day and ever afterwards he protested against the central government of the Institute, yet he later maintained, as the basis of his argument, that the old Rule was diocesan and that Mary had got it changed in Rome.]

> Sister Mary comes into this diocese without my leave;

[She had started off when she heard that Sister Teresa, the superior, was dying, and wrote to the bishop informing him politely that she was coming.]

> goes about all the convents

[Except the main one, which he forbad her to go near.]

> and secures the certainty of the Sisters obeying her

[She was bombarded by their declarations of loyalty and by their desperate pleas to be taken away from a place where their vocations were in danger.]

she orders them off at once to Adelaide

[She did it after much soul-searching, delay, and attempts to find a peaceful and legal compromise. Theological advisers had told her she had an obligation to do it. Her Council was unanimous about it.]

against the distinct promise made

[This presumably refers to the plan to delay the withdrawal. The promise was made with the distinct proviso that her Council approved, which it did not.]

and thus leaves my schools without teachers and she does this in the face of my appeal to Rome.

[She did her best to delay the withdrawal. Her jurisdiction and her obligation to the Sisters were not suspended by Quinn's request to Kirby to lobby with Propaganda.]

I will leave you to judge how far this conduct is respectful to the Holy See and Episcopal authority.

[Respect for the Holy See and concern to do what it had told her to do was what led Mary to defend the Constitutions against the illegal action of the bishop and the insults of his priests. Episcopal authority never had a more respectful client than Mary MacKillop, but in the case of Bishop Matthew Quinn the authority did not entitle him to bully Sisters into ignoring their vows and their Constitutions, nor to fail to discipline priests for their studied discourtesy to nuns.]

As far as I am concerned, I will still expect a just settlement of this matter.

[It is hard to know what he expected. Rome could tell him that he was free to found his own congregation (which he did in fact do); or it could take note of his suggestions for modification of the Constitutions, and in time refuse them or adopt them. But the bishop could hardly expect Franchi to tell Mary that she had been wrong to do what he had told her to do.]

Of course Kirby received the text of Quinn's letter without the comments that have been interspersed here. But he did receive a letter from Reynolds which made a number of points that should have alerted him to the truth: what Mary had done was in obedience to written instructions given to her in Rome; the old Rule was not based on diocesan government; and what Quinn was doing was contrary to the agreement made when the Sisters first went to his diocese.

Letters like this one of Quinn's from a few of the bishops in

Australia during the next decade turned Kirby from a friend of Mother Mary into a sour antagonist. She said later that it was a bitter cross to know that some of her friends in Rome died believing the things that had been said about her.

Kirby seems to have thought Quinn had won his point in September 1875, as he wrote to Franchi: "The Sisters of St Joseph with whom Dr Quinn had that little difference recently settled so wisely by Your Eminence . . ." How could he have thought this? It seems that Bianchi had been affected by strong Quinn lobbying, because there exists the draft of a letter, dated September 15, in which he tells Mary on behalf of Propaganda that it would be advisable to change the Institute to a diocesan one. Kirby evidently thought this letter had been sent, hence the compliment to Franchi about his wise solution of the problem. But the cardinal obviously did not approve of such a change in the Constitutions he had issued, and the letter was never sent. Kirby was soon urging the case again, referring to the inconvenience caused by whoever decided the letter should not be sent.

Whether or not Mary had begun to suspect Kirby's reliability, she realised that he was in a difficult position. She had continued to take him into her confidence, but when she became aware that the Quinns were using him as their agent too she saw that it could be embarrassing for him to have clients with opposing interests. She therefore began to write to Dr Grant, the Rector of the Scots College, and asked him to look after her interests in Rome. Grant did this, and his successor Dr Campbell proved in turn to be an invaluable friend to Mother Mary.

Rome's reaction to all the advice coming from Australia was summarised in a letter Grant wrote to Mary on 2 July 1876: "Propaganda has written to you approving of your conduct with regard to your religious. You have done nothing but what you were authorised by Rome to do." The fact that Bianchi's draft letter was never sent indicates that Franchi had not been affected by the arguments of the Quinn party. This conclusion becomes certain when we read what the cardinal said about the Constitutions on June 13, in the letter referred to by Grant:

> We see no reason why the religious should deviate from them. The Sisters of St Joseph may leave the above named dioceses if the Ordinaries continue to absolutely exact independence of the religious from the Mother House in Adelaide.

Quinn had still been urging his case with the cardinal in May:

> It is such a scandal, and such an insult to my authority and to yours, that I have no doubt Your Eminence will take the necessary steps in the circumstances.

By the time this letter arrived the necessary steps had already been taken. Mother Mary had been told that she was perfectly right to do what she did.

Footnotes

1. There were eight Quinn children, brought up on the family farm at Kilteel, fifteen miles from Dublin. A third brother was also a priest, and one of the sisters had four priest sons, the Horans, who went to Australia like their two uncles and played a notable part in ecclesiastical politics in Queensland.

   The Irish bishops in Australia were for the most part from the Irish College in Rome. There was loyalty among them as "Cullen men", but a number were also related by blood. Cardinal Cullen was the uncle of Cardinal Moran, the Quinns were brothers of each other and first cousins of Bishop Murray (himself the grand-nephew of an Archbishop of Dublin), and there is good evidence that the Quinns and Cullen were related. There was no love lost between this group and the English Archbishops of Sydney, Polding and Vaughan.

2. A sidelight on the lobbying was the cultivation of the Roman official Monsignor Rinaldini. This was of course quite legitimate, but it makes amusing reading. Quinn wrote from Dublin in August 1875: "Monsig. Rinaldini, who is in ecstasy at everything he saw, is gone round today in the Cardinal's carriage with Fr Wm Cullen to see some of the Churches and religious institutions. He has dined twice with the Cardinal and dines with him today again. I need not say we paid him all the attention in our power." We may be sure they did.

3. Woods wrote: "Some few matters of detail have been altered according to what a more mature experience seemed to require. But no change whatever has been made in its spirit, which is that of perfect poverty, true detachment and lowly humility." The more mature experience meant the will of Dr Quinn, and the perfect poverty meant the reintroduction of the rule rejected by the Holy See. The change from central government to diocesan was apparently a matter of detail!

4. The historical work of Margaret M. Press, a diocesan Josephite, has done much to clear away the traditional falsehoods about the events of 1876 in Bathurst, and to restore respect and veneration for Mother Mary there. cf. *Julian Tenison Woods*, Catholic Theological Faculty, Sydney, 1979.

EIGHTEEN

DRAMA IN
QUEENSLAND

The struggle of the Josephites to keep their Rule in Brisbane extended over a much longer period than it did in Bathurst. Dr James Quinn appreciated having them in his schools, but he had the same conviction of his authority over them as his brother—a fact clearly illustrated by his rejection of their 1875 Chapter.

There were several reasons why the story was different in the two dioceses: in Queensland the Sisters were unanimous in accepting the Constitutions; there was no group of postulants there brought from Ireland by the bishop; Father Woods was there in person, intervening to support the bishop's policy; there were more convents involved, and a more lively public involvement in the affair. These factors prolonged the conflict in the north and gave it a different tone from the one in Bathurst. Finally, no diocesan institute emerged in Queensland as in Bathurst. The bishop did make an attempt to start one, but after some years of frustration it ended in oblivion.

James Quinn spent twelve years (1836–1848) as a student at the Irish College in Rome. His flair for administration suggested that he might fill the office of Vice-Rector and later Rector, but it was Tobias Kirby who remained and became Rector while Quinn returned to Ireland. He founded St Laurence O'Toole's school in Dublin, and remained there until he was appointed to Brisbane. During this period John Henry Newman was establishing the Catholic University of Ireland, and lodged with Quinn until he could set up his own domicile. The two had much in common, but their friendship did not survive the pressures of a working relationship, and Newman holds a distinguished place as the first of the long line of Quinn's public antagonists. It was the question of authority that divided them. Quinn wanted his students to enjoy the privileges of the University without being subject to its rules or coming under the jurisdiction of its Rector.

Newman commented that "Dr Quinn liked power and intrigue".

Astonishingly diverse assessments have been made of Quinn's character. On his death, the chief local politician said of him, "There was not in this or any of the colonies a more enlightened or cultured scholar or a more perfect gentleman." Another admirer spoke of his grace and ease of movement, his high and noble qualities of head and heart, his mind as judicial in its decisions as it was statesmanlike in the breadth of its views, his courtly address, his grace of manner, his savoir-faire, which all "would have gained him the hat of the Cardinal Secretary of State, or that of the Cardinal Secretary of the Propaganda".

On the other hand, those who saw a different aspect of James Quinn used a litany of abuse to describe him: a scandal, a deceiver and swindler, devious to the point of dishonesty, full of a mercantile spirit and utterly indifferent to religion, arbitrary, a bully, revengeful, tyrannical and unjust, a seemingly impervious autocrat, pathologically unbalanced.

Whatever the truth of all this, it is clear that Quinn was a man to be reckoned with. His confrontation with Mary MacKillop was not an isolated instance of unpleasant discord in the life of an otherwise placid, genial, and tolerant man. But if he were ever to be looking for a character reference he would do well to go to Mary for it rather than to the historians. She never displayed disrespect or made unfavourable reflections on his person like those just quoted. She once said he was a "terrible man", but that referred to his effect on her, not to any personal deficiency. Anything she said about him had a direct bearing on their relationship; it was never a judgment on the man.

The drama of Mary MacKillop in Queensland may be divided into three acts. The first was the period during 1870 and 1871 when she was one of the pioneer Josephites in the diocese. The bishop was in Europe at the time and did not come into direct conflict with her, but his views were translated into policy by his Vicar General, Dr Cani. The second act could be divided into two scenes. Firstly, there was the bishop's refusal to acknowledge that the 1875 Chapter concerned the Josephites in Queensland in any way. Secondly, there came the later events of that year, when his opposition to central government and his attempts to draw the Sisters away from their Constitutions led to a direct confrontation with Mother Mary. In the end he reluctantly agreed to tolerate her authority, but the uneasy compromise could hardly be called peace. The third act took place after an interval of about three years. There were three scenes, each consisting of a visit to Queensland by the Mother General. In early April 1878 she went there for three and a half months, in late November she returned for a month and a half, and in April of the next year, 1879, she arrived for a stay of seven months during which the final withdrawal was decided.

In January 1880 Quinn sent two memoranda to Rome. Being aware that the Holy See was receiving unfavourable information about him he was anxious to clear his name. In brief, the world was against him, and the coordinator of the attack was the Archbishop of Sydney, Dr Vaughan, ably assisted by Mother Mary and some rebellious Brisbane laity. What he wrote was primarily an attack on Vaughan, but in the course of it he had much to say about Mary, as he considered her a kind of puppet of Vaughan's. He accused them both of using vicious means to blacken his reputation. But the man he was writing to, Cardinal Simeoni, had been in the thick of the negotiations about the Rule, and he knew Mary personally. He could see not only that the bishop was wrong about the Institute, but that its Mother General was being assigned a character which did not correspond to the young woman he had come to know and admire six years previously.

In the section of Quinn's first memorandum dealing with the Josephites, the falsehood that they were originally under the bishop appears very soon. Yet he had written five years previously that letters from Mary in 1870 caused him "to decide on separating the Queensland foundation from the central government whenever that could be tactfully done". Now, in 1880, we hear that things went well in Brisbane until "the Superior went to Rome and had the Rule of the Institute changed so that the Sisters were withdrawn from the authority of the Bishop and placed under a Superior General".[1] Mother Mary, he said, contacted all the convents and "obtained their consent to be united with the house in Adelaide and enjoined on them all to renounce the Diocese of Brisbane that very day". So that the schools would not be left unstaffed, he agreed that the Sisters would not be under his authority, but they would have to remain until replacements were found. Simeoni would have read the next paragraph with particular interest:

> She reclaimed the obedience of the Sisters, and said that, by order of the Cardinal Prefect of Propaganda, they were obliged to submit to the Mother House in Adelaide. The bishop replied that he had heard

nothing concerning the intervention of the Prefect of Propaganda and that the order she had referred to applied solely to Adelaide and that she herself possessed no document from the authorities to prove that things were otherwise.

The cardinal knew she did possess such a document, with his own signature on it, and he knew that it entailed the opposite of what the bishop was saying. How Quinn thought he would be unaware of these things is hard to imagine. He had himself been informed by Mary in February 1875 how things stood with the Roman authorities. He seemed to be less concerned with juridical facts than with putting down an ambitious woman who "recalled the Sisters in order to render obedience to her", "enjoined on them to renounce the diocese", and "declared her resolve to exact submission". The way he put it, her preoccupation was to demand submission to herself, whereas she saw it as protecting Sisters who were crying out for somebody to defend their right to observe their vows.[2] The bishop made no reference to his own failure and that of his priests to allow the nuns to live peaceably in the obedience they had professed. He complained of frequent changes of personnel, but these were often attempts to find nuns and superiors who were tough enough to survive the physical and mental conditions in which they were expected to exist.

In the bishop's eyes, Mary was upsetting the peace. He therefore considered he had a right to stop her from seeing her nuns. His document continues: "To this the bishop replied that, should she attempt to upset the peace of the Sisters in his diocese, he would command her to reside in the convent of the Sisters of Mercy." He does not mention a detail Mary later revealed to Annie: "He threatened to remove me by the police if I attempted to go to my own. Of course I did not mind his threats but told him I would do my duty."

The existence of a conspiracy involving journalists is then given full coverage, climaxing in the allegation that the activities of the Mother General and her followers were "thrust to the very limit of open rebellion". He is not sparing in his accusations against her, identified as she is with her partisans: "They had notoriously and shamelessly lied both in private and in the public dailies." He had, he says, received a petition from this group, in which they made insinuations and false assertions against him. The evil genius of Dr Vaughan appears in the summing up: "The conclusion of all this would seem to be the result of the conduct of the Archbishop of Sydney against the Bishop of Brisbane." With regard to Mary, there is a thinly veiled hint at collusion with Vaughan: she came back "and took the Sisters holus bolus to Sydney". A remark Mary made to Annie a year later shows that if there was a conspiracy Vaughan was not the only notable person involved in it:

> I did what I believed to be my duty. The Jesuit and Marist Fathers, the Archbishop and the Bishop of Armidale, the Vicar General of Sydney, some of the best priests in Queensland, and many more upheld me in what I did. They could not do this if the fault were mine.

This has been history according to Dr James Quinn, with some comment. What do other documents reveal about his problems with the Josephites in Queensland? It has already been seen that he told the superior there after the 1875 Chapter that she could come back only if she agreed to sever relations with her Mother General. He told the Mother General herself:

> I hope therefore that from the receipt of this letter you will cease to exercise any authority over the Sisters in Queensland and from sending them any communication which might tend to disturb or distract them in the discharge of their duties.

The parallel with Bathurst is exact. The Quinns knew the same facts, had the same mind and the same determination, and were working towards the same goal with the same methods. In Bathurst, Matthew had acknowledged that the Sisters were under central authority from the start, but he was treating them as if their vows bound them to whatever he said they bound them to.

In Brisbane, the Sisters were likewise told they could leave if they chose to be faithful to the terms of their profession. Those who had what was looked on as a strange hankering after Adelaide could return there at some indefinite future date, but in the meantime they were to have nothing to do with their legitimate superior, and they were to have no support, no information even, in coming to a decision. On the other hand, not only did the bishop intend to use his own persuasive tongue and forceful personality to pressure and bluff them (telling the acting superior how she was to assist in this) but he was planning to bring the influence of Father Woods to bear on them in favour of severing connections with their Superior General. The Sisters wrote to Mary in June:

> We have all become Sisters of St Joseph in the humble and firm hope of ever remaining in the closest union with our Mother House, and we find it hard to understand how any bishop could think we would separate from it.

In addition to this group letter, two accounts that came to Adelaide from individuals just at the time of the Chapter make it clear what the bishop was doing. Sister Catherine says he ordered a printed letter to be sent to all the convents declaring that he and Woods and the acting superior Collette were their only authorities, and that nobody was to hold communication of any sort with Adelaide or with Sisters outside the colony. But everything would be well:

> He said he would treat them very kindly and be a true Father to them, and he told us he was sending for Father Director. He said that he knows his wishes and with the help of God they will make the Sisters very happy.

In another letter Catherine has an invaluable narrative of how the bishop went about cajoling—"as sweet as sugar to all of us"—bluffing, and bullying the Sisters:

> I am your Father now and you are my child. Mind, be obedient, for you don't know the minute God will call you to Himself as you are in delicate health, and do whatever Sr Collette and myself order you to do. I appointed her Superior all over Queensland, and also Father Woods is your Superior as well, and I am sure you will do what he will advise you to do. Mind, Sr Mary has nothing to do with the Sisters here.

At the end of her long letter, Catherine shrewdly sums up the bishop's methods, and ends in a crescendo of loyalty:

> He thinks that if he gives us Father Director, we will do all he wants us to do, and then when he gets us under his thumb, he will send F.D. away and do what he likes with us. That is truth. I feel sure that is why he is so sweet and kind. Send for more wine, my child. I will not do it for any Bishop. I will not change my rule for anyone.

Mary's problem was to understand by what right the bishop could declare his intention to "withdraw the Sisters from subjection to central authority". Did he really think that she would cease to exercise her authority, or refrain from communicating with her subjects, because he told her to? The clue to his attitude is that he maintained she was not their superior.[3] He had relieved Sister Clare of her "Office as Head Superior of the Institute of Saint Joseph" in his diocese and he seemed confident that he could do the same to the Mother General.

Seeing it as her duty to resist this illegal act, Mary set out for Brisbane at the end of April 1875. She had hesitated, fearing that her presence could make things worse, but prudent people whom she had consulted told her that she had no alternative. She had known of the bishop's views for a long time, but kept hoping that he would accept what was given in Rome and approved by the Chapter. His continued opposition helped to teach her that others did not have the same respect as she did for what emanated from the Holy See, and that even good people were inclined to accept what Rome said only if it suited them. The formula she got used to hearing in defence of the process of continuing or initiating the opposite of what Rome had laid down was "pending an appeal to Rome". This somehow made her look like the one who was being disloyal in doing what the Holy See had told her to do.

In view of Quinn's wish that Mary abstain from contact with her Sisters, it is not surprising that her first meeting with him was a painful affair in which he uttered strong threats and told her she was obstinate and ambitious. She told him respectfully that she had taken advice before coming, and that she came in the cause of duty and peace. When she saw that he was determined not to tolerate the Constitutions, she offered to allow the nuns to remain a year longer, provided they had a superior appointed from the Mother House and could communicate with their Mother General. She even offered to allow the novices to remain if they were all brought to a central house under somebody appointed by the Mother General, but this too was rejected. Quinn insisted that they should be left entirely to himself, under the superior he chose, in no way connected with the Mother House, and forbidden to communicate with it.

With a letter describing all this to Franchi on May 20, Mary enclosed a copy of one she had written to Quinn on the same day. Having made as generous an offer as she could, she had asked the bishop: "I humbly ask you, can I do more? One simple but certainly just condition under such circumstances is given. Do I, my Lord, ask too much?" She had not asked him to accept the Constitutions, but she had reminded him that the nuns did. They had committed themselves to nothing else, and they resented his attempts to "explain away their vows", as one of them put it.

Writing to Cani in Rome, Quinn told him to inform them there "that the Adelaide Sisterhood is infected with fanaticism and insubordination to authority". He said Mary's purpose in coming to Brisbane was "to subvert the whole system here", and his view of the nuns' loyalty to their profession was that they "were unanimously decided to place themselves under the Adelaide government". By employing the tendentious term "Adelaide regulations" for the

Constitutions issued by the Holy See, and branding as "Adelaide authority" the central authority which could have been located anywhere, he was suggesting that the bishop of another diocese was usurping his authority.

Although he admitted to Mary on May 28, "My opinion may not be correct," Quinn insisted that it should be obeyed until the Holy See directed him to act otherwise. Thus, as he saw it, she had no authority until Rome said again that she did. As she saw it, he expected her in the indefinite meantime not even to visit nuns who considered their rights were being violated, while he organised their secession. There was thus to be a moratorium on her intervention, but not on his. But on June 18 she was able to tell Franchi that a kind of armistice had been agreed to.[4] The bishop would receive the superior appointed by the Mother House "pending the decision of the Holy See". It is clear, however, that he had merely taken a tactical step backwards when he saw that the nuns were serious. Still, after this his personal attitude became more kindly and tolerant.

The visit had cost Mary a great deal of physical effort, but the mental strain was worse. "No words can tell what a time of suspense and trouble we have had here," she wrote to Sister Andrea on June 10, adding a few details:

> I often feel inclined to envy my quiet country Sisters who have the same daily routine and so much peace whilst I am one day in a rough mail coach, again in a steamer, in rain and storm, but worse than all, when I have to see Bishops and Priests, and, in the cause of our loved work, have to hold out against all their arguments and threats.

In the same letter she spoke of the bishop both as "a terrible man" and as "a most winning man". When he thought it would be effective he used bluster and threats. "I have been threatened with the Police," she said, "and forcible detention in another Convent, anything rather than allow me to our own." No wonder she added: "This Bishop is a terrible man to deal with." "Yet," she said, "he can be frightened in the end." He did, after all, admit to her that he might be wrong, and he feared losing face with the Roman officials if they had to point this out to him. To his credit, however, his real fear was that damage could be done to his school system if the Josephites departed. He threatened Mary with these "consequences to Education and Religion" if she persisted, yet when he realised that she was not going to collapse under his threats he was frightened because he saw that if *he* persisted those consequences would really follow.

But the bishop's winning ways, not his threats and his bluster, were what Mary feared most when he confronted the Sisters. She was well aware of the danger of charm to somebody with the unpleasant duty of resisting the charmer. She said once that she feared Matthew Quinn more than James because she liked him more. When she put Josephine in charge in Queensland she advised her to give the bishop his own medicine as an antidote: "Don't argue with him, coax him rather by telling him how much the Sisters really do love him."

Though she could tell Kirby, "We have much to thank God for here—there is peace again after the threatened storm", there were still storm-clouds over the horizon. As she left to return to Adelaide she could not free herself of the suspicion that the bishop intended to continue the struggle when he had mustered his forces. He would then set about establishing a diocesan institute with the assistance of Father Woods, something he was quite entitled to do. But he also intended to enlist Woods in a campaign to draw the Sisters already there into the new institute. Aware that such trouble could arise, Mary gave some advice to Josephine, the one who would have to cope with it. She was to be respectful but firm in her dealings with the bishop, referring serious matters to her Superior General, and on no account to leave him with the impression that no such person existed. She should keep her eye on the common good and on future needs, rather than on what people were pressing for at the moment.

Mary struggled from a distance for five years to make the arrangement work. She did not visit Queensland again until April 1878, when she followed advice that the situation there demanded her presence. Writing to Josephine not long before she intervened, she relayed the cardinal's message that they should try to bear up as long as they could. She did not want to remove the strong ones with the weak if she could help it.

The nuns had been under constant pressure and needed encouragement. When some began to heed the persuasive words of the bishop and the blandishments of Woods, Mary urged, "Fly for refuge to obedience." She wrote to Grant on 23 March 1878 telling him that although some Sisters were not as humble as they should have been under unjust censure, nevertheless the priests tried them severely and the pressure made the inexperienced ones lose heart.[5] As a result, she had to go up to settle the matter, fearing that she might have to withdraw the Sisters if Quinn did not take more care of them. The particular trouble this time was at Townsville. A visiting priest had observed how abominably the four nuns there were being treated by the pastor and had advised Josephine to look into the matter. Among other things, water was a problem. It came down on them in torrents through the roof whenever it rained, yet they were not provided with tanks to keep a reasonable supply of it for their daily needs. The pastor "had plenty of water at his own house and at the church, but the Sisters had to carry theirs in buckets from a Jew's house, and this at great inconvenience".

But the physical hardships at Townsville were surpassed by the mental anguish. Josephine had seen a typical case herself when she was up there. One Sunday the pastor condemned a Sister from the Altar, calling her a teacher of false doctrine. Writing to the bishop about it, Mary said: "He actually maintains a thing to be false which all the Bishops and priests of the Church teach to be the reverse." The superior and another nun called on him, thinking they could explain what he had not understood. But they got only abuse for their trouble, and were again denounced publicly. When the thing began to rage in the newspapers, Mary thought it better to withdraw the nuns to prevent greater evils. She urged them to prudence and charity, and warned them not to speak a word in self-defence: "Give no reasons. In simple, honest obedience refer the people, if they question you, to your Superiors—to me, if you like." An enquiry was promised, but none was held. So she wrote to the bishop: "Many amongst us feel that justice was not done in the Townsville case. Under these circumstances I do not trouble you with detailed reasons for the removal of the Sisters from Gladstone and Gympie." She told Grant that the bishop admitted some fault on the part of the pastor, but was "very anxious to excuse him at the Sisters' expense".

Then a real storm broke around the Mother General. Quinn was spreading negative talk about her among the Sisters and the laity, trying to get them to believe (as she put it) strange things about her character. She could not understand why he was so hostile or how he could speak so injuriously of her to the two Sisters in charge: "He has done his best to induce them to separate from Adelaide and did not spare me in his remarks to them." Although upset by it all, she felt sorry for him—"Poor Bishop Quinn, he looks very ill." She wrote to Grant about it to ask him to take her part and act as a friend in Rome. In a letter to Simeoni she touched on the matter very lightly, not wishing her words to be taken as an official complaint but as a request for support in the troubled times that lay ahead: "There have been some troubles in a convent of ours here—a misunderstanding between the Sisters and their Pastor." But she added that the bishop had promised to settle it all.

During most of the years 1874, 1875, and 1876 Woods was in Tasmania. He was convinced that divine providence would re-establish him as guide to the Institute. He kept writing to the Sisters and took no care to conceal his injured feelings. These feelings and his rejection of what the Holy See had done were the raw material out of which James Quinn hoped to build his diocesan institute. The bishop was preparing the way with the Sisters who were already in his diocese. Mary wrote to Franchi:

> He told them that the Sisters in Adelaide had treated Father Woods badly, that they had cast him off, but that he would get him over and make him again their Director.

Quinn's cause would be assisted by Woods' sense of pique that Rome had cut across the designs of divine providence. Moreover, the former director was not only gifted with a charm of manner that matched the bishop's, but he was able, in addition, to count on the personal loyalty of a number of the Sisters who had been under his influence since the early days in Adelaide. In her briefing letter to Josephine, Mary did some straight talking about the founder's painful lack of candour, and spoke of her disappointment that "he has allowed his mind to become so prejudiced against some of our best friends that he does not see the gross injustice he does these by the way he represents their actions to others". Then she warned of more trouble to come:

> Ah Sister, if he would only tell me *the truth* and not let me hear these things from others. Forgive me for complaining—I am so disappointed to the heart in him. Our poor, poor Father, may God help him and save him ere he goes too far.

Some of the bishop's charm and diplomacy is evident in two letters he wrote to Woods in July and August 1875 about the prospect of setting up a diocesan congregation. Agreeing readily with his sensitive opinions, he deplored the alteration in the Rule, and assured him that "one can hardly anticipate anything but kindness and consideration from any Bishop, towards those who are so especially his own children as would be the members of such a Congregation as I suggest". But two things he did insist on: diocesan control, and no limit to the duties the members might undertake.[6] He seemed to expect that future bishops would pay more heed to the Holy See than he had done: "The protection of the Congregation against any unreasonable requirements on the part of any future bishop, will be guaranteed by the Holy See." At the end of August he was anxious to get started: "Send me the Rule as soon as may be convenient," he told Woods, and then asked, "When will you come?" He came in good time and stirred up plenty of trouble when he did.

The figure of Woods had been hovering over the Queensland scene since the Chapter early in 1875, not physically (he was in Tasmania) but as a promise on the lips of the bishop and a memory in the minds of the Sisters who had grown attached to him in Adelaide. Quinn promised that if they would abandon the Constitutions he would give them back their beloved Father Director, so badly treated by Adelaide and by Mother Mary, and everybody would live in harmony and happiness under a kindly bishop. But when Woods arrived he did not contribute to a solution—he had become a serious element in the problem.

After three years in Tasmania he turned up in Penola towards the end of 1876, and Mary interrupted her Spiritual Exercises to meet him there. But she was disappointed, as she told Josephine:

> I found him kind, holy and affectionate as ever—but that is all I can say . . . I cannot describe the anguish I feel when thinking of him and his views . . . He is too sensitive and tender-hearted to be a faithful guide of souls, poor dear Father.

Reynolds had not been very diplomatic in the way he informed Woods of the conditions under which he wished him to return. He did not write directly but relayed his message through Mary in a letter which she could scarcely refrain from producing at Penola. Its general tone and its references to fanaticism and sentimentalism can hardly have attracted the man to Adelaide. Still, Mary dreamt that he might come back and help the Sisters in an unobtrusive way without contravening any injunction of superiors. But Woods was unwilling to return on his bishop's terms, and therefore would not return at all.

The conversation at Penola reminded Mary how different the founder's views were from her own. She had had fair warning twelve months previously when he had told her that when she took over it spelt disaster and that things would not improve. She should have been warned by everything he had been saying since she went to Rome—in fact since he was superseded as director—that he was not prepared to accept the directives of anybody, be he administrator, bishop, episcopal commissioner, prelate, or cardinal prefect of Propaganda, about the Institute of St Joseph or about the apostolic vocation of Julian E. T. Woods. He even suggested at Penola that he could be director in Queensland, because that was far from Reynolds, ignoring the fact that he had been removed not by Reynolds but by the Roman authorities, and that what applied in one place applied in every place.

Mary told Josephine that she found it was labour in vain to remind him of what so many prelates and cardinals had said, or to try to appeal to his reason. But she kept hoping he would go back to Adelaide, both for the sake of his own obedience and for the sake of the Institute in Queensland. His views about obedience and the obligation of vows amazed her. He could see nothing wrong in encouraging Sisters to leave the Institute to join another one he proposed to found—it would simply be another work of God's—so Mary was anxious that the Sisters be reminded that a vow to live under a certain Rule was a serious matter.

She had been holding off writing to the superior in Queensland while she had hope that Woods might return to Adelaide. But when it became clear that he was not going to, and that he was likely to end up in Queensland, she was so acutely aware of the threat he would be to the peace and stability of the Sisters there that she felt obliged to write. "Oh Sister, this is breaking my heart," she told Josephine early in 1877. Though he had said he would not go, he was so changeable that his words could not be relied on. If he did go, Josephine was to make sure he had nothing to do with the guidance of the Sisters. Mary spoke of his bitterness towards the Institute, and of the conflict between her own emotions and her sense of duty:

> Surely never was a work more tried than ours. If other works had enemies to contend with, they were outside; we have our own dear Father both with us and against us. He is with us in affection and against us in opinion. Our hearts would lead us to him and what would please him, but our *wills* and *sense of duty* must lead us to displease or pain him, so that we may do right in the sight of God and the Church.

Woods did go to Queensland, and the result was the awful trial that Mary feared. As she became aware of what was happening, she was astounded at the extent to which his creative imagination had been drawn into the service of his convictions. As Quinn's instrument in the work of prising the Sisters free from the Institute, he was giving an account of past events which had very little relationship to the facts. In a letter from Adelaide in November 1878, Mary used some

219

very plain speaking to warn the Sisters against the snares being set for them. She reminded them that in spite of their love and veneration for the founder they were not to have him as director: "Be kind, dutiful and affectionate to our poor Father, but do not ask him to do anything which may put him in a false position. Let him see that you respect and love him, but that you *obey* for God and not from love of creatures." He was not to give instructions or retreats, and if the bishop were to arrange them and he were to consent to them, she was afraid the Roman authorities would have to be informed that their directive was being ignored. This was possibly meant to find its way back to the bishop, as he would not like to receive a direct reprimand from Rome for disobedience.

The Provincial and seven others wrote to Mary in December 1878 asking for an enquiry into Woods' allegation that he had been treated unjustly by Mary, and that Mary had asked for the change in the Rule on poverty and for his removal as director. Things were so serious that although she was not well she found it necessary to go up and spend the month of December with the Sisters. "I had to visit Queensland last December," she told Campbell in March 1879, "I had to save some of our Sisters from leaving there to follow the directions of our poor Father Founder. It was a sad painful mission."

What she discovered was even more painful than she expected. She got a fleeting glimpse of the founder, but he disappeared immediately—an incident which opened the eyes of some of the nuns. He was merely feeling his way at this stage, to find out which Sisters (his "true faithful children") were prepared to join in the secession he was planning for Easter. In a long letter to Bonaventure in Northern Queensland early in the year, Mary used words like deceit, insincerity, plotting, startling things, to describe what was going on. Woods had not a good word to say of Adelaide, and told the superior in the presence of others that *now* was a golden opportunity to separate from it.

One of the reasons Mary wrote to Bonaventure was to counteract the falsehoods on which Woods was basing his campaign. She dealt with three accusations he was making: 1st, that she went to Rome without his knowledge or consent; 2nd, that she asked for the Rule to be changed; 3rd, that she had petitioned to have him removed from the direction of the Institute. In handling the first two, she mentioned that she had his own letters to prove what she was saying. She added with regard to the third: "He has my letters telling a different tale, and if he does not believe them, need not go farther than to his friend the Bishop of Bathurst to know why Propaganda removed him."[7]

The situation was clearly serious. Mary was determined to destroy the net of falsehood that had been woven to ensnare the minds and hearts of her Sisters. She found the whole process painful, but the crisis demanded it. Her tone throughout was kind, she assigned no personal blame, judged nobody's conscience, never said anybody was lying or malicious. But she did point out in the clearest terms that *what* was being said was not true.

Yet the evil continued and nine months later, in September 1879, she found it necessary to set down these same arguments in a long letter to Woods himself to refute what he was saying about her and to induce him to stop it. Her citing of his praise of the pamphlet she wrote to plead for the old Rule on poverty, and the reference to the Bishop of Bathurst, should have been enough. But she added a personal appeal to his memory and his conscience:

> You know how you hurried away from Brisbane last December, being there a whole day and night after you heard of my arrival and not granting me even five minutes conversation. You know how disobediently and deceitfully you had allowed some of the Sisters to act, how your remarks about me and Adelaide had prejudiced them against the Superior they were bound by their vows to obey; and you wonder that I felt called upon to ask the Archbishop to speak to you?

She asked him as a priest to confront her personally with his accusations, or to speak to those who should bring her to account, but not to traduce her in front of the Sisters or to attack their Rule. Citing particular instances they had told her about, she said it all could have been avoided if he had not connived at their disobedience. With regard to the delicate matter of their personal attachment to him, she told him something he should have been telling everybody: where there is a conflict, feelings and affections must yield to duty.

She had returned to Adelaide in January 1879, having done what she could in Queensland. But the main problem there remained unsolved, and by April she was on her way to Brisbane again. This time a stay of seven months culminated in the decision to withdraw from the northern colony.

In March, just before she left Adelaide, Mary wrote to Kirby and Campbell in Rome. The letter to Kirby was very friendly, but her approach appears to have grown cautious. There is much about the recent deaths of great ones in the Church; she thanks him for a relic;

she tells him of the children's gifts being brought to Rome by Bishop Reynolds. But she says very little about what was really on her mind, apart from references to unwelcome publicity. From what she does say, it is clear that no solution was in sight. She finds it hard, she says, to keep up the courage of the Sisters, and the efforts of lay people to do some good through the newspapers only cause them more distress, as well as annoying the bishop.

Her letter to Campbell was much more informative. It is evident that things cannot go on for much longer in Queensland. The bishop will not work with the Sisters, yet he does not want them to leave. She explains that she does not like to write too much about it to Kirby, as he and the bishop are friends, and she fears placing him in an awkward position. Announcing that Reynolds is on his way to Europe, she remarks: "He is a good, holy, hardworking Bishop, but not what many would call a *clever* man. He has enemies who hope he may never return here again." Another person who might come Campbell's way was a Reverend Mother from Brisbane. Mary alerted him to the fact that this lady was no friend of the Josephites, and was likely to do all she could to promote Quinn's views about them.

The next few months saw a delaying action on Mary's part. She did not want to take the Sisters away, but as each convent came under intolerable pressure, or as the bishop told her to make way for others, she did so. She told him towards the end of November that she had no need to remind him that the first duty of a superior was to look after the vocations of those under her care: "Where external circumstances place such vocations in danger, and where nothing is done to remedy such circumstances, it becomes her duty to remove them."[8] The Townsville case shows that she did not take nuns away before she was forced to act according to these principles. Those who left waited in Brisbane for the bishop's judgment, ready to return or to work elsewhere in the diocese. But there was no investigation; he simply wrote to Rome that the local synod (without taking evidence) concluded that "the Sisters were seriously at fault, and that the priest in correcting them had acted indiscreetly".

Mary had said in a letter to Bonaventure, "Please send this on to S. M. Josephine. May God teach us all patience and the prudence we require." In spite of the prayer, it was this S. M. Josephine (Carolan, not McMullen) who lost patience and acted imprudently. On October 18 Mary had told the bishop that she sent Josephine to explain to Father A. Horan why she would have to withdraw the nuns: "I am sorry to say that his Reverence spoke of our Sisters in such a way that I should have been quite justified in recalling them at once." This was not the only time there had been trouble with the Horans, the bishop's nephews. When the nuns had asked for the proceeds of a concert organised for them by a Mrs Constable and got Horan's hard words instead of money, Mary wrote to Reynolds: "I am sorry to say that I think them capable of endeavouring to injure us in every way. They are fearfully bitter, and can abuse well."

But what caused Josephine to explode was a contribution of the bishop's spokesman to a public controversy about the nuns. This had been going on for some time, but it grew vicious when on November 22 a petition appeared in the Catholic journal, *The Australian*, on behalf of the Josephites. Mary loathed any public airing of differences with the bishop, but she could not control the public. Some angry people sent the journal a letter addressed to the bishop, deploring his action in dismissing the Sisters and asking him to reconsider his action. They spoke of the humble spirit and the simple and self-sacrificing lives of the nuns, and made reference to the "warm feelings of attachment" that had sprung up "between them who made such generous sacrifice and us for whose benefit it was rendered".

This brought an immediate reaction of a very negative kind from the bishop and the journal. A statement about the Mother General appeared which (the petitioners commented) should never have appeared in a Catholic journal. This is what led to the intervention that landed Sister M. Josephine in trouble. In a letter to the journal a week later, twelve of the leading petitioners said: "The entire statement has already received an unqualified denial from the only person (Sister Mary Josephine) who was in a position to do so." But poor Josephine, for all the approbation of the twelve signatories, was in trouble with the Mother General to whose defence she had so swiftly flown. She had to make a public apology. Mary herself wrote to the bishop regretting the intervention, but she pointed out that there had been, after all, great provocation. At no stage did she suggest that what Josephine had said was false. She merely indicated that what she had done was imprudent and unfortunate.

With regard to what was actually said against her, Mary was not indifferent to the effect it could have on the Institute, and appealed to the bishop for a tribunal to investigate the charges. She would, if necessary, go once more to Rome. The petitioners themselves vehemently rejected the charge that she had attempted to lead them "by a partial statement of facts into error prejudicial to the Bishop". In order "to relieve the good Mother General of the most serious charges which you have levelled against her by insinuation", they told the editor that not only was the accusation false, but that Mother Mary had done the very opposite of what she was accused of. She had tried to excuse the bishop, and begged the petitioners to avoid newspaper controversy. They summed up: "You are doing her a grievous wrong totally unwarranted by the circumstances." Mary had in fact also specifically warned the nuns,

> against taking part *in word or act* in anything that can possibly annoy the Bishop. If deputations wait on him, have you nothing to do with them, and be careful not to supply them with information against the Bishop or Priests in any way.

In his report to Rome early in 1880 the bishop included Mary with the petitioners in his accusation of barefaced lying. But her own view of the overall effect of the attack was a positive one. She was convinced that the Roman authorities would recognise at once the absurdity of the statements and get a better appreciation of what the Sisters were up against.

On November 29 she wrote to a Queensland priest: "Late last night and after I had seen *The Australian*, I decided upon going this morning to Sydney. If spared, I shall return in a few days." A final decision was obviously close, and she did not want to take such an important step without consulting Vaughan and her other advisers in Sydney. She was most charitable, and respected priests, but she was not stupid, and she could not close her eyes to what was going on. Her sense of duty, together with her love of the Church and of the Institute, was expressed in this moment which she recognised as critical:

> My one prayer is that God may bring glory to Himself out of all this confusion and that He may protect the interests of our Holy Church and not suffer anything but good to come out of the present sorrows.
>
> From my very heart I forgive Bishop O'Quinn the wrong he is trying to do me through the agency of his paper, but this does not prevent my seeing that justice to a certain extent is done to the Institute.[9]

When Dr Quinn heard where she had gone it would not have been hard for him to guess why, and his dislike of her chief consultant would have added fuel to his wrath. The next day, Sunday, he attacked her in the cathedral and in two other churches. A concert organised on behalf of the nuns was attacked in the strongest language by one of his priests in a letter to the secular *Courier*. But in the same issue there was an advertisement for the concert, announcing that the bishop and clergy patronised it and intended to be present. The editor made the most of it, and Brisbane laughed.

It was just as well there was something to laugh about, as things on the whole were grim for the Josephites in Queensland. But as their hopes faded there, new possibilities opened up elsewhere, even as far away as New Zealand. Vaughan promised to receive some Sisters in Sydney if the superior wished, and guaranteed that their Constitutions would be respected. The new Bishop of Armidale, the Capuchin Eleazar Torreggiani, was also anxious to have Josephites there, and he likewise had no problems with the Rule. Quinn saw a sinister link between the advice given to Mary by Vaughan and the invitation to make a foundation in Sydney. The fact that Vaughan was an Englishman and a religious did nothing to allay the suspicion that the support he offered Mary was part of a plot against the authority of the Bishop of Brisbane. Quinn made much of the fact that some Sisters went to Sydney when they left his diocese, whereas Mary had said there was plenty of work for them in Adelaide. This was irrelevant, as they were not leaving to go anywhere but to get away from where they were.

Bathurst and Brisbane in Perspective

The conflict between the Josephites and the Quinns was not a theoretical debate about the advantages of central government over diocesan for Sisters working in Australia at that time. Mother Mary could see excellent religious living under diocesan authority, but central government had been enshrined in the Josephite Rule as better suited to the aims of the Institute and the Holy See had reinforced this decision. The fact that in 1875 the Constitutions were provisional was irrelevant. The instructions given to her in Rome were not provisional. "It is not *implied* wishes but *positive injunctions* I received when there," she wrote to a Sister. She was told to take the Constitutions back to Australia and test them for some years. If experience indicated that changes were desirable, suggestions were to be submitted to the Holy See. In the meantime the Constitutions were to be observed.

Mary MacKillop did not think for a moment that a bishop was obliged to have any group of religious in his diocese if he did not wish to have them. This is clear from the statement of the signatories to the petition to James Quinn late in 1879: "She dwelt particularly on his right to judge whether the services of the Sisters of St Joseph or those of the Sisters of Mercy were best suited to the wants of his diocese." At the same time, Mary was convinced that religious, once accepted in a diocese, should be respected in their Constitutions, and should be allowed to live by the terms of their profession.

In the case of the Sisters of St Joseph in 1875, a bishop was entitled to suggest modifications, even essential changes like diocesan government, but these were to be submitted for the decision of the Holy See as indicated by Cardinal Franchi. No bishop was entitled to act in the meantime as though the nuns in his diocese did not have vows, or did not know what they had vowed, or had vows of a general nature whose substance was to be determined by the bishop in whose territory they happened to be. They were not chattels or units of labour to be shipped about, even for holy purposes. They were free agents, bound as religious only as far as their vows extended. Nobody could tell them that the vows they had made years ago no longer bound them to the Rule they knew, but to one substantially different.

Before this could happen, each Sister would have to be dispensed from her vows and then freely bind herself by new vows to the new institute. This is what should have been done, but was not done, in the case of Sister Hyacinth at Bathurst, and that is the reason why Mary was disturbed about this Sister's juridical position ever afterwards. What troubled her was not so much the departure of Hyacinth as the fact that she was never dispensed from the vow of obedience she had ceased to observe in 1876. As Mary saw it, no bishop had the right to tell any Sister that on his word her vows could be observed in a new institute, one in which she was to be completely withdrawn from the superior to whom she had promised obedience for life.

What the bishops were trying to do would be comparable to telling a Jesuit that he is no longer under the jurisdiction of his General Superior because it is more convenient for the local bishop for him to be under diocesan rule; or that his vows bind him henceforth to observe the Franciscan Rule, because it is a better one, a holier one, and likely to lead to a more fruitful apostolate. He should reply that the vows of a religious can never bind him to anything but his own Rule. The convenience of the bishop and the undoubted excellence and possible superiority of another Rule are irrelevancies.

There is a passage touching on this very point in a letter Cardinal Moran wrote to Bishop Gibney in 1890, when that bishop was attempting to do in Perth what Matthew Quinn had done in Bathurst in the case of Hyacinth. Moran wrote:

The Sisters . . . have no more power to withdraw themselves from the authority of the Mother General than the Jesuits here would have to separate from their Provincial.

Your Lordship has, of course, authority to erect any Diocesan Institute that you may deem useful in the interests of religion, but the Sisters of St Joseph can no more take part in it than the Sisters of Charity or any other approved Sisters.

Even though the Sisters, when asked by your Lordship, may have said that they would remain in the Diocesan Congregation, you will easily understand that such a promise has no force. The Sisters erred in making it and they would err still in carrying it into effect.[10]

Mary MacKillop also saw this juridical point clearly, and with an eye to threatened danger she had obviously discussed it with people in Rome, such as Anderledy. She was not free in conscience to "obey" the bishops on the point. Her obedience was already clear. Rome had given her a set of Constitutions and told her to go back to Australia and organise a Chapter to elect a Superior General. The Sisters had vows to live by these Constitutions—there was no other Rule. As Moran pointed out to Gibney, neither a bishop nor the nuns themselves had power to change the substance of vows once they were made.

Mary was the one elected as Superior General. Her duty was to protect these Constitutions and to help the Sisters to live by their vows. It would not be a matter of personal choice if she were confronted by a bishop's demands to neglect a substantial matter like central government. When such obstacles were placed in her way as she set about fulfilling her duty, the resulting tension can hardly be adjudged "a clash of personalities", as has been done. It was a clash of illegality with law.

Mary's problem was not to decide what she had to do. The problem presented by the personalities she had to deal with was how to do her duty with the minimum loss to the children and others under the Sisters' care. She was also greatly concerned to behave respectfully towards the bishops. How far she succeeded in this is evidenced by the letter to *The Australian* already cited in connection with her attitude to James Quinn:

She . . . urged on us by every means in our power to discountenance any attempt to annoy him on the subject, especially to avoid newspaper controversy; and, in general, sought to make things as pleasant for his Lordship as she possibly could.

If she could have helped a bishop to see the legal situation as it really was, she would have been very gratified, and only a superficial observer could have described such a solution as the bishop bowing to her opinion. But if she failed in this (as she did) she would be faced with the unpleasant duty to direct her nuns elsewhere, so that they could work under some bishop who respected their Rule. There was no question about what the Rule said. The bishops knew and had admitted that it was based on central government, and they wanted this changed. The way they went about it was to act as if, simply because of their desires, things were already what they wanted them to be; and to support their action by speaking repeatedly as if the situation had been like that from the beginning. They stressed the provisional nature of the Constitutions, but lost sight of the fact that the nuns were already under vows, and ignored the injunctions of the Holy See about what was to be done if changes were suggested.

So the dispute in both Bathurst and Brisbane was not about "what would be better here", but about whether the Sisters of St Joseph were to be allowed to keep their Rule. If another Rule were adjudged better in a given place, or better adapted to Australian conditions, each bishop was of course free to bring in other religious or to found a new institute to suit his needs. Matthew Quinn actually followed the latter course in Bathurst. The issue there, however, tends to be clouded by three facts: by the historical (but not juridical) continuity of the new congregation with the Sisters of St Joseph of the Sacred Heart; by the bishop's employment of Father Woods to draft the Rule of his Bathurst group; and by the transfer of Sister Hyacinth from one group to the other.

But Hyacinth's irregularity did not affect the bishop's right to set up a new congregation which was much like the original one but under diocesan rule. The postulants who came from Ireland with him, and the others who joined from the Bathurst area or were sent by Father Woods, were all perfectly in order. They had taken no vows to live by the Constitutions of the Congregation of Sisters of St Joseph of the Sacred Heart, and they needed no dispensation. They simply joined what they saw as "the Sisters at Bathurst", and would have been largely unaware of these important juridical distinctions. The bishop was quite within his rights in founding the new congregation, which in fact is one that has borne much fruit.

The attack directed at Mary MacKillop in Bathurst and Brisbane was not based on juridical argument but on irrelevancies and personal abuse. It was irrelevant for a bishop to recall how much he had done for the Sisters,[11] to guarantee that he would be a most kindly father to them if they abandoned their Mother House, to speak of how much they were needed and how awkward it would be for him if they clung to the Constitutions, to repeat his conviction that those Constitutions were totally unsuited to Australian conditions,[12] or to declare his determination never to accept the government of a woman.

It did not concern Mary MacKillop, either, that she was accused by Dr James Quinn of being young,[13] sentimental, colonial (that is, born in Australia), of non-Irish stock, female, the daughter of a bankrupt colonial seminarian, a former excommunicate, a strong personality, obstinate, ambitious, based on Adelaide and controlled from there, influenced by the Jesuits, a friend of Archbishop Vaughan.

"Yes", we can imagine her replying, "many of these things may well be true. But if I yield, am I doing my duty to the Sisters, and am I being faithful to the mission entrusted to me by God through the Holy See?" She herself had no doubt about the answer to these questions. It is the key to her steady obedience to Rome's directives, in the face of constant pressure from local authorities who were determined men of strong character and persuasive tongue. In the course of exercising this obedience she manifested many other spiritual strengths as well—understanding, wisdom, prudence, fortitude, courage, patience, courtesy, humility, and above all, charity.

Footnotes

[1] His language—"she had the Sisters withdrawn from the authority of the bishops and placed under a Superior General"—suggests that the Propaganda officials, cardinals and all, were easy to manipulate. Even worse, in a letter of Sister M. Teresa Maginnis to Mother Mary in 1879, we read how an astonished priest heard Dr Quinn say that Mary MacKillop "must have bribed some of the Cardinals, or they would not have taken such an interest in the Institute".

[2] The Quinn file in the Brisbane archives contains some notes of the bishop on the early history: "In the year 1869 I met the Rev. J. T. Woods, Founder of the Sisters of St Joseph and agreed with him to establish a branch of the Institute in my diocese on the following conditions: (1) that I would allow their Rule to remain as it was up to the time application would be made to the Holy See for the

approval of the Congregation. (2) That when such application would be made I should be at liberty to apply for a change of the central into diocesan government for the branch of the Congregation in my diocese. Father Woods said he could not act without the consent of the Bishop of Adelaide. (3) In September of the same year I met His Lordship the late Bishop on board the steamer *Geelong* in which we were fellow passengers to Europe to attend the General Council. Father Woods had spoken to His Lordship in the interim. We then and there agreed that the foundation should be made on the conditions above specified."

In setting down the second of these conditions, Quinn seems to regard his right to set up a diocesan congregation as overriding the nuns' rights to observe their vows. They were there to be shipped around by the decision of people like himself and Woods, with no consideration being given to just what it was they had vowed themselves to.

3   At one time the bishop said that there never was any central authority, at another time he maintained that it was abolished when Mary was excommunicated in 1871: "On my return to Brisbane in May 1872, I found that the office of Superior General had been suppressed . . . I talked the matter over several times with Father Woods pointing out that there was no ecclesiastical authority except my own over the Congregation in my diocese at the time . . . I agreed not to make any communication with the Sisters generally, but said that I would maintain the existing state of things, that is the dependence of the Queensland branch of the Congregation on the Bishop of the Diocese."

This dependence was never a reality (the nuns had never heard of it when they made their vows) but Quinn seems to have convinced himself that it was. In any case the primitive situation had certainly been restored in March 1872.

4   Sister Mary Josephine was responsible for the agreement being in writing: "I was with Mother at the interview and the Bishop was very nice, but determined to have his own way. The promises on both sides were verbal. So when he went out, I said to Mother she ought to give her promise in writing and so should he—that was what business people did. She asked him for it in that way. He got very red and then he gave his written promise not to interfere with the Sisters, and she gave hers not to remove them until he was ready to supply our places." Mary could have done with Mary Josephine at Baggot Street, Dublin, in 1874.

5   This letter to Grant opens with a reference to the death of Pius IX. The new pope, Leo XIII, made Franchi Secretary of State. Simeoni had held that office since 1876, but now switched jobs with Franchi, who had been Prefect of Propaganda. Mary wrote letters of gratitude to both cardinals. She warned Simeoni that he might have to protect the Constitutions whose birth he had supervised: "There are holy prelates and priests who do not yet understand them and who would wish them other than they are."

6   It seems that the spirit of the Institute was an elusive quality. Woods thought it was destroyed when the Holy See insisted that the Sisters own the Mother House, but he did not seem to think it was affected by "accomplishments" ("The more accomplishments of every kind the candidates possess the better," said the bishop) and the teaching of instrumental music, nor by openness to whatever a bishop might require, such as select schools and secondary schools for the well-to-do.

7 It had been the Bishop of Bathurst who, as a member of the Commission of 1872, had recommended the dismissal of Woods.

8 The bishop tried to get Mary to tell the newspapers that the nuns were leaving of their own accord. She refused, on the grounds that it was not true. One might compare the bishop to a landlord objecting to a tenant having a baby on the premises. The mother is told *she* may stay, but she cannot keep the baby there. So she leaves with her baby. Did she leave of her own accord, or was she evicted?

9 Late in life Quinn prefixed the "O" to his name, and it is sometimes confusing to come across the form O'Quinn.

10 The letter concludes with a diplomatic threat: "As the Holy See entrusted this matter of the Sisters of St Joseph to my care, your Lordship will at once understand that the duty will devolve on me of acquainting the Propaganda with this matter, unless perhaps you may relieve me of this very unpleasant necessity."

11 This was a favourite appeal of the Bishop of Brisbane, but it would hardly have impressed the Sisters. They had to beg their way up there in the first place, their living conditions were often not only inconvenient but constituted a health hazard, and many of them were scarcely shown common courtesy by his priests.

12 The Roman officials would not have been too pleased with this judgment, but there was a place for it. It should have been submitted with other suggestions, so that they could consider possible changes to the Constitutions. But they said that *they* would be the ones to make the changes, and that in the meantime the Constitutions were to be observed.

13 She was thirty-three at the time this was supposed to be a significant charge against her. It was the age at death of Alexander the Great, of Catherine of Siena, and indeed of Jesus Christ.

PART VI

Progress
and
Checks

NINETEEN

DAILY TOIL
AND CARE

Nine years elapsed after the Chapter in 1875 before Mother Mary transferred her base to Sydney. She spent all but two and a half of those years in South Australia supervising the growth of the Institute, overseeing its works, and defending its rights. She was no less concerned about the personal care of each Sister.

Within two years there were forty-three schools around Adelaide, and requests for ten more could not be met because there were not enough nuns. But as the numbers kept growing accommodation became a problem. Trainees would need a roof over their heads. There would also be sick nuns, and eventually old nuns, to be cared for. The government of the Institute had to be located somewhere and there would be need for a place for retreats and other gatherings. Kensington was the answer. The property had been secured for the nuns in August 1872, but it was not until May 1876 that the new convent and novitiate were ready. In the meantime the inconvenience was great. Mary did her best to ease things by reminding everybody of the calm and peace they would enjoy when at last the new house became a reality. Even close to the opening date there was uncertainty. "Fancy," she said, "the opening to be in less than a fortnight and no painting done yet. It really is too bad. No one seems to urge the men on but myself." But finally it was ready—they had their Mother House, a centre around which they could rebuild the Institute. Along with its obvious advantages, spiritual and social, this brought also the nagging disadvantage of debt.

The Holy See had insisted that the Institute should own property. It was pointed out very firmly to Sister Mary in Rome that the security of owning a place like Kensington would mean that no bishop could now throw the nuns into the street as Dr Sheil had done. Subsequent events were to prove that no command was beyond the imagination of his successor. At the moment, however, this successor was friendly and had grand things to say at the opening of the new convent. But he was the last person in the world to be able to pull money out of a hat, and the Sisters were dogged by the Kensington debt, however Spartan the accommodation there. Mary was concerned about it, but she kept a sense of proportion. She told the bishop:

> When we take into consideration the little help we have been able to get from our schools the last two years and how we have had to assist country convents, the new building here and all, it does not after all seem so great a sum . . . Considering that this house has to train all the Sisters for the Institute and to maintain the invalids, the debt in proportion is very little.

She could have added that the education of the whole of the Catholic poorer class was being handled by the nuns. At that time (1880) Dr Reynolds agreed with her view. He wrote from London:

> I trust the new mortgage may be the means of giving you more confidence in your endeavours to clear off the debt. Our debts are not so bad if there was a little more confidence amongst our fellow labourers.

Stanley James, a journalist who crusaded against social evils under the pseudonym *Vagabond*, did what he could to work up support for the Josephites.[1] He was impressed by their work in the schools, but it was their activities outside the classroom that particularly caught his eye, as they cared for "the sick, the orphan and abandoned child, and the poor victims of a vicious life". He said of the place where they cared for the destitute: "Providence is its name, and on Providence they depend alone for its support." He liked their simple direct methods:

> They take baskets with them for broken victuals and they have acquired by practice an expert ingenuity in converting provisions which in most houses are thrown away into very useful articles of diet.

James often mentioned public admiration and Protestant support for the Sisters of St Joseph, with a hint of wonder that "the only troubles they had were with the officials of their own faith". In their coarse brown and black alpaca garments, with "their bandaged features" and the rosary hung from the waist, they were well known in the streets of Adelaide, in the tram cars, and in the back slums where there were "vile dens and haunts as bad as any in Australia". They wished to be as near as possible to the haunts of squalid poverty. James knew there was more to it than met the eye: "These are the Sisters of St Joseph, who are ever to be seen busy in the cause of their Master, but of whose inner life and works even Catholics know so little."

He knew there was a clue to that inner life in their sharing of poverty with the poor. When he was shown over the convent at Kensington, he said, "I find that the Sisters are lodged and fare more humbly than any servant girls in the city." What Annette remembered years later bore him out: "Many times at Kensington we were half starving not having sufficient to eat." Casimir recalled that outlying communities hesitated to ask Mary for help because the Adelaide nuns were no better off than they were. As for the Mother General's personal lifestyle, Laurence said:

> At Kensington she had a very small room for herself. She had no office of her own but used the common room. Sometimes she interviewed the Sisters there, sometimes in a cellar underneath the house. When she came to Mount Street she did not have an office till the new wing was added.

Probably very few people at the time realised how poorly the Sisters lived. In 1927 Mechtilde told how in one place they had to go out after school and beg their dinner nearly every day. "They often had to sit in the dark and I heard the Sisters who lived there say that they had to eat raw cabbage because they had no wood for a fire to cook it." This was indeed frugal living. But although the Sisters lived so far from luxury, it was impossible to do what they were doing without running into debt. The schools brought in a little money, but it was pitiably inadequate to meet expenses. Most of the people for whom they were working had no means of support and could contribute nothing, so the Sisters found themselves trusting to the "Bank of Providence" to solve their problems. The officers of this bank were often Protestant servants of the Lord. Laurence said:

> Mrs Barr Smith was a particular friend. This lady was very wealthy; not a Catholic. Mr Barr Smith was a leading man in Adelaide, a politician, who gave Mother Mary £2000 for the building of the Kensington Convent. The Baker family, a wealthy family in Adelaide, prominent in the political life of the colony, were very friendly towards Mother.

Another example of Protestant help was Dr Benson, who never charged the Sisters for his services. When he died, Mary said:

> Oh! Sister I feel this death more than words can express. Poor dear Doctor, he is universally loved and regretted and his Funeral on Tuesday was one of the largest ever seen in Adelaide . . . His too generous heart never allowed him to save. We have offered to educate for the present Lottie and the younger boys. Poor Mrs Benson is so

grateful. When I made the offer she cried and embracing me said, "He told me you would be kind!"

In a postscript to one of Mary's letters at this time she explained a pencil scribble on the page: "Little Harrie [indistinct] Benson took my letter out of the envelope and commenced to write . . . so he said when I came in and caught him. He is such a dear child." The Josephites gave a few square yards of their property for a memorial to Harrie's father. This reminder of Dr Benson's kindness still stands after more than a century, in a little corner outside the fence of the Kensington property.

Apart from extraordinary challenges, the Mother General had to keep her eye on many things at once. In assigning people to jobs, she had to allow for the strengths and weaknesses of individuals and the varying demands of different schools and institutions. One Sister is not so good in school, but marvellous in the kitchen. Another has not fully recovered from a shipwreck, a third is easily disheartened and depresses those around her, another is timid, yet another is only now becoming her old self. And it was no easy matter to find people to put in charge: "There are plenty of good Sisters, good in their way— but few who have the tact to govern."

Mary was a tireless letter-writer, and many hundreds of these have survived. Some went to cardinals, bishops, and such dignitaries, but more were to people of humble standing. Some dealt with critical problems, but most dealt with routine matters. Some were circular letters to the whole Institute or to a Province, but more often they were letters of encouragement to particular Sisters, with or without reference to business. Many were to people who were not Josephites. Besides all this, she was often up to her elbows in domestic chores, helping at the Refuge, at the Providence and the orphanage, and visiting hospitals, homes, and gaols.

She spent much time and energy trying to control the debt. Begging for money and organising bazaars and art unions were not overtly religious occupations, nor were they very glamorous. It might have been a more satisfying policy, less troublesome, less worldly too, to put these things aside altogether as not spiritual enough for a person dedicated to the service of God. But Mary saw they were part of what God wanted of her. She apologised to Josephine for her "scraps" of letters: "You can have no idea of how hard it is to write when going about begging from place to place."

Collecting money was not a matter that could be neglected, but it did not have top priority. Nor did the problems involved in arranging the appointments of hundreds of Sisters and providing staff for scores of schools and institutions, but they could not for that reason be ignored. It was no simple matter to transfer Sisters from one place to another. The travel had to be timed so that there was no hiatus while an interchange was in progress. The hundreds of miles to be covered in moving from one colony to another posed problems that may have been child's play compared to the battles of Bathurst and Brisbane, but they had to be faced nonetheless. And it all cost money, even when you went steerage.

The Josephite ideal was a grand one, but it was not easily achieved. Mary put her finger on its demands in August 1877:

> The true Sister of St Joseph should never think of herself, her tastes, her spiritual conveniences, etc., but go where obedience calls her, and she should never think she has the true spirit of her vocation were she to find herself attached to place, person or circumstances.

She was far from thinking that she and the Sisters were faultless and that all the troubles were caused by outsiders. In 1875 she went so far as to write to Josephine: "I often think of late that a terrible *Devil of Disobedience* must be at large tempting the Spouses of Christ from their sacred duties." Seven years later she reminded Bernard that "Rome was not built in a day. Neither can such work as we are engaged in become what God wills without a painful struggle." Little-mindedness and murmuring are poor substitutes, she says, for generosity and trust. But it is God's work, and they should be confident that he will protect it "not only from the attempts of those who did not understand it, but from evil consequences of our own faults and want of experience."

She knew her own weaknesses, and this made her all the more sensitive to the problems of others: "In better moments we wish to be strong . . . A little contradiction comes—and away with all our good generous resolutions." She knew that what they needed most of all was encouragement. It was no easy life these young women were taking on, and she was anxious that newcomers should spend the proper time in a good novitiate with somebody reliable to train them, even though some of the clergy "were clamouring for Sisters and saying, 'What is the good of them being in there when they can be out doing good?'" Kensington provided the novitiate, but there had to be a constant follow-up. The need for instruction and encouragement would never end.

Mary was well equipped to provide what was needed. She knew what it was like to feel discouraged, and she knew only too well what it was like to be overwhelmed by pressure, and how desperate one felt when high-ranking people were the ones responsible for the distress. She was able to speak of this to a few of her old friends, such as Josephine:

> Sometimes I have wished as far as I dared without sin, that it might please God to take me away . . . Sometimes I feel so sad and so grieved that there cannot be more peace among those who strive to live for God alone.

Some months later she took up the same theme: "I am ashamed to tell you that I have been tempted to fly from you all—and from the eye of any mortal who would know me."

Of course she was not alone—she had some fine assistants around her. Calasanctius, for example, was a tower of strength. She lacked confidence, and suffered from the effects of a terrible shipwreck of which she was one of the few survivors, but Mary said of her: "She is invaluable to me in her sincerity and straightforwardness. I can ill spare her but she must go as I cannot possibly do so myself." Another treasured assistant was Monica, especially when she heroically held the Adelaide Sisters together after their Mother General had been taken from them later in 1883.

But, however helpful such Sisters were, it was no secret that Mary herself was the inspiration and support of all in rough times and smooth. Through letters and frequent visits she reminded them of the love of Christ and the glory of his Cross. She never ceased to stress the importance of charity and prayer and obedience. Her words were a reflection of her own soul: "Work on with constancy and courage— bear your little trials with patience and love." Whenever a Sister was dying, she took it for granted that she should be with her:

> Sister Mary Louis seemed to be dying on Friday. I could not leave her since—so had to give up my retreat again. Three times I had to disappoint the Bazaar Committee, or rather Dr Gunson, acting for them. Each time she was so ill that I could not leave her.

Mechtilde spoke of the effect of her presence:

> Anyone who would go to Mother in trouble would tell you that they felt better after . . . These things were so general in her life that we scarcely noticed them. We took them as a part of her life . . . She seemed to be able to throw oil on troubled waters.

Her role as comforter extended to outsiders as well as to the Sisters.

Her words of condolence, too, were full of faith and hope, and clearly came from the heart. Mechtilde said:

> If anyone ever went to her in trouble and distress, she would encourage and help them and draw the good that was in them out. She did a lot by correspondence. She could not do too much for the Sisters and for the families of those who were bereaved.

Mary did not confine her encouragement to words. She had a deep feeling for all who were in distress of any kind, and in spite of so many official duties she was often seen directly involved with people who needed a friend. Visiting the imprisoned was one of her frequent works of mercy. Casimir said: "She used to go to the prison generally on Sundays. This was when she was in Adelaide." Laurence, the Mother General in 1928, had learnt this lesson from the start. She said: "I remember very well my first day in the Congregation because Mother Mary made me accompany her while she visited the poor and prisoners in gaol." Annette also remembered:

> She had the greatest compassion and love for the poor girls and the poor orphans. She used to make us visit the gaol, the hospital, the reformatory girls, and if there was no one else to go she went herself.
>
> Many of the girls would not have stayed except for Mother's influence. We had bad characters who came from the gaols, the streets and everywhere. She said they were to have every comfort.

She added a memorable picture of a problem girl:

> There was a girl there whom they called 'Scotch Bella'. She came from Queensland. She had committed a murder. She dressed as a man for three years and worked on the roads. Nobody could do anything with her. She was sent to gaol in South Australia. Mother Mary got her out and she was brought to the Refuge. She was like a raving lunatic when they brought her there.

Not only did Bella calm down—she was eventually baptised, married a husband, gave up drink, and died happily. Annette had a vivid memory also of a condemned murderer "said to be one of the worst of criminals they had there", and spoke of the effect of Mary's presence on him:

> There was in Adelaide a man named Fagan condemned to death for murder. Dr Reynolds and the priests went to see him but he was like a lion and had to be chained down. He was just like a wild animal. Mother Mary and Sister Felicitas went to see him. The warders told them not to go in. They went in and prayed and Mother was so affected that the tears poured down her face. This so moved him that he knelt down and prayed with them. At the beginning he was abrupt

with Mother but he calmed down and became as gentle as a lamb. Mother prepared him for Confession and Father Williams heard his Confession and in the morning Mother went again with Sister Felicitas and he was without the chains, and received Holy Communion between the two of them. Mother Mary wished to ascend the scaffold with him but this was not allowed. Father Williams however did.

Mary's own love for the poor and needy, and her gentle personal concern for all, were the best sermon she could preach on the spirit in which daily work could be performed. Her health was often poor but she showed little sign of slackening in her prayers or her work. "I am writing this at one a.m." she wrote once, apologising for a hurried scrap, "and have had a hard day's writing yesterday, so am sure you will not wonder that I am sleepy and tired now." She apologised that there were times when she could not manage even the scrap: "Though I do not write in return to each dear Sister, it is not but that I would gladly do so, were I always well and able."

Sometimes her time and energy were taken up by domestic work mingled with spiritual ministry:

> I have four Sisters in Retreat whose meditation I have to give out, and besides this we are all kept so busy here. There are not enough of us for the work to be done. I had to go to the wash yesterday, and now find that I must go to help at the ironing.

It was not just the washing and the ironing she put her hand to. Annette recalled: "She would do what other Sisters would not do. In those days there was no water drainage, and she would clean those places out. Other Sisters refused to do this saying a man should be employed."

The duties of the Mother General involved a lot of travel. Apart from her four journeys to Queensland and several other visits to New South Wales, she was constantly on the move within South Australia during these years. It was all Institute business, mostly organising and encouraging people, but also looking for money—seeking loans at five per cent when the bank wanted ten, or asking friends who would lend it free.

The physical demands of this travel would be daunting enough to a person in robust health with modern transport and none of the harrowing concerns of high office. Mary MacKillop had to be generally on the move, often with a raging headache, and this in nineteenth century Australia when travelling even short distances was not recreation. Once in 1877 she wrote: "I kept up until Saturday, but nature gave way then, I could do no more, and had even to give up all thoughts of my home mail letters." There were these hundreds of miles to be covered, around Adelaide and up and down South Australia. But there were also Sisters in distant Queensland, and at the end of the long weary journey into Quinn territory there was no consolation awaiting a Mother General who upheld Constitutions. To one who loved peace and harmony it was a dreadful prospect to be obliged to resist the bullying tactics of a man whose sacred orders inspired her with a deep respect. "Mine is a weary, weary load," she said, "but then it is God's Will, and what else can I, or ought I, to desire."

As in Queensland, so elsewhere, not all the difficulties were created by nature. She had a distressing experience in 1881 when she had to wait overnight at Albury on a journey from Sydney to Adelaide via Melbourne:

> I was so tired and ill that it was a relief to think that we would have some rest and, not doubting but that we would get that at the Convent, gladly went there. To make a long story short, the Vicar General *refused* to let us stay there on the plea that I had not a letter of introduction. He came over when sent for by Rev. Mother, but did not come in to see me.

She was too ill to eat any lunch, wanting only somewhere to lay her head. A cab came (two hours after it was ordered) and took her the few miles to a hotel in Wodonga across the river. She had to start at six the next morning.

A visit to Penola in which she was to find little joy awaited Mary towards the end of 1876. Her health being seriously affected by the burdens of office, she had had to postpone her retreat, but even when she was well enough to undertake it she had no peace. The opportunity she had long awaited had presented itself—Father Woods was in Penola, and that was about as close to Adelaide as he ever seemed likely to be. Things had become so critical with him that she interrupted the retreat and set off at once by land, sea, and land again, to cover the 70 miles to Adelaide and then the 250 miles to Penola via Robe.

She described it to Josephine: "I had to stop and come to Adelaide to go on next day by steamer to Penola to meet our poor and ever dear Father there." Then, after a disappointing encounter: "Tomorrow I have to start on the overland journey home. The very thought wearies me, but as it is a necessity, I trust in God for the strength required." A month later she told Josephine how the experience had affected her: "Knowing his opinions as I do—and our obligations to Rome and the Constitutions, it has been my painful duty to tell you to beg of him not to assume any direction of the Sisters. Oh, Sister, this is breaking my heart."

The pity was, Woods had no friends to turn to, and lacked a superior at hand to help him. He was in fact avoiding his bishop as carefully as he was avoiding Mary. She summed it up early in 1876, though the coming years would reveal further developments:

> If I *dared* I would complain for my heart is literally crushed with sorrow. The stand-off coldness of Father Director, the inconsistencies of his letters at one time telling me that he cheerfully accepts the decision of Rome, and at another writing in the reverse strain, misunderstanding me so grossly, and avoiding me as he does. I tell you Sister these things have crushed me to the heart, and I have even dared to envy the *dead*.

The threat represented by Father Woods is exemplified in the case of Sister Francesca. This lady suddenly disappeared and sent back her habit with a note saying that she could not wait for a dispensation from her vows. She had been in charge of the Solitude, all honest and pious, but had abused her trust by being in secret contact with Woods and some ex-Sisters for months, because like them she wished to be under his direction. It was because they would not accept any other director that these people had left the Institute. "Fr Woods thinks them very perfect," Mary told the cardinal, "and it is said that he is forming them into a new and austere order." They were circulating talk that "Fr Woods had been harshly treated, and that the ex-Sisters were persecuted saints; that the Institute under the Constitutions would come to ruin". In August 1877 Mary wrote to him very plainly about his contribution to the infidelity of this Sister and of some Magdalens at the Solitude. He was encouraging deceit and disobedience. It was a serious matter—they had vows. "If I had had any suspicion," she said, "that they were in secret correspondence with you I would have been prepared for all, but I *trusted* them—and you too."

Mary's own fidelity to the directives of her superiors was unhesitating. For her they indicated God's will, and Woods' failure to think the same way never ceased to astonish and pain her. Whereas she had no mind to doubt the proposition that obedience means doing what you are told by legitimate authority, he always insisted on his own way. There is a gentleness and sadness in what she had to say about his behaviour, and she was always able to distinguish between her rejection of his spirituality and her affectionate memory of him:

> I *do* give him credit for being a holy Priest, I love him as our first Father and Founder, but here I stop. I do not like his spirituality. I have no confidence in it, and now less than ever. Loving and esteeming him as I did I could not for one moment doubt whom I should obey when Rome spoke.

He meant well, she told Josephine, but many of his views on spiritual things were clearly unsound. He did not see the harm he was doing. The Sisters should pray for him, love his virtues, and as far as possible be silent about his faults. "But with all my sad misgivings about him," she said, "I do not like to hear him spoken bitterly of, nor do I think any Sister should encourage such feelings against him."

Writing to Grant a few months later about this distressing development, she began with a fine account of the gifts and positive qualities of Father Woods. He is amiable, has a winning manner and great powers of persuasion, and never spares himself in his zeal. But of his devotees among the nuns and former nuns she remarked: "There is something too human, too like idolatry in the feelings I have heard some express towards him. He in his own pure-minded charity cannot see any danger in this." Then she touched on his basic weakness—he practised no obedience to anybody: "If he could but have some Bishop or Superior to moderate his zeal, I would be so happy and hope so much for the future." Alluding to the way he encouraged Francesca and others in their deceit and disobedience, she spoke of the painful fact that he who was "so holy and so amiable in every way" had been trying to draw them away to join "one or other of the several orders he has in contemplation".

In this same letter we catch a glimpse of life behind the scenes, in the utterances of Mr O'Brien (the father of this Francesca and of Ignatius the visionary) who clearly shared the admiration of his daughters for Father Woods. Mary wrote:

> Mr O'Brien is a good pious man, but reports strange strange things. He went to one of our convents one day and being unusually excited said, "that the Institute had never prospered since Sister Mary had taken to Popedom and given up Father Woods," and again that his children could not be wrong—that they had been sanctified before their birth, and something else really too painful to write.

She refers elsewhere to this interesting theological point:

> I believe the *visions* still go on in Sydney. Old O'Brien told our Sisters at Maitland that his children were sanctified in their mother's womb, and that our B. Mother would lose her place in Heaven before they could do wrong. Only fancy such awful talk. It can give you an idea of how our poor Father is deluded when he believed in any of them.

The thing had its funny side, certainly, but the situation was serious. Mary's logic suggested that Woods should either be approved in Rome and restored as director, or be officially and effectively stopped doing the damage he was doing.

Until the withdrawal from Queensland, one of Mary's most important duties was to keep in contact with the nuns there (especially with Josephine, the one in charge) by letters from Adelaide. Her health was being affected by concern about their situation, and by her own uncertainty about what was the best thing to do. As it turned out, she paid four visits to Queensland between 1875 and 1879.

She needed to encourage the Sisters not to lose heart, and to caution them to be prudent. This prudence involved two things: firstly, not to say or do anything that could possibly annoy the bishop; secondly, to be careful of seeming friends, and never to say anything that could be twisted against the Institute. They were being asked to tread on very thin ice in the interests of maintaining the schools. Woods was not helping by his attempts to get them to leave the Institute and join him in one of his new ventures. In Adelaide Mary was being told by Abbot Alcock that vocations were too precious to be subjected too long to this tension. His view was that the bishop should agree to respect the Rule in full; if not, the Sisters should be withdrawn at once. Any loss to the diocese would be on the bishop's head.

It was a delicate and explosive situation. A most unwelcome element in Mary's anxiety was the difficulty she had in imagining how the bishop could think that what he was doing was just, or that what he was saying was true. He seemed to treat vows so casually. Nevertheless, she saw it as her duty to help her Sisters to live by their vows. She warned them that it was easy to be "led away by the powerful reasonings of strong minds", and her advice was to be humble but firm, and to tell the bishop "that much as you might wish to please him, you cannot do so in any matter interfering with your obedience to your Superiors and the Constitutions". Obedience is due, she said, not to those we love, but to those placed over us.

It must have seemed very strange to her that the chief external threats to fidelity to the Constitutions came from the revered founder and the respected bishops of Bathurst and Brisbane. It was not just Woods' personal refusal to accept these Constitutions but his determined efforts (more or less secret and subtle) to wean the Sisters away from them, that created the need to be on the alert against his influence in Queensland, and also (though he was not there in person) in Adelaide itself.

The stories of Bathurst and Brisbane centred on this danger to vocations. The Josephites lived their lives in the service of God's poor, teaching and succouring them, but if the conditions of life put too much strain on them, and became a danger to their religious welfare and their health, it was the responsibility of the Mother General to intervene. She had to see that they did not have the spirit crushed out of them. In a letter to Josephine in February 1878 she showed how seriously she took this matter. She felt she had already too seriously endangered the Sisters, and to leave things as they were would be criminal on her part: "We have decided upon withdrawing the Sisters from Townsville, and that *immediately*. We cannot upon any consideration expose the Sisters to the dangers they are in there." She pointed out the same thing to Bishop Quinn in November 1879:

> I surely need not remind Your Lordship that the first duty of a Superior is to look after the vocations of the souls under her care. Where external circumstances place such vocations in danger, and where nothing is done to remedy such circumstances, it becomes her duty to remove them.

Although Mary was saddened whenever a Sister left the Congregation, she was sensitive to the differences between one case and another. How she regarded Francesca's departure has already been seen. In the case of another Sister, who left because of the pressures of life in Quinn territory, she did not absolve herself from blame: "I blame myself for not having removed herself and the Sisters who were with her sooner." Her sympathy for young women struggling along in quite unacceptable conditions is clear in another letter about the same Sister. She told Franchi:

> She lived in the most remote of our Queensland convents and was a good, honest, painstaking Sister. Whilst in that convent she had many trials, especially from the Pastor, yet she always bore up against them, concealing many of them from us and hoping that they would

be removed from the place. In the end, about six months ago, she suddenly lost courage and wrote telling me that she could never again be happy in Religion.

A notable feature of Mary's letters to those close to her during 1882 was the repeated suggestion that it might be better if she resigned and made way for someone who could handle the problems better. She was honest enough, though, not to blame everything on her own inadequacy. She recognised deficiencies among the Sisters, especially the cult of individual opinion against the known wishes of a lawful superior: "I grieve because some I have loved and expected more from do not come up to what I think they should." She wondered—was it wisdom, or was it a temptation to run? She wrote at various times to Bernard:

Do you know, dear Sister, that I am praying God to remove me, or to show my Sisters what I believe He wants from them?

I often do feel so tempted (is it a temptation?) to send my resignation to Rome and to implore the Holy See to appoint some other Superior for a time. Pray for me.

Do you know that my heart sinks from time to time and more than once since Easter I was greatly tempted to write to Cardinal Simeoni and entreat him to let me resign.

Mother Mary's Health

It is clear from Mary's letters that she suffered much from a distressing chronic illness. The doctors could provide no cure, but they told her that brandy would enable her to avoid its worst effect, namely the sheer exhaustion that made it impossible for her to carry out her ordinary duties.

With the ill health referred to in her letters there are two levels of indisposition. One was of the type, more or less serious, that humanity at large suffers from. It can be given a name readily enough, and this she often did: headache, severe cold and cough, rheumatic pains, bilious fever, danger of heart disease or of apoplexy, exhaustion of body brought on by overwork, mental fatigue, anxiety, and disappointment. But there was also a second attack which laid her low regularly, something she had come to expect even when she was otherwise well, the symptoms being headaches and other pains so severe that she simply could not keep going at all. She found it convenient to say that she could not keep her head up, and that the remedy was to go out of circulation, to bed, until it passed.

People around her knew of this condition, and Mary referred to it as something well known, in phrases like: the attack, my attacks, my monthly attack, an attack of the ordinary illness, the attack at Bundaberg. The letters frequently contain vague descriptions of this very troublesome condition: "My attacks do not come so frequently now, but are terribly severe when they do come." Or: "Though I never had so severe an attack." Or: "[I] could not go to the funeral—had to come home and go to bed—my monthly attack had come on severely—otherwise I am well thank God." She seems to take it for granted that even if she might manage to evade the nameable ailments that strike her frequently, this attack is something she has to live with.

Writing to her mother in February 1885, she referred to something they both obviously knew well, but which others could not so readily know about:

> The illnesses you know of try me terribly. Dr orders quiet and freedom from care. Dr Cani lectures me about keeping well and not being too anxious, that I must do this for the sake of the Institute. Of course he does not know what is the matter. I have determined when the next is coming to go away for a few days where no one can see me or bother me, and try what effect that can have.

Medical interpreters of the evidence are of the opinion that she suffered from dysmenorrhoea. Besides suggesting quiet and freedom from care, the doctors of those days used to prescribe brandy for such an ailment, and indeed until quite recent times brandy or gin was regarded as the only prescription that would bring any relief and enable the patient to spend less time in utter prostration. It is clear that Mary's doctors followed this common practice, and that she obeyed them in this as she obeyed them in anything else they prescribed for her. When this medical recourse became the substance of slander, she wrote:

> God knows I had the shame and humiliation of often taking stimulants, and of knowing that I was kept up by such, when I should otherwise have sunk and not been able for any duty, but far better to have yielded and to have given up than to have this shame and sorrow brought upon me by the false tongues of those I loved.[2]

Osmund Thorpe, Mary MacKillop's historian and a witness at the canonical enquiry into her life, said that her innate modesty was the reason "why not all of those who lived in intimate association with her knew that it was her custom to take alcohol as an analgesic for her regular pains". "I cannot enter into particulars," she told Donald in January 1883. Could she not just as easily have said, as she did on other occasions, that she was suffering from rheumatism, a bad cold, a raging fever, or whatever other name fitted the ailment of the moment?

If, like her fellow Scots, Mary MacKillop saw no wrong in using whisky as a beverage, she could hardly have regarded brandy as wrong when taken as a medicine. Still, she always seems to have had it measured out for her. Sister Teresa McGinnis said in 1926: "I was appointed to give her a measure of brandy before meals according to the Doctor's orders." Annette said the same: "About a tablespoonful twice a day, and she would never allow it to be in her own hand. It had to be given by me and Mother Bernard."

Footnotes
1   In 1986 the first feature film made on the life of Mary MacKillop was based on one of James' stories. *That Very Troublesome Woman* was written by Dion Boehme, produced and directed by John Mabey. The story begins in 1879 when James was a fellow passenger on the steamer *Egmonton* with Mary MacKillop and two other nuns as they were leaving Queensland.
2   She can only mean that, when she is in a sorrowful and depressed mood, the evil that has resulted from gossip makes her think that it would have been better to allow her physical indisposition to run its course without remedy. This would often have prevented her from continuing the struggle to do her duty, but it seemed to her at times that this could have been the lesser of two evils.

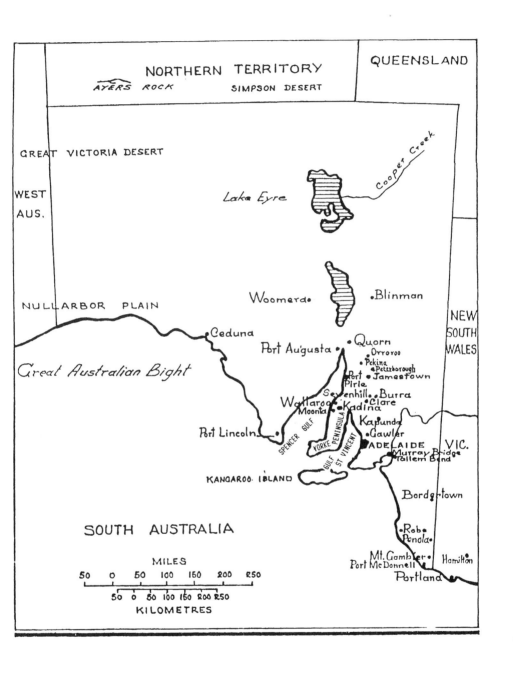

Fr Julian Tenison Woods.

Above: *The Alexander Cameron home, Penola Station, SA, where Mary lived as governess, 1860–1862.*

Below: Main Street, Penola, SA (c. 1866).

Above: *The Royal Oak Hotel, Penola. Mary's Uncle Donald was the licensee, and she stayed here on her arrival in 1866.*

Below: *The "stable school", Penola.*

Bishop Lawrence Bonaventure Sheil,
third Bishop of Adelaide, 1866–1872.

Above: *Fr Julian Woods (centre), with Fr Fitzgibbon of Mt Gambier and Fr S Carew of Kapunda (c. 1866). [Courtesy of Adelaide Catholic Archive]*

Below: *Penola school and hall (c. 1867).*

Sr Mary (c. 1870).

Above: *Bishop Sheil
with a group of his priests
(c. 1868). Fr Woods is
standing third from the left.*
[Courtesy of Adelaide
Catholic Archive]

Left: *Fr John Smyth,
Vicar General, Adelaide
1865–1870.*
[Courtesy of Adelaide
Catholic Archive]

*Sr Mary with Josephine McMullen, the first Adelaide resident
to join the Institute (c. 1870).*

Mary's fine handwriting is evident in this page from
her treatise on St Joseph.

Letter from Sr Mary to Fr Woods, 8 February 1870; an example
of her "crossed" letters—a technique to save paper, which was scarce.

Right: *Fr Charles Horan, OFM, close friend of Bishop Sheil.*

Below: *Archbishop John Bede Polding of Sydney (1842–1877).*

Right Above: *Fr Joseph Tappeiner, SJ, spiritual director to the Josephites, 1872–1882.*

Right Below: *St Joseph's Convent, Kensington, SA (c. 1870), which became the first Mother House of the Sisters of St. Joseph.*

Mother Mary MacKillop (c. 1882).

Above: *Archdeacon Patrick Russell,*
Vicar General to Archbishop Reynolds,
Adelaide. [Courtesy of Adelaide
Catholic Archive]

Right: *Archbishop Christopher*
Reynolds, of Adelaide (1873–1893).

Below: *St Joseph's Providence and Provincial House at 3 Cumberland Street, The Rocks,*
Sydney (c. 1881). Mary stayed here when sent from South Australia in 1883.

The Brothers Quinn: (Above) Bishop James of Brisbane (1859–1881) and (Left) Bishop Matthew of Bathurst (1865–1885). Both created painful problems for Mother Mary and the Josephites.

Archbishop Roger Vaughan of Sydney (1877–1883).

TWENTY

A NOBLE
ARCHBISHOP

T he English Benedictine Roger Bede Vaughan was appointed Coadjutor Archbishop of Sydney while Sister Mary was in Europe in 1873.[1] He succeeded Polding to the see in 1877. It was no secret that this appointment of another English Benedictine was unpopular with the Irish bishops in Australia.

Vaughan was a scholar of distinction and a notable orator.[2] He quickly came to the fore as the leader in the struggle against the secularisation of education in Australia, and when it became evident that the cause was lost he turned to the religious orders to take up the challenge. It is not surprising then that he took a lively interest in the work of Mary MacKillop. She quickly discovered in him a man of God—prudent, balanced, kind, and patient. He proved a steady counsellor when she was burdened with her Queensland problems, and the knowledge that she had been consulting him did nothing to calm the temper of Dr James Quinn.

It was all too easy for unfriendly minds to interpret Vaughan's interest as self-interest. He could well afford to be friendly, they said, when he stood to gain by a Josephite withdrawal from Queensland. He could pick up labourers as they moved south on their exodus, and in time this could lead to a shift of the centre of the Institute to Sydney. Mary was aware that some took this cynical view of his motives and she defended his conduct as always "honest and open and nobly charitable". Vaughan was large-minded as well as large-hearted, and history shows him not only as a pillar of strength to the Josephites in their troubles, but a loyal servant of the Church in every way. The untruths uttered about him reflected little credit on the highly-placed enemies responsible.

"The Archbishop is more than kind," Mary wrote to her mother in January 1880, "God has raised up a true and powerful friend in him, and just when we most needed such aid as his." She took up this same theme in an important letter to Simeoni a little later. After mentioning that Quinn had asserted "things against us which we believe to be incorrect", she went on to speak of Vaughan's support during a very critical time: "Were it not for the action of the good Archbishop of Sydney in receiving the Sisters who had to leave Brisbane, it would have been hard to have kept up the courage of some." This was such a contrast to what she had met in Bathurst and in Brisbane. Although he lived only three more years, Vaughan's openness became an important factor in the history of the Institute. Mary MacKillop never allowed the memory of his kindness to grow dim in the twenty-six years of life that remained to her.

When the leaders of the Church in Adelaide turned openly against Mary, their attack was also directed at the deceased Archbishop of Sydney. She had become used to personal attacks on herself, but this smearing of the name of a departed friend moved her to an indignant protest. If she would not speak a word against living mistaken bishops, she was not prepared either to allow mean talk about a dead Archbishop who had stood by her loyally "raising by his kindness my spirits and hopes which had nearly been crushed out of me". She wrote late in 1883: "Ah, Sisters! It was a cruel, I almost think a wicked thing to misconstrue that noble man's conduct towards me."

The Josephites opened their first school in the Archdiocese of Sydney in 1880. This was at Penrith, not so very far from the border of the Bathurst diocese. Other schools followed. But the very first sojourn of the Josephites in Sydney itself was at Woolloomooloo for the Christmas retreat of 1879. In addition they had from the start an interest in founding a Providence in an area called Dawes Point, or more familiarly *The Rocks*. In the course of its history the location of this work was moved several times, but today there is no trace of it left. The huge structure that became the southern approach to the Bridge was built in the early 1930s right on top of the sites where it had stood. It was in fact only a short walk from the spot where Alexander MacKillop had landed in Australia in 1838. The Sisters cared for the poor, the aged, and the orphans in two successive locations in Gloucester Street; then Number 3 Cumberland Street became a well-known address for many years, just near the junction with Lower Fort Street and George Street North. They had a school in nearby Kent Street in 1881, with a rented convent, and later moved to the corner of High Street. Although this area now has an historic aura about it, it was at the time a scene of much human misery. That is why the Josephites went straight into the middle of it.

In a long letter to Reynolds in March 1880, when he was abroad, Mary spoke of Vaughan's kindness, and introduced a new name and new possibilities with the mention of the Bishop of Armidale. This was Eleazar Torreggiani, a Capuchin, derided by the Irish as an "Anglicised Italian Monk". Vaughan had made himself more unpopular by not seeing to it that an Irishman was appointed to succeed in Armidale. Torreggiani was from the start sympathetic to the things Mary MacKillop stood for, but she had learnt to be cautious about the possible fate of the Constitutions in any new diocese the Josephites entered, so she sent him a copy and awaited his reaction before she made any move. He passed the test and remained a great friend over the years.

The principle of the single novitiate had been an important element in the Institute's policy until 1880. The Quinns had wanted their own novitiates, for purposes of control, so Mary was relieved for the sake of the Institute's survival when Rome strongly supported this policy and laid it down that only with the permission of the Holy See could a second novitiate be opened. In telling Simeoni how Vaughan welcomed the Sisters to Sydney, she mentioned his suggestion about a novitiate there:

> I have the utmost confidence in His Grace's disinterested goodness.
> I know that he will support and strengthen the Sisters in their love of
> the Constitutions . . . and that, in short, they will have every facility
> afforded them of being trained in the true spirit of the Institute.

One obvious reason for a Sydney novitiate was the number of candidates offering themselves in that part of the continent and the difficulty of providing financially for their passages to Adelaide. There would be long-term advantages to the Church in the educational struggle if the Josephites had a centre in Sydney. This would also help to untangle the confusion caused by the existence of the Bathurst community bearing the same name and wearing the same habit as the Mother House Sisters. A Sydney novitiate would make the distinction clear and candidates would know what they were joining. When Mary told Vaughan that the Constitutions made provision for a second novitiate (with the permission of the Holy See), he said he was confident that rapid expansion would follow such an initiative. Once she was sure that he was prepared to respect the Constitutions and did not threaten to take over as the Quinns had done, she also favoured the idea. In March 1881 Vaughan sent her a copy of the permission the Holy See had given him to have a novitiate opened, but he left it to the Sisters to decide when this should be done. Mary expected that the coming Chapter would approve of the step. But the Sisters were cautious, and although the Archbishop was only forty-seven, they were concerned about protecting their Rule against a possible successor in the Quinn mould.

The second novitiate proposal caused Mary to be criticised for inconsistency in her policy towards bishops. She called this "a weak, if not silly argument," and regretted that it should have been imposed on Dr Reynolds "who at least should have known its falseness". She told Mechtilde:

> Dr Torreggiani laughed when I told him that some said I had conceded to Dr Vaughan in the matter of the Noviciate what I had refused to the Bishops Quinn. He told me that without any word of mine he had the *word of Bishop Quinn* himself to the fact that nothing short of *absolute* control would satisfy them, that the granting or not granting of a second Noviciate had nothing to do with it.

Her letter from Adelaide on 2 April 1880 to Reynolds in Europe was written after her long absence in Queensland. It touched on topics that were soon to assume unexpected importance and to prove explosive, though at the time they seemed ordinary enough. There is a revealing paragraph about debts. She is obviously concerned, but she is confident that God will look after those who work for him and trust him: "I think of all the schools that would have to be closed and the poor children that would be deserted if some such responsibility would not be endured." Reynolds at first showed no resentment at the foundations in Sydney, but in time his advisers were able to work on the idea that another diocese was being supplied with labourers at the expense of his section of the vineyard. At this stage, however, amidst all his troubles abroad, he would have been pleased to read that Vaughan "was most kind in his enquiries about you and would, I am sure, like to hear from you. He at any rate is your friend and that of your children."

When the unexpected death of Vaughan in August 1883 deprived Reynolds of a source of stability and removed a true friend, those with opposing views had unimpeded access to his mind. Mary said that the change in his attitude could be dated from the time he knew of Vaughan's death: "All the change in the Bishop towards me has appeared since the sad tidings of the Archbishop's death."

The second General Chapter was due to open in Adelaide on 19 March 1881, six years after the first. But the bishop was away, and it could not begin until he returned. Some of the nuns saw the delay as a sign that a deed of suppression might be on the way. "Silly ones of little faith," Mary chided them. Instead of what they feared, "a formal recognition from Pope Leo himself has come, in which he grants us permission to establish a second Noviciate in Sydney". The bishop arrived on June 10, and the Chapter was scheduled for July 19. Mary urged the Sisters to have the right frame of mind: "Pray that *self* may be forgotten, buried in the one great aim of our lives, God's glory."

The most important piece of Chapter business was the election of a Mother General. Expecting to be able to lay down the burden of authority, Mary wrote on July 12 what she thought would be her last official letter to the Sisters, urging them to be good and faithful children of her successor: "Always remember to love one another, Superiors—and all—in God and for God, and beware of any earthly motive marring this proper spirit."

When the Chapter opened, a question arose about whether Mary could be re-elected. She herself maintained that she was not eligible, because she had already held office for more than twelve years. After consultation with Father Tappeiner, the bishop announced that she was eligible, as her term of office only dated from the first Chapter, when the Constitutions came into force.[3] Mary accepted this decision and the subsequent vote of the Chapter re-electing her.[4] "It was with great grief that I found myself re-elected," she wrote to Simeoni, "and, but for certain circumstances and the fear of offending God, I would have appealed to Your Eminence against it." She wrote to the Sisters in Sydney: "I did not and do not feel able for another six years of office—the prospect frightens so pray hard for me. I have been much disappointed too at the postponement of the 2nd Noviciate which now we cannot open before 1883."

There were differing opinions at the Chapter about the second novitiate. It was not approved for the time being (17 votes to 10); but the Mother General and her Council were given the discretion to open it from the end of 1882 (14 votes to 13). A study of the background of this decision, as far as it is known, reveals an important fact about the Bishop of Adelaide, already a very sick man—although he was externally still friendly, his mentality was basically that of the distraught man of 1883.

The papal permission granted to Vaughan to open a novitiate in his diocese spoke only of observing the Church's canons. It had said nothing about approval by the General Chapter or the Council. The Chapter's holding decision, including the reference to the Council of the Institute, was made at a time when they expected to be living under normal conditions, with the Mother General accepted by the bishop in Adelaide. Two and a half years later, however, conditions had changed drastically. There were postulants waiting in Sydney, but the Adelaide situation made it impossible to send them over there. So, early in 1884, exiled from Adelaide and deprived of contact with her Council, Mary followed the advice of theologians and canonists and established a novitiate in Sydney. In April she wrote to Rome telling Bianchi and Campbell about it, asking that Simeoni be informed.

The Mother General was blamed for having gone ahead, but the new Archbishop, Dr Moran, supported her decision soon after his arrival. She was relieved: "I am so glad that Your Grace is satisfied that we were justified in commencing it as we did." Her Sydney consultants, in fact, had gone further than to say she was entitled to act—they held that the Sisters and the powers in Adelaide had been blameworthy in not taking up the papal permission, and that their attitude had been a slight to Archbishop Vaughan. Had he not been the mildest of men, they said, he might have insisted on what they had refused.

In 1884 Josephine Carolan revealed something about the Chapter that is not to be found in the minutes. It throws light on how the bishop created confusion:

> It was at the General Chapter three years ago he told us also that Rome did not wish a second Novitiate, that Mother General could and possibly would be censured and that he himself ought to have been consulted before it was asked for.

This was sheer bluff on the part of the bishop. The Holy See knew all about it, and had already given the permission, and he knew it. So how could he say that Rome did not wish a second novitiate, or that there was some irregularity in the way it was asked for? But it gives a clue as to how the novitiate was blocked at the Chapter. The statement that the Mother General possibly would be censured for asking for the permission (actually it was Vaughan who asked) was also quite groundless, yet it would have created fear and hesitation among the nuns. They would have been impressed by the presence and the utterances of the bishop, especially as he had just returned from Rome. For his part, resenting Vaughan's request and the response of the Holy See, he was determined to block the whole thing.

Reading the account of the various sessions of the Chapter, one senses that the bishop was manipulating things. The issue of the second novitiate was introduced in the first session, then dropped, delayed, taken up again, delayed again ("before the question was decided, the bishop said that important business called him elsewhere"), and finally handled in the sixth session—a treatment that looks questionable for an important piece of business. Mary told Vaughan on August 8: "All would like to have it as you wished but many did not seem to see that they could vote in favour of it and do what they thought to be their duty." What that sentence does not say is as important as what it says. The confusion in the Sisters' minds is not surprising in view of the bishop's scarcely veiled threats about the Mother General.

The minutes of the Chapter do not give an account of the course of the discussions, but it is clear that there was some factor operating behind the scenes that made the delegates hesitate about voting for the novitiate in Sydney. Of the first session it is simply said: "His Lordship then spoke of the proposed novitiate in Sydney—this was postponed for another session." What he said is not recorded, but it is clear from later recollections of the Sisters that his remarks were aimed at killing the idea. Tappeiner was against it too, and it would be interesting to know why. He may have seen intrinsic reasons, or perhaps he saw danger in the mood of the bishop.

The response to the proposal of the Sydney novitiate was a fairly strong message that Adelaide would call the tune. The Archbishop of Sydney should be asked to prepare a written statement of his intentions. There was a party in favour of total rejection, and it is not hard to see that its policy was based on things the bishop had said. The outcome was that in the meantime any attempt on the part of the Mother General and her Council to consult with Vaughan was effectively blocked until 1883.

Mary was sensitive to Vaughan's feelings. "I regret the delay exceedingly," she told him on August 8, "the more so as I did not expect it, and fear it may cause annoyance to you who have been so kind to us." But her last paragraph is even more delicate in not saying directly what she was beginning to see—Reynolds was part of the problem. He was in very delicate health, they owed him much gratitude for former kindnesses, and so on, but would the Archbishop please ask him to help the second novitiate on. Her gentle language obscures but does not entirely conceal what went on in the Chapter. In order to make sure that the Sydney novitiate would not be approved, the bishop evidently "came to the aid" of the Sisters by saying he would "let his schools suffer" by consenting to exchange more senior Sisters for postulants in Adelaide. The fact that Mary asked Vaughan to bring his influence to bear on Reynolds indicates that the trouble did not arise merely from the hesitation of the Sisters.

Along with the report of the Chapter, a strongly worded document was sent to Rome about the conduct of the former Sister Clare Wright. She has acted shamefully, it said, and is deserving of severe censure so that others may realise the seriousness of what she has done. The peace and unity of the Institute have suffered for many years from her secret activities and her neglect of duty, she has been the cause of the loss of vocations, and she has practised the grossest deceit. The Sisters think it was her fear of an investigation that caused her to abandon the Institute in March 1881 "without informing or asking anyone". She was not prepared to face the superior on whom she had practised such deception. To this lament about Clare's behaviour was added a protest against the Bishop of Brisbane and Father Woods. They had both shown themselves sympathetic by receiving her, in spite of the fact that she had left the Institute and laid aside her religious obligations without a dispensation.

In her personal report to Simeoni, Mary gave some facts and figures, and added some reflections on matters she was concerned about. After mentioning the troubles in Bathurst and Brisbane, and Vaughan's helpfulness, she spoke of the encouragement given by Woods to "disobedient and troublesome religious", and said she hoped Clare's case would open the eyes of his admirers. A great part of the trouble was that "he has a way of making it appear that he has been injured, and this appeals to the affection of those who know him".

In April 1881, when she returned to Adelaide from Sydney, Mary had written to Vaughan about the trail of deception and unfaithfulness Clare had left behind her:

Many things that were a mystery to me before now have come to light . . . Amongst the Sisters she has been secretly advancing Father Woods' views—whilst to me she always expressed the greatest disapprobation of them. I leave Your Grace to imagine how well the Institute is rid of such a person—but I tremble to think of what her end will be.

She also wrote to the Sisters about Clare's departure, warning them against pride and disobedience. But they were not rid of her influence. Her former status made it easier for her to unsettle Sisters who were attached to Father Woods. She had also been treacherous in her conversations with influential clerical enemies of the Institute, sowing seeds that bore fruit in 1883.

A few months after Clare had protested, "I will be glad if you will contradict anyone who asserts that I am going back to Brisbane as it is quite untrue," she had followed her sister Gertrude out of the Institute without dispensation, and was on her way back to Brisbane. She intended to exploit her influence and was apparently expecting a good number of the Adelaide Sisters to follow her. A citizen up there, Patrick Ahearn, kept his friend Mother Mary informed about what the people thought of Clare and her group, and it was not a favourable assessment of her character or her prospects. He wrote like Geoffrey Chaucer:

> i suppose you now Sister Clare is arived hier and her Sister Gerturde they are goun to do wonders hier they say ian told that Sister Clair said she never tuck her vows for Life she only pretended to take them and if that Be the way it seems she had Bad idays in her head all along ihapened to beComing over Spring hill afue days sins ithink it was Last thursday and imet her rite unawares quite cloas to her and we Boat steerd Each other in the fais she looks very bad there was some other of what they call the Black Sisters with her they expect to do agraite stroake hier But they mite find oute there mistake.

This represented the outlook which made it impossible for these "Queensland diocesans" to survive. Quinn and Woods might have been able to accept Clare's faithlessness, but the Patrick Ahearns of Queensland were not.

The priest in Bundaberg, Father Rossolini, was friendly to Mary but she feared that "the Bishop may give him orders to leave or send them a priest unfriendly to us". This eventually came to pass, and the Sisters withdrew in July 1880. A small group of diocesan Josephites arrived a fortnight later. Rossolini was not impressed: "I saw these unfortunates and I think your order lost nothing by losing them, but gained a good deal."

Mary was not so much concerned with her own losses and gains as about the fact that the founder and a bishop were encouraging Sisters who abandoned their profession without dispensations. She found this a great puzzle. To her it was not just a difference of opinion, it was a matter as serious as the obligation to observe vows. Woods had written on 15 May 1875: "I am as faithful to them and to the Institute as ever I was and will, please God, fight this battle out to the ending." What he could have meant by these fighting words Mary probably found it hard to guess at the time, but when she discovered that he intended to cajole as many Sisters as he could away from their obligations—dispensation or no dispensation—her reaction was not merely dismay, it was amazement and utter incredulity. When she remonstrated with him in September 1879, she did so with great restraint and respect, but with a firmness and clarity that should have alerted anybody whose brain was not befuddled that the situation was serious. She said:

> Pardon me if I frankly tell you that I think you could have prevented all this had you not spoken of me and the Institute as you did, and had you not encouraged them by conniving at their disobedience in hiding it from their superior.

That Rossolini shared Mary's bewilderment at Woods' conduct is clear from his comments on the way the diocesan community was being set up in Queensland: "At present they have no rules here. I was told that the Rev. Woods is to be here soon; if I shall see him, I will tell him a few things about his stupid doings." Two Sisters who came from Adelaide—"outlaws and ranaways," he called them—had reputations for instability, one being described as deranged and the other as giddy. They openly favoured Woods. At least the two from Bathurst who joined them in late August seemed to be "pretty fair".

In July of the next year the two Wright sisters, Clare and Gertrude, brought the number to six. This enabled them to open a second school in Bowen, a further 400 miles north—a foundation taken over by the Sisters of Mercy in 1885. The Bundaberg community received candidates and carried on the work of education until it was disbanded in 1896 by Bishop Quinn's successor. One of them once met one of Mother Mary's Sisters at Quirindi and told her that she had thought she was joining her community and discovered her error too late.

Josephine McMullen mentioned in a letter to Mary in 1889 that Clare had been at the house of Mrs Gertrude Abbott (Ignatius O'Brien). Some time after 1897 Clare abandoned religious life; she was killed in an accident in Melbourne in 1925. No record of a dispensation for her has been found, as there has for her sister, Gertrude. Little is known of the others, though some apparently joined the Bathurst community.

Mother Mary was well aware of the Institute's deficiencies. In her letter to Simeoni accompanying the report of the second Chapter, she told him of this realistically, but spoke also of her hopes for the future. Very few of those who had caused trouble had had proper novitiate training, but that had now been remedied:

> For the rest of the professed Sisters I can only say that we have many faults, but as far as I can judge the will of each is good, and with the blessing of God, and the help of the spiritual aids afforded to us by our kind Bishop, we all hope to advance in the spirit of our holy state.

She was clearly looking to the bishop for encouragement and assistance, and she did not dream that the 1883 visitation, which she regarded at first as a genuine attempt to help the Institute, would take the vicious form it did.

Footnotes

[1] Roger Vaughan was born in 1834. He had five brothers priests (including a cardinal, a bishop, and an abbot) and four sisters nuns. He joined the Benedictines in 1854, studied in Rome, and was ordained in 1859. Before his appointment to Sydney he was Prior and Rector of the monastery in Belmont, near Hereford. On 18 August 1883 he died unexpectedly at the age of forty-nine at Ince Blundell, near Liverpool, soon after arriving in England on a visit.

[2] A sample of his style as he dealt with Henry Parkes: "He thinks to silence me with the cowardly cry of 'sedition', and to make the world believe that whenever I open my mouth on the education question and denounce his odious bill, that I am disloyal! Cannot I appeal to the past, to many a bloody struggle since Agincourt, when he, whose name was given to me, Sir Roger Vaughan, was knighted in the field of battle by the Prince himself? Does my accuser imagine that though the people of the country are opposed to my religion that they will stand silently and approvingly and see me gagged?"

[3] The rule said that a Superior General who had been elected twice in succession and so had been in charge for twelve years, could not then be re-elected. Mother Mary had been *elected* only once—in 1875. So Tappeiner (who was clearly the brains at the consultation) concluded that, since she had not been twice elected, the restriction did not apply. Her period as guardian before 1875 was irrelevant.

[4] The voting was by a majority of 23 to 4. The four consisted of two votes for Calasanctius, one for Bonaventure, and one for Monica. It is interesting that no one voted for Bernard. Four General Councillors were elected: Calasanctius, Monica, Michael, and Matthew.

PART VII

The Second Adelaide Crisis 1883

TWENTY-ONE

CHRISTOPHER
AUGUSTINE REYNOLDS

Christopher Augustine Reynolds played an important role in the life of Mary MacKillop as friend and foe in turn. Together with the Jesuits, he was her main support in the critical days of 1871 when the Institute was threatened with disbandment. As caretaker of the diocese after Sheil's death, he halted the process that had been set in motion against the Sisters, and sent Mary to Rome in 1873 to seek approval of their Rule. When he became bishop he helped the Institute to rebuild, supported it during the difficulties at Bathurst and Brisbane, and showed no overt ill will when foundations were being made in New South Wales in 1880.

But at some moment late in 1883 his mind was taken over by Mother Mary's enemies, and he became the most bitter of foes. What he had to say was gross and personal and (objectively speaking) slanderous. Moreover, being a bishop, he attempted to use his authority not merely to shove her out of his way, but to pursue her with the calumnies that had been fed to him, and to crush her. Bewildered by his conduct, she remarked to Campbell: "Our good God allows us to have much opposition from some of His best servants, and to me this is a painful cross."

Reynolds was born in Dublin in July 1834. At the age of eighteen he volunteered to join Dr Salvado, a Benedictine bishop who was looking for recruits for the Northern Territory mission in Australia. In 1854, together with Frederick Byrne, a fellow countryman, Reynolds went to the Benedictine novitiate in Subiaco, Italy, as the first step in his preparation. After a year both young men left for Australia as members of a missionary band led by the Benedictine Dr Serra, Administrator of the diocese of Perth. They were not professed, but they had a document from the Abbot explaining that this was for reasons of health and that if things improved in Australia the superiors there might see their way to professing them.

The trip was not a happy one, and when they arrived in May 1855 the Australian scene was not what they had imagined. For a start, the diocese of Port Victoria in the north never came to anything. The site was abandoned in favour of the modern Darwin, and Salvado never even went there. To make matters worse, the life provided for Reynolds and Byrne in Perth was a disappointment.[1] Whatever their visions might have been, the reality was intolerable. By May of the next year they had written a long letter of complaint to Dublin, destined for the eyes of Cardinal Cullen, laying the blame squarely on the arch-villain Serra, and declaring that it was "the part of honest men to expose oppression and maladministration of public affairs especially to those by whose influence they can be remedied".

Hopes for a novitiate in Perth came to nothing and it does not seem that the young men ever resumed the religious habit. Instead, they were set to teaching school in Fremantle in conditions that did not please them at all. Far from improving their health, the classroom made things worse. There was talk of ecclesiastical studies, but it came to practically nothing—hardly a one-semester course in one subject, at night.

It comes as no surprise then to learn that within eighteen months, by January 1857, the two had left Western Australia. They were headed for South Australia, apparently encouraged by the Bishop of Adelaide, Dr Murphy. The details of the next few years are vague. There was possibly more schoolteaching, there were studies with the Austrian Jesuits at Sevenhill (a school for boys where the Fathers tutored would-be priests from time to time), there was continued ill health, there were sojourns in Adelaide, there was the death of Bishop Murphy in 1858. Eventually, however, they were both ordained for the diocese of Adelaide by Bishop Geoghegan in April 1860. In 1873 Reynolds became bishop of the diocese, and Byrne his Vicar General.

Reynolds could not but be aware of the difference between his preparation and that of his fellow bishops like the Quinns and Cardinal Moran with their extended Roman studies, their doctorates, and their experience of ecclesiastical life in high places; of Archbishop Vaughan with his deep scholarship and culture added to his profound Benedictine spirituality; of the Austrian Jesuits at Sevenhill and Norwood with their prolonged scholastic and spiritual training; and indeed of the priests around him and under him who had been educated in Rome at the Irish College and at Propaganda, or at regular seminaries in Ireland. Whereas Woods had been able to make up to some extent for his lack of formal training by applying a sharp mind to private study, Reynolds was, according to even such a gentle commentator as Mary MacKillop, "not what many would call a clever man". His title *Doctor* was not earned in the schools; it was honorifically attached to every bishop, whatever his background. As can be seen, in this case the scholastic background was minimal.[2]

There is every reason to think Reynolds would have maintained his uncomplicated reputation as a good priest if he had remained a parish pastor. The story of how he came to be in charge after Sheil's death is told variously according to the prejudices of the narrator. Some said he had intruded himself and assumed power illegally. Polding passed no judgment on the issue; he simply confirmed him as Administrator. There can be little doubt that Reynolds honestly did not expect to be the next bishop. His lack of ambition was probably based on self-knowledge, and there is no reason to suggest that his distress at the appointment was feigned.

Although he was a good and zealous man, Reynolds was not a success as head of the diocese of Adelaide. Not only was he devoid of any business sense and even average ability to manage money, but in the realm of the spiritual and personal he was unable to handle anything but normal and regular situations. Spiritual insight in his letters is restricted to a few stock phrases which, however pious, reflect the limits of his mind and his lack of ability to relate to his fellow humans. He was very sensitive about his authority, and quickly reacted to anything that could be construed as an offence to it. He saw himself as the heroic victim of his own devotion to duty, and never failed to mention how much thought and prayer he had given to the consideration of some unpleasant decision, usually the suspension of a priest or the expulsion of somebody from his diocese. He could speak confidently when he had statistics at hand about the number of churches opened, foundation stones laid, schools inaugurated, sacraments administered, Catholics doing this or that. His theology was sound as far as it went, but his handling of canon law, of the rights of his fellow man, and of the truth, could only be excused on the plea of invincible ignorance, encouraged by skilful and interested assistants.

It was no secret that the bishop was not popular. Mary MacKillop accepted it as a fact; no matter how warm a friend he was to the Institute of St Joseph, she knew there were many who did not share her admiration and loyalty. "He has enemies who hope he may never return here again," she told Campbell in March 1879. Reynolds himself clearly knew it, and his response was to make a habit of assimilating himself to his "sorely tried diocese". His self-pity deepened with the years, and as his problems grew so did his awareness of his incompetence. He was intolerant of priests with problems, reacting to them with rhetorical personal abuse.

A document of protest was sent to Rome in September 1877 by six priests who had left Adelaide to serve elsewhere, either expelled by Reynolds or choosing not to remain longer in his diocese. It is a devastating attack on the person and the performance of the bishop, beginning with the fact that it was "a matter of notoriety that he never received any ecclesiastical training", moving on to the allegations about his appointment as Administrator, and not sparing him in any aspect of his exercise of authority. It is openly political in its spirit, typical of its kind, professing only the interests of the Church and of religion, but full of acrimony and spiteful abuse, conceding nothing praiseworthy in its victim. The signatories all professed to be supporters of the good Bishop Sheil and his Franciscan friends, and were therefore opposed to the *Irish Harp*, to Reynolds, and to everybody who thought that Sheil had acted imprudently and unjustly. The spirit of the document may be deplored, and much of its gossipy, petty, spiteful detail may well be doubted. But the fact remains that a number of priests felt they had good reason not to admire or trust Reynolds, and much of the evidence they cited was public knowledge.

These priests alleged four signs of the thinness of their bishop's theology: that he never preached in his cathedral, never issued pastoral letters, never held clergy conferences, and avoided discussing theological matters in private conversation. With regard to his handling of finances, they were equally merciless, recalling the fact that the judge in a civil case against the bishop had described his conduct as "an open attempt to defraud" and had added "that if there was any possibility of such an attempt succeeding there would be an end to all commercial transactions in the community".

The bishop's treatment of his clergy is presented in the letter of protest as deplorable, cruel, and unjust. Certainly Tappeiner was not a little critical of them in his 1872 report, and there were instances where priests behaved unworthily—some charges of excessive drinking and sexual immorality do not lack evidence. But they could hardly have been such a consistently unpriestly and unsatisfactory lot as appears from Reynolds' statements. Money and drink were his bugbears, especially drink. The protest letter gave the stories of twelve priests who had left the diocese, showing incidentally that Mary MacKillop was not the only person to fall victim to the bishop's sensitivity in these areas. But whereas she was content to point out the factual errors in what was alleged against her, others were much more vocal in rebutting charges, adding lively colour and spirited protests against the bishop's injustice.

The stories are often substantiated by other documents in the Roman archives. A Father O'Brien was under threat of automatic suspension the moment he took a mouthful of beer or wine or anything stronger. Among other instances, the two sides of the story of Father Jörgensen in 1886 are extant—the bishop's story, and the victim's. The bishop lamented:

> With my own eyes I had to witness your public and open violation of the law of the Diocese, enacted at Synod. In your Bishop's presence you broke that law. You will know that to stop abuses I have decreed that none in this diocese should take drink before dinner . . . I now declare you suspended from your priestly functions.

The facts seem to be as follows. One Sunday this priest was in charge of the arrangements for the blessing of a church close to his own. After celebrating an early Mass, he walked two or three miles to this church, heard some confessions, and had everything ready by 11 o'clock. After the blessing ceremony he was the celebrant of a sung Mass, during which the bishop preached for an hour and a half. It was about three o'clock when the function was over, and it was a hot day. As they gathered before dinner, Father Jörgensen (still fasting since midnight from all food and drink, including water, and very thirsty) was offered a glass of wine by the Dean in the presence of the bishop. He took it gratefully without a worry. The next day he accepted an invitation to dine with the bishop, sitting next to him, but during the whole day not a word was said about the glass of wine. It was on the following day that he received the devastating letter from Reynolds suspending him for his open and public defiance of the law.

In the 1877 protest there are thirteen pages of examples, stories, and letters cited to illustrate the bishop's deficiencies as a man and as a pastor. They speak of his gross mismanagement of the financial affairs of the diocese and the misapplication of funds contributed for specific purposes. Hence, they say, "the people have ceased almost unanimously to contribute towards the liquidation of the so-called diocesan debt". They speak of lying, and cheating with money. Whatever his acts should be called, the evidence for these accusations makes one suspect that in his desperation to survive the poor man had became insensitive to important values like truth and honesty.

If this document were a single disgruntled protest against a man of otherwise unquestioned trustworthiness and ability, it could be left in its place in the annals of slanderous invective. But its substance harmonises with evidence that comes to the surface in Reynolds' dealings with the Josephites and Mary MacKillop from 1883 onwards. Statements that the six protesters would have called lies, slanders, injustice, dishonesty, gullibility, gross insensitivity, and inhumanity, were called "unfortunate mistakes" by Mother Mary of the Cross. But the evidence of their nature is too stark to be ignored.

It is all very pathetic, and might well be buried. But Reynolds expelled Mary from his diocese as a drunkard and an embezzler of money meant for the poor. This was in fact a gross slander, contradicting everything everybody knew about her, but because he was a bishop his action lived after him and delayed the Process of Canonisation for twenty years. When Cardinal Moran's 1884 report to Rome eventually came to light in 1951 it was official documentary confirmation of what everybody knew. Reynolds was a bishop, but he was a distraught, unfortunate bishop; his judgment was neither serene nor objective, his acts often bore the mark of irresponsibility, and his word could be accepted only with extreme caution.

While he was absent from his diocese for twenty-seven months from March 1879 until June 1881, Reynolds was in constant contact with his Vicar General, Frederick Byrne, his long-time school friend and fellow Benedictine novice. The letters reveal the bishop's preoccupations, his state of health, and his attitude towards those under him. Three recurring themes (in the form of charges against various people) are excessive drinking, the squandering of funds, and betrayal by old and trusted friends. Mother Mary is hardly mentioned, and never at all in connection with such charges.

Lack of funds could be called the leitmotiv of the letters. Reynolds certainly was in need of money, especially to pay for the outfitting and transport of the clergy he hoped to recruit. It could hardly be denied, either, that the poverty he saw about him in Italy and Ireland made it impossible to expect help from there. But it must have grated on the Vicar General to hear the constant refrain about money and debts, repeated not only in every letter, but many times in each letter. As his nerves became frayed, the bishop hit out at everybody:

> I have to relinquish every personal comfort to meet the wants of a *thoughtless* if not ungrateful flock, for had they done their duty by me I need not be in such straits for means.

There was physical distress behind this, but Byrne had not only to listen to repeated reminders of the suffering and the apostolic heroism of his bishop, but he had to bear the sting in the tail of his boyhood companion's lament that he had to travel second class: "Your waywardness has placed me in a miserable condition in this terrible winter." Injured dignity was plainly visible on several other occasions: "Like other matters, you have treated it with the *Veni, Vidi, Vici* style which pervades so many of your letters to me lately." He showed a special sensitivity to betrayal by an old friend. "I never expected that you would be the one to add the bitterest portion to my cup of affliction," he protested, when Byrne had mocked him about two priests he had sent from Ireland being drunkards:

> I do not deserve the uncharitable bitter taunts you have heaped upon me! You calmly write, "Behold the first fruits of your labours, at which everyone is astonished knowing how bitterly you inveighed against Dr Sheil's want of judgement in selecting priests." You also say, "Don't take any more priests like Guinane and Sheridan; the scandal they have given is awful," thus concluding that I had known all about them.

The theme of the unworthy priest was a sensitive one, and that is why Reynolds was so touchy about drink. Byrne's taunts about Guinane and Sheridan obviously hit the mark. The startling story of their first days in Adelaide would have caused any bishop to raise an eyebrow, and the Vicar General made the most of it. But it was not an isolated instance. Similar stories were told about other Adelaide priests, about some who wandered in from elsewhere, and about laymen in responsible positions.

The demon drink is a recurring theme in the letters. In fact, even before the main body of his volunteers set foot in Australia he was issuing orders for earlier arrivals to be expelled for their drinking. His action was approved by the Vicar General, who began by coming straight to the point: "I will begin with the notorious drunkard you sent out in the person of the ex-Dominican Guinane," and ended with the plea: "I don't think of anything more to say—only don't take any more priests like Guinane and Sheridan; the scandal they have given is awful." This kind of thing did nothing to improve the bishop's confidence, or to strengthen his attachment to Frederick Byrne.[3] But there was worse to come. *He* was being blamed in Rome and London for the drink trouble! Reacting to this shock, he sent home strict orders: "*I forbid under obedience* either ale, porter or brandy to be brought to the House. Give a due supply, at meals, of good red or white wine, which is sufficient for health and nourishment."

If Reynolds was convinced that somebody in his service was drinking, that person's cause was lost. He or she would be shipped out at once and there would be no appeal. Anybody looking for an opening to destroy an enemy had only to look for it here. The problem would be, how to convince the bishop. This seems to have been the politics behind the organising of the 1883 Commission in Adelaide.

It would be tedious to run through all the details of the bishop's troubles as narrated in his letters to Byrne. Drunken and unsatisfactory priests, and the debts, occupy the stage for the most part. The only note of joy is the memory of the audience with Pope Leo XIII—"Truly the sorrows of the past ten years, a hundred times over, would be more than compensated for by such a consolation as this hour and quarter's audience all alone with the Vicar of Christ!"—and the only positive news he has to report is the recruiting of ten priests. The rest is woe. The lack of money is chronic and serious, his health is consistently poor, the political situation and the poverty in Italy and Ireland make distressing reading, and the weather is bad from start to finish. In addition, he was not long in Europe before he realised that enemies had been at work, and that he had much to do to set the record straight: "I had a good deal of uphill work to show what manner of man I was." Much of it had to do with versions of the troubles of 1871 that had been brought home by those who had been repatriated because of their part in them; but later years had made him plenty of enemies also.

There is very little about the Sisters of St Joseph in the letters, and in the light of the great fuss created about them a couple of years later this is surprising.[4] Mary was engaged for much of 1879 with problems in Queensland, and on the only occasion Reynolds adverted to this he included a very uncomplimentary reference to Bishop Quinn: "I have a letter from Sydney and one from Mother Mary with a hurried account of that poor madcap's doing in Brisbane."

As to the Adelaide Josephite affairs, Byrne made a few references to the debt, and threw in a hint of indiscipline, but he was aware that it was not luxury living that was running up the debt: "The Sisters in Macclesfield want a little house very badly; it is a shame to have them living in a miserable hut with the cold winds and rain blowing into it." But the bishop was not worried about the debt, remarking only that it was a pity that "there has not been that support given the Sisters in many districts that they should have had".

Some light is thrown on Bishop Reynolds by the details of a running battle that was waged for some months in 1879–80 over a small Benedictine community in his diocese. They were a valuable adjunct to the parish clergy, and the bishop was anxious to retain them. When their superiors indicated that they were to proceed to New Zealand, he sent counterorders that they were not to go. The Vicar General expressed doubts about his right to do this, but the bishop had already sent cheering news from Rome—he had been told at his private audience with the Pope that the Benedictines were to stay:

> The Holy Father has *overruled* the decision previously given. [He] sent me with special directions to the three Cardinals who have the Commission of these affairs.

The Vicar General shared his joy: "I am very glad that it was so gratifying to you and that you were successful in keeping Abbot and companions." But then clouds appeared on Reynolds' horizon: "I cannot but feel I have a host of opponents—in one single Cardinal and that one Simeoni." In fact his hopes were dashed, and New Zealand got the Benedictines.

This saga seems to have given Reynolds cause to think that Simeoni was less than fully sympathetic to him. In hard terms, we wonder just what the Pope did mean to tell him during the private audience, and whether the decision on the Benedictines was really a reversal of anything but the bishop's hopes. It would seem a strange proceeding for a pope to tell a bishop by word of mouth at a private audience to instruct three cardinals to reverse some official decision.

What is clear is that both Pope Leo and Cardinal Simeoni got a good look at the Bishop of Adelaide. We are told that the private audience took an hour and a quarter. We are also informed that the bishop was asked to work for a time in a Vatican office, and to attend some meetings "by the wish of Sacred Congregation and under instruction from His Holiness". As he remarked, it all seemed very flattering, but it may have left Simeoni and the other curial officials with a less than flattering picture of the man they had good reason to wonder about before he arrived. When it came to the moment of truth, it was Leo XIII and Giovanni Simeoni who were behind the eventual approbation of the central government of the Josephite Institute in 1888, contrary to the express wishes of Reynolds and other bishops in Australia.

The conclusion is forced on one reading the documents a century later, that Simeoni did not believe what Reynolds had to say on the subject of Mother Mary and the Josephites after 1883. That the bishop had himself become aware of his lack of credit with the cardinal is clear from the pathetic climax to a long letter he wrote to him against Mary in November 1884: "I am treated by Propaganda as if I were some chierichetto [altar boy]. I said I am too ill and tired to make a copy of this in the Italian language: as it will take too much time, just now."

Christopher Reynolds lacked confidence, and he tried to make up for it with bluster; he was nervous about the superior ecclesiastical training and human culture of the other bishops and many of the clergy around him; he was oversensitive about his authority (so painfully aware that it was practically all he had) and invoked it petulantly to quell any doubts about the prudence or justice of what he was doing or not doing. He had a supply of Homeric adjectives to apply to those who did not conform to his desires, and these poured out the moment he sensed any provocation.[5]

To sum it up: Reynolds seemed to find finance a mystery; he suspected alcohol in any form but wine in the liturgy and a "good red or white" for dinner at Bishop's House; he was under constant pressure because of the lack of clerical and religious personnel. These three sensitive issues were cunningly discerned by those around him who bore no good will towards the Josephites or their Mother General. The motives of such people are of concern only to God and themselves; what is of concern to history is how they induced the bishop to throw the weight of his authority behind their cause. They studied his frailties and played upon them, timing the attack well. His health was wretched, he was consistently depressed and pessimistic, he could scarcely conceal his incompetence any longer even from himself, and his only resource was to rely on strong-minded men with superior training who were standing by, apparently ready to help him do his duty.

Reynolds' volte-face in 1883 was really not out of character. A study of his life up to that time makes it clear that he had been a time bomb waiting to explode in Mary MacKillop's life, and explode he did. Enemies primed it well and made sure it contained just the right ingredients: accusations about money and drink, disappointment in a trusted one, and the threat that personnel would be lost to Sydney through Vaughan's initiatives there. The sound of the explosion was still reverberating in 1931 when the Process of Mary's canonisation was suspended because of what Reynolds had said about her in 1883.

Footnotes

[1] There was no Benedictine foundation in Perth. One had recently been made at New Norcia, eighty miles away, but it is doubtful if the two delicate young men would have been happy with a diet of lizards and insects, or with other conditions of life there in those early days.

[2] Questions are often asked about the appointment of Reynolds. Vatican records of the discussion preceding it throw little light on the puzzle. Nothing about his background and training is mentioned. The recommendations of the bishops are noted, but not their change of mind. Polding, who favoured bringing in an outsider, did mention Reynolds (with diffidence), but a few days later he backed Goold's three nominations without mentioning Reynolds. Matthew Quinn forwarded a list of four names without including Reynolds (though he had mentioned him earlier); James Quinn, Murray, and Lanigan all sent lists that did not include Reynolds.

[3] Byrne was relieved of his post after the bishop's return, and given extended leave of absence. The same thing had happened to Russell after one of Sheil's absences. It was Russell, however, who now replaced Byrne as Vicar General, until he too resigned in 1889, after a quarrel with Reynolds over the diocesan debt and His Grace's own personal holdings. Both Byrne and Russell were later reinstated after the death of Reynolds.

[4] Byrne told the bishop about the arrival of the Sisters of Mercy, but not about the total lack of preparation for them. Nor did he mention that Mother Mary invited twenty-four of them to live at her main convent for a week, then gave them one of her houses and offered them a choice of the Josephite schools.

[5] Writing to Bishop Murray in 1888, Reynolds fired a broadside at Moran, paused for a pious phrase, and then resumed the attack with a double shot at the two cardinals, Moran and Simeoni: "I will not trust myself with any remarks on the insolence, and I may add cowardly insolence, of the Chief *Actor* in all, as he passed here it was so wanton. Yet may God forgive *Him*. I have nothing now remaining to hope for excepting the justice of God, who in His own time will give what he and his brother at Propaganda have persistently denied me."

TWENTY-TWO

TWO BAD

ADVISERS

Archdeacon Russell and Father Polk

In the two years between the second Chapter and the Commission of 1883, there were two changes of personnel in Adelaide that seriously affected the Josephites. The first was the appointment of Joseph Polk as their director when Joseph Tappeiner died in February 1882; the second was the substitution of Patrick Russell for Frederick Byrne as diocesan Vicar General in February 1883.

Tappeiner had always been a wise friend of the Josephites, with the genuine good of the Church at heart. When he died Mother Mary said: "We have lost a treasured friend and father. In dark and trying moments—who so patient, hopeful and kind? May we hope to meet him again and to see him smile upon us with his own dear kind smile." Tappeiner had maintained his good cheer in difficult times. He was not a partisan, but a prudent man of God who knew how to be silent and what to say when it was time to speak. He had no delusions about the defects of those around him, but he did not believe that discouragement and division were means of healing. He was a steadying influence on Reynolds, but the association of the two did not always please the other bishops. Reynolds wrote to Mary from London in 1880:

> I need not assure you more than I have done with reference to my many, but I may not add, disinterested friends. Bathurst says I am led by the nose by Jesuits! Jesuits say I am haughty and the mitre has turned my head!

When Tappeiner died, neither his official position as director of the Sisters nor his unofficial role as counsellor to the bishop was filled with distinction. The Jesuit Father Polk, the new director, was, to speak plainly, a disaster. That is evident from the words of even the most charitable of his victims. It was clearly implied in a plea made more than forty years later by the head of the Josephites to Father George O'Neill, when he was writing his *Life* of Mother Mary. The Sisters knew that the truth would not always flatter some of the clerical characters in the story, and Mother Laurence (who had lived through those times) gave away more than she suspected by making her request. After referring to the spirit of Mother Mary of the Cross, O'Neill wrote:

> One of the last requests of her successor (in 1929) to the writer of these pages has been: "*Please* do not be hard on Dr Reynolds; he was kind to us for so long! *Nor* on poor Father Polk!"

It was safe enough to say, as Mary did, that Father Polk was "good and holy" and "a strict upholder of discipline", but even there one gathers a hint that he was hard, unsympathetic, unimaginative. He was in fact a dangerous, gullible, incompetent busybody, ready to believe the worst, who thought he was doing a service to God. Like Mother Laurence in 1929, Mary revealed much between the lines when she wrote in 1882:

> He really is most kind and does his best to make all feel at home with him . . . May God be with our dear departed Father. He is, I am sure, praying for us now in heaven.[1]

But things did not go well, and in spite of Polk's efforts to make them feel at home most of the Sisters would have preferred any other confessor. This was stated by Mother Mary, and supported by Osmund Thorpe, who knew many of the Sisters in Adelaide later on. It is clear from letters Mary wrote early in 1885 that Polk's effect on the Sisters was of grave concern to her. She told Archbishop Moran that it was cruel to force on the Sisters somebody they did not trust. She had considered writing to her friend Anderledy in Rome, now in charge of the Jesuits, but hesitated to trouble him. It was no laughing matter, but some of the nuns' letters show that it did have its funny side:

> [*From Philippa*:] Sister Francis Xavier and Father Polk had a great row a few weeks ago. He frightened her. He put his fist up into her face and said she was an impudent bold woman and that she ought to be ashamed of her Protestant name [*Blanche Amsinck*] and her Protestant face.

> [*From Ambrosine*:] Fr Polk makes me mind my P's and Q's, I can tell you. He said the novices could never be heard when they were answering Mass. He said we ought to speak like him, plainly and distinctly. Fancy all the Sisters imitating his roar. If the people were passing they would think there was a menagerie in the Convent grounds.

Mary's Jesuit brother Donald knew Polk personally. When he heard what was happening in 1884 he recalled a previous warning he had given her, and added a reassurance: "I know him well, know him to have some strange fancies and to be very headstrong where he can. I did not fear much from you—you would be more than enough for 50 Father Polks." There are hints here and there that the Jesuits around Polk were not as reticent about his lack of prudence as the Sisters were. Annette wrote to Mary eighteen months later: "Father Polk is looking ten years older. I think he gets it hot from the other Fathers."

Some of these Fathers seem to have suggested the unthinkable in 1885, namely that the Sisters should ask to see the written authority the bishop claimed to have for serious things he was doing—the second time in three years he had made such a claim. They did ask him, and his answer was an indignant declaration that his word was sufficient, and that they would get nothing else. But the Jesuits may well have asked Polk if *he* had seen the document, and from his answer realised that it did not exist.

Annette said Polk "got it hot" from his brethren, but we do not know whether this treatment was sufficient to wake him up to the truth. It was probably not. After all, he could have been forgiven if, like the Sisters in 1883, he found it hard to believe that the bishop and the Archdeacon were not speaking the truth when they said they had letters of authority from Rome. It is unlikely that he was accustomed to deception at such a high level. Although he must have known, as everybody else did by this time, that the 1883 claim was false, it seems that he was convinced that Rome was behind what was being done in 1885. He said to one Sister, "Ah, but what if Rome has spoken?" Presumably he meant he had reason to believe that orders had come from Rome cancelling the Constitutions and the instructions given to Mary, and turning the Congregation into a diocesan one. Otherwise it is hard to see how even a foolish man could be so wrong about the Rule of an institute of which he was official director.

Polk must have had his head in the sand if he had not heard during the troubled years that the Constitutions were based on central, not diocesan, government. Had he not heard of Bathurst and Brisbane, and wondered what the fuss there was all about? He must have known the Rule was not diocesan. The only explanation of his attitude was that he was under the impression that the bishop was authorised by Rome to ignore the Constitutions. He had been impressed by the letters of authority he had never seen and he would naturally have been upset when his Jesuit brethren asked him if he had seen them.

Father Polk, to say the least of it, did not inspire confidence. The evidence shows him as a foolish mischief-maker with good intentions. With such a man at one ear and Archdeacon Russell at the other, the bishop certainly had what Mother Mary kindly called bad advisers.

Patrick Russell, fifty-three years old and twenty-eight years a priest of Adelaide at the time of the Commission, was an Irishman with a well-known bias in favour of his own countrymen. His family was well-to-do, and this gave him social status and influence above that of any other priest in South Australia. He had fallen out of favour with Bishop Sheil, who sent him away from the diocese on indefinite leave after his own return from Europe in 1871. The most publicised reason for the bishop's displeasure was the enquiry conducted by the Archdeacon about what had been going on in the diocese, and the report he sent to Rome. According to one witness, another reason was that he talked too much and too loud about the bishop's drinking habits.

Though it may not have been entirely his fault, there never seems to have been a period when Russell was favourably disposed towards the Josephites. Mother Mary, who always weighed her words carefully, was stating an experienced fact when she told Dr Campbell in 1884:

> I have every reason to think that the Vicar General, Archdeacon Russell, is not, and has not for years been my friend, nor can I think that in many things he has been the Bishop's. I tried hard to think otherwise, but ere the Visitation ended, had to return to my first opinion.

Russell's antipathy had been sharpened by the episode of the disappearance of the hosts from the tabernacle in Franklin Street. The bishop was in Europe, and when Father Smyth died unexpectedly Russell took over the role of Vicar General. Unimpressed as he was by the stories of the visionaries, he thought he should investigate an occurrence that certainly reflected no credit on the Institute of St Joseph. The cardinal in Rome approved of his action, and told him to bring the matter up with the bishop on his return. The bishop also received a letter in the same tone, but his reaction was a hostile one. He sent Russell away on compulsory leave of absence, from which he did not return to Australia until June 1873, well after the bishop's death.

From the outline of Russell's troubles given in the report of the

1872 Commissioners, it is easy to see how even a neutral person could have become unfriendly towards the Josephites because of what had happened to him on their account. He had seen their deficiencies at close quarters, and had taken steps to remedy the situation (maybe more than willingly, but justifiably) and what he got for his pains was banishment. His subsequent hostility was not praiseworthy, but, human nature being what it is, it was understandable.

So far Sheil had been defending the Sisters against Russell. But then Cardinal Barnabò, to his surprise, received a strongly worded document from a group of laymen protesting against the action the bishop had taken meanwhile against the Sisters. Allies never seemed to stay together for long, and the cardinal found it hard to keep up with the latest developments. Letters expressing this bewilderment were sent on 29 February 1872 to a number of bishops in Australia, namely Polding, Goold, J. Quinn, and Murphy, as well as to Sheil himself.

The heart of the matter seems to have been the fact that the Josephites did not represent the social status with which Patrick Russell was familiar. He was more at home and far more friendly with the Dominican Sisters. He was a kind of relative-in-law of the Prioress, through the marriage of his sister to her brother, and he sympathised much more readily with the respectable schoolwork these Sisters had undertaken than with the ragtag teaching of the Sisters of St Joseph. He shared the reassurance felt by many Catholics, clergy and lay folk, when they saw in the Dominican nuns the traditional style they had known at home. The Josephites who went about the streets visiting the shops and the markets with their begging-bags were an embarrassment.

To make matters worse, the Dominicans fell badly out of favour with Reynolds when he was Administrator after Sheil's death. Having been protégées of Horan, they found themselves in the centre of the faction opposed to Reynolds. They had to put up with treatment that was not gentle and probably far from just. Reynolds wrote a long letter to Rome revealing not only that there were problems with these Dominicans, but that he was not a man who could handle pressure well. The report of the more balanced Tappeiner, however, shows that his complaints were not without some justification.

Reynolds told how Horan presided at the nuns' annual entertainment before an audience of his partisans, a large group of suspended and suspect priests and a number of Protestants and Jews.

"I was not invited," he said, "the whole affair was of course intended to insult me." One priest publicly expressed the community's gratitude to the Dominicans for giving "a tone to Catholic education in this colony" and added other things hardly calculated to please the friends of the lowly Josephites. According to Reynolds, "They have given the portraits of the friars Horan and Nowlan to several persons, done up in vignette style by Mother Subprioress, with an inscription *The victims of tyranny and misplaced power.*"

The Archdeacon, then absent in Europe, would not have been at all happy about the way his friends the Dominicans had been treated. His resentment would have been deepened by Reynolds' support of the Josephites, which was adding fuel to Russell's disapproval of these Sisters. Dean Fitzgibbon indicated in an 1872 letter to Rome that Russell was already critical of the financial situation of Woods' Sisters, arguing against their education-for-the-poor policy, which he saw as the cause of the troubles of the diocese.

Russell disagreed from the beginning with the Josephite schools, at which all were welcome but to which only those who could afford it were asked to contribute. His policy was that all poor children should be sent to a *Poor School*, and that no children should be received at other schools without full payment of fees. His reason was that the Josephites were being imposed upon by people who could pay. Although Mary was aware that there was some truth in this, she always strongly opposed the segregation idea. The Archdeacon would have been particularly annoyed by her removal of a partition he had built in the Glenelg school to separate the poor pupils from the others.

An incident that will make Russell's 1883 behaviour less surprising was told by Annette at the Process in 1926. When asked a question about Mary's trust in God when things were difficult, she confirmed under oath a story that had long been well known among the Josephites. There was a bill for boots and no money to pay it. Sister Clare went to the Archdeacon and they plotted to get the boot merchant to summons Mother Mary so that when she did not pay she would be sent to gaol. But Father Thomas Lee overheard them from the nearby waiting room at Bishop's House. He made straight for Macclesfield and saw to it that Mary was put in a buggy and driven over the border. "I don't mind," she said, "it was not for myself but for my Sisters. I could not let them go without boots. St Joseph will provide."

Bishop Reynolds had been aware in 1880 that Sister Clare was a sower of discord, as he wrote to Mary from London:

> I have often told of the ill effects of Sister Clare's conduct . . . I know
> well what a role she has played and the effects are too apparent in the
> spirit of discontent and criticism that has been going on.

Much later, Annette spoke of Clare's fall from grace:

> She formed a party in opposition to Mother. Mother was always nice
> and kind to her and told the Sisters to be kind to her, but moved her
> from her position. Mother never showed any resentment towards her.

Annette also revealed a remark made by Clare in 1925 that throws
some light on the events of 1883. Even then, more than forty years
afterwards, she was still bitter. After pouring out her grievances—
"nothing was right and everything was wrong"—she said : "I told
everything to Archdeacon Russell and Father Polk, S.J., and they
promised me that they would consult Dr Reynolds and have an
investigation." The ill will of the Archdeacon, the foolishness of
Father Polk, and the incompetence of the bishop did the rest.

Footnote

[1] The departed was Father Tappeiner. Sister Bernardine was inclined to wish that
Father Polk could share his bliss. She wrote to Mother Mary on 29 March 1886:
"Oh, dear Mother, I wish he would die and go to Heaven. It is so hard to have to
go to Confession to him."

TWENTY-THREE

INIQUITY
UNLEASHED

The Adelaide Commission of 1883

T he history of the year 1883 is dominated by the Commission
set up by Bishop Reynolds in July to enquire into the affairs of
the Josephites, culminating in the expulsion of Mother Mary
from Adelaide in November.

Throughout 1882 Mary had been trying to fulfil her promise to
visit the Sisters in Sydney, and several times she seemed to be on the
point of succeeding. But one thing after another prevented her until
she had to send Monica to visit Sydney on her behalf, keeping
Reynolds well informed of all that was happening. Eventually, in early
December, Mary was able to set out herself. On her way through
Victoria she visited her sister Lexie, who was dying at the Good
Shepherd convent at Abbotsford.

Vaughan gave her great support during the several months she was
around Sydney. But when he set out in April to visit Europe, the grand
farewell given him on the harbour was in fact to be a long farewell, as
he never saw Australia again. He died in the following August, not
yet fifty, during the first night he spent in England after ten years
absence.

Just before Vaughan left, a letter arrived for Mary from Reynolds.
He recalled her to Adelaide in terms indicating that he was acting in
obedience to higher authority: "Last mail brought me despatches from
Rome which necessitate my calling you back to Mother House,
Adelaide, as soon as possible." He then said she was not to do
anything about the New Zealand foundation "until we have had an
interview and carried out the *instructions given me*". When she
returned to Adelaide she was confronted with a letter dated 4 July
1883 announcing an Apostolic Visitation. In the bishop's

handwriting on paper surmounted by an imposing episcopal crest and (in Latin) *Christopher Augustine by the Grace of God and the Apostolic See Bishop of Adelaide*, it began:

My Dear Mother General,

In virtue of our letters of instruction from the Holy See, as well as for the mentainance [*sic*] of order & discipline in the Religious Houses of this Diocese, We are to hold Visitation of the Convents and examine into all matters, *Spiritual and Temporal*, either by ourselves or by our officials.

There was then a lot of detail about how the nuns were to be notified that the Visitation would begin on the 10th (tenth) day of July 1883, and how diaries, account books, and bank books were to be ready. It was signed: "+C. A. Reynolds, ut supra", and "Patrick T. Russell, Vicar General."

The "letters of instruction from the Holy See" following the April reference to "despatches from Rome" would have convinced any reasonable person that the bishop had received some special authority for what he was doing. It would also seem perfectly clear that this was the impression the two signatories intended to convey. Mary was convinced of it until she received the astonishing news in April 1884 that it was not true. Campbell wrote from Rome that neither Cardinal Simeoni (to whom he had put a direct question about it) nor any of the other officials knew of any special powers given to Reynolds. "He certainly did not receive them from Rome," he said. Part of Mary's reply ran:

I had not for a moment allowed myself to doubt but that the Bishop had received some power from Rome ere he would have acted as he did. The Bishop is really a holy, hard-working man . . . I cannot believe but that he meant all for the best, and if in saying that he acted in virtue of instructions from the Holy See he has made any mistake, I believe that he has been urged to it by others.

But meanwhile the Commission had been conducted, and submitted to, as though the claim were true. The bishop time and again used solemn phrases to remind the Sisters that he was acting on behalf of the Holy See, so it is not surprising that at the conclusion of her long memorandum for Archbishop Moran in November 1884 Mary wrote: "All this time I firmly believed that the Bishop was, as he said, acting under instructions from Rome."

The announcement of a visitation in itself caused the Mother General no surprise or concern. Indeed she had been expecting one for some time, and she hoped much good would come of it. While reassuring her in September 1879 of the good general state of the Institute, Tappeiner had agreed that many things needed improvement. The prevalence of harmful gossip, and even a campaign of bitter criticism being conducted by some malcontents among the Sisters, made it clear that there was much to be desired. Writing to Campbell after the event, Mary referred to the need for a purification which involved suffering: "For a time I hoped for great and lasting results for good from the Canonical Visitation lately made in the Adelaide Diocese in the houses of the Institute." Monica, who had had similar hopes, reflected later: "If we had exactly obeyed our Mother and followed her instructions we should not have required reproof."

The members of the Commission were, in addition to the bishop, Archdeacon Patrick Russell, Dean William Kennedy, Father A. Herberg, S.J., Father T. F. O'Neill, and Father M. O'Sullivan. The driving force was the Archdeacon, with the Dean apparently in general agreement.

Dean William Kennedy, the 42-year-old pastor of North Adelaide, had spent his early years in the diocese far from the centre of things, and when he arrived in the highly charged atmosphere of the city he came under the influence of the Archdeacon. Father Herberg was an Austrian who had been in South Australia since 1875. There is not much about him in the records. It is hard to see why he was on the Commission—it was possibly to make up the numbers. He did not understand English well, so he could not have been a very live member of the team. Father Michael O'Sullivan, who acted as secretary, was ordained by Bishop Reynolds during his visit to Ireland. A few years later he fell into disfavour and was expelled from the diocese. When he came to Sydney, Mother Mary gave him her own watch and bought an outfit for him.

Father T. F. O'Neill, 30, also ordained in Ireland by Bishop Reynolds in 1879, came to Adelaide the next year. He was on the Commission as a financial expert, and at least some of the records of evidence are in his handwriting. He lived on for more than forty years, and in later life explicitly repudiated the whole thing. Evidently he and the other priests did not have the courage to suggest that they be shown the letters of instruction from the Holy See. He wrote of Mother Mary two days after her death in 1909: "She was truly a marvellous woman and seemed especially fitted by Divine Providence for the wonderful work she accomplished. Great indeed will be her reward and glorious is the crown she now enjoys in the Kingdom of her Divine Master." Shortly afterwards he wrote in reply to the acknowledgment of this letter: "I looked upon the whole circumstance as a huge mistake and think so still. . . . You may not be aware that I never signed the report prepared by that Commission."

But these four members of the Commission were ciphers. It was Archdeacon Russell who was its soul. He nursed a resentment that seemed to blind him to the injustice of the means he employed to crush the Josephites. Mother Laurence, who had been a young Sister at this time, was questioned later about Mary's kindness in speaking of others and put the finger on the Archdeacon as the one there would have been most reason to speak against: "Dean Russell was the hardest of the opposing clergy. Yet I never heard her speak against him."

There is no extant official record of the sessions of the Commission. Such was the nature of the proceedings that there probably never was one. The archives in Rome contain short reports, amounting to verdicts of condemnation, from the Archdeacon and Dean Kennedy, a letter from Father Herberg, and a statement from Fathers O'Neill and O'Sullivan about the accounts. Although the bishop said several times just after the interrogations that a report had already been sent to Rome, the Roman officials denied that any such document ever reached them, just as they denied that they had ever authorised the Commission in the first place.

A number of accounts of the Commission are extant, written in answer to requests from Church authorities who, when they heard that an "Apostolic Commission" had been at work in Adelaide, wanted to know what had been going on. There are two lengthy texts from the pen of Bishop Reynolds. One, dated 14 June 1884, was sent to Kirby; the other, dated 4 November 1884, was sent to both Moran and (an extended version) to Simeoni. In none of these documents does the bishop mention the fact that he had claimed to be conducting an Apostolic Commission in obedience to letters of instruction from the Holy See. To Moran he simply says he called the senior priests together and decided to put the Sisters under oath; to Simeoni he speaks of "a council, or commission"; to Kirby he says, "I was about to hold the visitation of the convent . . . I formed a commission of priests to aid me in the work".

Reynolds' letter to Simeoni is a very sad document. It would be better forgotten, but because the writer was the chief authority involved in the events of 1883, and the letter was his *apologia* to his superior, it has to be noticed. It is long, hopelessly confused in its sequence of events, emotional, strongly partisan, self-justifying and defensive, manifesting a creative imagination (especially in the citing of dead witnesses), as well as betraying a disturbed mind and a heavily burdened heart.

Apart from a sentence in which he says Mary had done much with the Sisters for the welfare of religion and education, he has not a single good word to say of her. It is a document of unrelieved abuse of her habits, her methods, her motives, and her duplicity. She had done nothing right or honourable for a long time. It is by far the most sustained attack on the character of Mary MacKillop ever penned. However, because it contains so many statements contradicted by a mass of reliable evidence, and because other documents have shown that there are good reasons for great caution about its author's use of words, it could not be treated as a guide to the historical truth on any topic, incident, conversation, or other detail with which it deals. To speak plainly, one would be rash to believe a word of it without strong corroborating evidence from elsewhere.

On the death of Mother Mary, the Sydney recipient of this letter (Cardinal Moran) declared that he was confident she would be raised to the honours of the altar, so he could not have been too impressed by its contents. A gentle warning about truthfulness from Bishop Murray of Maitland on 12 June 1884 seems to indicate that the weakness of the Bishop of Adelaide in the matter was recognised by his peers in the hierarchy:

> If she and her party have written to Rome against you, you will then have to tell the truth, the whole truth, I mean and of course nothing but the truth.

The last phrase is really an extraordinary thing for one bishop to write to another.[1]

When the air cleared, various Sisters wrote to Cardinal Simeoni about the affair. They mentioned that the bishop "did not read any decree or show any document from Rome showing what powers he had received from the Holy See". We read that the oath taken by each Sister bound her,

> first, to answer truthfully all questions they should ask her, second, not to repeat to anyone what passed during her examination, and third, to make known any abuses or anything she saw wrong or that needed reforming in the Institute.

Not all the members of the Commission were present at all the interrogations. Sometimes it was the bishop and the Archdeacon, sometimes the latter alone—he would administer the oath, ask the questions (often putting answers into their mouths, they said) and write down their evidence himself. Some of the country Sisters were not examined at all.

Although there never seems to have been an official report, what did reach Rome eventually was a transcript of notes made by the secretary as the Sisters answered questions. The questions themselves were not recorded. These notes were never read over to those whose evidence they represented, and they were never signed either by the witnesses or the secretary. What makes them particularly untrustworthy as evidence is that the oath bound the Sisters not only to remain silent until death about everything that transpired during their interrogation, but also to mention to the Commissioners anything they knew, or had heard, that indicated any weakness in the Institute. As a result, hearsay evidence abounds on every page, the Sisters evidently being under the impression that to pass over in silence anything they had heard would amount to perjury. They felt themselves bound by the oath to repeat any gossip they had come across, even at second, third, or fourth hand, if it was detrimental to the order and in particular to the Mother General about whom they were closely interrogated. When they had in their nervousness said something that was not true, and later tried to correct it, they were told that they were not now believed.

Moreover, a reading of the notes suggests that the form of the questions put the Sisters under explicit pressure to mention anything negative they had "heard". The evidence of Sister Matilda, Sister Elizabeth, and Sister M. Joseph leaves little doubt that they were asked to support hearsay by additional hearsay. Of Matilda the notes say: "Heard of scandals but attach no importance to them." Of Elizabeth: "The rumours about Mother General drinking are unfounded." Of M. Joseph: "Heard that Sisters took drink cannot say whether it is true." Whatever gossip any Sister had heard, however unlikely or unfounded, she felt bound by oath to repeat. What she then said was simply written down—there was no cross-examination, no challenging by the defence, because there was no defence. The reason there was no defence was that the accused was unaware she was being charged. But, whatever might be said about the legality and the morality of the procedure, the cumulative effect on the distraught bishop of all this insubstantial chatter was precisely what the Archdeacon was aiming at. In her letter to Campbell on 7 December 1883 Mary commented: "That some extraordinary evidence must at times have been given is manifest."

At the beginning of August, before she was herself called before the Commission, Mary received two written commands in language calculated to reinforce the impression that they had the authority of the Holy See behind them:

> In virtue of the obedience you owe to the Holy See, we direct that you by *this day's post* summon Sister Mary La Merci and Sister Mary Collette, now in N.S.Wales, to come at once to Adelaide.
>
> In virtue of your Vow of Obedience, we, as representative of the Holy See, forbid you to borrow any money or contract any further debt under any pretext whatsoever without our written authority.

The second one had serious implications. "The bishop," Mary said, "very bitterly upbraided me with having borrowed money, and kept the place in debt." She told Moran:

> One of the Sisters asked me where the book was in which we had the Bishop's *written authorization* to do that for which he was now blaming me. I produced it and said I would show it to him the next time he would come out. Some advised me *not* to give up the book, but a copy of it; however, I trusted my Bishop and gave up the book when he asked me for it.

That book has not been seen since. More than this, it appears that money collected for the Sisters had never reached them:

> In one case only had we failed in returning the amount at the exact date, and that was an amount of £100 lent in a difficulty by an immediate friend of my own. The same good friend had often aided us, and told me he was only too glad to do so, but on the occasion I speak of the money with which he was to have been repaid should have come to us from the Bishop himself and did not. This is a painful truth. It was money which was collected in the Churches of the Diocese for an Institution under our care.

The Commission condemned the Sisters' financial records as unsatisfactory, disgraceful, and "so badly kept that an experienced accountant could not understand them". The situation clearly called for a joint perusal of the books by the Commission and the nuns, to see what light could be thrown on the obscurities. Yet the nuns were never given a chance to explain their bookkeeping, as the books were in the hands of the Commission and were never produced. Mary was confident that everything was there, but she could not prove it without the books. Monica asked to consult them one day when she was speaking with Russell, but she was told: "None of the books can be given up until the Visitation is ended." Mary told Moran:

> I cannot write upon this subject without expressing what I feel, and that is that we were very unjustly dealt with about our books. We might at least have been allowed to go over them and to clear ourselves if we could. But at the time of my examination I had not a suspicion that they were going to blame us as they did later, nor had I the most remote idea of their questioning my own honesty. All that was to come later.

When the Mother General's turn came to be questioned, she was not only not given a chance to refute the gossip that was being treated as evidence against her conduct and character, but she had no suspicion of the nature of the charges that were being built up against her. The bishop referred to the brandy in a private conversation—"in his usual kind fatherly way cautioned me against some of the remarks made of me"—but his words did not suggest that intemperance was the chief concern of the Commissioners. They seemed to be interested in matters of general discipline and in the finances. Herberg asked her about receiving delicate Sisters too easily, "their training and matters of that kind"; O'Neill asked if she thought a particular mistake in the Balance Sheet was intentional; the bishop asked about lessening the debt; Russell, Kennedy, and O'Sullivan did not question her at all. The notes make dull reading, for example: "Baking would reduce expenses. Sister Mary Ann is a good housekeeper. A cow would be good. I think the land about the convent should be let to a kitchen gardener and let him have it free but supply us with vegetables." Not a word about drink, and (she told Moran) not one reproachful word from the bishop:

> No question about the local Superiors, or fault found with any of them, nothing to lead me to suppose that any of the charges made later were even thought of, not a hint at the charge made later against me by the Bishop of "squandering the means of the Diocese upon my own friends". Like some more of my Sisters, I left the presence of the Commission full of regrets for having thought any of them prejudiced.

Up to this point it would seem that bookkeeping was what concerned the Commissioners, and that they were not dissatisfied with Mother Mary. She certainly had that impression. But because of what came to light later the next part of her report to Moran is significant. Somebody was making her out to be a cheat and a deceiver:

> During our retreat I was much surprised by Father Polk telling me

that I had previously violated poverty in buying 20 pounds worth of books for my brother. I told him that I had not as much as bought him a sixpenny Imitation or any book of any kind. He replied that it was on the books that I did, and something else equally false.

Though she was becoming aware that her honesty was being questioned, she still had no idea she was being represented as a drunkard. She was never questioned on the matter. It was many months later that she was shocked to discover what the bishop had been led to believe about her as the result of the Archdeacon's skilful manipulation of witnesses.

When Sister M. Borgia Fay was able to open up to Mary about the injustice of it all, she spoke of the Archdeacon as the one in charge. His tendentious questions and his insinuation that the Sisters were guilty of dishonesty and deception are evident in her lively recollection of the interrogation:

Now, on your oath are these the true convent accounts? Were not these accounts made out or entered in view of this Visitation taking place? Do you know of things that were got, drink for instance, and not entered? Were there sums of money received and the account of them suppressed?

Was not Mother Mary in the habit of taking brandy? Was I not disedified at this practice of Mother Mary's?—No, not when she did not do it of her own wish but by the doctor's orders.—Now, conscientiously, do you not consider it a scandal that the Mother General should be addicted to drink?

These were no-win questions—like the classic: Have you stopped beating your wife? But Borgia was evidently able to handle them. She told Mary: "The Archdeacon immediately classed me among the flatterers who, as he said, pampered you up. The Bishop said that I had prevaricated very much and refused to give me his blessing."

The notes, written by the Archdeacon, say: "Sister Borgia's evidence was not satisfactory." This was true enough, as the questioning was clearly not directed at finding the truth, but at supporting a conclusion Russell had already determined. Although one or two like Borgia seem to have been able to handle his bluster, he generally avoided tangling with strong and experienced Sisters who would have used the same vigorous language in their Mother General's defence at the time as they did later when they discovered what had really been going on at the Commission. He recalled witnesses he thought might contribute to his case, but Sisters of high standing who knew Mary well were not asked about her at all. Monica wrote: "When I was brought before the Commission, I was not asked any question about Mother General." Calasanctius was questioned, but the Commission's reaction to her evidence was not only to ignore it, but to make sure that she was sent as far as possible from Adelaide, namely, New Zealand.

The news that "Mother General took drink" was no news at all. The fact that her doctors prescribed fluid that contained alcohol was never a secret. It was not something that had to be admitted and then somehow defended. In a healthy society it would have passed with no more comment than the taking of medicinal liquids about whose pharmacological composition nobody had the faintest idea, nor would it have occasioned more gossip among people of good will than the use of a walking-stick by the blind Mechtilde. But in that milieu, terms like drink, stimulants, and liquor suggested excess, intoxication, and moral degeneracy.

Russell won the day with the help of a few malcontents. The question naturally arises: Who were these accusers? A study of the notes that were sent to Rome shows that seventy-five Sisters were interrogated.[2] A number were recalled several times; Sister Michael, for example, paid four visits to the Commission. Not all of those called in were questioned on the subject of drink, Mother Mary herself being the outstanding example. While many simply denied any abuse in the matter of alcoholic drink, only four could be said to have made accusations of excess.

The Commission called Sister M. Joseph Dwyer twice. The first time nothing was said about drink, but on the second occasion she was questioned about it thoroughly. What she had to say referred not to what was going on at the time, but what had occurred more than two years previously. It was of little value as evidence, as it was clearly hearsay that she was forced by fear of perjury to repeat. She explained it by further hearsay. They wrote down: "She heard it was through the infirmarian giving her too much. It was a common rumour that Mother General took too much."

Sister M. Michael Quinlan, sister of Hyacinth, is recorded as having made a serious accusation against the Mother General on the second of her four visits to the Commission:

> There has been an excess in the use of stimulants. Much liquor is got but do not know how or when . . . It has been taken to excess by Mother General. She takes it unnecessarily. I heard it remarked by Sisters Mary Joseph and Francis Xavier. Mrs Baker mentioned it to

me once. I do not know whether the doctor ordered it. Noticed the
effects of liquor three times on Mother General.

Much of this is hearsay and the private opinion of the witness. We
might ask how she knew Mother Mary took brandy unnecessarily if
she did not even know whether or not the doctor ordered it; and the
same would go for Mrs Baker's views. The phrase "the effects of liquor"
is a blank cheque to be filled in by the prejudice of the listener. As it
stands, it could mean the effects desired by the doctor who prescribed
it. In any case, Michael's evidence was undermined by her volte-face
some months later. Perhaps the minutes of her evidence are
untrustworthy, or she was an unscrupulous and unreliable person, or
there is some other explanation, but the fact remains that she was
one of the signatories of a letter to Moran in October 1884, which
stated "that this scandalous charge is entirely false and a gross
calumny on the fair name of an innocent person".[3]

Sister M. Matthew Walsh was called before the Commission three
times. Part of her evidence on the first occasion was the compound
hearsay that she "heard that the Sisters spoke of Mother General
taking too much". The second time she said:

[As *superior*] I provided drink for Mother General. She would take a
wineglassful of spirits in a little water. She has taken it at other times.
I saw her when it went to her head.

This could mean anything a listener might wish to read into it. In all
of Matthew's evidence there is very little of real substance, and
perhaps that was why she was recalled a third time by somebody
wishing to get something more specific out of her. But on this
occasion she spoilt her earlier impression by saying: "I have heard and
seen a great deal, but my memory is very defective." As well as this
apparent attempt to free her conscience from responsibility for what
she may have said, she later repudiated completely not only the
interpretation put on her answers by the Commissioners, but
everything she may have said against Mother Mary. For she too signed
the statement to Moran already quoted, that is, that the charge was a
gross calumny on the fair name of an innocent person.

It was Sister Mary Ignatius McCarthy whose evidence seems to
have fuelled the destruction of the bishop's respect for Mother Mary.
Her long and rambling evidence is an unrelieved flood of nasty gossip
and innuendo. The transcript reads like *Finnegans Wake*. She has not
a single good thing to say about anything or anybody—except to refer
to somebody's kindness, as ammunition for a broadside at somebody

else. Most Sisters were unsuitable, the Mother General was a schemer and a deceiver, there was a clique to keep her in office, and Ignatius herself had been wrongfully excluded from the Chapter. She accused Mary directly: "I have observed her under the influence of drink. About a year ago I wanted to see her. Sister Matthew would not let me.[4] I got to her. She knew me for a minute."

The evidence of Sister Ignatius suggests that she was out to curry favour with the bishop, a thing she succeeded in any case in doing. In the years immediately following the Commission he sent her and another Sister (without any permission from their Mother General) to New Zealand, South Africa, Europe and the U.S.A. in order to beg for money to pay off the debt the Institute had incurred in South Australia. It is not known how much they collected or to what extent the money was applied to the needs of the Institute and the diocese, a point which perplexed Cardinal Moran. On 6 March 1889 he wrote to Reynolds saying that his question about the sums of money collected by Ignatius and her companion had not been answered.

How unsuitable Ignatius was for this work, and what her reputation among the Sisters was, can be gathered from what some of them wrote about her to Monica when she was on her collecting tour. Mary Gertrude Dewe, the former Benedictine Sister, said:

> I hope and trust that wild little creature will not disgrace us ... I really wonder what kind of a conscience she has. However, we need not be surprised, for in every Community, even enclosed Orders, there are found suchlike members.

Opening up about Ignatius at the Process in 1926, Annette gave a clue to the venom that Sister directed at Mary in 1883:

> In Adelaide Sister Ignatius ordered a case of wine and said that someone had sent her a gift. Mother Mary was very angry and made Sister Ignatius send it back.

In answer to a direct question, Annette said she knew by experience that Ignatius was unreliable. For her part, Mary was not unaware of the part played by Ignatius in the 1883 episode. This is clear in something she wrote to Annette from Sandringham after her near-fatal illness in 1892:

> She came here one day when I was still very weak and wanted to justify herself for the past. I advised her to leave *well alone*—that I was willing to forget, but, no, she must go on with her say—blaming others and making out that she was faithful. It was too much for me and she got an expression of my *true opinion* of her conduct that astonished her.

On September 13, after the Commission had completed its interrogations, Reynolds had told Mary that "though the Visitation had been made in the strictest form, no grave evils had been met with", and that he had been able "to send a most consoling report to Rome". He was quite pleasant to her on the 14th, on the 22nd, and on October 2. A letter he sent her on September 26 is more remarkable for what it does not say than for what it says. All the Commission evidence had been given by this time, yet the letter gives no hint that the person being addressed was soon to be expelled as totally unfit to deal with.

But on October 10 the bishop came to the convent with the Archdeacon, bearing a *Memorial of Directions*. It was the first clear usurpation of jurisdiction within the Institute, but because the words "In the name of the Holy See" were used more than once, the impression was maintained that what was being done had Roman authority behind it. It was a prolongation of the deception on which the whole Commission was based, and which had been expressed formally at other times during the Visitation, for example in the orders of August 1. Typical of the *Memorial* was number 5, which forbad the nuns "to hold any communication by *letter or otherwise*, with any ex-Sister under pain of deprivation of the Sacraments. Nor shall any Confessor have power to absolve from such violation of the Rule—the case is absolutely reserved to the Bishop." The Sisters commented: "Our Constitutions or Rules make no mention of ex-Sisters, so how can seeing them be a violation of Rule?"

New appointments were made of Sisters in charge of various works, others were changed from place to place, one with life-vows was summarily dismissed from the Institute, and a great number of directives were given about the daily life of the nuns. Neither the Mother General nor her Councillors had been consulted about any of this, except that Mary suggested Francis Xavier for the orphanage. But there was one positive result of the bishop's visit with the Memo. He permitted somebody other than Father Polk to be assigned to the Christmas retreat. Telling Moran of this, Mary said that few had any confidence in Polk, and that the general feeling was that he "was doing us much harm and indirectly encouraging the troublesome few".

One particular piece of interference with the jurisdiction of the Institute's superiors had nothing to do with Adelaide at all, and could have been justified only on the grounds that the Holy See had given the bishop power to do what he was doing, which it certainly had not. This was the ordering of Calasanctius to New Zealand. If he did not wish to tolerate this Sister in his diocese, Reynolds could have asked that she be sent elsewhere, but he had no authority to say where she was to go. When Mary had made the ordinary representation allowed, or rather required, in the obedience of one who sees some serious difficulty in what is ordered, her action was regarded as opposition to the Commission. She mentioned Calasanctius' dread of the sea—she had once survived a shipwreck—and stated that the Sister they were sending in charge could do without her. The Bishop insisted that she should go, saying it was the decision of the Commission. But Calasanctius was so distressed that Mary wrote him a note asking if he would see her and hear what she had to say; after which, should she still have to go away, she would surely acquiesce. Up to this time the bishop had been friendly to Mary, and she said, "I had no reason to fear that he would resent my writing to him on so important a matter." She had no fear, either, that her note would be misunderstood. But it was. The bishop would not see Calasanctius, but wrote her a most bitter letter against Mary, insisting that she should go as directed.

There was another case in which Mary was accused of opposing the Commission. The Memorial required the immediate expulsion of Sister Angelina. This was contrary to the Constitutions; so Russell was asked, in what seemed a friendly conversation, if the Commission was independent of the Constitutions. He said no, it was upholding them. But then Mary received "a most bitter letter" from the bishop accusing her of opposing the Visitation. "He plainly told me this," she told Campbell, "and a great deal more that I shudder to think of." So Angelina went, and her dispensation was sent after her when it arrived in proper form.

The Commission Passes Judgment

The verdict on Mother Mary, although not a formal one, was "guilty". The written statements of Reynolds, Russell and Kennedy acquired a peculiar status in spite of the vigorous repudiation of their contents by nearly all the Sisters. One curious aspect of the three documents is their date—they were not written until well over a year after the Commission had concluded its interrogations. That is longer than the span of ordinary neglect. The bishop and the Vicar General, it seems, had hoped to take over the Josephites without reference to Rome or anybody else from beginning to end. Archbishop Moran put a stop to this. When he arrived in Australia in September 1884 he was commissioned to ask questions, and the Adelaide men had to put something in writing.

Kennedy's statement, dated 23 October 1884, grants that the Institute of St Joseph had been very useful in promoting Catholic education, but then everything is negative. The debts are large, the finances are in a deplorable state, the accounts are badly kept, the Constitutions are not observed, there is carelessness in the admission of postulants and the training of novices, there is dissipation, and there is disrespect and disobedience among younger Sisters towards superiors. Of Mother Mary he says:

> I am grieved to find that the Mother General of the Institute as well as a few of the older Sisters have been guilty of intemperance as is only too manifest from the evidence. This is known to many of the Sisters who have lost respect for and confidence in their Superiors.

In Russell's document, dated 21 October 1884, exactly the same points are covered and substantially the same things are said. About Mother Mary he wrote:

> It has been proved that the Mother General has been edicted [sic!] to drink, that she has failed to correct other Sisters edicted to drink and other faults. All this has been known to many of the Sisters hence their want of confidence and respect for the Mother General . . . I judge that for the good of Religion and the stability of the Community that it is necessary for the Mother General to retire from her office.

The bishop's views were enshrined in his notorious letter to Mary on 13 November 1883, and in his letter to Simeoni a year later. She found it hard to believe her eyes when she read this:

> Dear Mother General,
>
> Owing to an exceeding pressure of duty I could not go out today as I had intended, and you are aware that my being one of the deputation on Monday at 10 a.m. to the C.E. Soct'y I could not see you on that morning. I do the next thing in my power—write, as I am not sure of the moments tomorrow.
>
> (1) The letter your Maternity addressed to me was far from being either an explanation *of* or a reply *to* my statements. The letter was plausible enough, but did not meet my cases. After due consideration and prayer, I feel that I have but one course now left me consistent with my duty to my God, to my office, and to those Sisters of St Joseph who are committed to my care by the Apostolic See.

(2)   I told your Maternity during the first days of the Commission (which you have made so painful to me) that "I wished to make all changes through you, and that I did not wish to appear to act myself, though specially directed to do so—with a discretionary power". I need not allude to your profession of gratitude, etc. etc.

(3)   You have done your best to keep me in the dark, to conceal the scandalous habits of some, notwithstanding your promises of "being open and candid with your dear Father in Christ". Well! Well! I have often told you that my object was to heal, save, and not to punish, to lift up and not pull down, to build up, to consolidate, and to have the Constitutions observed at all hazards. The Searcher of all hearts knows what pain and anguish I have undergone to bring about a result so holy, so *necessary*, and so desirable, but you—from whom I expected every assistance—did your best and still continue to do your best *for your own* ends to frustrate all my best efforts and intentions. You govern by party spirit and by clique. Hoodwink the Bishop— that is your motto.

(4)   I am but too well aware of how you have violated religious poverty, how you have squandered (I will refrain from a stronger term) the means of the Diocese given for the Institute of St Joseph, and the charities under its care. I connived at some of your excesses as they came out *from your books*. My Council would fain do the same to save you. One or two instances for example—your supplying furniture and piano to McDonalds and having them sent as Convent property. My priest and the Sisters at Penola were constantly dunned for payment.

(5)   I did not recall about the money you so often promised to pay to Convent Account. It is true you spoke of it to me at your last interview with me previous to *your running away* to Sydney. Your ingratitude stunned me *that morning*. I thought you were above such—but then—"The Bishop was responsible—let him pay it."

(6)   I will pass over, as they were uttered under excited feelings, your menaces to Dean Kennedy and the Bakers. You would go to Rome—and what would they say there at the Bishop's allowing such a state of debts—aye, what would they say!!! It has been said of a great writer of (the) present age—"That a straw, tho' a trivial thing—tells the current of the stream." But let it pass.

(7)   I was not, nor am I now unmindful of what you formerly did when you were "true to your trust", and I will consequently lay aside all feeling of self in the matter, but I have a duty that I

may not shrink from, as I shall be responsible *here* as well as hereafter—for its fulfilment or neglect.

(8) I therefore notify to your Maternity to prepare at once to leave for Sydney, as you have no longer the confidence of the Sisterhood, nor is it in the interests of good order and of discipline, of peace or religion that you should remain in this Province.

(9) This is the easiest and most charitable mode for me to adopt consistent with my duty. Were I to act upon instructions, I would insist upon your resignation of office. This course would necessitate a new election, and what I wish to be forgotten, as I hope God has forgiven, would have to be fully detailed in Chapter—and besides this, the unavoidable exposure to the Public.

(10) Your state of health I know is far from being satisfactory; this— with the assumed fact of some duties calling you to Sydney will save appearances so that you can go in safety to your character and to that of the Institute until this storm subsides, and the wishes of Rome are expressed.

(11) You will bring Sister Collette with you.

(12) I will appoint a Mother Vicar and make other arrangements for the maintenance of order and discipline, and also see to the due and proper observance of the Rule and Constitutions.

(13) Your Maternity will see that the Misses Woods now supported at Mitcham seek other homes. It is high time that they seek to support themselves by going to situations.

(14) I will shortly make arrangements for the O'Reillys as economy and order must be preserved in Mitcham as well as in other Convents.

(15) I must again remind your Maternity of what I before commanded in the Name of the Holy See that under no conceivable pretext is it lawful for you to borrow money.

(16) I deeply regret for your own sake that a subterfuge was made by you to Rigby under plea of getting books for Wellington. The account has been sent to Dr Redwood. Your want of candour has made matters known in such a way as will, I fear, be very detrimental to the Institute.

(17) May God give you grace to perceive, and fortitude to perform all your duties in Sydney with religious candour and fairness. I mentioned to you before the necessity of a proper settlement of the Convent properties in your name in N.S.W. It will spare you many embarrassments with a coming Archbishop. Take counsel, however, of someone in whom you have confidence. I

have given you my opinion, take it for what it is worth. Rest assured matters will take a very different turn ere long in New South Wales.

I pray God to guide, keep and direct you in all your ways. May you shortly have peace of heart and mind, which—blessed be His Holy Name—you have not let me enjoy.

I remain, Your Maternity's truly in Christ,

+ C.A. Reynolds, Bishop of Adelaide.

With this notification all jurisdiction with the Sisterhood in this Province ceases. +C.A.R.

Throughout this tirade of abuse, there is not a single hint at intemperance. The bishop's party possibly feared that it would have been too much for Mary to accept quietly along with the rest of the slander, and that she would have protested vigorously and publicly. She replied to his historic document on November 16. Her words are also historic, and as a monument to humility, obedience, patience, kindness, and incredible mildness, they would be hard to surpass:

My dear Lord,

The instructions in your last letter surprised me but I submit. All is, I hope, for the best—at least, I know *you* so intend it. I have no hope that any suggestion of mine would have any weight under present circumstances, therefore do not make any unless it be an earnest entreaty that you hear what Sister Monica can tell you, and which it may help you to know.

I have made all the haste possible and will leave by the Penola tomorrow. The Sydney Sisters had written to ask me over on some business about our property there, so I am able truthfully to give that as my reason, or one of the reasons, for going. May I tell you that many of the Sisters have sad misgivings, and really want encouragement. If you appoint a Vicar, please let it be one in whom they can confide.

I can say no more, but grieving deeply for having caused you any sorrow,

I remain, my dear Lord, Your humble child in J.M.J.,

Mary of the Cross.

In the document Mary prepared for Moran in November 1884 she made the following commentary on Reynolds' letter:

Note 1. The letter referred to was in answer partly to one the Bishop had some time previously written to me, and partly an explanation of the motive I had in asking him to see my Assistant before insisting on her going to New Zealand. That letter was unfortunately destroyed, but one of my Council took a copy of my reply—which should be amongst some of our papers, though I have not got it at present.

Note 2. The Bishop did tell me so, adding that if I did not work with him, he would act without me. He spoke so kindly about everything and seemed so truly to seek our good that I, on many occasions, expressed gratitude which I really felt.

Note 3. (Keeping the Bishop in the dark—party spirit—clique.) I must in all truth deny this charge, and can only suspect to what in particular he refers. I knew that a Sister was blamed unjustly, and wished to mention what I knew to the Bishop *himself* and therefore cautioned a very uncharitable Sister to be silent until I would see him, but this she was not—and my motive in this seems to have been misrepresented, whilst no opportunity was afforded me of telling the Bishop what I knew. He may also mean another case in which he was led to believe that I had encouraged a Sister to leave one Convent for another because she could not agree with the Superior of the first. Without consulting me, or waiting to hear what penance she had got, he gave instructions of his own which completely upset our arrangements, but all submitted in silence.

I don't know what is meant by *"your own ends"* unless that I wished to keep power in my own hands. As my Council were all with me and aware of my views in most of the matters then under discussion, he surely could not have meant that they were a clique. "Hoodwink the Bishop" was a term I never used—nor heard used. Neither was such a thing thought of.

Note 4. (Violations of Poverty) The next painful accusation I also positively deny, that is, in the sense in which it appears. Unintentionally and thoughtlessly I fear I have too often offended against holy Poverty, but not wilfully, or in the dishonest manner of which the Bishop speaks. The charge is a very serious one—and I would much rather that I could remain silent than vindicate myself at the Bishop's expense. He says he connived at some of my excesses as they came from the books—there he alludes, I suppose, to an extraordinary accusation to the effect that I had bought 20 pounds worth of books for a brother of my own who was on the Continent studying for the Church. I have mentioned this before—and that it was utterly untrue—and that I told the Bishop so, and he at the time believed me, saying *my word* for it was sufficient.

There is truth in the fact that eight pounds worth of furniture having been sent by a very officious Sister to my Mother—*without* her instructions, and then, through my absence and carelessness on the part of others, the account was not furnished, so that some time elapsed before it was paid. But that was not my Mother's fault, nor— if the truth were known—was she in any way bound to pay for the same furniture as she had left its equivalent in the cottage she had occupied, but which was taken by us for poor Father Roache, the Bishop wishing the same to be done. The piano was *Convent property*, got at the request of the Sisters, and to aid them in keeping their pupils. Miss McDonald was simply their Music Teacher, and as her cottage was near the school, the Sisters left the piano there rather than have it in their own community room, and to be spared the annoyance the practice of the children would cause them there.

Note 5. (Running away) The money referred to was a sum of £700 to be paid later into the Bank Account. Of this I sent £400 from New South Wales (all I could get; it was, besides, money that had come in a legacy from home to one of the Sisters who had joined in South Australia), and proposed to the Bishop that some other means should be employed to get the rest required, and for other expenses. Instead of *running away* as stated, I had—after many delays caused by the Bishop—represented that my duty to my Sisters in N.S.W. demanded my presence there. After this, in the most friendly way, the Bishop agreed to my going, only asking me to delay for a few days until he could make arrangements with the Sisters of Mercy at Mt Gambier for the reception of a boarder he wanted to send under my care as far as Penola. I waited for the required answer, received my instructions and His Lordship's blessing, and left—as I thought—upon the happiest understanding with him. I really cannot understand what he means.

Note 6. (Menaces to Dean Kennedy) I did speak to Dean Kennedy, thinking him a sincere friend, and showing him how, up to that time, no help had been *practically* afforded us from the Diocese save what we got from begging and Bazaars, that few if any of the schools really supported the Sisters, that certain moneys supposed to have been given to us had not been given, and I did then say that if they went too far, I would go to Rome and state our case. This was before Archbishop Vaughan died for in him I knew that the Institute had a true friend. In speaking of this to the Bishop (if he did so), I think Dean Kennedy must have intended to put matters before him from our point of view, hoping to do us good, but in that he certainly failed. The remark to the Bakers (friends and benefactors) was but a passing one—drawn forth from something they had just told us.

7. I make no remark upon this passage.

Note 8. My Council took a copy of this letter to read to the Sisters at the Xmas Retreat, but later it was thought better not to do so as we preferred waiting to hear what complaints had been made to Rome, and I thought it better to keep quiet rather than discourage the poor Sisters too much. But as they had been given to understand that the Bishop said I no longer had their confidence, they have ever since given me every proof that I have—all but the few we have known from the beginning to have been insincere.

9. I make no remark upon this passage.

Note 10. As far as possible, I have tried to act upon this advice.

Note 11. Sister Mary Collette was local Superior of the Mother House, a most exemplary Sister, but much disliked by those who all through were giving the Superiors so much trouble. She was a comfort to me and to all my Council who recognized her worth.

Note 12. Before leaving, I myself—acting upon the right the Constitutions gave me—appointed Sister Monica as Assistant General instead of Sister Calasanctius who had been sent to N.Z., and later the Bishop confirmed this, or as he thought *appointed* her himself. The Local Superior he wanted to appoint instead of Sister M. Collette was, or had been, a little more than a year ago, quite insane, and it had been a question whether she would not have to be put into an asylum. Sister Monica succeeded in getting the Bishop to agree to Sister Mary de Sales (whom I had, after consulting with my Council, named for the office) in her stead.

Note 13. The Misses Woods were nieces of Father Woods, whom we had brought up from childhood, and whom only a few years back the Bishop had, through me, refused to give up to their Father (they being for good reasons unwilling to leave our care). The Bishop was not aware that *both* were earning their living, one as a Music Teacher and not staying with us at all, the other as a most useful Pupil Teacher in one of our schools.

Note 14. The O'Reillys referred to were two boarders whose father, as an *alms* to us, was paying the large sum of £70 each a year for them. He was peculiarly circumstanced and a very bad Catholic—and it was with much difficulty that I got him to send them to school. He would only send them to me—as he was a very strange man. I had a little influence over him having known his family before I became a Religious. The Bishop knew his history.

Note 15. I have already explained that when I did borrow money it was with the Bishop's consent, and from kind friends who were only too glad to assist us.

Note 16. The Bishop has got hold of some wrong story again. I was authorized by the Priest to whose Mission our new foundation was going to provide them with all required books, etc. etc. which could not be got where they were going. Our Procuratrix ordered the same and instructed that an invoice should be sent to the Priest, and one to me for the Sisters.

Note 17. Our pecuniary position in New South Wales is very

different to ours in Adelaide, but we have taken the Bishop's advice and legally secured any property we have for the Institute there.

In this same document Mother Mary tells Moran how she left for Sydney in obedience to the bishop's orders:

> I had little more to add. As soon as possible I left Adelaide. Feeling that I could not do anything to help my Sisters there, I was only too glad to come away. I had a consultation with my Council the night before I left and then appointed Sister Monica Assistant . . .
>
> I made no attempt at any further explanation with the Bishop, feeling that it was utterly useless to do so, but full of hope that he would soon find out the truth. I merely sent him a short note testifying my willingness to obey him.
>
> At this time I firmly believed that the Bishop was, as he said he was, acting under instructions from Rome.

Neither at the time nor at any period in her subsequent life did Mary show the slightest sign of rancour or resentment towards Reynolds. She was an intelligent woman, and she knew quite well that things were not right, but she gently and persistently deflected the blame from him. In a letter accompanying her statement to Moran she spoke of her disinclination even to write about what had happened:

> It has cost me a great deal to write it, for I would rather suffer any blame than reflect in the least on the Bishop of Adelaide. I am confident that he meant everything for the best, and that most extraordinary evidence must have been given against me ere he could write to me as he did.
>
> If in my statements I have written anything uncharitable I beg Your Grace to believe that it is not so intended. I only tried to tell the truth.

Except in this statement requested by Moran, she never made a detailed defence.[5] With quiet dignity she simply trusted to the power of truth, hoping that the Sisters would assist in making this truth appear. She wrote to them about the charges that she allegedly had lost their confidence:

> I do not enter into any explanations—I simply *deny the charges* made against me . . . Surely those who know me so well—who were constantly with me or in my confidence, ah, surely they could tell a different tale . . . If, I say, you believe these things to be true—say so honestly, but if not, let our poor Bishop know the truth.

History Judges the Commission

It seems to be one of the ironic dispositions of providence that Causes for canonisation not only reveal wonderful reflections of the divine in the souls of God's special friends, but also bring to light the limitations of others of his servants who in their days of power never suspected that their weaknesses would be scrutinised along with the rest of the historical farrago that goes through the Church's mills of investigation.

It would be pointless to take morose delight in this anticipation of the day of judgment, especially as no one can judge another's conscience. But the Josephites, and especially their Mother General, suffered a great deal through the 1883 Commission, and it is not at all irrelevant here to examine exactly what happened. Although Mary was charitable she was not stupid, and the word *lie* must have crossed her mind when she discovered that the bishop and his Vicar General had no letters of instruction when they signed a formal document saying that they did. It is not a complex issue. You either have a document, or you do not. It would be hard to find a court of law or a historical commentator ready to accept a statement from either of these men that he thought it was the truth he was signing. Such a claim would have indicated a lack of intelligence that would have rendered the claimant unfit for office. Whatever about the bishop in his distraught state, the Archdeacon was no fool.

So it was really a moral *tour de force* for Mary MacKillop to write so much about the subject without using the word lie. *Mystery* was the word she preferred. She wrote to Dr Campbell:

> I had not for a moment allowed myself to doubt but that the Bishop had received some power from Rome ere he would have acted as he did. The whole affair is a mystery to me, but I hope God will be glorified in the end and His most holy will worked out.

Her letter to the Sisters on 24 March 1884 (after the discovery that there were no letters of instruction) opened with the comment, "God's ways are most mysterious"—echoing again the theological word play which designated the collusion of Rebecca and Jacob as *mysterium* (a mystery) rather than *mendacium* (a lie). Mary exclaimed: "What can the poor Bishop have been thinking of?" And she wrote to Calasanctius: "From all I can gather our poor Bishop has made a great mistake." Archbishop Moran, referring in his report to the claim about *letters of instruction*, also spoke diplomatically of what the bishop had done as a mistake, a grave error.[6] But really, it was not something that had slipped out under the emotional pressure of the moment. It was a signed, sustained, and repeated statement that was simply not true. When the truth came to light, were Cardinal Moran and Mother

Mary convinced that the bishop really thought he had received authority to institute a Pontifical Commission? For her part, Mary probably regarded this question as none of her business.

Even so, whether it was a mistake or a lie, this false claim was introduced only as a means to an end. The end was a worse mistake. This was to depose the Mother General and to usurp control of the Institute.

In spite of these mistakes and juridical errors, it was probably the attack centred on money, leading to the treatment of the Sisters as criminals and pariahs, that was from a human point of view the worst aspect of the whole business. In all the talk about debts, it seemed to be suggested that the nuns ran up bills because they were thoughtless and irresponsible, and were living in some kind of luxury. It seemed to be supposed that it should have been possible for this group of women, housing and feeding hundreds of needy people, and charging nothing for educating most of the Catholic children of South Australia, to sail through life in difficult times without ever being in debt. Bishop Torreggiani was later telling Mary of some big developments in his diocese: "You might wonder where we get so much money to do these things. I answer from the Bank of Providence which will never fail those who trust in God and try to do the best they can for his eternal glory and the salvation of souls." This was Mary's view too. When thoughtless criticism of the nuns developed into persecution, she wrote to her advocate in Rome, Dr Campbell:

> From the little aid we received from those who should support us, it seemed indeed folly to go on. That it was folly in the eyes of the worldlywise I had long known, but from year to year I hoped for the best, and so long as the Bishop was satisfied, and the interests of the poor children's Faith served, I did not care for the anxiety and suspense to be endured.

Knowing that the nuns shared the poverty and wretched conditions of those in greatest need, Adelaide people responded to appeals for help as generously as they could. Yet it is names like the Protestant Barr Smiths and the Jew Emmanuel Solomon that are remembered as effective supporters of this work of God at this time. The hard fact is that the Church dignitaries, while professing "the good of religion", were taken up, either as principals or as instruments, in an attempt to slander Mary and her nuns into oblivion. One wonders whether they had ever seen the Josephites' living conditions, or taken a close look at their work, or had ever stopped to wonder what motive drove young women to such a life. If we can feel the edge of it at such a distance, those who actually suffered it must have had their faith and charity severely tested. Yet Mary MacKillop always spoke kindly and respectfully about these people. She was particularly concerned that the truth should be known in Rome in a way that would not injure the bishop. This concern appears in everything she wrote to the nuns on the subject. "Mind, my solemn charge to you", she said, "excuse the Bishop in what you write."

The debts attack may not have been the most surprising tactic of the Commission, like the lie; or the most spectacular of its accusations, like the drunkenness; or the most illegal of its acts, like the usurpation of authority; but it is the most galling thing to read about after a hundred years. It told the nuns that they were not trusted or respected. One Sister wrote from Adelaide to Mary, as one of her desolate children who got little encouragement from the bishop: "Of all the things he said, I think his choice of adjectives is the most disgusting ever heard of. I really don't know where he got his list."

There is a moving phrase in a letter Patricia wrote to Mary about a conversation with the Archdeacon. She had told him that it had lately been very discouraging to see so many of the Sisters going into the grave without a Requiem after so many years hard labour:

I then spoke of poor Sister Magdalen who was buried a day or two before with apparently as little sympathy from the Ecclesiastics of the Diocese as if it had been a duck that died at the bottom of the yard.

Instead of regarding it as a privilege to be associated with the Josephites in assisting the poor, the authorities pointed accusing fingers, browbeat witnesses, and twisted evidence in order to make out that the nuns were dishonest, deceitful, scheming, untrustworthy self-seekers. There were indeed a few Sisters, very few, of whom something like that could have been said. But these were the very ones who had become confidantes of the bishop and Father Polk, and who had convinced them that the Mother General and the body of the Institute were unworthy.

Mary always spoke objectively about the affair, making no secret of the effect it had had on her. She wrote to Mechtilde a month after she received the bishop's letter:

I am so sorry for him but night or day cannot forget his cruel writings to me. It is strange but last night is the first time that I did not wake up dreaming of some thing or other that he wrote.

Some months later she said:

Our good friends of the Visitation have done their best one way or the other to ruin my reputation, but God's will be done. I don't care for any sorrow this causes me save that I feel as if death would be preferable to returning to Adelaide.

Little did the Bishop know the injury he did me in writing me those cruel letters, and thus breaking all my trust in him. Poor dear Bishop, and yet I would save him from sorrow if I could.

Her kindly spirit, which forbade her to speak against Reynolds and Russell, hardly imposes an obligation on posterity to conceal the truth about what she suffered. It is not adequate to say that Caiaphas and Pontius Pilate were badly advised and made unfortunate mistakes in the case of Jesus of Nazareth. Certainly, no human being is competent to pass judgment on another's conscience, not even in the case of these two or of Hitler and Stalin. But it is objective evil (like killing), not the conscience of the perpetrator, that harms people and causes suffering, tests endurance and reveals moral calibre.

After due allowance has been made for the mistakes of leading churchmen, for the pathetic mental state of the bishop and for the possibly guiltless consciences of all, it is no service to the Christian or human cause to be mealy-mouthed about what happened in Adelaide in 1883. Mother Mary and the Sisters of St Joseph were the victims of gross breaches of justice and charity.

Footnotes

[1] Reynolds does not seem to have heeded his friend's suggestion. On Easter Wednesday 1885, he addressed the Sisters: "I, as Bishop of Adelaide, received letters from Rome during Passion Week which empower me to act, and it has been decided that the Institute of St Joseph is to be divided into Diocesan Communities, and the Bishop in each case to be Superior in his own Diocese." He had received no such letters. In fact the Holy See was just at that time sending the very opposite message to Australia.

[2] Some Sisters have half a column of the notes devoted to their evidence, some a quarter of a column (50–60 words), and some just a name. Mother Mary's evidence occupies two columns, that of Sister Ignatius ten.

[3] Some time later Sister Michael became very unhappy and discontented. She sought out Mary in order to deny that she had ever accused her of intemperance. She was met with kindness and was allowed to occupy responsible office. Her view of the bishop was: "I think he is one of the weakest-minded and worst principled men I ever knew."

[4] Ignatius O'Brien had a similar story in 1925. Unenthusiastic about the Josephites because of her own history, she told George O'Neill fifty years after the event that Mary had once been in a state of inebriation. This sounded serious, so she was put on oath. It turned out that Mary was ill, and Ignatius had wished to see

her before going away. When this was not allowed by the Sister in charge, she concluded on no further evidence that Mary was affected by alcohol. But the heat of the oath caused the alcohol to evaporate. Ignatius would swear to nothing, except that Mary was kind, sweet, and good.

5   Though she would not defend herself, Mary quickly jumped to the defence of Woods when he was attacked. At a time when he was outside Australia, and in any case would have nothing to do with her (March 1884), she told the Sisters: "The tongue of cruel slander has not attacked me alone. Most wicked charges are said here about poor Father Julian, and I had to give an indignant protest against one charge to a Dignitary whose name I had better not mention."

6   On the same terms, David made an error with Bathsheba, Judas made an error in his dealings with the High Priests, and Adam and Eve made an error in the Garden of Eden—these statements are true, but they are not adequate accounts of what happened.

PART VIII

The Institute's

Affairs

1883–1888

TWENTY-FOUR

AN EXILE FINDS A NEW HOME

Mother Mary Settles in Sydney 1883

In a short letter to the Sisters before she left Adelaide in November 1883, Mother Mary referred thus to her departure: "Circumstances call me to Sydney. S. Bernard says that if I go for one week they will be satisfied, but I have reason to think that I shall be longer than that away." She could not tell them that she had no idea when the Bishop of Adelaide would allow her to re-enter his diocese, but she could tell them how they should conduct themselves meanwhile:

> The Institute is passing through a severe trial but with humility, charity and truth on the part of its members all will in the end be well. Have patience, my own loved children,—pray—pray humbly and with confidence and fear nothing. Our good God is proving His work.

Some weeks after her arrival in Sydney, she wrote the Sisters a Christmas letter full of hope, although things certainly did not look too bright for the Institute:

> We have had much sorrow and are still suffering its effects, but sorrow or trial lovingly submitted to does not prevent our being happy—it rather purifies the happiness.

She reminded them that not all the faults could be laid at the door of outsiders. Charity was often thoughtlessly wounded within the Institute, there were deviations from obedience in little matters, and criticism and murmurings were frequent. God had chosen his own way to correct them, and with regard to herself: "It is but right that He should let the heaviest part of the cross fall upon your Mother who was so little able to be to you what the Mother General of such an Institute should be."

In her concern that things be made as easy as possible for Monica, now in charge in Adelaide, she gave them three practical pieces of advice: not to murmur or listen to a murmurer, always to be sincere and open with Superiors, and never to exaggerate. She returned to these precepts at the end of the long letter, making it clear that her recent experiences had taught her a lesson about the damage done by murmuring and criticism. Referring to the Commission, she warned against hard feelings towards the bishop, and turned the blame rather on those who had misled him. With regard to herself, she simply appealed to their own knowledge of her, without attempting any detailed defence.

Although the death of Archbishop Vaughan was a blow, Mary was not by any means without friends in Sydney. She quickly sought out priests whose position and character led her to believe that they would provide good advice. She got from them not only good advice but much needed encouragement.

Mount Street, North Sydney

A historic moment is touched near the end of Mary's letter to the Sisters on December 17—she referred to the small beginnings of what was destined to become the new Mother House of the Institute in North Sydney. This was where Mary herself was to die, and where today her tomb is visited by many pilgrims. She wrote:

> A dear benefactor, a good old priest, is giving us his own home to serve as a future Novitiate. It is beautifully situated, so retired and quiet, and is to be our own property. Another friend has offered £500 when we start the Novitiate.

Until this house of Dean Kenny became available on the north shore, the Sydney Josephites were lodged on the south side of the harbour. The move created a new atmosphere, reflected in Mary's letters. On May 9 she wrote to Monica from Alma Cottage, Mount Street, North Shore:

> The place is beautifully retired, though near one of the chief streets, it is as quiet as if miles away from other people. We have no noise, bustle or excitement, have a nice little garden and paddock with high fences, and little birds singing around us.

The Sisters gradually took up residence at North Sydney. Dean Kenny was leaving them his little oratory with its furnishings, and allowing them free use of his library of ascetical books. He proved to be a good friend, taking an interest in the novices and sharing in their instruction. "May God reward the dear old man," Mary wrote, "his ideas in most things quite agree with those that I believe to be God's for the Institute."

In spite of the spirit of hope in Sydney about the new novitiate, some Sisters in Adelaide still had misgivings. Mary's advisers not only failed to share this hesitation but declared that it was positively wrong. If the late Archbishop had been less tolerant, they said, he would have been justified in objecting to it strongly. In the light of this professional advice, Mary was sure she was justified in going ahead. But knowing that some were critical of her decision, she urged Monica to encourage them to be more large-minded, pointing out that they had "very few practical opportunities of judging of the necessities of the Institute in other places". She appealed also for a large-heartedness more worthy of a Sister of St Joseph than a spirit of carping criticism based on ignorance of the facts. She dealt with this practical matter on a spiritual level:

> As long as I hear that any Sisters murmur, I shall not feel that the lesson our good God wished us to learn from the recent Visitation has done its work. I shall feel that more pruning and sorrow must come ere my Sisters will have the spirit I wish to see in them, or what is far more to the point, ere I can believe that we are . . . what the Sacred Heart of our Divine Spouse expects us to be.

The Arrival of Archbishop Moran

When Patrick Francis Moran arrived early in September 1884, Australia was to him by no means a *terra incognita*. Born in 1830 and orphaned young, he had gone to Rome at the age of twelve, where his uncle Paul Cullen was Rector of the Irish College. After ordination in 1853 and doctorate studies, he was Vice-Rector of the College for ten years. He was thus a thoroughly romanised Irishman, having spent twenty-four of the first thirty-six years of his life in the Eternal City. He knew how things were done there and he was familiar with the people who did them. Returning to Ireland in 1866, he became secretary to Cullen, now Cardinal Archbishop of Dublin. In 1872 he became Bishop of Ossory, and often acted for the Irish bishops in their Roman business.

Not only had Moran learnt much while acting as ecclesiastical agent in Rome for the Australian bishops, and later through association with his influential uncle in Dublin, but his appointment would have stirred him to inform himself as fully as possible about the personalities and the problems of the country of his adoption. His visit to Rome on the journey out gave him an opportunity to extend his knowledge of the Australian Church. He would not have believed all he heard, but he had a chance to hear a lot. Reynolds was writing to Kirby, and Mary had kept up contact with Simeoni and Bianchi as well as with Campbell.

There are twelve extant letters to Moran in Mary's hand dated in the four months beginning 19 September 1884. The first began:

> If at your convenience you will kindly grant me an interview I shall be most grateful. I humbly wish to submit certain anxieties that I have got to your Grace's kind consideration with a view to obtaining such advice as may enable me to discharge my duty.

A week later she was able to tell Monica that the Archbishop had been twice to see the Sisters, once at the Providence and once at North Sydney. He told her that Dr Reynolds had tried to prejudice him against her by talk of debts and drink. "Imagine my feelings when the Archbishop told me this," said Mary, "I did not think he would dare to go as far as the latter. Dr Reynolds now wants to crush me." She asked Moran whether he was a Delegate of the Holy See with the right to settle Adelaide's difficulties, as Reynolds was saying. He replied that he had no such authority and did not want to have anything to do with Adelaide's troubles. Even when later he was asked to hold an enquiry, he made it clear that he had no right to settle anything.

Mary alerted Monica in Adelaide to the fact that it was an important moment for the Institute, urging her to encourage the nuns to be "unflinching in their defence of the right". She also spoke of the effect of the crisis on her personally:

> Sorrow at the insincerity and unfaithfulness of some I have loved is telling upon me, and I feel more unable than usual to meet my crosses, but when I am a day or two well, I gain heart again.

She summed up her situation in a very incisive way for Monica:

> From what has been told to Dr Moran I can judge of what has been told to others. The character of your M. G. is at stake. She is guilty or not guilty. If guilty in the eyes of the Sisters, let them say so, if not let them clear her, or she must cease to be their M. G.

Just at this time members of the hierarchy were visiting Sydney to welcome the Archbishop. Reynolds was among them, but he went away without seeing the Sisters. Arrangements for a meeting came to nothing. He did not come on the day arranged for him to visit Dean

Kenny at Mount Street, and when he did come to see him it was on the very day Mary was due to be absent visiting the Archbishop. She gave an account to Monica:

> When the latter asked him before leaving if he would not come in to see the Sisters, he excused himself and said something about another day. I then decided that two, S. Bernard and M. Veronica, should go and see him, but the same day was told that he had gone back suddenly to Victoria. Evidently he did not want to see me.

But there was good news too."Everything does not look so dark," she wrote, "Drs Torreggiani and Cani were almost daily with us, and only yesterday I had a most kind letter from Dr Redwood." Cani was now his own man, no longer an instrument of James Quinn.

On September 26 Mary sent the Archbishop copies of the Rules and Constitutions, also Vaughan's letter about the Novitiate "and his attested copy of the permission he had received from Rome for its establishment in the Archdiocese". On October 2 came the reply that "the letter of the late Archbishop and the permission granted by the Holy See for establishing the Novitiate in Sydney are quite satisfactory".

On October 20 Moran had an important message for the Mother General to forward to the Sisters. He had received a rescript from Rome indicating that the Pope had absolved them from the oath of silence about the 1883 interrogations in Adelaide. In her acknowledgement of this on 22 October Mary referred to the great distress that had been occasioned by this oath.

Although the Bishop of Adelaide did not venture to express his opinion to the Archbishop, who would not have been pleased to know that doubts were being cast on his ability to read a Roman document, he told the Sisters that the papal dispensation was not valid, and that they were still bound by the oath of silence. Well aware that it was possible to cite non-existent documents from Rome, he demanded to see the alleged dispensation:

> As this document was obtained under a mistaken plea, it is of no effect, pending further letters from Rome. Mother Mary of the Cross should have notified me of her sending you such. She has not done so. To prevent further scandal bring in that document to me, as I wish to satisfy myself of its genuineness.

But the Sisters preferred to believe Archbishop Moran, and when he made the long-awaited official request for information—"the Sacred Congregation of Propaganda has been pleased to instruct me to make some inquiries"—they proceeded to reveal what Dr Reynolds had done in 1883. In transmitting this message, Mary warned the Sisters against pettiness and resentment:

> Whilst speaking the truth to the Archbishop . . . let no Sister worthy of the name yield to bitterness or want of charity in anything she may have to say about the Bishop or those concerned with the Visitation.
>
> Let us all believe that everything was done with a good intention, and let us not forget what the good Bishop was to us in a very painful past . . . If we cannot excuse everything, we can at least excuse the intention.

Whether or not the Sisters heeded this exhortation to avoid offending or annoying Reynolds, he was being occasioned the greatest annoyance by what Propaganda had instructed the Archbishop of Sydney to do. He reacted by writing long letters defending himself and renewing all the charges against the Mother General.

His direct reply to Dr Moran's request for information is dated November 16. The questions are easy to deduce from the answers. He made no reference to his authority for holding the Commission, although later he said that his claim to Pontifical authority implied more than he had intended—a phrase to soften his admission, made in reply to Moran's direct question, that he had no letters of instruction.

Reynolds had told the Sisters on several occasions that he had sent a report to Rome, but had to admit to Moran that all he had done was to write to Kirby. He gave three reasons for not sending any report to Propaganda: his desire to screen the Mother General, his desire to show the minutes to the Archbishop, and his hope that the latter would have some instructions about them "and thus save a world of trouble, for it's most unsatisfactory to have to deal with Propaganda in writing". His second reason, "I wanted to show them to your Grace", could only refer to some as yet unappointed Archbishop of Sydney. It is not clear how he expected Rome to instruct a new Archbishop a year later about a matter it was not officially going to know anything about.

With regard to his authority over the Institute of St Joseph—"the Authority which Propaganda seems to call in question"—Reynolds wrote the unfortunate sentence:

> It is quite evident that Cardinal Simeoni has forgotten the letter of late Cardinal Franchi, a copy of which I append, or rather a translation as Mother Gen'l has taken the original.

If there is an implication here of anything unworthy, it is unjustified. The original was a letter addressed to Sister Mary, so she had every right to take it. The translation bears the signature of Reynolds himself attesting to its correctness. It was the fact that Simeoni had *not* forgotten the contents of the letter, signed by himself as well as by Franchi, that made him so cognisant of the status of the Josephites. It was exactly the opposite of what Reynolds was maintaining.

As for the oath, which Moran was to say later could have got Reynolds into gaol, the bishop said:

> I more and more see its painful necessity—for even on oath, I would not get at the abuses were I to have to examine today. I am not alone in this view of the case. Sad facts have made the Vicar Gen'l and Dean Kennedy say the same.

This could have made the Archdeacon and the Dean accessories in any criminal proceedings against Reynolds in the civil courts for his administration of the oath. The danger of such proceedings, referred to by Moran in his report, was one of the reasons why he had to go quietly about his investigation.

Reynolds then attacked Mother Mary, with specific reference to her unworthy motives and her duplicity, for establishing a Sydney Novitiate, remarking that she sheltered her act "by an alleged dispensation by late Abp Vaughan". He was to resume the charge, with the same personal innuendos, in his letter to Moran on 22 January 1885. This would hardly have impressed the Archbishop, who had seen Vaughan's papal document and had told Mother Mary it was "quite satisfactory". Finally, with regard to the finances, the hand of the Archdeacon appears again—Reynolds asked leave "to give this part into the hands of Vicar General".

On November 16 Mary asked Moran for an interview. She was aware of a certain tension between the demands of truth and of charity, and wanted guidance about just how much he wanted to know. Anxious to shield Reynolds as much as possible, she feared, "were I to write everything, and Your Grace have to use the same officially I might have to add much more to his already heavy sorrows than I wish". By November 26 she had finished her "sort of statement concerning the principal circumstances of the late Visitation in Adelaide", and sent it with an apology:

> It has cost me a great deal to write it . . . If in my statements I have written any thing uncharitable I beg Your Grace to believe that it is not so intended. I only tried to tell the truth.

Moran acknowledged receipt of the statement on November 28, adding a restrained word of reassurance:

> When you have done what you judged best and when you have placed matters in as clear a light as you could before the duly constituted authorities, you should rest quite satisfied and attend to every duty as hitherto.

Meanwhile, letters poured in from the Sisters, and Moran sent them on with his report to Rome. Many Sisters sent their letters directly to Simeoni. They amounted to a chorus of protest against the action of the Bishop of Adelaide, of praise and support for Mother Mary, and of indignant repudiation of the charge of intemperance. On October 1 Moran received a letter from the four Councillors—Monica, Michael, Matthew, and Mechtilde—in which they stated: "This scandalous charge is entirely false and a gross calumny on the fair name of an innocent person." Mechtilde also lodged a personal protest:

> I have known her for 17 years, she has been my superior for 15 years, and I have lived in the Mother House for the last 11 years and I can state with truth that she never gave way to intemperate habits to my knowledge. Surely in all justice each one of the sisters should have been questioned on this point, in particular those who have lived in the convent with her.

Another declaration was signed by four Sisters, including the future Mother General, Laurence:

> Trusting you will do all in your power to vindicate the innocent whom we have known for more than six, twelve and fifteen years, and of whom we can say in all truth and sincerity that we have never known her to be guilty of any such crimes. The only crime we can accuse her of, if such it can be called, is her very great charity and generosity . . . We sadly deplore her absence and find it hard to feel the same interest in our duties . . . We believe a few murmuring members of our own, aided by enemies of the Bishop and Mother General, have been the cause of it all.

Mary Gertrude Dewe revealed her high esteem for Mother Mary:

> For many years I belonged to a Benedictine community in England . . . With the sanction of all my Superiors I came out here three years ago with our worthy Bishop Dr Reynolds, and to whom I am greatly indebted, as well as also to our respected and much esteemed Mother General. From what I have myself seen and heard through the different Sisters, it appears to me that things have been misrepresented to the Bishop.
>
> Since I became a member of this Institute I have never seen

anything in our Mother General but what was edifying, besides her constant endeavours to do all in her power for the happiness and spiritual advantage of the Community under her charge.

Two Sisters who had held the office of infirmarian protested about the accusation of intemperance and the fact that they had not been questioned. Annette wrote:

With regard to the scandalous falsehood that she was intemperate I deny it utterly and I had good opportunities of noticing her. I have been ten years professed in the order and spent the greater part of that time in the Mother House. I was Infirmarian there for two years, attended Mother in her illnesses and never saw in her any sign of such a thing. Whatever stimulant was ordered her by the doctor I measured out in small quantity.

I was never brought before the Commission and several of the oldest Sisters in the Institute were not questioned. When such grave accusations were brought against one whom we so loved and revered *at least* our opinions ought to have been taken. I am sure that our Bishop had a good intention in what he did, but fear that others put false suspicions into his mind.

Philippa wrote:

I for one declare that to be a falsehood. During all the years that I have known her and been in her company night and day I never saw anything that could give the slightest foundation to such a malicious statement.

I was her infirmarian. It seems strange to me that when the Commissioners accused Mother of such a gross thing they did not take the evidence of *all* the Sisters and of those who are the longest in the Institute. They did not ask me any questions on the subject.

Patricia Campbell stated that the Sisters from places under the care of the Jesuits—Willochra, Yarcowie, Jamestown, Caltowie, Laura, Georgetown, Gulnare South, Sevenhill, Auburn, Mintaro, Manoora and Tarlee, were not questioned nor "acquainted in any way with the removal of our esteemed and much respected Superioress", and she went on to make her opinion very clear:

We consider it an injustice on the part of the Commission to lay accusations against our Mother General without having the opinion of at least all the senior members of the Institute. Those accusations we most positively deny.

Besides the individual protests, there was a document sent to Simeoni in elaborate hand-printing signed by almost all the Sisters in South Australia, to the number of 117:

We hereby unite in declaring that this malicious report is a base fabrication, and is entirely untrue. It has also been stated that Mother General had no friends among the Sisters in this Diocese, and that they have no confidence in her. This statement is also false; we all most positively deny it.

This declaration of solidarity with the Mother General provoked an anonymous letter which said that the nuns were terrorised into signing by threats of reprisals. It claimed to be written by a Josephite, but it could have been sent by anybody.

Archbishop Moran's Report

Moran wrote a short letter to Propaganda on 27 January 1885, saying that he hoped for a peaceful outcome of a dispute in which there were faults on both sides. His report, he said, would be delayed until after a visit to Sydney by Bishop Reynolds. At last on March 7 the document was ready. He began by expressing his confidence that the controversy between Reynolds and Mother Mary would be settled peaceably. Then he went on to assure Simeoni that both sides were prepared to abide by the decision of Rome. This may have been conventional language, or he may simply not have understood the mind of Bishop Reynolds. But the fact is that Reynolds was at that moment busily engaged, not in preserving the *status quo* until a Roman decision came, but in attempting to wrench the Adelaide Josephites from the authority of their Mother General and to set up a *fait accompli* in his own favour.

Then follows a short account of the origin of the Institute in 1866. The foundress, Moran notes, is a very able woman of good education and has been in charge uninterruptedly since the beginning. The paragraph about Woods mentions the thinness of his theological education, his scientific work, and the fact that he is currently occupied, not with the sacred ministry, but with a scientific expedition in Malaya. It suggests that the rumours against his good name may have some foundation. [1]

The next paragraph shows that at this stage Moran did not properly understand the status of the Josephites. He says it was a misinterpretation of Franchi's letter to Mary on 21 April 1874 that led them to imagine that they were exempt from diocesan authority and subject immediately to Propaganda. In their reply to this report on May 8 the Roman authorities were quick to point out that the Institute of St Joseph was *not* diocesan and *was* indeed immediately subject to the Holy See.

The Visitation is the next topic in the report. Moran states very plainly that Reynolds made a serious mistake in claiming papal authority through letters of instruction that had never existed. Moreover, when he imposed the oath upon the Sisters he was committing a serious offence in civil law and was liable to a heavy penalty if the Courts ever took the matter up.

The report then moves on to money matters. The Bishop of Adelaide is concerned about the heavy debt incurred by the Institute of St Joseph, a particularly serious thing in a diocese notorious for its financial problems. It was after Sister Mary's return from Rome that the real trouble began, when the Sisters imagined they were exempt from the authority of the bishop. What the report does not say is that while the debts were being contracted Reynolds knew and approved of everything Mary was doing, and that she had presented him with documents signed by himself to remind him of this. It was only when he turned sour that he disapproved of what he had previously supported.

The Archbishop goes on to state that the books were not well kept and that accountancy was not one of the Superior's strong points.[2] It had been pointed out to him that the miserable state of many of the convents was the reason why money had to be spent on them from time to time. He mentions the cost of travelling Australia's great distances as an important expense that sometimes passed unnoticed. Reynolds' accusation that Mary was spending money on her relatives is mentioned, but Moran rejects it as quite unfounded.

It might be remarked in passing that although some of the saints may have been good accountants, it is not a characteristic that has a high place among their recorded virtues. It would be surprising to hear that Francis of Assisi was a good bookkeeper, or that the Institute's patron Joseph was noted for his careful balancing of accounts. But open-handed charity and trust in providence are different matters, although they can seem "folly in the eyes of the worldly-wise" as Mary knew.

The Archbishop then takes up the accusation of intemperance. He starts with some remarks about the habit of doctors in Australia of prescribing brandy for women with all kinds of petty illnesses. Many of the patients end up by taking too much, and this includes nuns. In the case of Sister Mary of the Cross, she admits that for some years doctors have directed her to use brandy. From the evidence of the Sisters it is clear that she has drunk much of it. The bishop was aware of it and shortly before the Visitation he called her attention to the obligation to give it up.[3] Moran notes that Sister Mary herself denies absolutely any suggestion of excess, and adds that the accusation of some Sisters that she drank too much is quite compatible with what she says. She does not deny that doctors frequently told her to take brandy and that she obeyed them. At times when brandy of poor quality made her sick some Sisters rashly judged that she was drunk. There are cases where the illness itself, without any use of brandy whatsoever, was rashly interpreted by a few Sisters as due to drinking.

His words are careful and measured. He does not say, much less prove, that the doctors were wrong to prescribe brandy. His statements about petty illnesses and abuse of the remedy by some women, including nuns, may or may not be true; but they are sociological background, not evidence against Mother Mary, and certainly not a verdict against her. Her periodic illness was, we know, not petty; and we also know that the brandy prescribed was the only remedy that kept her on her feet and enabled her to go on with her work.

There is a tendentious use of the word *admit* in Moran's account of what Mary said. The word suggests a presumption of guilt or imperfection. But she did not have to admit she took brandy, she stated that she took it. There was no question of being unable to deny it, regretfully, as it were. "She does not deny that she has made much use of brandy" is one way of stating that she told him that over a period of years the doctors often prescribed brandy and she took it. That was common knowledge among the Sisters, just as Mechtilde's blindness was common knowledge. Mary regretted the necessity of the medicinal brandy, as she regretted Mechtilde's infirmity, but her real sorrow was that some of her Sisters were not decent enough to think on her brandy as they did on Mechtilde's walking-stick.

The most important point Moran makes is that what Mary herself says can be reconciled with the evidence alleged against her. What she says is that she is perfectly guiltless in the matter, therefore he is saying that the charge of intemperance is not sustained by the evidence.

The Archbishop then treats of the support given to his own conclusion by the flood of letters from Sisters favouring their Mother General and strenuously denying the charge of intemperance. He remarks in passing that it proves at least the falseness of the statement that she has lost her good name with them. Then, after wisely noting that many who wrote (and this would apply to many who signed the communal protest) would not have been in a position to know much about the matter, as they did not live in the same house as the Mother General, he came to the point. There were strong letters from wise and virtuous Sisters, respected people who *were* in a position to know the facts, and these explicitly denied the accusation.

Reynolds' citing of doubtful medical witnesses against Mary is treated by Moran in the report with what amounts to contempt. One is dead, he says, and the other—"I don't know who he could be."

The report concludes with a statement about the present position of the Institute. It refers to weaknesses in observance of the Rule, to the admission of unsuitable candidates, and to the efforts being made to reduce the debt. But at this time Moran did not seem to grasp the importance of the constitutional issue at stake in Reynolds' usurpation of authority. He says that the bishop has taken over in Adelaide, and that the Superior General is now in Sydney busy governing the houses of the Institute there. They are doing much good and he has no reason to complain of her. He is in favour of maintaining this *status quo* until the coming Synod of Bishops makes some decision about the Sisters of St Joseph. The diocesan Sisters, originally at Bathurst and now at Maitland and Goulburn also, have turned out well; he is personally inclined to think that this would be the best solution for the Josephites everywhere. Propaganda promptly pointed out his error, and made it clear that the Institute of St Joseph to which it had issued Constitutions was *not* diocesan.

To Moran's credit, when Rome had made the situation clear and he understood it correctly, he was faithful and meticulous in maintaining the proper juridical status of the Sisters. This brought him into conflict with some of the other bishops, notably Reynolds, and in the course of the next few years he wrote some masterly letters pointing out the demands of law to men who simply wanted their own way.

When Moran arrived in Rome shortly afterwards, there was a reply awaiting him, dated May 8. On his return to Sydney six months later he announced an important decision it contained. In telling Mother Mary about it, he did not say it was waiting for him in Sydney. He said it had "come to hand". The document identifies two main topics: the nature of the Institute of St Joseph, and the problems concerning the Mother General.

In treating the first, Propaganda pointed out that although the

Constitutions had not received final approval they were for a general, not a diocesan Institute. The Sisters being therefore immediately subject to the Holy See, the matters in which they were subject to the local bishop were limited to those explicitly mentioned in the chapter of the Constitutions dealing with this matter. With regard to the separated houses of Bathurst, Maitland, and Goulburn, the Archbishop was referred to a former letter of Propaganda so that the status of the Sisters in those places could be regularised by a clear decision to belong to the Mother House or to withdraw from the Institute.

With regard to the second topic, there is no mention of the accusations against the Superior General, but Propaganda says it had become aware that she had occupied her office illegally since the second General Chapter in 1881. Only two periods of six years are allowed by the Constitutions, and she had already been more than twelve years in charge at the time of her re-election at that Chapter. This difficulty had in fact been proposed by Mary herself, but it had been dismissed by the bishop. He was following the professional advice that since the Constitutions had not existed before 1874, her time in office began with her election in that year. The restriction applied only to somebody who has been "elected twice" and she had certainly not been elected twice before 1881.

But her 1881 election was now seen as illegal. Moran was instructed to declare her out of office and to arrange for a new Superior General to be elected as soon as possible by a Chapter. It has been suggested that he was the one who engineered this directive, basing it on an idea Mary herself had planted in his head. During the previous two years she had spoken of her weariness, and expressed the desire, sometimes strongly, to escape from the responsibilities that were pressing on her. Her performance of duty, she knew, had been a potent factor in bringing on the troubles that engulfed her and the Institute. It would be most unlikely that she said nothing to the Archbishop about these feelings, or about the doubt she had expressed before her re-election.

Although he had a very high personal regard for her, his subsequent action in keeping her out of office for a proposed seventeen years indicates that he was convinced there was some advantage in having her out of the way. It is unlikely that Rome would have proposed this course of action as a solution without the knowledge of the man to whom it had entrusted the supervision of the affair in Australia. Moran never gave a reason for keeping his nominee in office, other than that he was directed by Rome to do so. The invalid election idea was obviously a mere cover-up, as Rome and Moran could quite easily have authorised Mary to continue, with their authority, until an election. Keeping one woman in office for seventeen years seems a bizarre way to remedy the illegality of another woman being in office for more than twelve.

It has generally been said that Mary was removed to placate the bishops with regard to a woman who had a bad record for resisting attacks on her Institute's rights. As most of them were Irish, it is said that Moran's concern to foster peace among them led him to see the Irish Mother Bernard as an acceptable change after one who was colonial and Scottish as well as troublesome. As Bernard did not have either Mary's intelligence or her strong character, she was more likely to be pliable with regard to suggestions that were in doubtful harmony with the spirit of the Institute.

But this is simply speculation. The Quinns were dead, and Reynolds died four years before the last extension of Mother Bernard's term of office. One or two other bishops who had shown themselves less than fully enthusiastic did not have the Sisters in their dioceses. On the other hand, there were a number of bishops who were positively friendly to both the Institute and Mother Mary. If Moran hoped at first that things would improve in Adelaide if somebody other than Mary were in charge of the Institute, he was soon to see that the determination of the bishop there to crush the Josephites was not affected by the substitution.

Probably the whole matter, including the setting aside of Mother Mary, was decided on Moran's 1885 visit, in the light of what he reported orally as well as in writing, and that this part of the reply to his report, though dated May 8, was composed while he was in Rome. It certainly seems strange, as it seemed strange to the nuns at the time, that it took the people in Rome four years to discover the flaw in the 1881 election. They were probably glad that someone suggested a solution to the tension in Adelaide that would not seem to favour one side or the other.

An impasse was latent in the next sentence of the long 1885 letter from Propaganda to Moran. The Mother House, it reminded him, could not be moved from Adelaide without the consent of the Holy See. Now if a new Mother General were to be elected she would be no more likely than Mother Mary to be tolerated in Adelaide by a bishop energetically engaged at this very time in forcing the Sisters to withdraw from their Mother General.

Propaganda's final paragraph expressed satisfaction that the Bishop of Adelaide has been able to resolve the problem of the debt contracted illegally by the Josephite Superior; and it hoped that Dr Moran would be able to continue his good work and settle the conflict peacefully. Two remarks might be made here. Firstly, the debt problem was by no means solved; in fact, Moran was to devote much of his time to supervising its solution over the next few years. Propaganda was a little sanguine too in expecting that the Bishop of Adelaide would come to any agreement except on his own terms, and Moran was to learn from personal experience that dealing with Christopher Augustine Reynolds was a very prickly business indeed.

Secondly, there is no evidence that the Mother General ever contracted any debt illegally. Moran does not say so in his report. The adverb is used in Propaganda's reply, with the remark that expenditure over a certain amount requires the consent of the Holy See. But no specific accusation is made against her, or was ever made, much less proved. It is hard to do much about such a floating adverb except simply to deny it until proof is forthcoming. If there were anything illegal, it would have been traceable to the Institute's advisers, including Reynolds, whom she consulted consistently. It was the bishop's frustration in the face of a large diocesan debt that turned Mother Mary into a scapegoat. There were instances where he accused her of contracting debts without his knowledge, but she was able to show him his signed authorisation for everything she had done. She wrote to Dr Campbell:

> I think he has allowed himself to exaggerate our pecuniary difficulties without remembering that he had known of their existence before, and forgetting that the whole Catholic education of the poorer class had been carried on by us in his diocese when, for the little aid we received from those who should support us, it seemed indeed folly to go on.

She summed it up for the Sisters late in 1884, urging them to ignore criticism and not to desert the poor children:

> Don't let yourselves be dismayed at the Adelaide debt. It is little in comparison with the work done and the means for it; but had I been wise for myself I should have held out against it long ago. But would the work have been done? If man forgets, God does not.

Footnotes

1 Moran calls Woods an English convert, which is not true, except in the sense that at a certain moment he began to take his Catholic religion seriously. The suggestion that his good name was in some doubt may have been a true statement as it stood—that is, there were rumours. But historically there has never been any doubt about Woods' goodness and fidelity.

2 It is impossible to draw a picture of the finances of the Josephites at the time in question. In 1983 they were given back any surviving material that concerned their affairs, but there was no sign of Bank Books, Bank Statements, the Mortgage Book, Balance Sheets, or of the famous Loan Book recording the bishop's approval of everything. Most of the books and records of 1875–1883 were given to the Commission on demand and simply disappeared.

3 This means that Reynolds said later that this is what he did. In fact he had mentioned in a friendly way to Mary that some Sisters were taking scandal, but he had not spoken of an obligation to take no further notice of the doctors. Even if he had, his remark would not have constituted an obligation.

TWENTY-FIVE

HARASSMENT
IN ADELAIDE

The Institute Under Pressure 1884–1885

Meanwhile the campaign against the Constitutions continued in Adelaide. The nuns were so upset by three visits Bishop Reynolds paid to the convent early in 1885 that they described what they lived through as worse than the excommunication. Monica's long reports to Mary about these events may be regarded as being as accurate as any account written from notes taken at an interview or a discourse. Mechtilde also sent a vivid narrative of it all, her memory possibly sharpened by her blindness.

On the feast of the Epiphany in the first week of the year, and again in Easter week, the bishop came with his entourage—Russell, Polk and O'Sullivan—and addressed the nuns in a very domineering manner. He had not a good word to say about them. He was their only superior, he claimed, and he demanded that each one give him an assurance of submission to diocesan government. He told them again that the dispensation from the oath was not valid, and that they were all still bound to silence about all the details of the Visitation:

> By a falsely obtained dispensation you were freed from that oath. It was by a false representation of matters and by not telling the whole truth, Monsignor Campbell, the *poor old man*, was deceived, a venerable priest made a dupe of, but I tell you now that dispensation is not valid.

But it was not Dr Campbell, it was Pope Leo who had granted the dispensation. And whatever anyone may have said to Propaganda, it was Archbishop Moran who had been the intermediary. The bishop was never specific about why he considered the dispensation to have been granted through false pretences. The facts about the oath itself were plain enough: he forced an oath of silence on the Sisters, they took it, the Pope dispensed from it.

Before long the nuns were pouring out their hearts in letters to their absent Mother General. "Here we are," said one after the bishop's first visit, "in misery and disgrace ... Poor Father O'Sullivan had to write everything that he said because the Sisters are such liars." Another said: "Oh, dear Mother, if you were here, I could tell you some strange things that I never thought anyone could say or do." Another wrote of a Sister who "says she can never tell anyone what she felt when she heard him raging in the oratory". Calasanctius was the one he identified as ringleader of rebellion and indiscipline. She went about during the Retreat disturbing everybody by talking and gossiping. When Monica ventured to come forward and tell his Lordship that Calasanctius had left the Mother House four days before the Retreat, she was waved out of the way with the remark, "If Sister Monica is to be believed."

"I appointed Mother Monica," said the bishop on his first visit, "I and I alone had the right to do this; from me she received her authority and she is my representative here." Whatever he may have imagined, it was Mother Mary who had designated Monica to act as Vicar, according to the Constitutions, in the enforced absence of both the Mother General and her Assistant. Monica's intense suffering during these months made her realise what Mary had been going through. Her defence of Calasanctius reminded them all of the excom-munication scene when Mary was defended in a similar manner by "poor Sister Teresa that's dead". Bernardine wrote:

> You really would pity the poor old Sister after she came from the Bishop. She said to me that she did not know how you stood it so long as you had, that if she had very much to do with them she would lose her senses, and I believe she would.

In spite of what the bishop was doing to them, many of the Sisters wrote of him with pity and sympathy. Typical was:

> When I think of the last 17 years that I have been in the Convent, and now to hear the Bishop say such things . . . that Bishop that I always loved since a child, and I love him still. He looked so old after he came out of the oratory.

The blame was reserved for the unfaithful few among the Sisters— "someone must take tales to him," said one. Another wrote: "I cannot understand how it is that he hears everything we say and do. There must be some busybodies amongst us." Another: "The Bishop hears everything. They pretend they do not speak to Father Polk, but they spend hours with him on the quiet." The busybodies are not always easy to identify. Not all were like Ignatius McCarthy. Some, like Francis de Sales, seem to have acted out of sheer weak-mindedness. Francis Xavier was for a time unreliable, and they never trusted Matthew.

During Easter Week, Reynolds claimed to have received written authority for what he was doing, and the Sisters wondered if they were really being told by Rome to forsake their Constitutions. They were startled to hear in the chapel on Wednesday April 8:

> I as Bishop of Adelaide, received letters from Rome during Passion Week which empower me to act, and it has been decided that the Institute of St Joseph is to be divided into Diocesan communities, and the Bishop in each case to be Superior in his own Diocese.

Mary de Sales, remembering no doubt the bishop's earlier claim to authority he did not have, was courageous enough to ask to see his document. Monica told Mary about it:

> Sister M. de Sales then respectfully asked his Lordship would he not read his Roman document. He replied, "No. Am I so untruthful that I cannot be believed. etc." Sister M. de Sales rejoined, "Oh no, my Lord, but it will be more satisfactory to the Sisters." His Lordship replied, "My word is sufficient and they will get nothing else."

He told them that their choice was to accept his demands or leave, and he would come for their replies the next day. If they chose to leave, they would not be received elsewhere: "They will not be received in the Archdiocese, believe me; the Archbishop is not hoodwinked." A telegram went straight off to Sydney:

> Bishop has just addressed the Sisters here told them they must decide on being diocesan communities and give their answers to him tomorrow morning all not acknowledging him as their superior must leave at once but will not be received by your Grace is this so? and if so can we not have longer to consider kindly reply.

Moran quickly assured them in reply that what Reynolds had told them about his attitude was not true: "I have not made any rule such as that referred to in your telegram."

On the next day the bishop prefaced his private interviews with some public instruction about his authority. The chapter of the Constitutions relating to the bishop of the diocese made him absolute Superior of the Institute there. It was as clear as daylight, and he did not know how it was that they all understood the Constitutions so badly. [1] He was the one to make changes, and the nuns were to submit, whether they liked it or not.

Annette wrote Simeoni a vivid account of what was happening.

After making sure he knew the bishop had claimed to have authority from Rome to divide the Institute into diocesan communities, she spelt out clearly and powerfully where she stood:

> I now wish distinctly to state to Your Eminence that I do not acknowledge His Lordship, Dr Reynolds, as my Superior. I adhere to our Mother General, Mary of the Cross, and I shall always uphold the Central Government. As a Bishop I shall always respect His Lordship, Dr Reynolds, and obey him in all things which come within his jurisdiction.

On Friday, April 10, the bishop told the Sisters he was removing Monica from office and replacing her with Michael. This caused a crisis. They obeyed Monica because they knew Mary had appointed her before leaving. If the bishop made a change now they would not accept it, because it would be clearly invalid according to the Constitutions. Monica therefore had to tell him that the Mother General had appointed her before he had. He would not accept this, and insisted that she leave, announcing that Michael would take her place as "my Mother Vicar". Michael refused to cooperate, but he prepared a document appointing her.

Michael saw him again on Monday, and urged the impossibility of having her in place of Monica and of putting Francis de Sales ("many of them had seen her when she was quite out of her mind", "a poor lunatic") in charge of the Mother House. He finally yielded about Francis de Sales when the Archdeacon "observed that it was of no use to enforce on the Sisters a Superior whom they would not recognise". Matthew and Michael waited on him the next day to beg him to allow Monica to remain, pointing out that the nuns would not consent to her replacement and would leave the colony. He tried to tell them that they would not be received in Sydney, but they had Moran's telegram to the contrary; so he "commanded Michael by his authority as Bishop of the Diocese, and in virtue of Obedience, that she was not to give the passage money to any of them". Michael said they would go anyhow, and another Sister later told Russell that Monica's departure would be the signal for them all to go. This state of affairs went on for several days, until Russell saw that the Sisters were not to be bullied, and he somehow convinced the bishop to let the matter drop for the time being. So Monica stayed.

The case of Calasanctius, the General Assistant, is astonishing. She had returned to Adelaide from New Zealand with the full approval of her Mother General. On April 8 the bishop assembled the Sisters, and referring to "*Miss Howley*, running about the country making mischief and sowing discord", announced that he had sent her out of the diocese and had not given her permission to return. Whatever his purpose in insisting that Calasanctius be in the first New Zealand group, he had said nothing about not wanting her in the diocese, much less about expelling her under pain of refusal of the sacraments if she returned.

In the course of time, Mary felt she was within her rights in sending her Assistant back to South Australia. She knew, and the Institute's enemies knew, that she was sending back a strong upholder of the Constitutions. "There is one thing that I feel sure of," Bernardine told her, "and that is that your enemies are also Sister Calasanctius', and that is the reason that they dread her coming home. They know that she would defend you." The bishop reacted with a circular to every priest, forbidding them to give Calasanctius the sacraments. It was Annette who braved his wrath, and by powerful and passionate pleading eventually won Calasanctius the right to receive the Eucharist.

A week after the Sisters had been told they would not be received in Sydney, and after Moran had assured them that this was not true, he received a letter from Russell asking him not to receive them. The Archdeacon also tried to enlist the support of Bishop Murray of Maitland in ensuring a Sydney boycott. Moran not only refused the request, but made it clear to the Adelaide authorities that although it was not any business of his "to inquire what may have been his Lordship's motives", he was not impressed by what was going on there:

> Well I frankly say that I will admit them. I would be unfaithful to the duty imposed upon me by the Holy See were I to prejudice its decision by refusing to receive them. My duty to the Holy See requires me in dealing with any Sisters who may come to Sydney to completely ignore any new regulations that his Lordship may have made.

Mary received many appeals for help from distressed Sisters. Scholastica's clearly came from the heart:

> Fancy our Institute being on the point of being suppressed. His Lordship said so after our nice retreat. We were all nearly brokenhearted at what he gave out about . . . It's more than we can bear up against much longer. I never knew religious tried beyond their strength until I have witnessed this most terrible of all trials.
>
> Oh dearest Mother, what are we, your faithful ones, to do, or how are we to act? Is it possible we will be driven to destruction after our

long years in religion through the bad members that are in our Institute running with their dreadful lies and tales? Must we all perish through them?

I feel very lonely indeed. I hope in God our awful trials will soon have an end, that we can serve God in peace somewhere or other for it's really too much altogether, dear Mother. I beg of you to take me to you and send me to New Zealand or any place out of this. I am really sick thinking of the state of affairs here.

From her distant exile in Sydney, Mary did what she could to encourage the writers of such letters: "Rome is watching to see how the Sisters behave and is not insensible to their suffering. Courage, then, and pray." In time, she reminded them, those who have been patient won't be sorry. They had the right to protest, but it should be done humbly and quietly. At the same time she firmly disowned anyone who said, "Go with the stronger party; there is no use in struggling more for Central Government." After a time she adopted a policy of writing only to Monica. This seemed strange to them, but she explained on October 16: "You can now say that I have not sought to attach you to myself."

She wrote confidently to Monica on April 21, when she had received strong assurance that what Reynolds was doing was illegal: "Rome is very jealous of its authority, and the manner in which it has been set aside in Adelaide will not help the Bishop's cause." Then comes some sound practical advice to the superior on the spot: to keep as quiet as possible, to keep on the schools if you can, and to suffer anything short of consenting to separation. The bishop will be told: "The Sisters may stay with you if they like but if they prefer their Constitutions and cling to their Superior, they can certainly do so."

On a more mundane level, she had earlier had a word of caution for Monica, because the postal officials had assured her that one of her letters to that Sister had been opened illegally and in some way detained in Adelaide. "Mind who posts your letters," she warned, and "notify the postal authorities that your letters are not to be given to anyone but yourself or to your order."

As early as February, Mary revealed something of her personal feelings about all this in a letter to Laurence:

I now feel the effects of years of care and anxiety. It seemed only to require this quarrel with a Bishop I loved to make me *almost* completely break down. I say *almost* for I am trying hard for my Sisters' sake to keep up, but there are times when the effort is too much for me and I break down and am quite helpless. It is so hard to know that many faithful children are suffering and that my hands are tied and I cannot help them, oh, it is very hard.

By mid-April she saw that she could no longer regard the action of the bishop as merely personal injustice to herself, and realised that she would be forsaking her duty to her Sisters and to the Institute if she did not protest strongly and clearly in the right places. She wrote three letters to Rome: to Cardinal Simeoni and Father Bianchi on April 17, and to Dr Campbell on the 22nd. These had substantially the same content, but the message was adapted to each person.

She told Bianchi she was pained at having to write critically about a bishop who was once so kind a friend, but he was now openly setting the Constitutions aside, and she felt the Sisters had endured far more than the justice and charity of Rome would allow if the truth were known. As a prelude to her appeal for support, she made sure Bianchi heard what was being said in Australia about his Constitutions—they were bits of paper of no value, drawn up by someone who knew nothing of what was required in Australia, and not in any way binding either on bishops or Sisters. As the Sisters owed them to his charity in the first place, they now appealed to his charity to protect them.

In her letter to Campbell, Mary began with some personal reflections, as she had become aware that her own character was being blackened and that her bad name was being used as a stick to beat the Institute. Moran had told her the character he had heard of her in Rome, and when the oath of secrecy was lifted in Adelaide she at last came to know what was being said about her there. "They were not honest enough," she said, "to accuse me to my face when I was examined." Then she gave Campbell an outline of what the bishop was saying and threatening. It was his claim that he had authority for what he was doing that most upset the Sisters, as they were divided between fear of abandoning the Constitutions and fear of disobeying a legitimate ruling from Rome if they held out. Mary asked:

Why cannot the Bishops who desire their services work with them in peace according to their Constitutions or do without them if they are not willing to do this.

Does it not seem a cruel injustice that Bishops should expect Sisters to turn from their Rule and Superiors whenever they, the Bishops, wish them to do so.

She began her letter to Simeoni rather solemnly, to let him know that the situation was serious:

> The sufferings I may say persecutions of our Sisters in Adelaide have become so great that I am reluctantly compelled to appeal to Your Eminence's Fatherly protection against the acts of the Bishop.

She gave a sober and factual account of what was happening, reminding the cardinal of the origin of the Constitutions: they "were given to me by the late Cardinal Franchi, together with a letter instructing me how to act". She could have added, "your signature was there too, and if the truth were known you probably drafted the letter". The Bishop of Adelaide now "quite ignores the Constitutions" which he calls mere bits of paper of no value, and claims authority to demand that the Sisters separate from their Superior General. Mary was aware that she was making a strong point, as the cardinal knew only too well that the Constitutions were based on central government, and it was hardly likely that he had issued secret orders to the contrary. She begged him to save the nuns "from a repetition of these terrors".

The Adelaide Sisters meanwhile had prepared their own appeal to Simeoni. It is not only an expression of the way they felt and what they thought, but also a clear statement of the facts and of the juridical issues involved. They have been told by the bishop that the Holy See has authorised alterations in essential parts of the Constitutions it issued in 1874. But having taken perpetual vows under the Rule given by Rome, they wish to retain the form of government they understood they were embracing. Besides, eighteen years of experience "of the vast work of the education and protection of the poor in this great colony" has taught them the benefit of central government. "We have also seen," they concluded, "what our fate would be were this local or Diocesan government forced on us."

During this same year, 1885, the Sisters also prepared a petition for Rome seeking a dispensation from the "two elections" limit, so that Mother Mary could be re-elected at the General Chapter due in 1887. With strong support from New South Wales and New Zealand, the idea of re-election developed into a request that Mary be elected General for life. This petition was sent, but by that time Rome had other plans.

Mary had alerted Simeoni to the fact that even an intelligent man like Moran failed to see that the provisional nature of the Constitutions did not mean that they could be ignored or changed by a bishop. For all the good will he had shown towards the Sisters, he had said that Reynolds was in a manner able to do what he was doing, as the Constitutions were only on approbation. It seems strange that he was not quicker to grasp the issue. He may have been influenced by his personal opinion that the Sisters *would be* better as diocesan, and did not see, until Propaganda spelled it out for him, that they were *in fact* not diocesan.

Mary was nevertheless confident that Moran's integrity, intelligence, and sense of law would win the day, so much so that she hoped the Mother House would be moved to his diocese. She told Bianchi that although Moran did not think the Constitutions were binding, she was sure he would maintain them if advised to do so from Rome. In writing to Campbell, she saw this as a solution of the serious difficulty about the children in Adelaide whom the Sisters did not want to desert. If Rome made sure Moran was properly informed, if the Mother House were shifted to his diocese, and if the Sisters were not forced to stay with any bishop who would not have them on the terms laid down in the Constitutions, Mary believed that Reynolds would yield sooner than let them leave his diocese.

As things turned out, the difficulty was settled in this way. Fortunately for the Institute, Moran was a man who respected law, and Simeoni had, as Secretary of Propaganda in 1874, been officially involved in briefing Sister Mary. He knew that the course she had followed since her return to Australia was exactly the one she had been told to follow. It was a further benefit to the Sisters that Simeoni was personally acquainted not only with their Mother General but also with the Bishop of Adelaide.

Footnote

[1]   Chapter VI of the Constitutions says: "A diocesan bishop cannot change the Constitutions nor can he abrogate or lessen the authority they give to Superiors in matters concerning appointments, visitations, the holding of Chapters and such matters." Chapter III says: "Only the Holy See can remove the Superior General from office or accept her resignation." Yet Bishop Reynolds said: "Mother Mary's authority here has ceased."

TWENTY-SIX

THE THICKETS
OF THE LAW

A New General, A Synod, An Approbation

T he Archbishop of Dublin, Cardinal McCabe, died in February 1885, and when Dr Moran left Sydney for Europe a few months later it was surmised that he would be his successor. There was more to it than rumour, but Anglo-Irish political tensions seem to have influenced the decision finally in favour of another. The Archbishop of Sydney was given a cardinal's hat, and returned to Australia to be the acknowledged leader of the Church there for another twenty-six years.

On his arrival in Sydney in November, Moran's agenda included three items that concern this history. Firstly, his welcome as Australia's first Prince of the Church. This new dignity, together with authority he received from time to time to carry out particular commissions, gave him a status among the bishops which had a significant effect on Josephite history. Secondly, he was soon to preside at the first Australasian Synod of bishops—a synod that issued a decree touching the heart of the Josephite Constitutions. Thirdly, he had to inform Mother Mary of the Cross that she was holding office illegally, and that he was commissioned to appoint an interim Mother General until a successor was elected at Chapter.

A New Mother General

This commission was performed immediately. The Archbishop wrote to Mother Mary on 9 November 1885:

> It is my duty to intimate that the Sacred Congregation holds your last election as Superioress to have been invalid, and from receipt of this note you will be pleased to resign and lay aside all exercise of the office of Superior General.

339

A few days later he consulted with Mary and the members of her council at North Sydney, and on November 16 it was announced that he had appointed Sister Bernard as Superior General.

So began in 1885 the long period of Mother Bernard's Generalship, which would have lasted seventeen years if she had not died after twelve. Her appointment was made and renewed twice by Moran; she was never elected by Chapter. The election of a new Superior General by a Chapter—which Propaganda had said was to be held as soon as possible—did not take place until 1899, after her death. Two Chapters were held during her term of office, but they had no power to elect a Superior.

Although Propaganda was perfectly within its rights in giving Moran this power over the Institute, it was not acting according to the Constitutions but from outside them. When Mary wrote to the Sisters about it, however, it was the Holy See's protection of the Constitutions that she emphasised. The hierarchy had been reminded that the Institute was not diocesan, that it retained a Mother General, and the limit on her term of office as laid down in the Constitutions was to be respected. Mary wrote:

> God is so good to us, we should be so grateful and prove our gratitude by our deeds. The Constitutions for which we have all suffered so much are upheld by Rome.
>
> My last election as Mother General is held to be invalid, and His Eminence was empowered to appoint a temporary M. G. until such time as there could be a fresh General election.
>
> Be then, in love and devotion to your new M. G. what most of you have so long been to me. Try to make her cross as light as possible. Obedience and charity will help you to do this.

In this letter Mary blends a hope that the Sisters will be good daughters of the new Mother General with thankfulness for Rome's protection of the Constitutions. She refers to two future events about which she is quite confident, namely, confirmation of the Rule by the Holy See, and the election of a new Superior at a General Chapter. The first was to come long before the second, though this would have seemed unlikely at the time. She continued:

> Rome, in its wisdom, rules that the last election was invalid and some of you will remember that I thought so too, though another ruled otherwise. How grand for the Constitutions that Rome so strongly upholds them . . . Be of good heart and be one with the Superior God has given you through His Church.
>
> From my heart, dearest ones, I thank God for this decision and

am delighted to be as one of the least children of my new Superior. Shortly after she took office, the new Mother General wrote to Dr Campbell with some important things to say about the prelude to the election of 1881. She had prepared a letter for Cardinal Simeoni, thinking he should know that Mother Mary had herself proposed the twelve-year objection to her own re-election and only acquiesced when the bishop told her that it was groundless. But Mary had entreated her not to send Simeoni this letter, lest it should seem to be questioning the decision. So Bernard thought it her duty at least to alert Dr Campbell to keep his eye on things.

Reynolds wrote one of his catty letters to Kirby about the subject on 2 January 1886. In mentioning Mary's dismissal, he says nothing about the fact that it was his decision that overrode her objection to re-election:

> The object of Propaganda, I dare say, was to let her down easily. It's certainly less painful to all to say "that she was set aside through an informality in her election" than to say she was deposed for drunkness [sic] and misappropriation of funds.

He told of a sinister spirit in Mother Mary's reaction to Propaganda's support of the Constitutions it had issued:

> Well what is the result. She and her party are loud in their cry of victory . . . She at once issued her pastoral as her party call it to all the Sisters in South Australia. It speaks for itself, it shows her spirit. I endorsed a certified copy of it. For obvious reasons I keep the original. It was not intended for my eye, no doubt, but it fell into the hands of a secular, hence to me.

What was this pastoral? It was not the letter written to all the Sisters on November 16. It was a private letter written to Monica in Adelaide a few days previously, containing much of the same matter, except that the name of the new Mother General was not then known. The text of this private letter was presented by Reynolds with changes and omissions of as much as eight lines (signed and certified by him nevertheless as a genuine copy) as a circular letter from the former Mother General rallying a party around her in preparation for re-election. It must have been stolen by somebody close to Monica and given to the bishop. A copy was made with changes appropriate for a circular letter, the greeting "My own dear Sister" appearing as the plural "Sisters", which is maintained where necessary except two or three times where the original slipped through.[1]

The strange thing is that although the falsified text is as harmless and edifying as the original, Reynolds sent it to Kirby as a sample of Mother Mary's spirit as "she sounds the note of revolt and is now canvassing for re-election". She certainly did not conceal from Monica her relief that Rome had maintained the view of the Constitutions it had held from the beginning. But her only reference to the bishop was: "I dare say Dr Reynolds now understands the mistake he made in treating me as he did. I am so sorry for his many troubles and will do all I can to help him." This is a very sympathetic reference to a man who had done great wrong to both the writer and the recipient of this private letter. It was reasonable to say she expected he would understand his mistake, although this was a more sanguine hope than events were to prove. In her real letter to the Sisters she made no reference to the bishop at all, except to say "though another thought otherwise" in referring to her invalid re-election, and very vaguely in mentioning "the past painful ordeal".

The Plenary Council (or Synod) of the hierarchies of Australia and New Zealand assembled in Sydney in November 1885. Moran had invited the bishops to submit topics for consideration, but Robert Dunne of Brisbane was the only one to mention the Sisters of St Joseph. Both the Quinns were dead by this time, and Reynolds evidently said nothing. The Sisters were not mentioned in the printed circular listing themes to be discussed. Propaganda had sent a list of recommended topics, mentioning complaints from religious men and women about bishops encroaching on their rights, and complaints from bishops that religious would not submit to their jurisdiction. This was not just a veiled reference to the Josephites, as there were others, such as the Patrician Brothers, who had the same problem.

The Sisters were well aware that the Synod was going to discuss their status. While experience had taught them that strange things could happen in Australia, they also knew that the Roman authorities, having a more delicate sense of law, were not always impressed by the decisions of ecclesiastical authorities in that distant land. So just after the Synod, but before the decrees were known, Mother Bernard sent the cardinal in Rome a petition, with 175 signatures, begging his protection for the central government of the Institute. The text alluded to the fact that, although the bishops had discussed the matter, it was the business of the Holy See to decide it. The Sisters asked that the protection hitherto given the Constitutions be maintained.

Bernard also wrote a personal letter to the English Cardinal

Howard in Rome, appealing to his kindness and his sense of justice. She referred to "the late lamented Archbishop Vaughan, who upheld Central Government and greatly encouraged our Mother. For his sake, too, we hope your Eminence will do all you can for us." This was done clearly at the suggestion of the former Mother General, who knew Howard personally and had been advised by him in England in 1873 to ask Vaughan to do what he could for the interests of the Institute when he went to Rome.

Monica also wrote to Simeoni begging him to preserve the unity of the Institute. Her letter showed not only that she had her preferences but that she understood the juridical situation. The Sisters, she pointed out, had made perpetual vows under the impression that the form of government they accepted was to continue. Some of the bishops now wished to have the Institute broken up into diocesan congregations. In a matter of such vital importance she trusted she would be pardoned for appealing again on behalf of all the Sisters before the final decision was made.

When the decrees of the Synod became known, it was clear that the concern of the Sisters had been justified. The bishops had voted that they should be a diocesan institute. Decree 99 read:

> With regard to the Congregation which is called Sisters of St Joseph of the Sacred Heart, the Bishops think fit that the Convents or Religious Houses in each Diocese should be subject to their respective Ordinaries, like the Sisters of Mercy.

The voting for this decision was 14–3. There were eighteen bishops present, no absentees, so one did not vote. It is more than likely for several reasons, but not certain, that the presiding Cardinal Moran did not vote. It will probably never be known for certain who the three negatives voters were. From what we know of the men concerned, we might have expected the number to be four. Mary had written to Monica in April: "We have Bishops Torreggiani, Cani, Luck and Redwood for us at the Synod, and the Archbishop will be with us too if the Mother House be here and Rome expresses the slightest wish on the matter." Yet only three votes favoured central government. It would be surprising indeed if Torreggiani was not one of them, but of the other three any one could possibly have voted the other way in the circumstances. In any case all four remained supporters of the Institute.

Writing to Kirby shortly after the Synod, Bishop Murray gave him a glowing account of the harmony that prevailed there:

If the Pope himself were present presiding over our deliberations there could not prevail greater union, accord and charity than prevailed amongst us. I have reason to know that this union has astonished all non-Catholics in this country, while it has been a source of the greatest edification to our Catholic flocks.

But there are two letters in the archives of Propaganda that do not reflect this union and accord at all. They are from the Marist Dr Redwood of Wellington and the Benedictine Dr Luck of Auckland, both from New Zealand, both Religious, and both non-Irish. Neither touches directly on the Josephite question, but both speak very strongly about the antagonism towards religious orders and the pro-Irish bias of the Irish bishops at the Synod. They also pointed to Murray, the very man who had written so glowingly to Rome about harmony, as "the soul of the conspiracy". Murray did not have direct dealings with Mother Mary, but his shadow was behind those who did, especially his first cousins the Quinns and later Reynolds. There were apparently some fiery scenes during discussions about choosing the Metropolitan See of New Zealand and nominating a bishop for Christchurch. The Marist Bishop of Wellington was particularly incensed that Monsignor Moran of Dunedin spoke so disparagingly and so untruthfully of the contribution of the Marists to the Church in New Zealand. These letters of Redwood and Luck make it unlikely that they would have voted with the Irish bishops on any controverted topic involving a religious order.

In a long letter Mary wrote to her sister Annie during the synod, she spoke of common friends among the clergy and others, and relayed the news of what was happening about the Institute. A kindly and charitable view of everybody, forgiving those who have injured her, is blended with a practical wisdom. As Annie has evidently voiced some sharp views about the clergy and religious and all their goings-on, Mary does her best to broaden her sister's spiritual and historical outlook:

> There is no Order in the Church doing any good that has not been so tried, and often by some of God's greatest servants. See how the work of Teresa was persecuted, how she and St John of the Cross suffered, and oh, ever so many more . . . Our many trials have done us great good and serve to strengthen us.

Knowing that Annie is a chatterbox, Mary warns her to watch her tongue: "Know nothing when speaking to priests etc. , but that Rome upholds the Institute—and the Cardinal is our friend. Be kind to Dr

Reynolds if you meet him, but allude to nothing." But in addition to all this, the letter contains an unexpected piece of news—Reynolds actually came to see the Josephites, and spoke as if nothing had broken their friendship. Not only that, but Russell turned up too. Mary was convinced that Moran had put the pressure of Christian charity on both. She reflected on Reynolds to Annie: "From all I know he is much to be pitied, and has very few friends. His will is good, but his health makes him hasty and irritable, and he has not the best of advisers near him." In spite of the visit, the bishop's subsequent bitterness was to show that his attitude had not changed.

Propaganda Rejects Decree 99

It was sixteen months later, in March 1887, that the decrees of the Synod were considered by the Congregation of Propaganda. Cardinal Luigi Serafini presented the background to Decree 99 in no. 19 of his summary. The facts are there, though the chronological order is at times confused. He opened with the statement that the Institute of the Sisters of St Joseph "was established as a non-diocesan Institute, that is, with a Superior who has authority over the houses in various dioceses". The unsatisfactory nature of the first text of the Rule meant that it had to be amended, and while it was awaiting approval there came the troubles with the Bishop of Adelaide, the Visitation, and the deposing of the Superior General. Cardinal Moran had been asked by Propaganda to investigate these matters and sent back his report. The bishops in Synod have now "for no known reason" decreed that the Institute "would cease to have a Superior General and that each diocese would have its own independent Superior subject to the authority of the Ordinary". The strong pleas of the Sisters for the retention of central government were noted. Then the question was put:

> Whether the Decree 99 by which the Institute of the Sisters of St Joseph is declared diocesan with an autonomous Superior subject to the Ordinary of each diocese, should be approved.

Their Eminences replied:

> Let there be a special position and let Decree 99 be deleted.

Some months later Mary wrote to Laurence about the protection thus given to the Institute, adding some good advice to pass on to the Sisters in Adelaide:

> The Bishops have not the settlement of our affairs . . . Let us only do our work humbly and quietly, and instead of impatiently wanting to

hurry things, quietly await God's own time, and pray with all our hearts that His Will alone be done.

But the matter was by no means settled, as is clear from a letter Mary wrote to Campbell some weeks later, asking him to continue his interest, as bishops were still writing against the Institute in an attempt to swing the final decision against its unity.

So the months passed. The Sisters tried to do their work as well as they could, in Adelaide in spite of the obstacles placed in the way of their obedience to legitimate superiors, and everywhere with uncertainty about the future. Eventually their patience and fidelity were rewarded late in 1888. While Moran was on another visit to Rome in the middle of the year, he received the final decision of the Holy See confirming the central government of the Institute of St Joseph. On his return to Sydney he read it to the Sisters on December 1.

There were three points that interested them. The chief one was that they were confirmed as an Institute with central government. In addition, the Mother House was now to be in Sydney. Moreover, Mother Bernard was to remain in office as Mother General for a further ten years. The Decree read as follows:

1. That (whilst reserving to the Apostolic See the approval of the Constitutions of the aforesaid Sisters) the said Institute be erected into a Regular Congregation having the Mother House in Sydney.

2. That in the event of the Bishops who have communities of the aforesaid Sisters in their Dioceses being unwilling to have such Houses connected with the Mother House in Sydney, it shall be lawful for those Bishops to constitute their Houses as a Diocesan Institute, in which case however, it shall be permitted to the Sisters who are at present in the said communities, either to remain in the Diocesan Institute or to proceed to the Mother House.

3. That in regard to the communities which in union with the Mother House in Sydney constitute the Regular Congregation, the Actual Superior General shall continue in office for ten years from the date of the present decree; the election of Superior General shall thereafter be made by the chapter as laid down in the Constitutions.

4. That the Diocesan Institutes which are distinct from the Regular Congregation shall make some alterations in the Habit and in the Rule, and shall be approved by their respective Bishops.

The document is dated the 25th day of July, and signed by John Cardinal Simeoni and by the Secretary. It notes that the papal consent was given at an audience on the 15th day of July.

Annie, Mary and Donald (c. 1898).

Mary a few years before her stroke.

Patrick Francis Cardinal Moran, Archbishop of Sydney
(1884–1911).

Mother Bernard Walsh, second Superior General of the Sisters of St Joseph (1885–1898).

Bishop Eleazar Torreggiani, Bishop of Armidale
(1879–1904).

Julian Tenison Woods (c. late 1870s).

Right: *Fr Woods in the 1880s, towards the end of his life.*

Below: *St Joseph's Convent, Mount Street, North Sydney (c. 1905).*

ST JOSEPH'S CONVENT. NORTH SYDNEY

Mary (c. 1892) recovering from severe illness in Victoria.

385

good and faithful Sisters, but had
a plan to propose which I hoped
would clear them up and be for
the general good. However the
election was unanimous, and
the Cardinal was graciously pleased.
He complimented me upon it, and
said many kind things. Dr.
Sharon told some of the Sisters afterwards that he had never seen any
thing like it, and that he had
been at many elections. In every
way in their power the Sisters have
proved to the Cardinal their perfect
trust in me. Matters that in
the previous two Chapters they
in G. Chapter took into their own
hands, in this they decided to
leave entirely to the judgment of
the M.G. & her Council. saying
they wished in this manner to
show their perfect trust. God
draw me. I will not fear them
...

Mary (in the wheelchair) about six months after her stroke; she is at Remuera, New Zealand, with a group of the sisters, her nurse, and her sister Annie (seated in front).

Another photo of Mother Mary after the stroke of May 1902.

With her right hand paralysed, Mary used her rheumatic left hand to write this letter to her brother Donald on 15 June 1903. She is happy that her Life of Father Woods has been completed.

*Mrs Joanna Barr Smith, Mary's good friend and benefactor;
though not a Catholic, Mrs Barr Smith contributed to the
Sisters' charitable undertakings over a long period,
right up to the last years of Mary's life.*

Mary, c. 1908.

Above: Mary, with Donald and Annie, about a year before her death.

Below: The old novitiate and memorial chapel at Mount Street, North Sydney, site of Mary MacKillop's grave.

Above: *The final resting place*.

Below: *The inscription on Mother Mary's grave*.

In telling Mother Bernard to be in Sydney to receive this decree, Cardinal Moran did not tell her its contents, only "that the Holy See has wished to reconcile the desires of the Sisters and the opinions of the Bishops". This phrasing was not quite fair. It seemed to be setting the Sisters up against the bishops, whereas it was the bishops who had set themselves up against the directives of the Holy See. "The desires of the Sisters" were exactly what the Holy See had told them to observe in 1874. However, not all the bishops disagreed with this thinking. Shortly afterward Torreggiani wrote a most encouraging letter to Mary, congratulating her on the success of her cause, and remarking, "St Joseph is more powerful than some people thought." Then he added some colour: "I did not call to see you and your Sisters when I was in Sydney lately to avoid remarks of partisanship, especially under the existing circumstances. Feelings run high."

Mary wrote to the Sisters on December 3, full of joy that the Institute had been erected into a Regular Congregation, "a privilege I scarcely hoped to live to see". She reminded them that nobody could be forced either to leave the unity of the Institute or to remain in it. "Those who are dissatisfied are now free to go, and in the name of peace and charity I hope they will do so." She also wrote to Reynolds, now an archbishop:

> I have often wished to write to you but had not courage until today. Cruel and mischievous enemies of yours and mine have come between us. There have been times when I have felt most keenly and I fear for the moment resented things I have heard you said about me . . . but I always wished you well and longed at any personal sacrifice to assist rather than to cause you any personal annoyance.

Asking his forgiveness for anything in which she had pained or disappointed him, and recalling his kindness and friendship in the early days, she pleaded with him to be a friend of the Institute and a good Father to the Sisters:

> I dearly love South Australia and wish it every blessing. I hope to live to see its Archbishop and the Sisters of St Joseph working heart and soul for the one great cause, the one supporting and encouraging the children of the Congregation who are working under his Fatherly care and the other repaying with grateful affection the kindness bestowed upon them.

Mary MacKillop could hardly have extended a more gracious hand of reconciliation to Archbishop Reynolds than this beautiful expression of humility and charity, but it was to no avail. Writing to his friend Kirby, Reynolds described the letter as insolent.

The Role of Cardinal Moran

As with the earlier decision of Propaganda that Mother Mary should stand down as Mother General, it would be strange to think that the decision to extend Mother Bernard's term for ten years was made without consulting Cardinal Moran. He had been entrusted with the care of the affair in Australia, he was in Rome at the time the decree was issued, and he brought it back to Sydney five months later. It seems reasonable to suppose that it was he who suggested the idea. Certainly if he had advised that the Josephites should be allowed to elect their Superior General according to their Constitutions, it would be hard to imagine Propaganda ignoring him.

Besides, there is in the Roman archives an earlier draft of the decree, subscribed June 26 and bearing the note that it received papal approval on July 15. But that was not the version that Moran took back to Sydney. By July 25 something for which no documentary evidence is available led to the insertion of an extra clause—the one extending Bernard's term for ten years. Then in 1897, towards the completion of the ten years, Propaganda empowered Moran to extend her term of office until the next Chapter in 1902. There had been two General Chapters in the meantime (in 1889 and 1896) at neither of which could the Sisters exercise their right to elect their Superior General. It was not as if Bernard were a great success in the office, because it was not long before it became evident that it was too much for her.

The reasons behind the decision were of course never stated, but it seems that Moran judged that the best interests of the Church in Australia would be served by his action. It was a fact that Mother Mary's performance of her duty was the irritant that had upset the bishops who wanted to impose their own Rule on the Sisters. Mother Bernard was a more pliant character; she was also Irish, and this would do something to assuage the nationalism of the bishops which was criticised so truculently by Redwood and Luck after the Synod. Mother Mary told the Sisters in 1885:

> Mother Bernard's appointment as Superior General is also a wise act on the part of the Holy See. She is popular with the Bishops for more reasons than one, and I am not; I firmly believe that those who have been against us hitherto will now unite.

Moran knew as well as anybody that if the Sisters had been allowed to elect their Mother General they would have chosen Mary, and he apparently judged that this would be an unnecessary disturbance of the peace among the bishops (though since Reynolds died in 1893 the 1897 extension could not have been made to placate him). He could also have been of the opinion that it would be a better thing for Mary herself, and who is to say he was wrong? Still, it was a great cross for the Sisters that they did not have a Mother General of their choice.

Other Bishops

Among the questions discussed at the Synod in 1885 was the creation of new dioceses in Australia and New Zealand. The Holy See took cognisance of what was recommended, and eventually made the decisions in 1887. There were three that concern this history. On May 10 Adelaide was made an Archdiocese, with territory including all South Australia and the Northern Territory. The town of Port Augusta, 186 miles north of Adelaide, was named as a new see. On May 13 Father John O'Reily, an Irishman in Fremantle, Western Australia, was nominated as first bishop, and on May 15 Bishop Reynolds was declared the first Archbishop of Adelaide.

The birth of the new diocese was not without travail. There was much discussion between Moran, Reynolds and O'Reily about the boundaries and the debts. As delineated, the diocese of Port Augusta would take from Adelaide 9000 (others say less) of the people and £17,000 of the debt. Moran suggested that these might be adjusted to 15,000 people and not more than £15,000 of the debt. Reynolds was indignant at the suggestion, and resented what seemed to be a conspiracy between the other two. Although he had previously accepted, O'Reily wrote to Rome shortly afterwards declining the appointment. He did this after consulting men well versed in Church affairs, in view of his very limited business experience and his fear that he lacked the ability to administer a diocese with such a small and impoverished flock and such a large debt. The effect of this letter was twofold—the Holy See ordered another investigation into Adelaide finances, and it refused to accept O'Reily's resignation. So Murray went to Adelaide to conduct the enquiry, and O'Reily was consecrated in Sydney in May 1888.

Although his problems were so daunting, the new bishop set about his duties of spiritual leadership and financial administration with great faith and energy. In time he solved not only Port Augusta's difficulties, but also those of Adelaide when he succeeded Reynolds in that see in January 1895. He was always a kindly and helpful friend to the Josephites, and it seems that his influence made Reynolds somewhat more tractable.

In the meantime, however, the Archbishop of Adelaide continued to be antagonistic. He made the financial question the pretext for refusing to come to a decision about the Institute. After the Roman decree of 1888 it was necessary for each bishop to declare whether he was prepared to accept the authority of a Mother General in his diocese. The Sisters would then know whether they had a decision to make about remaining in his territory. Reynolds appeared to want the Mother General to get out and to take the Adelaide debt with her, but to leave her Sisters behind. Mother Bernard wrote to him in distress:

> I entreat Your Grace to consider my position and to give me the answer I beg from your hands. Do you agree to the Central Government? Will you let the Sisters in your Archdiocese remain united with the Mother House here, or do you insist upon having a diocesan community?

It is clear that Moran was guiding the Sisters in handling the problem with the Archbishop. He was himself constrained to write to Reynolds on 25 February 1889 reminding him that he was the only bishop who had so far failed to indicate his decision to the Mother General: "I have told her it is her duty to ask Your Grace's decision, and in accordance with the Decree of Propaganda she has a strict right to such a decision."

Reynolds did not reply to the question, but treated Moran instead to another diatribe against the Sisters. The cardinal calmly pointed out that the contents of this latest letter were not relevant, and repeated the question with a hint that it would be more convenient if His Grace answered it:

> It appears to me that you leave the question in *statu quo*, and I do not see any grounds on which I can ask M. Bernard to alter the present arrangements. There are two points, however, on which there appears to be some misunderstanding.
>
> 1. Should Your Grace constitute the Sisters of St Joseph as a Diocesan Institute, the property belonging to the Sisters would be handed over to the local Superiors and other Sisters whom Your Grace shall appoint.
>
> 2. I have asked for information regarding the sums collected by the Sisters deputed with your sanction to collect. I have been told

that the sums collected were handed to Your Grace, though it would appear from your letter that this fact was overlooked by Your Grace.

I beg Your Grace to rest assured that if I appear to differ from your views in the present matter it is solely on Canon Law principles and not on the question of expediency regarding the debt itself. Neither have I the slightest bias for either arrangement regarding the communities in the Diocese of Adelaide which Your Grace may decide upon. But I fear that the Holy See will regard it as a slight upon the authoritative Decree relating to the Sisters if you persist in declining to adopt either of the courses set forth in the Decree.

Reynolds really had only one choice, because if he decided against central government he would have no Sisters. But it was months before he ultimately chose the lesser of two evils. The Sisters could stay.

As well as confirming the Institute of St Joseph centred on the Mother House, the 1888 decree contained a provision that Josephites who wished to belong to diocesan congregations were free to do so. Bishops were entitled to have whichever type they preferred in their dioceses. But the Sisters also had freedom of choice, and nobody was obliged to belong to the Mother House or to withdraw from it but by her own choosing.

The law was put to the test in two places—in Wilcannia (a diocese cut off from the western part of Bathurst) and in Perth on the other side of the continent. Each case illustrated the point that had been at issue in Bathurst and Brisbane in earlier days, namely that a Sister who had taken vows under one Rule could not be treated as if she had vowed obedience to a different authority. Only by a dispensation and a new profession could that be done.

The first bishop of the diocese of Wilcannia was John Dunne, consecrated in August 1887. When the decree on the Sisters of St Joseph was published late the following year, he wrote from Broken Hill to Bishop Murray at Maitland saying that he was not clear about the significance of the Roman ruling: "Will it be necessary," he asked, "to consult the Sisters in the Diocese as to their option?" It seems that he did not do so, as a letter written in 1905 by Aquin, one of these Sisters, tells how in 1901 they saw the Maitland Rule: "It was not until we read the same we saw we were at liberty to withdraw to the Mother House, if it were not agreeable to us to accept changes which would distinguish us as diocesan." Yet in his decree erecting a diocesan congregation in 1899 Dunne had said, "after the receipt of the Decree

... having notified to the Sisters their liberty to join the Congregation in Sydney".

But Dunne agreed to the amalgamation in December 1901 because the Sisters desired it strongly, and the Mother House continued to maintain schools in the diocese to his satisfaction. Aquin ended her days with the Sisters of the Mother House.

The Perth Josephites had a different history. In one way it was an exact parallel to what happened in Perthville (Bathurst) in 1876. The first ones went there in 1887 from Adelaide, and others followed from Sydney. But in 1889 all except one returned to Adelaide when Bishop Gibney declared them diocesan. He wanted his own novitiate, like Matthew Quinn in Bathurst, and when this was delayed he decided that the Perth Sisters were no longer to be under the Mother House. He imagined like Quinn that the Sisters would simply become diocesan by his decision, but they all departed except one, Ursula Tynan.

The Sisters appealed to Moran for help. When he wrote to the bishop on their behalf, he said exactly what Mary had been saying all the years she was Sister Guardian and Mother General. It was what had caused her all the trouble with the Quinns and later with Reynolds. Moran pointed out that Gibney would have to make a fresh start, as the Sisters of St Joseph in his diocese had no more power to withdraw themselves from the authority of the Mother General than the Jesuits in Sydney had to separate from their Provincial. His Lordship was free to erect any diocesan institute he might wish, but the Josephites could no more be part of it than the Sisters of Charity could. A Sister would err in promising to join, and she would err in putting such a promise into effect.

Gibney insisted on his right to institute diocesan Sisters even more than a year after the publication of the decree, and in this, of course, he was quite justified. But he showed that he did not really grasp what Moran was saying, when he replied in relation to Ursula's case:

> I can produce two witnesses as well as the Sisters who lived with her to show that *she* did not unite with the Mother House but kept her disposition unfettered so as to serve the Diocese in the manner God's Providence would dispose.

He did not appreciate the fact that Ursula *already* had vows binding her to the Mother General. Sisters with vows were not "unfettered", and Bishop Gibney was not an instrument of divine Providence free to make dispositions contrary to vows already binding Ursula to the Mother House.

But if a bishop could be so confused about the binding power of vows, it is hardly surprising that Ursula saw no difficulty in remaining, any more than Hyacinth did in Bathurst under Bishop Quinn. Before her death, however, Ursula advised the Sisters to amalgamate, and this is what they did under the next bishop, Dr Clune. John O'Reily, now Archbishop of Adelaide, cordially endorsed the proposal with his usual calm wisdom, writing to Clune in May 1911 that it would be good for the Sisters, good for their work, and good for religion.

Footnote

[1] What she wrote to Monica at the end was: "God bless my darling Sisters and reward them for their constant love." The changed version reads, very strangely: "God bless you my darling Sisters and reward them for their constant love."

In one omitted section Mary told Monica that Cardinal Moran had told her not to sign a paper by which Bishop Reynolds was trying to get her to make herself responsible for the debt.

PART IX

Mother Mary's
Affairs
1884–1898

TWENTY-SEVEN

DAUGHTER, SISTER, AND FRIEND

O ver the years Mary had seen her mother from time to time, and had kept in touch by letter. She carefully avoided any mention of the Institute's problems, except when false rumours had to be corrected or when she thought it wise to warn relatives to be discreet. "Be as reserved as possible," she wrote once, "when mentioning our affairs or speaking of our dealings with the Bishops and Priests. Uncle Peter will, I am sure, understand this." What she told her mother was positive and encouraging—news about the work of the schools, together with little pieces of information about Sisters and other people they both knew.

Just after the withdrawal from Queensland, she wrote to Flora about the first foundation of the Josephites in Sydney. She said much about what people were doing for the Institute, but nothing against Bishop Quinn and no details of the major crisis that had been preoccupying her for months. She made no secret of the anguish it all caused her, reflecting sadly that the work had to be left, but she was full of praise for the goodness of the Brisbane people. She wrote of old friends in Sydney, Mrs Finn from Portland days, and Dean Kenny who "spoke so much of old times, of Papa, of yourself etc., and of a visit he had in Geelong from Uncle Peter and Aunt when they were newly married".

The letters always contain greetings and remembrances to relations and friends, and mention of matters of family interest: "We have so many anniversaries this month", she wrote in December 1883, "but I shall have Masses on each please God." John, Papa, Maggie and Lexie had all died in the month of December. When Mary wrote this, Lexie's first anniversary was three weeks away. Her death had taken them by surprise, no one more so—Mary imagined— than Donald, who had departed for studies in Europe not long before.

She wrote him a long letter full of gentle humanity and deep faith:

> I saw our dear one on the way here. She was then very weak and
> propped up in her bed by pillows . . . Most of what we said was about
> you . . . She had no desire but to do as God willed. I feel that our
> darling Sister is with God, and that this earth did not deserve to hold
> one so good.

She concluded with something Donald would also have reflected on:
"There are only three now left out of eight."

Six months later, on the eve of the terrible events that overtook
her in Adelaide in mid-1883, Mary wrote to Donald again about
family matters, reminding him how much his letters meant to Flora.
Whether or not she adverted to the irony of it, she mentioned that
the Good Shepherd Sisters had sent a copy of their little printed
account of Lexie's life and last hours to the Duck Ponds Mrs
MacKillop, Aunt Julia, when it was meant for Flora.

Donald had been at his studies in Europe, at first at Innsbruck and
later in St Beuno's, Wales. Anton Anderledy, Mary's helpful friend
of 1873–74, still at Fiesole and now Vicar General of the Jesuits with
right of succession, wrote to her late in 1883. He referred to the
Institute's troubles, but it is not clear how much he really knew of
what had happened:

> I received your kind letter by your dear brother, who called at Fiesole
> in 1882. He is a very good, religious man, and I am happy to have
> made his acquaintance. Now he is doing well at Innsbruck, and he
> shows a solid virtue and a firm character. I trust he will become a very
> zealous Missionary and do a great deal of good in Australia. . . . Your
> Congregation is going on, I hope, increasing in number and virtue,
> and you will, after so many difficulties and persecutions, have the
> happiness of seeing a great deal of good being done by your Sisters.
> Pray, remember me in your prayers, and not only me but especially
> our whole Society. . . A. M. Anderledy S. J.[1]

Nearly a year after her expulsion from Adelaide, Mary wrote to
Donald about what had been happening, obviously recalling
conversations they had held together. Crosses—God's "presents"—
are the main topic. She mentioned where they come from—"some
whom I have loved most. Dr Reynolds and I are no longer as we were."
But there is not a word against anybody. Crosses are from God, and
he draws good from them, but they are often hard to understand. An
added sorrow was "our noble Archbishop's death. The Institute lost
its most powerful earthly friend in him".

When she arrived in Sydney after experiencing the surprising unkindness of Dr Reynolds in Adelaide, Mary wrote to her mother about the kindness of the people who surrounded her in Sydney, like Dean Kenny. "Just fancy," she wrote, "the dear old Father proposes giving up his house to us and retiring into an old cottage on the grounds." There is not a word about Adelaide. The Sisters are toiling along happily and their schools are doing well. Not only are they in great demand around Sydney and in Armidale, but pressing appeals are coming from New Zealand too. The Bishop of Auckland is using every inducement to make her go over and see for herself what is to be done. In Sydney Archbishop Moran is very kind and encouraging, and Dr Cani, now Bishop of Rockhampton, is no longer the Dr Cani of 1870. "He made for us at once when he arrived on Sunday," she wrote in February 1885, and they chatted over many things:

> He reminded me that I was "Mary of the Cross" and asked need I wonder. Dear Mamma, Dr Cani is a saint—he put fresh heart into me. I think he will come out and stay a night at the Dean's (who told me to invite him) and thus say Mass for us in the morning.

Mary's favourite uncle, her mother's brother Donald MacDonald, had a series of strokes and was taken by his wife Eliza to live in Sydney in 1884. Mary kept her brother Donald informed of what was happening. At one stage Uncle Donald had lost his memory and "only knew those who were about him and as long as they were in his sight . . . he had no idea of anything relating to his soul . . . he had no thought about us, not even of his absent children no more than if we had never been." Mary encouraged them to bring him over to Sydney. There, she said:

> To our great joy he knew us all, and when a little later he was speaking to me, he began to cry saying he did not know what had come over him, that he could not say his prayers, that he forgot everything. Next day he attended Mass with the greatest devotion and has been getting better ever since. His affection for me is most touching.

Now that Uncle Donald lived in Sydney, Mary was able to keep her mother up to date with news about him. He and Eliza were now in a little cottage with a lovely view, quite close to Mary's convent, and he was quite delighted. When he finally died on 8 July 1887, Father Woods, sensitive to the significance of the occasion for the MacKillop family, broke his silence to write Mary an extraordinary tribute to her beloved uncle: "A kind husband and a good son, with certainly the kindest heart I have ever met in my intercourse with the world."

Meanwhile, on 20 September 1885, the younger Donald had been ordained priest in Wales. The Father Provincial was waiting on his knees for a blessing while the newly ordained penned his first blessing to his dear ones in Australia. He wrote to Mary: "You have your long-cherished wish. I am a Priest of the Society of Jesus. What a fine cry you will have over this!" "I can scarcely realise the joyful news," Mary told Annie, "May God be praised for it all." They were all looking forward to attending his Masses in Australia.

Flora was never to see her priest son. In the March of the following year she set out for Sydney to help with the bazaar, but she never arrived. On May 30 her ship, the *Lyeemoon*, was wrecked not far off the coast at Green Cape, near Eden in southern New South Wales, with the loss of sixty lives. Flora was one of the victims. When Mary heard the news, she went to the Oratory and spent two hours on her knees. She wrote to Annie on June 1:

> My dearest Annie, God help us all. The hand of God is heavy upon us, but His Holy Will must be done. Oh Annie I had so yearned to see her again and all the Sisters were planning to make her visit a bright and happy one. Poor, dear, long-suffering Mamma.

Her letter to Donald on 17 June 1886 is a beautiful document, full of humanity, faith, and sensitive love:

> My dearest brother, How can I write. You must ere this have heard from Adelaide of our sad, our terrible loss. Everything was too bewildering at first, then the efforts to recover the dear remains, the funeral, and then came the reaction. Between all, you, for whom my heart ached, have been seemingly neglected by me. But don't think so, dear Donald. Our darling unselfish Mother true to her character to the last, has gone to receive her well-earned reward.
>
> I cannot now attempt to describe the dismay with which I heard the sad news. It was too terrible to be true, but its truth was too soon proved. Fortunately John was here and he went down. He found the dear remains awaiting him. Hers was the only body picked up by the pilot boat, and the only body found anywhere without being injured by either the rocks or the sharks. The scapular she had so loved was on her neck. How it remained on seems miraculous, and is I believe. John says she looked as if she were asleep.

Archbishop Goold, who had been bishop in Melbourne since 1848, died a week after Mamma, and for Mary MacKillop these two deaths would have been an occasion to relive her earliest memories. They would have reminded her vividly that the things that are seen are temporal, the things that are not seen are eternal. Of her family of ten, now only she and Annie and Donald survived.

Comforter of the Afflicted

Mary had written to Donald when Lexie died in 1882:

> Ah Donald, charity to the afflicted must be dear to the Heart of Him
> who knew so well how to sorrow with those He loved. I hope we shall
> ever bear this in mind.

She certainly remembered her own advice and observed it
faithfully. "She could not do too much for the Sisters and for the
families of those who were bereaved," said Mechtilde. By her presence
or by the written word she extended a transparent personal sympathy
wherever she heard of grief. She wrote many a letter breathing
Christian faith and hope on the occasion of a death in the family of
some Sister or other friend:

> From my heart I sympathize with you in your great sorrow, and wish
> that I could relieve it. It was indeed hard that you should not have
> had the comfort of seeing your poor Father in his last moments. But
> a Heavenly Father willed that you should have this trial—take it
> therefore in love from His hand.

When the mother of two Josephites died at the very time one of these
daughters was dying, Mary wrote to the other sister:

> Dearest Sister, do not fret. None of us live for this world. We know
> that we have been created for a better one. Your dear mother has, I
> trust, made a bright exchange. Her sorrows and cares are now over
> and in the bosom of her God. She blesses the day that she gave up her
> two children to His Service . . .
>
> Should you not rejoice that your Divine Spouse has so favoured
> your young sister. We shall miss her—yes, I cannot tell how much we
> shall do so here—she has endeared herself to all—but blessed be
> God's Holy Will.

At times Mary was the one who had to break the news of the death of
a parent to a distant Sister. She wrote to Sister M. Lucian Brosnahan
in New Zealand:

> My dearest Child, it has pleased our good God to end your good
> Mother's sufferings, and to take her to Himself. Hers indeed has been
> the death of a saint, so you, my child, while you naturally must grieve
> for her, cannot but thank God for all He has done for her.

A special case was the death of Mrs Howley, the mother of
Calasanctius and Andrea, two of the early Josephite stalwarts. Mary
wrote to Andrea in August 1891:

> You have all lost a good mother, one of whose memory you may justly
> be proud. . . Surely, if ever a woman deserved a reward, she did. And

most certainly she obtained it. Naturally you must grieve at your loss
but the thought of her much greater gain must console you for all.
Some of these letters are quite long, like the one of over a thousand
words to Sister Benedict on 4 November 1892:

I am writing this in the Oratory near the holy remains of your dear
Mother. She looks so sweetly peaceful and pretty one can hardly
imagine that she is anything but sleeping... You must not grieve too
much. It would not be natural if you did not feel your poor Mother's
death, but there is much attending it to give you great consolation.

Aware of the importance of detail, she told Benedict about a lot of
things that happened in her mother's last hours, recalled words that
were said, and spoke of the quiet way death had finally come. "Poor
dear Mrs Hickey was a friend to your Mother," she said, "no daughter
could have done more for her, nor in a more loving manner." Then
she turned to the funeral arrangements, speaking of the exact location
of the grave, which ones were close by—"Dean Kenny's is the nearest
to hers"—the Mass that was being planned, who would be there,
which priests, what altar boys (even their names, Arthur and Dick),
which buggies the mourners would be travelling in (such as the
neighbour Mr Jenkins and Mr Murphy the grocer). It is the letter of
one who not only wishes to do something for an absent daughter, but
who knows just what to say, and realises the importance of little
things: "We have your dear mother's rings and I shall myself cut off a
little hair for you before we put the lid on the coffin."

When a family suffered the loss of a small child, Mary must have
thought of little Alick. She hastened to comfort the parents:

My dear Mr O'Brien,

I am so grieved to hear of the death of your dear little boy, and beg
that you will accept my deepest sympathy with Mrs O'Brien and
yourself in your affliction. Great as your mutual sorrow must be, for it
is always hard to lose a loved child, you will both, I trust, find
consolation in bowing to the will of God. He gave the dear little one
to you, and for some wise but hidden motive, He has taken him from
you again.

Mary had lost both her mother and a grandfather by drowning, so she
could write with genuine feeling when a Mr Casey was drowned:

My dear Mrs Casey, Words cannot express the deep sympathy I have
for you and yours in your present great sorrow. God alone can comfort
you and I pray that He will do so. For some mysterious reason He has
permitted this great affliction but as He is a just and merciful God,
you may be sure that the trial is sent in love... Dear friend, put your

trust in God, and keep up for the sake of those depending upon you.
James Woods and his wife Catherine had given two daughters to the
Josephites. On the occasion of the death of another daughter, Katie,
Mary wrote to her sisters, Mechtilde and Eustelle Woods:

> The news of dear Katie's death came as a great shock to me and from
> my heart I feel for your dear family in this great sorrow . . . I pity her
> poor husband. Tell him that he has my deepest sympathy. Dear bright
> Katie. I had so hoped to see her once more but she is better off for I
> am sure she loved God and submitted herself to His Holy Will. You
> must not, my dear Sisters, fret—rather bear up and comfort the other
> poor mourners.

Mary MacKillop moved easily in two worlds, the one that is seen and
the one that is unseen. On the occasion of a bereavement, her
sympathy took account of both. Her consolation grew from her faith
and her hope in Christ. The faith was the truth of things. But she
remembered that "nature must grieve and feel too", that "Jesus wept"
at the death of his friend Lazarus, and she did not hesitate to express
human feeling in her letters of sympathy. She understood, moreover,
the feelings of the widows in chapter 9 of the Acts of the Apostles,
who "stood around in tears showing Peter the tunics and other clothes
Dorcas had made while she was with them". This made her sensitive
to detail in writing to a friend who had lost a loved one: the lock of
hair and the careful description of her mother's grave site for
Benedict; the consolation for the distant Lucian on the death of her
mother—"Hers indeed has been the death of a saint"; the assurance
to the grieving widow of the drowned man—"Depend upon it, poor
Mr Casey had time when in the water to recommend his soul to God".
And some of her phrases were like jewels—the Woods family would
long remember "dear bright Katie".

Footnote

1   Father Anderledy had been elected Vicar General of the Jesuits on 24 September
    1883, and in the first weeks of 1884 he had in effect taken over the government
    of the Society. He became General on the death of Father Beckx, 4 March 1887.

TWENTY-EIGHT

"OUR POOR DEAR FATHER IS AT PEACE"

The Death of Julian Woods

Father Woods died on 7 October 1889. Apart from a few months in Brisbane, he had spent the last three years of his life in Sydney, in the care of a group of devoted women friends who had previously been Sisters of St Joseph. The chief figure among these was Mrs Gertrude Abbott, the former Adelaide visionary Sister Ignatius O'Brien. Although always polite in his refusal to resume friendly contact with the Mount Street Sisters, the founder treated them in effect as if they did not exist.

Apart from his few days at Penola in 1876, Woods never returned to his diocese after visiting Adelaide for the Episcopal Commission in 1872. With at least the tacit approval of the hierarchy, he fulfilled his vocation in tireless missionary activity, at first in Tasmania until 1876, and then in Queensland and the various dioceses of New South Wales. At last his amazing energy began to fail, and in any case by 1883 he had become a *persona non grata* in one diocese after another. So it came about that in the August of that year he accepted an invitation of his old admirer Sir Frederick Weld to undertake a voyage of scientific observation for the British Government in a number of countries north of Australia. The principal aim of this undertaking was to provide information about likely sources of coal and minerals.

This three-year interlude of travel and exploration in Java, Borneo, Singapore, Malaya, Siam, China, Hong Kong, the Philippines and Japan contributes a colourful chapter to the life of this extraordinary man. His notebooks are filled with careful descriptions of what he observed, illustrated by his own fine sketches of places and people. Though his voluminous correspondence with Mary MacKillop had ceased years previously, the letters he wrote at this period to friends like William Archer are interesting, bright, and at times witty. They betray no sign of the imprudence and lack of balance that had become characteristic of his style of spiritual direction, and of course none of the domineering possessiveness which he had developed towards the Institute. They are attractive human documents, revealing from time to time glimpses of a wounded heart: "I dare say too," he wrote to Archer from Malaya in 1884, "I had grown rather weary of trying to do good in another way in the face of so much unkindness, hard usage, and is it too much to say envy and bitterness?"

Arriving back in Port Darwin in June 1886, he spent four months on scientific observation in Australia's Northern Territory. In April and May of 1887 he contributed a series of letters to the *Sydney Morning Herald*—"Explorations in North Australia" and "A Trip to the Victoria River"—which are full of acute observation and fine writing. In October he proceeded south to Brisbane, where he spent some weeks with his Sisters of Perpetual Adoration. After a short period in Sydney, he was with these Sisters again in the following year, 1887, from February to May. By June he was back in Sydney for the last time.

At first he could move about a little, but by the end of the year he was confined to the house. A small group of admirers surrounded him with attention and affection, and provided amanuenses for his scientific writing, his letters, and his memoirs. But in time his powers were so diminished by his distressing illness that he could no longer manage even the labour of dictation. He suffered a great deal, very patiently, and was always spoken of as gentle and most charitable. Some of his friends from the scientific world came to see him, and a few priests like Father Ambrosoli—who had once called him the St Bernard of the Antipodes—but on the whole it was a lonely time.

He had made it clear that he did not wish to resume contact with Mother Mary or her Sisters, however much they were anxious to see him. Some had tried to keep in touch by letter, but the correspondence was one-sided. Mary sent him greetings regularly on his birthday, and she received brief polite replies. He considered that his attitude needed no explanation, as he told Monica in replying to her letter on the death of his brother Terry: "As circumstances then were, it was not advisable for me to reply to you." It is evident from this letter that Mary had been trying to resume contact, with little result:

Mother Mary was kind enough to ask permission to come and see me, but I was obliged to decline. Under no circumstances could I consent to renew my relations with your Institute.

He seemed to think that there was no third path to choose between total lack of contact and what he called "interference"—"It would be useless for me to interfere"—which apparently meant a resumption of some kind of control over the Institute. Ordinary friendly contact, such as good Christians maintain with each other, seemed to be out of the question. He could not consider treating his old friends, the Sisters, with the civility he extended to people like William Archer and his other scientific acquaintances. In spite of his gentlemanly politeness, the bitterness in his soul was clear.

How deeply he had been wounded by Rome's treatment of his Rule, and by Mother Mary's obedience to the Holy See, can be seen in the letter he wrote to the diocesan Josephite Sisters on 9 September 1887. It must be borne in mind that when he speaks of "your rule" he means the Rule as it came from his pen in 1868—the Rule rejected by Rome—with the "unimportant" modifications necessary to take the Sisters from a Mother General and place them under the Bishop of Bathurst. The opposition, the lack of respect for the rule, the wayward spirit of novelty, the experiments, the snares—by all these terms he is referring to the Holy See's directive and Mary MacKillop's obedience to it. However incredible that may seem, it is perfectly true. He wrote:

> I ask of you to remember all the dreadful consequences which we have seen following on a neglect of the rule or want of love and respect for the rule, and I ask you also to bear in mind what struggles our holy rule has come through and what opposition it has had. But look around and see what has become of the efforts to change its spirit. You can all see that God has not blessed these undertakings nor will they flourish in future.
>
> But I think the time will come when the wayward spirit of novelty will depart from these experiments and all St Joseph's children will be brought back together again and be what they were in the beginning. We have gone through many trials and difficulties and many snares have surrounded us, but what has it all meant except to show us the value of the rule and what would come of the destruction of what seemed unimportant portions of its spirit or principles.

It seems that when he cited the words of Christ, "If you love me keep my commandments", what he was really saying was, "If you love Father Woods, do what Father Woods says and not what the Holy See says". The switch from Jesus Christ to Father Woods is effected without an eyelid blinked. The pious language he could use so fluently probably concealed the truth even from himself.

Sourness about the past and dreams about the future were as far as he would go in his thinking of the Mount Street Sisters. He would not admit the idea of polite converse. He had dramatised himself into a tragic figure determined to suffer in silence and isolation. But Mary was not to be put off by such posturing, and her persistent efforts to break through his cultivated aloofness were rewarded at last by the slight crack that appeared in his defence when he wrote on 12 August 1887: "Well, my dear Mother Mary, if you insist upon this, I must defer to your wishes, but I must ask you to bear in mind that I utterly decline to renew any relations with your Institute."

He was dismayed when she wrote that the Sisters in Sydney still clung to him as their Father. "I do not wish to see any of them," he said, explaining that such expressions as she had used showed that she misunderstood the present position. They could lead only to confusion, pain, and disappointment. Though he was a very intelligent man, the only thing that can explain his attitude to what had happened is *his* lack of understanding of the issues. Otherwise he would have been subjectively as well as objectively guilty of setting himself above his superiors in the Church, a thing hard to associate with such a good man.

There can be no doubt that he suffered a great deal mentally as a result of his disappointment. But he habitually thought of *himself* as the victim, and he never seems to have considered that Mary suffered acutely through her sacrifice of his friendship for the sake of fidelity to the Church. However much Julian Woods felt that he had been wronged, Mary MacKillop knew that *he* had wronged *her* and the Institute, and her concern about seeing him again would have been partly due to a desire to express her total forgiveness in deed. She would never have been so insensitive as to express it in words.

Woods never seems to have grasped how intelligent Mary was. He seemed to think she did not understand what had happened! She understood it perfectly, and she alone knew what it had cost her. But she had a sense of history, and she knew that neither then nor at any future time could Father Woods lose his place as the Institute's Founder and Father. She also had a sense of loyalty to one who had been a close collaborator in a great work of God. But more than all, she wanted to pay her affectionate respects to an old friend in Christ who was close to death.

Her persistence was rewarded, for Woods wrote in a postscript to the "breakthrough" letter on August 12: "If you will write and say when you will call, I will take care to be at home for you. Between 3 and 5 in the afternoon is the best time, for I cannot always get up early in the day." Annette attested to a story that Mary had the door slammed in her face by one of his zealous friends when she appeared on the doorstep, but it can be safely said that Father Woods did not countenance this kind of thing. She did manage to get in to see him before he died, more than once, but her accounts of these visits are vague enough. It seems that she was discreetly refraining from any mention of the unpleasantness she had to face from the other occupants of the house.

There was never any serious suggestion that Woods had abandoned the priesthood, although his movements were so shadowy that unsympathetic people were inclined to say unfounded things about him. Never in the whole course of his varied and active life did he ever give any grounds for suspicion about his moral character, or about his attachment to his priestly vocation. Cardinal Moran, with his keen sense of law, had wanted him to place himself within regular ecclesiastical bounds by going to a parish residence or to St Vincent's Hospital. But he preferred to remain at the home that had been prepared for him by his old friends at 533 Elizabeth Street. His choice meant that he was deprived of priestly faculties, but in any case the days of his ministry were over.

When he felt himself at death's door, he made a pathetic appeal to the cardinal:

> I make bold to ask your Eminence to exercise the great charity of coming to see me. If I ask too much . . . I can only beg God to bless and preserve your Eminence and beg your blessing and prayers, for my pains and sufferings are greater than I can ever describe.

This letter does not seem to have been answered. There is a strange story repeated "with all reserves" in O'Neill's *Life of Woods*. According to the undertaker, there were signs that Woods' coffin had been opened during the night before the funeral. It was suggested that Moran had come into the cathedral with someone from his curia, in order to look on the face of this man about whom he had heard so much but whom he had apparently never seen.

Two days after his death, Father Woods was buried with honour at Waverley after a solemn requiem in St Mary's Cathedral. Mary was very relieved that everything went peacefully and with dignity. "We were in great dread," she wrote, "that the Cardinal would not allow the public requiem at St. Mary's—but thank God he did—and our good Father received honour in death that had not for long been his in life." Woods' failure during life to conform to some of the norms of clerical behaviour led to an isolation that explains Mary's relief when her fears about the funeral were not realised.

The day after the funeral, Mary wrote to Monica and Mechtilde, two Sisters who had known the founder since the earliest years of the Institute and before, Mechtilde being his niece. She enclosed a few flowers from his coffin, and gave some details of her last visit a quarter of an hour late to see him die: "I had no idea he was dying when I started to see him—of course, he had been so to say, dying so often and got better. I saw him about a fortnight before and then he said, 'It looks like the end but it's not.'" She had heard he liked a few strawberries, so she tried to send him some now and then. He suffered terribly in his last illness, but now "our poor dear Father is at peace. Let us try to imitate his virtues of charity and gentleness, and on no consideration forget him in our prayers."

At the time of his death Mary was under the impression that Woods had been readmitted to the Passionist Order, and spoke of her joy that she had played a part in bringing this about. But in her *Life* fourteen years later she wrote simply: "Father Marcellus, at the request of the dying priest, invested him once more in the habit of the Passionists." What had been done was that as a gesture of blessing and reconciliation the Passionists had allowed him to reassume, in the literal sense but not canonically, the habit he had been obliged to put aside so many years previously. The photographs of him taken after death show him in the habit.

At the end of the month Mary was asked by Bernard to write to the Sisters about the coming Chapter. After dealing with this matter, she spoke to the "children from whom he was separated on earth" of the gentle spirit of the founder:

> I ask you, my dearest Sisters, one and all—those who knew him personally and those who have only heard of him—to remember that he dearly loved the Institute and that he wished to see the Sisters humble and full of charity towards each other.

Mary would not have had to make a special effort to write this gentle letter. It was a sincere expression of her mind and heart. Even if he had rejected her, she was never going to repudiate his memory nor write anything that reflected poorly on it. Where a bishop or a priest or an old friend was concerned, she never allowed her faith or her memory of past kindness to be obscured by less auspicious events. She certainly never allowed the demands of any human being—bishop, priest, or friend—to prevent her from fulfilling the will of God, but at no time did she treat her differences with such people as personal issues. In spite of Woods' unfortunate reaction to her refusal to follow his views rather than obey the Holy See, she never showed any ill will towards him, or any lessening of her respect and esteem. Her greatness of soul is evident in the way she wrote of one who would have nothing to do with her for the last fifteen years of his life.

Mary's respect for the memory of the founder led her to wish "to start the building of an oratory, the Mother House Chapel, dedicated to St Joseph in memory of our departed Father". In addition, she wished that an account of his life might be written to remind the future members of the Institute what manner of man their first Father and Founder had been. She wrote to Sister La Merci in December 1900: "It wants someone who had more faith in him than I latterly had to do it, and it should be done." She at first suggested that Francis Xavier might be the one, but posterity can be grateful that the task devolved ultimately on Mary herself. Not only is it a most beautiful and informative account of the life and work of the founder, but it reveals the sensitivity and humanity of the writer. On 15 June 1903 she told her brother Donald that she had sent it to the cardinal, hoping for his permission to print it. A month later, however, Moran sent a message that he could not see his way to approve of the printing or publication of the volume.

Patricia Campbell, one of the postulants who came out with Mary in 1874, survived to write to George O'Neill in 1927, when he was gathering material for his historical works: "His Eminence refused. I never knew why." It is still hard to be sure why the permission was not given. Moran certainly had heard many strange things about Woods, some of them true, no doubt, and much exaggeration. But he was himself a historian, and had already published in 1896 his *History of the Catholic Church in Australasia*. Perhaps it was Woods' cavalier attitude to hierarchical authority that disqualified him from serious historical consideration, as it is clear from the cardinal's own *History* that edification was his touchstone. But in 1903 Woods had been dead for fourteen years, and it does not seem that a favourable version of the truth about one of nineteenth century Australia's most extraordinary personalities could then have done any harm.

From Moran's brief reference to Woods in his letter of refusal, it seems that he was more impressed by the man's literary ability and geological expertise than by his spiritual and priestly qualities. He did not say he had read the manuscript, only that he had read enough to come to a decision—which may mean that he read little more than the title, *Life of the Rev. J. E. T. Woods*. But Mary MacKillop, who knew the strengths of Father Woods as well as his weaknesses, gives a very different impression in the text, which has remained unpublished. What she has to say makes no pretence to be a scientific history—it is just "a labour of love". Everything is positive, and there is hardly more than a very general mention of the tensions that developed between the founder and the Institute. Much has been said in this present History about Woods' vagaries as a guide in spiritual matters and his temperamental abandonment of his Institute. Lest the fallout be a caricature rather than a portrait of this gifted priest, the contents of Mary's *Life* have already been cited more than once. Her presentation of him explains to some extent the attraction and the influence of a gifted man who appears at some times to have been out of his mind. No more sympathetic picture than what Mary MacKillop set down there is ever likely to emerge from anything that may be written about Julian Woods.

Mary took a broad view of his activities, not restricting her interest to his spiritual ministry. Her selection of quotations from his writings reveals not only his fine literary style and the variety of his interests, but also her own eye for colourful detail and for the natural beauty of the works of the Creator. It is clear from her treatment of Woods' scientific writings that her own love of the open countryside and of nature—evident in the vigorous and fearless young horsewoman Mary MacKillop, but kept on a tight rein in the dedication of Mother Mary of the Cross to God's service—was by no means dead. "This is pleasant reading for non scientists," she said of his *Essay on The Vegetation of Malaysia* where he introduces the betel palm, which is "gracefulness itself . . . the foliage is like a plume of feathers around a warrior's helmet as it waves to and fro in the breeze".

These later chapters of the *Life*, dealing with matters in which Mary was in no way personally involved, show the trouble she had taken to collect detailed material. She mentions the award of a medal and a prize in 1888 for his work *The Anatomy and Life History of Mollusca Peculiar to Australia*. The paper was read to the Royal Society of New South Wales, and she notes that "the author corrects an error he had made" in the work *Fish and Fisheries of New South Wales*. One may wonder if it crossed her mind as she wrote these words that Father Woods was prepared to admit errors in his scientific work, though never as a spiritual director.

She quotes some of his colourful passages of human rather than scientific interest, such as the reception by the Sultan of Sulu:

> It did not add to my enjoyment to find myself close to the Sultan, behind whom stood a murderous looking scoundrel in gorgeous livery, with a loaded revolver on his shoulder, and his finger on the trigger.

On another occasion the Father had to depart in the dead of night from the home of a rajah to avoid an embarrassing and pressing invitation to marry the only daughter of his host and become heir to the estates. Mary wrote: "Rajahs are not to be trifled with; and his highness could not be expected to understand the reasons which obliged Father Woods to decline the honour." When the host began to show signs of displeasure at the hesitation, the guest begged time to consider the important question, during which he prepared and executed a speedy departure.

Mary devoted several pages to Father Woods' last days. His struggle to keep at his writing became more and more difficult on account of the "paralysis of the hands and legs which was slowly creeping onward". But he never lost "the genial affability which charmed his friends", and he made no complaints:

> The remarkable fortitude with which he bore his sufferings, and the resignation with which he accepted his lot, so different to what he had wished and hoped for, edified those who were privileged to witness them . . . He had to endure nearly three years of slow torture. A doctor who attended him remarked, "He was the most lovable man I ever met."

Together with her own account of the funeral, Mary cited words from *The Freeman's Journal* describing the scene outside St Mary's Cathedral after the solemn dirge and requiem:

> When the coffin was carried to the hearse at the principal western entrance, the "dead bell" in the old tower was sounded, and the solemn ringing was continued till the funeral was out of sight.

Then, after mentioning various tributes paid by eminent people, Mother Mary gave her own reflection on the life of the founder:

> Certainly, when personages who have occupied far more important positions are forgotten, *his* name will be held in affectionate remembrance.
>
> "A Saul in stature, but a child in heart,
> God was his science, God's love all his art."

TWENTY-NINE

VICTORIA
AT LAST

In the beginning of the year 1890, Mother Mary's letters reflect a new phase in Josephite history—the first foundations in Victoria. In late 1889 approval was given for a convent at Numurkah, 120 miles north of Melbourne, in the Sandhurst (Bendigo) diocese. She helped the Sisters to settle in, and wrote from Numurkah in January 1890 of the "humble beginning of a great work".

Then a few months later the Sisters moved into the Melbourne Archdiocese for the first time—a school at Bacchus Marsh, about twenty-five miles west of the city. It was close enough for Mary to visit each time she was in Melbourne. She wrote about it in her April circular, and in May she was able to give some details of the warm welcome Archbishop Carr organised for the first group. In fact, within four years of his arrival in 1887 Carr had six communities of Josephites in his archdiocese. These first ones were the guests of the Sisters of Charity in Melbourne before being driven to the Bacchus Marsh train in the Archbishop's carriage. At their inauguration there, "sermons preached and great things said," wrote Mary, "and a grand address read to the Sisters. They tell me it was a hard matter to keep serious faces during the reading of this address." The *Advocate* report of the function indicates what it was that made them smile—the preacher said the Sisters were known "throughout the world for their piety and learning".

The Institute took a further step forward in May 1890 with its first foundation in Melbourne—a home for poor children in the suburb of Surrey Hills.[1] From the time the First Fleet landed in Australia in 1788, the poor, the homeless, and the destitute had been part of the country's social scene. The problems grew with the colonies and found a response in the efforts of individuals and church groups to provide shelter for orphans and abandoned children. In 1885 the

Society of St Vincent de Paul started a Home in South Melbourne, at first with three children under the care of a matron in a small cottage, and then in a larger house managed by a committee. They were soon looking for an even larger property to cope with all the children in need. In 1890 they found a good site in Surrey Hills, and in the first year fifty-eight "of the most helpless of all the helpless" were catered for, according to the first Report, "the waifs and strays of this great metropolis". Help came from the Council of the St Vincent de Paul Society in Paris and from some local benefactors.

But some of the children were in such a deplorable state that the committee found it hard to cope, and the official patron, Archbishop Carr, turned to the Sisters of St Joseph. Mother Bernard went to Melbourne in May 1890 with two invalid Sisters, hoping soon to be able to provide stronger workers, but as there were many demands on the Institute it was not easy to find them. Melbourne's disastrous financial crash occurred just at this time, causing acute economic and social distress, and the Josephites moved right into the middle of it. Mary wrote in July that she had been for some time busy as Beggar in Chief in her native city—it was "like beginning the work all over again".

As well as the challenge of collecting money, there was the difficulty of dealing with a committee. Mary was seen as the one to handle it, and so it came about that in June 1891 she began the longest sojourn in her native city since she had left it in 1860 to go to Penola as a governess. She was not back in Sydney before the middle of 1892. Her letters came from the Children's Home, Surrey Hills, until in October we find the first one written from the Providence in Latrobe Street, Melbourne.

The work of the Home involved three kinds of activity: managing the building, caring for the children, and finding money to offset the debt and to provide for the Institution's daily needs. With regard to the first, Mary had to keep one eye on earth and the other on heaven, symbolised by the kitchen and the chapel respectively. There was, for example, the earthy problem of a smoky kitchen—solved by transforming the place into a dormitory and setting up a new kitchen. The chapel was always Mary's first concern in any new house, and this was no exception. She was delighted when Maggie Cameron—"such a good girl"—donated some equipment for the altar, and linoleum and carpet for the floors. This young woman, born in 1868, was the eldest of the Penola King's children from his second marriage. As Sister

Raphael she was later in charge of the Sisters of Charity Hospital, Mount St Evins, East Melbourne.

There was nothing very special about these matters connected with the fabric of the building. But with the care of the children, and the financing of the whole enterprise, there were thorny problems, and Mary had difficulty in communicating effectively with the Mother General about them. She wrote regularly, but had few letters in return. The need for money was pressing and Sisters capable of handling the begging were urgently needed; de Sales was getting on nicely, but Gonzaga and Catherine were overworked and had no rest, night or day; Teresa was not much use, though she did her best; the woman in the kitchen was more trouble than anything—the cooking was most important and required to be well managed so as not to have waste; and there were a lot of Government and other Report Books to be kept. "Do you intend to come over?" she asked Bernard in June, "I hope so and that you will bring the necessary help. If you do not come be sure and send help."

But the Mother General did not come, and when she wrote it was sometimes to make a change that had not been discussed, or had been advised against. From Mary's letters it is clear that she was trying to communicate a realistic sense of the nature of the demands being made on the Sisters in Melbourne, and that Bernard seemed incapable of responding to the challenge. The problems presented by the children at the Home were not genteel ones, and they were quite different from the ordinary classroom challenges all the Sisters were used to. They could not be faced by just anybody who might be sent to deal with them. A willing spirit was not enough. A Sister missioned to the Home required strong motivation, a sound constitution, and a strong stomach. The Sisters did not all have the same gifts, and Mary mentioned frequently to her Mother General the great care that should be taken to suit workers to the work. Some Sisters were champions in the classroom; others were not, but were superb with the tough neglected little waifs who came to the Home. Thus, when Bernard was proposing to change de Sales for Bridget, Mary was forthright in speaking of "the really revolting duties" at the Home:

> Sister Mary Bridget has not the strength or stomach enough for what Sister de Sales has to do here. Some of the children are more like beasts in their habits than human beings.

The first annual Report had given further clues about this:

> Their clothes—if rags which covered them could receive such a

dignified title—were merely hanging together; their language was in keeping with their apparel, and although but mites, one may say that every sixth word was prefaced by either an adjective or an oath.

The Home was a heavy financial burden on the Institute, and the only solution was begging—for money in large and small quantities, and for food and clothing. The sole source of income was people's generosity, mostly those of ordinary means, but others also with more resources such as Mary's "very dear old friend" Mr Goldstein, not a Catholic, who like Emmanuel Solomon had extended her a helping hand during her 1871 Adelaide troubles.

Catholics were not always the most open and generous ones. As in Adelaide, some of them had resented the sight of the Josephites from the time they first appeared with their begging baskets on the streets and around the markets and in the shops. They thought that nuns should remain in their cloisters. There were plenty of exceptions, of course, like Mrs Cameron and Maggie, who kept an eye on Mary's needs and helped her generously.[2]

So, besides making the Home a real home for the children, where they could find the love and interest they had never experienced before, Mary was a kind of public relations officer. She made contact with rich and poor, with tradespeople and passers-by in the street, people she knew in her native city and many who were unknown to her. There was no other way to keep the Home going and to provide daily bread for the children and the Sisters. But she could not do it all without help, and she would not be able to do it forever, so suitable Sisters had to be made available for this exacting work. The work of begging was not everybody's field. They could all try it, but as a vocation it required certain gifts of character and education, as well as great stamina. Mary outlined to Bernard the different talents required. Besides, the ones who go out begging should have their night's rest, without any heavy house duties to attend to, and nobody should have to both cook and beg and then go without sleep:

As for Sr M. Gonzaga having the begging in turn with [Emelda], I certainly say NO to that. Sr M. Gonzaga must attend to the house and correspondence. She must be at her post when required for visitors too. She has things in good working order and has a great deal of correspondence. In this house the books must be *exactly* kept.

On June 16 Mary made a desperate plea to Sydney for somebody to do the begging, but by June 30 there was still nobody for the work, and July expenses were about to begin. She was not imagining problems—there were dozens of children waiting to be fed. She made another urgent plea to Sydney: "Tomorrow will be the first day, and we have no Sisters for the begging. I implore you to send two without delay." On July 8 she was still writing: "I am so anxious that you soon send help."

By July 20 there was some relief, not because Sisters had arrived, but because serious flooding in Melbourne and other reasons had made begging impossible there for three weeks. So Mary availed herself of the offer of a Railway Pass, and went begging around the country areas with Margaret Mary. This Sister had been spared by Bacchus Marsh because a young woman came in for a while to help in the school. Finally, help arrived in the person of Sister Emelda, and Mary started with her on a tour that took them through Kyneton, Daylesford, and Ballarat, and back by way of Geelong. They "did very well in the week". While Mary was chief beggar, Emelda was good as a companion, but she did not have the qualities to be anything more than that, and so the search went on.

Mary was anxious, too, to supplement the daily begging with a system of annual subscribers. As well as Bernard's slowness to see the need for current expenses, Mary had to cope with the complications presented by the committee. She was told that a falling off of subscribers would be checked when control of the Home was taken out of their hands and given over to the Sisters. She reflected: "As it was, the poor Sisters barely got enough to keep themselves in boots. Not a thing they got but had to be discussed by the Committee."

Because of the slow pace of dealing with the committee and Bernard's tardiness, Mary had approached the Camerons for help with the nuns' personal expenses. In answer to an urgent plea her old friend Annette in Adelaide had made her some tunics and a couple of nightdresses to replenish her bare wardrobe ("the Sisters here have not time to mend their own clothing") and sent a little money to meet an accumulation of daily expenses that was embarrassing her. But she was sensitive:

> I trust you not to speak of my wanting these things—charity might suffer if you did, and that would not please God. Some people are very thoughtless, and some the reverse, but God loves all and wants us to make allowances.

It was not only by her inaction in Sydney that the Mother General created problems in Melbourne. The work would suffer if directives kept coming from up there about changes in personnel without consultation, or if decisions were made contrary to the advice of the official who had been sent to supervise the demanding operation on the spot. Mary pointed this out firmly but gently, aware that there was "prejudice" around Bernard:

> You cannot change Sisters here without doing harm and bringing trouble on yourself, and I have good reason to put you on your guard. Besides, what is the use of being your Assistant if you do not let me advise you—I who am on the spot should be better able to advise than those who are not and who perhaps may not be free from prejudice.

The Latrobe Street Providence

On 2 October 1891 Mary addressed a letter from "St Joseph's Providence, Latrobe Street East, Melbourne". Six weeks before this, she had let the Mother General know how plans were progressing for this first foundation in the city of Melbourne proper. The caution she had learnt from experience is evident in her words. No matter how anxious the Archbishop was for them to take on the work and how willing they were to oblige, they could not "have anything to do with a Committee in the matter". When Dr Carr asked if they would have any objection to the locality, Little Lonsdale Street, Mary told him: "Of course we have no objection to the locality, it is there that the real work lies."

Archbishop Carr from Galway did not need to tell Mary MacKillop that the Josephites were walking into the toughest part of Melbourne. This was her home town. She had been born a few hundred yards away, and as a young woman she would have been well aware of what went on in that corner of the city. It was a block at the north-east of the grid of streets comprising Melbourne—the block now enclosed by Spring Street, Exhibition Street, Latrobe Street, and Little Lonsdale Street. In the early days there had been many struggling "squatters" in the city centre, but the blocks were sold over their heads and they had to move out to this corner. The area was never a prosperous one. The social conditions became deplorable during 1891 and 1892, when Melbourne's great depression was at its worst, and that was the time when Archbishop Carr looked to the Sisters of St Joseph to bring relief to the hungry and suffering people who had congregated there.

Nothing is left of the Josephite houses. Where they once were there now stands a tall modern building, and not far away is the City Circle underground railway. Although the conditions are totally changed, there are still plenty of Melbourne people who remember when "Little Lon" was an area where respectable people went only when necessary. The adjacent Exhibition Street would have been better known to Mary as Stephen Street. It had such a bad reputation that it was given a new name when the police tried to clean up the area in 1878, in preparation for the International Exhibition to be held nearby in the Carlton (or Exhibition) Gardens. But the old name lingered as a kind of symbol. For eighty years onwards from the early 1850s, mention of the area was equivalent to a reference to prostitution. In 1854, when Melbourne was hardly twenty years old, and Mary MacKillop was twelve, the *Argus* said:

> That part of Stephen Street between Bourke and Latrobe Streets on the east side of Stephen Street is a disgrace to the city and a greater disgrace to the police. Almost every house is occupied by females of the lowest and most disreputable class, who pursue their calling with the most filthy language and conduct.

Compared to what went on here, the poor little children at Surrey Hills whose "every sixth word was prefaced by either an adjective or an oath" would have been considered angelic.

The houses chosen for the Providence were in Latrobe Street, backing on to a lane that came to be known as Providence Place. Although the lane has been gone for years, the name still survives in the area, but few could guess the reason why it appeared in the first place. Just to the south there was a parallel lane, Cumberland Place, where the Josephites later set up a school for street urchins; Little Lonsdale Street is a further twenty-five yards to the south. Recalling in later years her sister's illness at the Providence early in 1892, Annie MacKillop described the locality of 43 Latrobe Street:

> It was a dreadfully noisy place—women screaming at night used to be so awful I thought it was murder; also cattle used to be driven past going to market; they and the dogs with them made great noise, and M. used to waken unless I kept on stroking her forehead.

The preparation of the houses for the Providence in Latrobe Street dragged on and on into September 1891, until Mary wrote to Bernard about her method of dealing with the delays. Up till then she used to go in day after day to find "people pottering about, doing nothing in fact", so she decided to move in and hurry the men on herself. The Dean was relieved to see that she was making light of the inconvenience. When she and Gertrude moved in, the Latrobe Street Providence became a reality, modest enough, but destined to bring relief to many a friendless and hungry unfortunate. Dr Carr was delighted and gave them some money for personal expenses. He and the Dean seemed to think it was all too good to be true.

But Mary knew that "not by bread alone does man live", and her concern went deeper than the bodily needs of those about her. Ethelburga, who was there, wrote of this in later years:

> My impression was from the first time I saw her that she was no ordinary woman, as time went on I felt convinced that she was a living saint, and I can honestly say I never saw anything in her manner or conduct that might cause me to waver from my opinion . . . I have known her to go into some of the slums of Melbourne, and get men and women from ill-famed houses, and got them to go to Mass, also to their religious duties.
>
> She had wonderful influence both with young and old, but would generally bring them to see their error. Mother often persuaded careless young men to go to Mass also to the Sacraments. She seemed to have great control over them.
>
> Some would say, "Mother, it is no use trying to resist you, for you will have your way." Mother would say, "No, and above all do not resist God, for your souls are very dear to Him, and Jesus Christ came into the world, suffered and died to save each one of us."

An important element in the planning of the Melbourne houses was the choice of personnel. Gonzaga at the Home and Gertrude at the Providence were wonderful women whose dedication to the needy was long remembered in Melbourne. The *Advocate* said many years later that the Home was "a standing monument to the fervour of the faith and persevering toil and heaven-granted optimism of the Sisters of St Joseph". Then it said of Gonzaga: "The remarkable personality at the head of affairs, a mother to all, she was beloved as a mother, while honoured and venerated as an ideal nun."

The Providence had a similar type of woman in Gertrude. Mary described her as "heart and soul in her work". She suggested to Bernard that Sister Lucy come as Superior of the Providence, as she was "prudent and a good manager in money matters—which we know Sr Gertrude is not and never will be".

Gertrude wrote to Mary in June 1897: "I need not tell you, for you know too well what this part of the city is and how much could be done for God." She took the initiative of renting a two-roomed cottage in Cumberland Place, and in October 1897 there were sixty children enrolled in a school she set up there. A year later a brick building replaced the cottage. In 1898 nearly a hundred children were attending, waifs and strays from the byways and alleys of the city. It was known to some as "St Joseph's Syrian School", as there were so many children of Syrian origin in that area. These and the many Chinese children spoke little English outside the school. The Sisters accepted everybody, and when it was obvious that there was no food at home, children were taken back to the Convent to be fed and cared for. The Cumberland Place school functioned until 1926. When the nuns no longer lived in the area, they came from the second Providence in Albert Street, ten minutes away.

The first two Melbourne works, the Children's Home and the Providence, were social rather than educational, but it was not long before schools began to appear. The "Syrian School" has just been noted. But it was in 1894 that the first regular Josephite school was opened in Melbourne, at Footscray in the western suburbs. In the next year they opened one at nearby Yarraville, and in 1900 and 1901 they went to Williamstown and Newport. There was also a school attached to the Home in Surrey Hills, and in 1903 Sisters stationed at the Home went out to schools at Surrey Hills, Camberwell, and Box Hill.

During October 1891 Mary spent a couple of weeks in the diocese of Port Augusta, where a problem about obedience was of serious concern to Bishop O'Reily. She in fact agreed thoroughly with all he had to say about it. She had to pass through the Archdiocese of Adelaide on her way to and from Port Augusta, spending some time at Kensington on the return journey because of ill health. Apparently this did not upset Archbishop Reynolds too much, although there is no evidence that he ever moderated his bitterness towards her. What she wrote about this visit to South Australia gives a good idea of how she frequently spent her time over these years:

> I managed to see all the convents in the North—besides calling at Clare, remaining a night at Seven Hill, a few hours at Gawler—(I saw the Hamley Sisters at the Station)—a night at the Port and then on to Kensington on Tuesday—but there I was obliged to rest, having an unusually severe attack of the ordinary illness.

In a letter on November 14 containing some very significant phrases, she told Bernard that her health was causing some concern. She apparently sensed some warning of the serious illness that was to bring her close to death a few weeks later:

> Another thing, dear Mother, that I must ask you to remember—I have had a very heavy strain on me and am now feeling the effects of it. Was very seriously ill in Adelaide, and just one week after I was

better, got very bad again—so bad that I had to keep as quiet as possible, in pain and misery for another week. Owing to your fears—and wicked minds—I could not take the remedy that would have done me good, so that I lost a week of valuable time.

The illness that had long been threatening finally overtook her late in the year. It was so serious that many of those around her thought she was dying. She told Annette on 17 February 1892 that for three days and nights she was "cold as ice all over—just like a corpse", though she never quite lost her senses. Annie, called in to help with the nursing, later remarked that her task had not been made any easier by the rowdiness of the area in which the Providence was located.

But the crisis passed, and Archbishop Carr, who had come to see her almost daily throughout her illness, saw to it that she was taken in his carriage to a convalescent home, *Ellesmere*, in the bayside suburb of Sandringham. There she gradually recovered her power to speak without terrible difficulty, but her legs continued to give her much pain and it was a long time before she could walk. For weeks she lived on "a little milk daily mixed with lime water". Ethelberg turned out to be a wonderful nurse to her, and the two established a lasting friendship during this time. Mary agreed with the doctors that her recovery was the result of prayer, and she spoke of making good use of the *extra time* she had been given. Telling the Sisters how grateful she was for the prayers, she said that when she thought she was going to die she felt quite happy about it "but oh, so lonely" at the thought that she would not see them in this world again.

Mary remarked that her illness had given her more rest and freedom from care than she had had for years, and the doctor wanted her to stay at Sandringham as long as possible. On March 19, she wrote that she hoped soon to be able to walk the five minutes to the beach. But we find that by April 8 she was recovering from some sort of relapse at Bungendore, in central New South Wales. She was obviously not fit to travel, yet for some reason Bernard wanted her out of Melbourne.

M. Bernard did not rest until she got me away from Melbourne. I am sorry she persisted in it against the Doctor's wish, for though he insisted that I should break the journey at Wagga and stay at a Doctor's home there, one of the things he feared has taken place, and I am obliged to stay here until I get better again.

We can only guess what was going on here, but Mary's differences with the Mother General were beginning to cause her serious concern. Bernard had taken little practical interest in her personal needs, not having sent her as much as a shilling. On March 19, embarrassed that she had no money to meet current expenses, Mary appealed to Annette:

> I wish more of my Sisters would follow your example and send me some help. *You* are the only one—and two others, one in N. Z. and one in Sydney, who sent me one pound each. May God bless you, but you might perhaps give some more a hint that I am not here without being under expense and that help from them would be welcome.

On April 8 she wrote to Annette again from Bungendore:

> I had to borrow 10 pounds from a friend of my own to pay some of our expenses down at Sandringham. M. G. never asked me if I wanted anything, or if I had money to pay for what was got. *All* my expenses have been paid by money from you, Sr Gonzaga, Dr O'Reily and about 3 pounds from other Sisters.

But her embarrassment about having no money for personal expenses, and Bernard's failure to think that she needed any, were matters of little importance—there were much more serious questions of Institute policy that upset the foundress. She always hated anything like double-dealing and insincerity, so she had spoken her mind openly to the Mother General about the false position she was in as Assistant General.

The delicate balancing of the personalities and talents of the various Sisters in these communities, constantly under great strain, was something that she took very seriously. That is why she was not happy with Bernard's wish to replace de Sales at the Home with a Sister quite unsuited to the work. It is also the clue to her strong objection to the continued presence of Ignatius McCarthy in Melbourne. She knew only too well the capacity of this Sister for making trouble, and she was concerned at the disaster her disrupting influence could bring to these small specialised communities. She wrote to Annette about her in February, and again in March: "I have been much annoyed at M. Ignatius remaining so long in Melbourne. *She is doing no good*, but M. G. thinks her almost perfection."

It is not known why Bernard was anxious to get Mary away from Melbourne, but it is likely enough that Ignatius had something to do with it. Ignatius was a dangerous person, as has been shown from the history of 1883, and part of her danger was that she was very plausible. She was the only one who had really fed the calumny against Mary in 1883. She completely deceived Bishop Reynolds, who then proceeded to combine with her to deceive her superiors about the begging tour which took her far from Australia without their knowledge. She now turned up at Sandringham and tried to exculpate herself, blaming others for the calumny that had embittered the bishop's mind. As we have already seen, Mary described what happened:

> She came here one day when I was still very weak and wanted to justify herself for the past. I advised her to leave *well alone*, that I was willing to forget, but no, she must go on with her say—blaming *others*, and making out that she was faithful. It was too much for me, and she got an expression of *my true opinion* of her conduct that astonished her.

So, smarting under this rebuff, and aware of Mary's disapproval of her prolonged presence in Melbourne, it would not have been out of character for Ignatius to work on Bernard's mind against her. It would harmonise, too, with what Mary had told Annette of the reaction of Ignatius when she heard the "true opinion" of her conduct. "Since that she has not come near me," said Mary, "and when I see her at the Providence (where I sometimes go, being driven to and from the train) she is very quiet."

After her remarks to Annette on April 8 about Ignatius, Mary said: "On this matter, and some others, M. G. and I have seriously differed, and if I can get out of being nominal Assistant General I intend to do so." As she shared her thoughts with Annette in this way, she told her she had been careful to let the Mother General know she was doing so.

From the start of the Josephites' work in Victoria, Mary was on good terms with the other orders of Sisters there, beginning with the Good Shepherd Sisters at Abbotsford, the companions of her late sister Lexie. These helped from time to time to care for girls she was interested in. Ethelburga wrote of one such occasion: "Mother took care of them for a few weeks, then she asked them if they would go with her to the Good Shepherd Convent. Mother took them there, and left them at the refuge."

It is evident that she maintained a friendly relationship with the Sisters of Charity, who provided her with hospitality when she was passing through Melbourne from time to time. She could write to Bernard on 15 June 1891: "I shall ask M. Gertrude to let me know if anyone will be going over to Sydney who could take Sr Teresa with them."

Mary often mentioned the Loreto Sisters as being friendly and helpful. She wrote to Mother Bernard on 15 June 1891: "Maggie Cameron drove me yesterday to Albert Park Loreto Convent. The Rev. Mother from Ballarat was there and had asked Maggie to bring me over. They sent us such a lot of things for the Home." And she added a few weeks later, after a begging tour: "The Nuns at Loreto, Ballarat, and all through Victoria have offered us hospitality." When the Loreto Reverend Mother and a companion intended going to Sydney to see about a foundation there, Mary wrote to Bernard to tell her that on her behalf she had suggested that they stay with the Josephites. She thought this might be some return for their constant kindness to her.

It is not clear exactly when Mary returned to Sydney after her illness in 1892, but she mentioned in a letter in September that she had not really been able to move about before July 16. Even when she considered that she had recovered, she was by no means free from health problems. Apologising for not writing earlier, she told Annette on 3 June 1893: "At first I was again very ill, and as soon as I got better had so many things to attend to that I was out every day, and really was always so tired when I came home." After that, she was certainly on the move—"to the Orphanage, Gosford, Lithgow, Penrith and other places".

An almost casual reference in 1894 to the problems she encountered as Assistant gives us a flash of insight into how they affected her: "I believe that another year in Sydney with its cares and annoyances would have nearly killed me." Her apologies for not writing, and her references to "circumstances" make it clear that things were not going smoothly. She had written in October 1892: "As things are it is perfect torture to me to write to anybody." On the same day she wrote to Raymond in New Zealand: "I know I have become a shocking correspondent but there are reasons that make it very hard for me to write to anyone. You must only have patience and not doubt my love."

There was obviously more than just work to be done in Sydney; there was something wrong, but in spite of it all she kept on, doing what she could. There seemed to be no limit to what she was prepared to tackle: consultations with prelates; interviews with businessmen; troubleshooting ("the dirty work", as she called it) which often involved long and uncomfortable journeys; begging for the works of the Institute and other causes; giving Confirmation classes; caring for people who depended on her in some way; visiting the sick; encouraging the weary.

On one occasion it looked as if the Sisters would have no midwinter Retreat because they were quite out of money and could not make the usual offering to the Director. "We were in a fix," she told Monica. But she described for Annette how she handled this piece of business. She went to the Jesuit Superior and put her cards on the table. He waived all idea of stipend and said the Josephites could have Father Power, even though he had been tabled to direct a Retreat elsewhere at the time. After the event she reported to Annette: "We had a lovely Retreat, thank God. I was able to attend all through. I hope to be better now and perhaps more help to my dear Sisters."

Mary MacKillop's love for people was not abstract; it was personal and practical and detailed. When two Aboriginal boys came south from the Northern Territory with her brother Donald, she told Sister Annette: "We are keeping the black boys at St Mary's near Penrith, but he is paying 10 shillings a week for them . . . They want care and *warmth* in the winter." Her concern for others was never simply, "God bless you!", but also, "I will personally make sure you keep warm". In a letter to her cousin John from Lithgow on November 9, she speaks of one of these black boys being with her there: "I feared they would never live the winter out unless very carefully housed during that time. They are dear boys, and so good and intelligent."

She kept a sisterly eye, too, on Donald himself, looking to his simple personal needs as well as arranging for contacts in Adelaide who might help him with his appeal for the Mission. She asked Annette to approach Mrs Barr Smith on his behalf. "So far the Bank has got all he collected," she said, and then added: "I am sure, dear, that you and Sister Bernardine will look after his clothes, socks and pocket handkerchiefs."

Mary did not forget any part of the Institute, encouraging the Sisters by the written word when she could not be present in person. Knowing the unfortunate atmosphere in which the Adelaide Sisters had to live, she saw them not only as "those over there" but as individuals. She loved them all, though one or two were not enthusiastic in their response—somebody sent her back the circular she had written for St Joseph's day. She said she had her suspicions who it was, and we might have some too.

Dr Reynolds was not making things any easier. In December 1892

Mary wrote to Annette: "It is very painful about the Retreat not being allowed, but our good God will make up the loss to you in other ways." She encouraged them to be patient about this spiritual inconvenience, but made no mention of the source of the trouble. Reynolds had, in fact, but six months to live, and when it became clear that he was dying Mary was full of kindly sympathy:

> Is it not wonderful how long the Archbishop lingers—I am so glad he has the two Brothers with him. Sometimes I have thought of writing to him, but fear I might do more harm than good by doing so.

She had done her best with her conciliatory letter late in 1888, and being well aware of his disposition she feared another letter might upset him in his last days. But she organised all the spiritual forces she could in his favour, having many Masses and prayers said for him, and when he died in his fifty-ninth year on 12 June 1893 she asked Sister Annette, "Please send me all the news you can about the last of the poor Archbishop."

In a letter to Annette at the end of August 1893 Mary spent some time sympathising with the sick, especially the rheumatism sufferers, and then made a passing reference to her own health: "I manage to keep about, but am nearly crippled with rheumatism." This trouble was never really to leave her from now on, but her "old visitor", her chronic problem, seems to have abated. At the start of 1894, within a week of her fifty-second birthday, she was able to write to Annette:

> What the doctors said has come true of me—those terrible past attacks have ceased, and the Doctors have all said that if I could survive them, I would be healthier than I ever was, and so it is. Oh, how I used to dread every fortnight as it would come around. Now there is no trouble and I don't know what it is to get a headache. Won't you thank God for me?

Footnotes

[1] Mary later reported to the Mother General about the possibility of acquiring a much more ample property for the Home in another area of Melbourne. From all that is said of the location and nature of the property, it seems that it was the one that eventually became the Convent of the Good Shepherd at Oakleigh.

[2] This Mrs Cameron was the Ellen Cameron, the second wife of Alexander of Penola, who had travelled to Europe on the same ship as Sister Mary in 1873. Alexander had died in 1881. As his first wife had been Mary MacKillop's Aunt Margaret, there was a relationship with his first family, but there was really none with his second family. Nonetheless, they were regarded as relatives.

THIRTY

A PAKEHA IN
AOTEAROA

Two Visits to New Zealand and
an Australian Interlude

Mary MacKillop spent three years of her life in New Zealand—Aotearoa, the Land of the Long White Cloud. She liked Auckland as soon as she arrived there in 1894, and proceeded to fall in love with New Zealand and its people. After her first six months she wrote: "I like New Zealand very much and have been so well here"—this was the pleasant memory she always retained. She was glad to be there for the sake of the Sisters too— "The poor Sisters over here needed someone from headquarters to encourage them"—and also because it gave her some relief from the tension in Australia: "I believe that another year in Sydney with its cares and annoyances would have nearly killed me."

Towards the end of 1893, plans were finally being made for somebody from the Mother House to visit New Zealand. The Institute had now been established in that country for ten years and there were problems crying out for solution. But Mother Bernard had never been able to realise her hopes of crossing the Tasman. "I think you should coax her over," Mary had urged the New Zealand Superior, "and then she would see for herself, and be in a position to help the Sisters very much." Now a visit could be put off no longer, as she told Monica: "M. G. wants me to go to New Zealand after the Xmas Retreat. *Some one must go.*" She wrote to Annette on January 10: "I leave for N. Z. on the 22nd, God willing." And so it turned out—her next letter was from Auckland on 25 January 1894.

The New Zealand foundation had been made at a time of great anxiety for the Institute, November 1883. It was the culmination of many years of effort on the part of the Marist Father Fauvel. He had

388

first heard of the Sisters from Father Woods at Villa Maria in Sydney in 1873, and when three years later he found himself pastor of Temuka in the South Island of New Zealand, he decided that he wanted them in his scattered parish. His efforts to procure them were long and persevering, and at last rewarded. He had even sent Mother Mary a little picture of St Joseph with the instruction that it was to come back to him only in the company of some of her Sisters. On 29 September 1881 Bishop Redwood of Wellington had promised the Bishop of Adelaide, at that time still friendly to the Sisters, that he would not interfere with the Constitutions or change any part of them.

This reassured them on the main point, but there was something else that could disturb the peace. In 1880 the diocesan Sisters of St Joseph from Bathurst had gone to Wanganui in Dr Redwood's diocese, and he must have known enough of their history to see the reason for Mary's anxiety about the Constitutions. In writing in January 1882 to thank him for his promise, she mentioned that her Sisters dreaded the possible difficulties of this situation, and to strengthen their "hopes of not clashing with others and working in peace" they would like to have them discussed with the bishop during his coming visit to Sydney. This point was apparently settled satisfactorily, as Mary told Father Fauvel in March that a letter from the bishop had set their minds at rest. She hoped to have four Sisters over there by June, but knowing the sort of things that could cause delay she was cautious about making a straight-out promise. Her caution was justified, as we find Father Fauvel writing in February 1883 of his disappointment that no Sisters had come. When he read out her letter to his people they were very sympathetic with her in her various trials, and their good will was in no way diminished. For his part, he would not give up, being convinced that the Sisters of St Joseph were destined by God to do much good in his parish and elsewhere in New Zealand.

Two months later, Fauvel was able to write of his joy that his desires were about to be fulfilled. In the following dreadful months in Adelaide, it must have been consoling for Mary to know she had such an enthusiastic supporter across the Tasman. The first party left Melbourne on October 24—Calasanctius, Raymond, and Immaculata. Calasanctius, Assistant to the Mother General, was in the party on the express orders of Dr Reynolds, who had his political reasons for wanting her out of Adelaide. The Sisters settled in well at

Temuka, but cries for reinforcements came very soon. Mary was in an awkward position. She could not go near Adelaide, yet most of her Sisters were there. Word sent from Sydney that two of them were to go to New Zealand was ignored. She apologised to Calasanctius, saying that she had believed the message from Adelaide that they were sending some. The entry in the Adelaide diary of the Institute for March 19 shows that the bishop was using his imagination: he did not consider they ought to be sent from Adelaide, it runs, but said that Mother Mary told him she would send two on from Sydney.

Now at last eleven years later Mary was in the Sisters' small cottage in Temuka. She was delighted to find a happy and united community—"they could not be otherwise under Sister Raymond". She noted that they really needed a new convent, and by the time she was visiting New Zealand for the second time in 1897, it was being built as the result of appeals to the people by Father Fauvel. On that occasion she wrote: "The Sisters will have a lovely convent there, and not too soon, for the old one is scarcely safe to live in." The school celebrated its Golden Jubilee in 1933, and its Centenary in 1983 under different social conditions. Father Fauvel's second school at Kerrytown, a few miles away, functioned from 1884 until 1945.

The distance of New Zealand from Australia is in the order of 1500 miles. One could sail from Sydney to Auckland in the north, or leave from Melbourne and arrive at Bluff in the far south. Wellington in the centre could be approached conveniently from either place. Movement about New Zealand often involved the hazards of sea travel, even when it was not a question of going from one island to the other. On her first visit to Meeanee, Mary's vessel once had a very rough passage from Auckland and could not put in at Napier. So it took her to Wellington and she had to go back 150 miles by train.

When Mary arrived in Auckland from Sydney in January 1894, the Sisters had two houses there (Surrey Hills and Remuera), two others in the North Island (Meeanee near Napier, and Matata on the Bay of Plenty, 220 miles and 120 miles from Auckland), and four in the South Island, roughly 600 miles from Auckland (Temuka, Kerrytown, Rangiora, and Waimate). Surrey Hills, Remuera, and Matata were in the diocese of Bishop Luck of Auckland. Meeanee was the only house in Dr Redwood's diocese of Wellington. The houses in the South Island were in the diocese of Christchurch under Bishop Grimes. At this time there were no Josephites in the diocese of Dunedin.

Mother Mary's itinerary on this first visit can be reconstructed to a large extent from her letters, but there are gaps during which it is not clear where she was. Many letters are obviously lost. What we do know is astounding enough—even with modern means of transport it would be remarkable—and it reveals her style of visitation.

Arriving on January 25, she stayed at first at Surrey Hills. On February 6 she began a visit to Matata, and on March 6 she was at Meeanee. By April 7 she was in the South Island at Temuka, and spent many weeks visiting the four foundations in the vicinity. On June 25 she was back in Wellington, then in the north visiting Meeanee again, and on August 8 she had returned to Matata. She was still in Auckland in early September, but back in the South Island in mid-November (probably by October), this time going to Dunedin and Invercargill in the far south. This visit to the southerly diocese of Dunedin was made at the express invitation of Bishop Moran. She told Andrea on November 28 in a little outbreak of Scottish fervour:

> Just fancy, I expect to spend St Andrew's Day in Dunedin, where I am going at the Bishop's invitation to visit him. Dr Grimes, our Bishop here, has spoken so much about our Sisters and the work they are doing here that he has gained us a friend in Dr Moran.

After returning for a further period in Auckland and the north she paid another short visit to the South Island, and finally left for Australia in March 1895 via Wellington.

Her life was full of activity: travelling, inspecting, supervising, instructing, correcting, protecting, arranging transfers of Sisters, helping with teaching methods and suggesting better ways to organise the schools, seeing prospective postulants, discussing problems with the clergy, helping to arrange and conduct displays, picnics, and bazaars, and begging for the needs of the Sisters (such as wire netting to enclose the chickens and ducks at Matata).

But her chief concern was to encourage the Sisters. She always spoke of the basic virtues, especially those proper to religious who were called to be children of the humble and hidden St Joseph. Harmony and kindness to one another was something she never tired of recommending to them. Devotion to Christ in the Eucharist in the Mass and the Blessed Sacrament was paramount, for it was in him that their union was founded.

Her letters to Sisters in New Zealand and in distant Australia at this time show a personal interest in each one, especially the "old" ones who had been with her from the start and had lived through troubled times with her. She loved to have news of them and asked repeatedly for letters, even though she had often to apologise for what she called her own poor record in answering individual letters. When someone suffered a bereavement, she was always ready with a consoling letter, and the death of a Sister always moved her. She was always interested in the sites of their graves, and she was especially pleased when they were kept well and situated where they would remind people to pray for those who had gone before. She was especially pleased at the way the Monsignor at Panmure kept the parish cemetery green.

Both in her letters and on her visits, Mary was always interested in the details of daily life. She loved to see an easy harmony among all the members of a community, and she hated thoughtless and unkind gossip and suspicion. She was ready with words of praise for individuals such as Sister Teresa at Surrey Hills, who "deserves great credit for her energy and perseverance. Her troubles there have been great, but she has bravely surmounted them." She spoke of her admiration for those she found living cheerfully at Matata, contented and at peace, in distressing conditions, where "the Oratory is the only good room in the house".

In a sense she was in her element. Her element was charity, harmony, and helpfulness, not the disputatious atmosphere she had been forced to breathe almost everywhere she went in Australia. Certainly there was much labour, some troublesome ill health, anxieties, and one or two unpleasant priests (like the one at Palmerston, "a queer man, and it is well that they got away from him as they did"), but nothing like the sort of thing she had been enduring in Australia for a quarter of a century. The problems here were the ones a religious superior might expect to find anywhere, but they could not be ranked with the succession of avalanches that had descended on her from the most elevated places in Adelaide, Bathurst, Brisbane, and again in Adelaide. She also enjoyed a temporary respite from the unpleasing developments in the Institute that were being tolerated in Sydney.

In handling Institute business she had learnt to get signatures to agreements before the Sisters were committed to anything. No bishop was forced to have them in his diocese, but if he did accept them it had to be understood that they brought their Constitutions with them. Experience had shown that this was not only to be understood, but confirmed on detailed and signed documents. The handshake and gentlemen's agreements were not enough; her astonishment to discover this had led her to a practical caution in organising any new venture. Her correspondence with Bishop Redwood before the Temuka foundation has already been noted. The origins of the Auckland houses demonstrate the point in a similar way. For her part, Mary was meticulous about keeping her side of any agreement. She had earlier explained to Raymond: "I know from two past painful experiences that it is no use to act as her Assistant and delegate should, and I value *my word and promise officially given*."

Similarly, in secular business dealings with lawyers she had a clear mind and a firm approach. She wrote, for example, to C. H. Tripp Esq. on 28 February 1895:

> Sister Raymond has forwarded to me your communication asking for two pounds sixteen shillings on Mrs Cregan's account. I am surprised at this as, in your presence, and at various times in the presence of other Sisters, Mrs Cregan herself proposed that if I would be satisfied to take 60 pounds as her daughter's claim upon the land, she would bear all expenses. *60 pounds—free of all expenses* was what was agreed upon. She knew at the time, and so did you, dear Sir, that according to New Zealand law, the Power of Attorney was defective and that the deed had to be sent to Melbourne for signature, but there was no word then said about having expenses to meet. Under these circumstances I really do not feel that I have any right to meet this demand—and, candidly speaking, have not the means of doing so.

Mary MacKillop had learnt that more formidable people than C. H. Tripp could try to bluff and bully their way out of an agreement, and she knew how to respond to his legal terminology, politely but firmly. He was not dealing with any overawed confused little nun.

She wrote in her first week: "We go on Friday to Matata, the Maori Mission." The amount of detail available about the life of the Sisters in this place gives an insight into the style of heroism the Josephites took with them everywhere. First, we are fortunate to possess a colourful account of the trip "on Friday to Matata". It comes from the pen of Annie MacKillop, who was in New Zealand at this time for the sake of her health and accompanied Mary and Teresa to Matata. It throws light on the implications of a simple sentence like, "Mother Mary went to Matata". Annie deserves to have her account perpetuated:

> We started (from Auckland) in a little and very uncomfortable steamer and were all seasick. We got to Tauranga next day, Ash Wednesday, and went to an hotel kept by Catholics. All we could get

to eat was some black tea and dry scones, and very little of that.

The Matata Sisters sent a man with a light wagon to meet us. There was only one seat. Mary sat on it, also the driver. A board was fastened across the back for Sister Teresa and me. The back was also filled up with all sorts of necessaries for people at Matata—I had a saddle up to my knees. We started on our fifty-six mile drive and got to our first stage eighteen miles away at about 3 p.m. The driver expected to stay there for that night, but Mary and Sister begged of him to get them to the Convent that night, not knowing how dreadful the road was. They did realise it a little when they saw how horrified the landlord looked when he found that we were going on. We again got nothing to eat but dry scones and black tea. I took half a scone with me and ate it later on.

A half-caste Maori rode beside us on a white horse until near dusk, when he went ahead of us, and made a fire and had billy-tea ready when we got up to him. Mary stayed in the trap, but Sister, the driver and I got out. Sister took her refreshment standing by the wheel, but I sat on the ground. By morning, all the Maoris knew that the *pakeha* (white stranger, me) sat on the ground just like a Maori and that made them my friends.

It was a dreadful road, up and down hills, with the road just wide enough for one trap. It was very dark, neither moon nor stars showing, but our eyes got used to it. I kept fancying that I saw shadowy figures flitting about, and at last whispered my fancy to Sister, of whom I stood rather in awe in those days. To my great surprise, she whispered back that she had been fancying the same thing!

I was starving, and told them that if it were anywhere near twelve when we got to the Convent, I would sit up and have some meat for supper. I could not understand why my remark made the driver laugh so much—he knew that there would be no meat.

Annie had a good memory, a helpful imagination, and a good simple style. These added up to a memorable description of the conditions of life at Matata:

Mary was very distressed about the Sisters' want of comfort, but they were quite cheerful. The Convent was a large unfinished building, the small windows very high up . . . The wooden partitions between the rooms were not finished all the way up and at night we would see a rat running up and along the top of the partitions. There was also a balcony unfinished and without a railing.

Meat was hard to get—I think that generally a butcher called once a week. There were only a very few white people among the Maoris, who were good to the Sisters (the Maoris) and sent them fish, etc, when they caught them. The curate went out on Saturday to try to shoot something for Sunday's dinner and only got a water-bird (like our waterhen or coot). It had to be skinned before cooking. The priests lived in a whare—Maori house—the Sisters cooked for them, so gave them the bird for dinner. I don't know what else they got or what we all lived on; my last meal there was dry bread and a tomato! The Sisters could not keep poultry then because they were surrounded by Maoris who had maize plantations and they had no wire-netting or other way of keeping them from the Maoris' places. There was neither butter nor dripping. Before she left New Zealand, Mary sent them kegs of butter, dripping, necessaries, and wire netting which she begged while travelling about.

The Sunday after we got to Matata was a great day. All the Maoris came to Mass, which they sang. Some were dressed only in blankets. They gave Mary a great welcome and made friends with me, too, after Mass.

Annie's next story would have been typical of the memories so many people had of her sister:

Mary had another great day with them in the school-room, during which she gave lollies to the children out of a tin. She gave each one two tablespoons at least. The two priests and the Sisters were with her when a dear little boy came clad only in a shirt which Sister had put on him when entering. He saw that his little hands could not hold the quantity, so he held up his shirt for it. Sister Teresa was so amused that she had to leave the room. I had thought her so severe and strict.

We returned from Matata by way of Rotorua, a sixty mile drive, and had the same driver. During the first part of it we realized how dangerous had been our first journey. The driver told us that in the dark he trusted to his horses as he could not see . . . Another Sister must have gone with us, because Sister Teresa and I returned by train to Auckland.

Mary herself gave a long description of conditions at Matata to Calasanctius during a later visit to the village that year. She wrote on 8 August 1894:

I must give you some idea of what Matata is like. Imagine a big straggling barn, but a two-storeyed one. On the ground floor we have entrance hall, reception room, and a large school—used as a chapel on Sundays, holy days and festivals . . . There are besides, downstairs, a sort of passage used for laundry work and a lumber room. Upstairs we have a *very nice oratory* with matting on the floor. We have our dear Lord always with us, and Mass is daily said by one of the Fathers.

Off the top landing a door leads to the kitchen, which is simply a passage fifteen feet long by six feet wide. At the end, opposite the door, there is a miserable stove with which cooking is done. Off this kitchen is a little closet used as a refectory—eight feet by six. A board two feet wide and about five feet long is fixed against the outer partition and this serves as a table. Shelves above this contain the crockery in use, knives, spoons, etc. All is very neat and clean. In fine weather it is all right, but when rain and wind come, the first pours in in all directions, and the second causes the whole place to shake and the fire to smoke. Indeed, at such times, to keep this fire alight and do any necessary cooking, Sister Genevieve has to stand in water—and for the purpose wears strong leather boots.

And so the description continues in similar detail. Mary was far from being the detached observer, however much she may have admired the devotion and selflessness of the nuns. As Annie put it, she "was very distressed about the Sisters' want of comfort". It was her business not only to see for herself, but to do what she could about their needs. The spiritual sphere came first, certainly, but she was concerned also to provide some heat in the house, and to supplement their sometimes near-starvation diet. After speaking of the community room she goes on:

Just imagine how cold this must be in winter. From the floor to the highest beam in the roof there must be a height of twenty feet, and *there is no fireplace anywhere in the house*—not even in the kitchen which has only a miserable stove.

She gives an account of the ingenious but uncomfortable way ("the Maori plan") the Sisters manage to get some warmth by squatting around an improvised fire on a metal sheet in the middle of a room with no chimney. And then:

Of course, this luxury of a fire is only indulged in *at night*. On the coldest mornings and during the day, all have to work and exercise themselves to keep warm. The cold is very much felt during school hours, but so far has had to be endured. Please God, this will be remedied next year, for when I return to Auckland I shall, God willing, not leave a stone unturned to procure a stove for the community room, school and kitchen.

As for the meals:

The food is the poorest, meat very seldom, once in a month perhaps—fish just as the Maoris please to get them any, wild duck, swans, or wild pig, whenever any of the fathers succeed in shooting or killing such. It is often a feast or a famine here. The chief food is the sweet potato. Butter and milk are luxuries for which they pay dearly and which they can only procure from one person—a Protestant, whose daughter is the only white child attending the school.

But she has already been at work since her last visit:

> Through the kindness of friends down South, I was able to send them six ducks, seven fowls, and wire netting to make an enclosed yard for same; so now they have the commencement of a poultry farm or *yard*, I should say. Other friends sent a quantity of beautiful butter which will last nearly until Christmas, ham, bacon and other housekeeping necessaries.

Whilst concerned with all these details, Mary did not forget the reason for the Sisters' presence among the Maoris at Matata. She set before their eyes as often as she could the importance of the work they were doing and its long-lasting effects, reminding them of the history of the people they were helping:

> The Maoris sing the Vespers through themselves in their own language, but the Litany and hymns for Benediction they sing in Latin. The Vespers were originally taught to the Maoris by Bishop Pompallier about 70 years ago, and the old Maoris of that time in their turn taught their children. This is an important thing to remember, as they were a long time without Priests, for, between wars and changes in the Auckland diocese, the poor Maoris had little to remind them of their religion.

She frequently stated her liking for New Zealand in so many words— "I like New Zealand very much". One particular paragraph of the letter to Calasanctius just quoted enables us to sense her reaction to the country:

> From the community room and balcony we have a lovely view. From where I sit writing this, there is a view of the ocean and several small islands—one being "White Island" which contains an active volcano, which is smoking away at present at a great rate. Looking towards the south east there is a range of hills—can hardly call them mountains. Between the Convent and the sea, just about five minutes walk from here, there is a fresh water creek running parallel with it and only separated from it by a sandy ridge, not many yards wide. This is a lovely day, and everything looks bright and beautiful.

The atmosphere of heavenly peace and the beauty of the day is reflected in her words. The day's date was in fact the one on which she would leave this earthly life fifteen years later. There had been a rare touch of the same peace in the way she spoke of the quiet seclusion of Mount Street when she first arrived, but it is only in her letters from New Zealand that this relaxed style really manifests itself. On this day at Matata, and the next (when it poured with rain), she wrote a number of long letters to her Sisters in Australia. Seven are extant. In the one to Andrea we catch a glimpse of the delightful relationship Mary had with the Maori children:

> Just now two little mites came up to me as I was writing and performed some wonderful Maori dance—or exercises rather. Their actions and the time, the beat, were wonderful.

By the second of these days her writing hand was affected:

> Owing to rheumatism in my hands, it is hard to write as much as I would wish. I wrote a good deal yesterday and today my hand is very much swollen.

She could not see fifteen years into the future, but she could look back over twenty-five years of the life of the Institute. This meant that a number of Sisters were celebrating Jubilees. She was not highly excited about the matter herself, but she wished to share the feelings of those who were. It was twenty-five years since 1869, a year the Josephite Register shows that the Sisters from number 41 to number 74 joined the order.

That in itself was a matter for rejoicing, since the great proportion of them were still Sisters, but it provided Mary with a problem. All her Sisters were dear to her, and if she were sure of not forgetting even one date as it occurred, she would be happy to make a habit of writing on these occasions. But as things stood, especially with all the travelling she had to do, she thought it better not to notice any particular one, except in her private prayers and at Mass. She made this point in her letters to Monica and Andrea, incidentally revealing the way she prayed for her friends. She could not remember all the dates concerning all those dear to her, so she prayed every day for anybody who had a birthday or a feast day or an anniversary on that day, for "by such means alone could I make sure of not neglecting any of my Sisters".

It seems to have been the Jubilees that turned Mary's mind to the past at this time in a way that is not reflected in many of her other letters. Her mood led her to share some rare personal thoughts with her old friend and Assistant, Calasanctius:

> I feel as if all my old friends are dead to me, and beyond trying to do my duty wherever placed, am, in a measure, dead myself. The past with its many sorrows and few joys is a dream.

She was writing in the mood of the psalmist's cry: "My life is worn out with sorrows, and my years with sighs." But then her prevailing mood appeared in some solid advice for Calasanctius: "Leave yourself in God's hands—willing to live and suffer as long as He pleases, asking

Him only to keep you in His grace and love." If Calasanctius also had, as Mary suspected, some "longing for release from this weary world", she had to wait another thirty-nine years for it.

Australian Interlude 1895–1897

After a long absence in New Zealand, Mary returned to Australia on 13 March 1895. A rough crossing of the Tasman brought her safely to Sydney; then a less troublesome crossing of the harbour brought her to North Sydney and a warm welcome at the Mother House. The little dog joined in the rejoicing too: "A warm welcome home awaited me. Even dear little Bennie (the dog) remembered me and almost went wild in his joyful welcome." She wrote back to Gertrude Mary about the building renovations that were in progress at Mount Street—changes which determined the form of the main entrance to this day.

She soon settled into the busy life that was to be hers until she left for South Australia in mid-1896. As Assistant she was likely to have to face anything at all "at home or abroad". At home she soon found herself in charge of the Mother House. In spite of the burden of work, her health was in general much better. She suffered from the normal colds and other ailments that were about, and spoke of tiredness, but she seems to have been free from her "old visitor": "I cannot understand myself, and sometimes think a miracle has been worked in my regard. May God be praised for all, and keep me strong and able to work."

The things that kept her busy included spiritual duties and much prayer. The hours she spent in the chapel do not feature in her letters, but others remembered them later. Her duties included such things as supplying for the lack of a priest to conduct the retreat, and caring for a deranged Sister, "quite out of her mind at times, and very troublesome". This latter call on her kindness and patience is mentioned almost in passing, yet those who have had such an experience will appreciate what her words implied.

A constant stream of letters flowed from Mary's pen. The total number must have been enormous—even the collection of those that are extant is very impressive. Some of the recipients, notably Annette, kept them carefully; but it is plain that many have been lost. More than once we read that the day has been occupied in busy writing, but the only surviving document is the letter in which such a remark is made. One "short note" of nearly five hundred words contains an apology for brevity and pleads the excuse of a very busy day.

Her New Zealand friends were constantly in her thoughts, and she kept in touch with them by writing regularly. Many letters to Gertrude Mary at Rangiora have survived, and it would be reasonable to assume that Raymond, in charge of the Province, also received her share. The young people got attention too. On one occasion, Mary wrote to them at Rangiora confessing that she did not have their letters with her and so could not send each of them a separate message. She was simple and affectionate in her words to children, but at the same time wrote as one who was well aware of their real needs and the kind of encouragement that would help them. To pay attention in class was important, she knew, but it was first necessary to *be* there. Her ideals were the highest, but she also had observant eyes, and she had learnt that the children not only had to be reminded to go to Mass on Sundays, but also to go to school on weekdays.

Along with the children, she remembered the priests in charge of the parishes where the Sisters had schools. There were always greetings and good wishes for Father Regnault, or Father Fauvel, Father Williams, or Father O'Connor. The latter, pastor at Rangiora, was seriously ill at this time, and she always reassured him of her prayers and those of the Sisters in Australia. She was saddened when he died late in 1896.

Another of her "dear good friends" whose death particularly affected her was Father Peter Hughes in Adelaide. He had been one of the friendly priests in the troubled days of 1871—in fact it had been he who had been commissioned to lift her excommunication. Always sensitive to the memory of kindness, she wrote of her distress at his death and thanked those who had sent her the particulars of his illness. She wrote to Adelaide some weeks later, saying that in spite of the scarcity of funds she hoped to contribute to the memorial they were preparing for him: "it will come very hard on me if I don't get some little thing to send."

Whenever Mary heard of a Sister in sorrow she always sent a short message of consolation. She had a wonderful way of combining a genuine feeling for human troubles with the reassuring word of faith that everything came from the hand of the loving Father in heaven. She was able to speak of people's interests in a most homely way, and yet without artificiality she could throw a ray of faith on every situation. She always presented obedience in the light of the divine, and never tired of urging its practice in everyday life: "Represent your difficulty humbly, . . . Don't refuse anything." At the same time she was realistic enough to know that perfection is not attainable in this world, and once sympathised with a superior: "It is hard for you to be troubled with the Sisters you so often have, but we all have such things to bear and must make the best of them."

The visitation of the convents and schools involved a great deal of travelling in the country areas of New South Wales. In the earlier days her travelling was done in uncomfortable horse-drawn vehicles on rough dusty roads, or in wretched coastal vessels. Now that a railway system had replaced Cobb and Co.'s coaches on the main land routes, travel was somewhat less harrowing. Though her normal second class ticket provided anything but a comfortable journey, there was an occasion when she could have said with the Apostle Paul, "I know how to live modestly and I know how to live luxuriously too". Mary's luxurious living was a free first class pass on the railways for a journey that took her 350 miles.

Though there are not many references in her letters at this time to her concern about the Institute in Sydney, it is clear that she was not happy with a number of developments there. She later wrote from New Zealand about the difference between some Sydney Josephites and the others. Her confidence in St Joseph was such that she did not regard him merely as the source of soft favours, such as supplying food when they were starving, and getting them out of other tight earthly corners. His interest in the Institute, she believed, had led him in the past to see that the Sisters met the hard treatment they needed from time to time to remind them of their high ideals, and she did not hesitate to tell them that he would do the same in the future.

Her circular letters, addressed to all the Sisters, generally dealt with the deeper principles of the spiritual and religious life. Experience had shown that the weakness of human nature was never to be fully overcome, and at times the signs of forgetfulness were only too clear. She hoped that constant reminders would inject new vitality into flagging spirits. It was always kindness, unity, humility, and obedience that she emphasised. On a few occasions the letter was long and the language strong.

In March 1893 she sent a memorable letter for the feast of the Institute's patron. It contained her thoughts on a topic she considered of supreme importance, and had in fact been composed for the most part more than twenty years earlier. It laid great stress on the value of

Joseph's hidden humble life, the vocation to which the Sisters were likewise called. The intervening years had convinced her even more deeply of the importance of the lessons referred to in the 1870 message:

> This humility is something wonderfully beautiful in itself. My Sisters, this was a *quiet humility* . . . grounded on submission to the adorable will of his God. It was a humility of heart, not of words . . . a silent not a noisy humility.

She noted that some things not obviously in harmony with this silent humility seem to be commendable in some rare cases. These things would include "heeding the esteem of men". One of the official Roman critics of her writings thought he had detected a false element in her thinking here—that she was approving of a showy humility that consisted in words only. But she was perfectly orthodox. She was led to make this allowance by remembering that some "saints and servants of the same good God" are called to an expression of humility in some ways different from the one she was commending to the Josephites. Their office requires them to draw attention to themselves in a favourable manner, like a pope or a bishop at a solemn ceremony, or a king at Court like St Louis or any head of state. Though not vain or insincere, such people are at times called to be on show. Their public have a right to it, so they have to concern themselves about external signs of respect and esteem—otherwise, why parade in eye-catching garments? Why be surrounded by splendid ceremonial? Pageantry has its place. The humility of those involved may be genuine and interior, but its expression clearly has to have a different quality about it from the "quiet hidden sort" proper to the Sisters of St Joseph.

During these years Mary was anxious to speak with some of her trusted advisers about her worries, but circumstances always seemed to defeat her. In mid–1895 she had planned a meeting with Archbishop O'Reily at Goulburn, but it was not realised, and she was to suffer the same disappointment on the occasion of the synod of bishops held later that year in Sydney. Dr O'Reily certainly made efforts to see her, but events once more seemed to conspire against them. She wrote on December 16: "Dr Carr kindly came to see me—he is always so kind in that way." She had waited at home for days expecting Dr O'Reily also, and when she was forced to be absent briefly it was precisely then that he arrived.

South Australia 1896–97

The active life of Mother Mary during her long visitation of South Australia as Assistant in 1896–97 was the normal kind of thing a busy religious superior might expect anywhere. She had much to do, but the atmosphere was a great contrast to the tension, intrigue, secrecy, and suspicion that had prevailed in Adelaide ecclesiastical circles when she had last lived there in 1883. At that time a few Sisters had occasioned much harm to the Institute, a number of priests had been actively unfriendly, and there had been much to suffer from the bishop. Now under Archbishop O'Reily the tone was quite different. There were problems, but nothing comparable to the crushing pressure of Dr Reynolds' last decade. Instead of that, Mary now experienced respect and kindness.

In a letter to Raymond a few months later she reflected on the worthlessness of human opinion and the wisdom of taking an eternal view of things, adding a wry comment on a puzzling word of praise that came to her from an unexpected source. The debts would be cleared away, a priest told her, as she was to come in for a lot of money willed by a gentleman whose name he was not at liberty to mention, and this (as he said) "for your fidelity". "Fidelity to what, I wonder," Mary remarked to Raymond.

She also found it consoling to be among the Adelaide Sisters now that the clouds of the '80s had cleared—"no contentions, strife or jealousies". A few shadows in this bright picture are referred to vaguely in a letter to Annette: "I confess that I dread Caltowie, Jamestown and Gladstone and will make those visits as short as I can—still I should not say this, even to you."

Relationships with other orders were friendly and helpful. In April 1897 the Dominicans at Kapunda were prepared to have the Josephites with them until their own house at St John's was habitable (though the pastor would not let them accept the offer). Mary retained a vivid memory of such kindness, and never missed an opportunity to repay it with a Josephite welcome. When the Mercy Sisters had trouble finding suitable accommodation for the ailing Mother Magdalen as she passed through Adelaide, the problem vanished as soon as Mary heard of it:

We all owe a debt of gratitude to Mother Magdalen for kindness to us when we had no Convent in Sydney. More than once she and some of her nuns gave up their cells and beds to us in our travels, and this when our Sisters came to them unexpectedly and at dead of night. The poor old nun cried with joy when she saw me.

Now that she was in Adelaide once more, Mary resumed personal contact with her old friend, Mrs Barr Smith. She had not been able to see much of this lady in recent times, but she did not neglect the little tokens of affection and gratitude for the kindnesses of the early years. In 1896 she sent a message from outside Adelaide for Patricia to handpaint a birthday card and let her have it in time to sign and forward to Mrs Barr Smith for the right day. She prayed for this lady every day, and her name occurs from time to time in her letters. The friendship was close enough to allow Mrs Barr Smith to remark to Mary that she did not think the Josephites had quite the same spirit of simplicity that was evident in the early days. She was still open-handed, and responded generously to a request for help in furnishing the chapel at St John's.

The work of the Mother Assistant was never ended. She had many routine duties, and extraordinary demands were constantly presenting themselves. Apart from visits to the country areas and to the Port Augusta diocese, there was much travelling to be done within the bounds of Adelaide itself. She kept up her letter-writing, although complaining that she could not write as many as she would have liked. One of her regular correspondents was Ethelburga, her nurse during her illness in Melbourne in 1892. Mary retained grateful memories of how this Sister had nursed her in those critical days, and always added a little note about her health, as to one entitled to know about it.

She spoke of tiredness and of the effect of the heat, but her general health was standing up to it very well. But as she never spared herself, it is not surprising that she became tired, and the heat (such as 104 in the shade) had never been her friend. She had thirteen more years of life, but the ailments that were to lead to the prolonged sufferings of her later years were already showing their signs. She told Annette on 11 May 1897: "My leg has been very bad. It is well I am able to rest it."

The visitation of convents and schools often took her far from Adelaide. She spoke to Annette of her reaction to this activity: "I feel strangely tired, but the work is exciting and keeps me up. The poor Sisters are all so good and kind." The impression one gets from these visits is of an angel of encouragement who had a keen eye for domestic detail and the little things that make up life on earth. The following passage, with its mention of the former orphanage boy and of the good horse, not to speak of the cup of tea, could only have come from the pen of Mary MacKillop:

> At the station there we were met by someone from Mr Kenny's who drove us to his hotel where we had a delightful cup of tea, bread and butter and cake, and then were driven out here in a nice hooded buggy—good horse—and had as driver Luke Martin once long ago an orphanage boy. We gave the Sisters a pleasant surprise.

While on these journeys, Mary looked out for opportunities to visit the families of Sisters who were on missions far away. After such a visit to the old mother of Sister Raymond, she wrote to Raymond in New Zealand with all the details, ending up: "I told her not to despair of seeing you yet." Her description of this visit shows the sort of schedule she had, and incidentally reveals that she sometimes exercised her old skills by taking the reins herself:

> Was driven yesterday to see Sister Raymond's mother who was so pleased—drove myself with Sister de Sales over there today to finish the school work and return to Caltowie. Tomorrow I go to Gladstone—Wednesday night back to Caltowie and Thursday morning will be driven from there to Pekina. Friday will go on to Petersburg, stay there that night and Saturday go to the Burra.

The foundation at Kapunda—St John's—fifty miles north of Adelaide, was not without an element of melodrama. Mary told Gertrude Mary about this Home for young girl prisoners: "This is the place which has so long had the name of being haunted, but we have seen no ghosts—though there are plenty of graves near us—the cemetery is quite close and a nice one too." But the first days had not been so smooth. There may not have been any real ghosts about, but the arrival of the Sisters seems to have been haunted by the ghost of the ambiguity displayed towards them in the old days by Frederick Byrne when he was Vicar General.

From an old Dominican nun who was there, we learn that there was only an empty house awaiting the Josephites at St John's, and that her community offered them hospitality until their own house was ready. Mary thought it would be polite to greet Father Byrne before even taking a cup of tea, but when she did so she found that he refused to allow them to stay at the Dominican Convent. In giving her own account she laughed off the predicament—they lacked the necessities of life, but they had soap, candles, and mustard! She made but a vague smiling reference to Byrne's strange intervention, with no mention of his name:

After a time we walked over to Rodgers where we got something to eat and drink. Then Mrs Rodgers had the horse put in the buggy and drove us back, bringing some cups, kettle, etc. etc. and sheets . . . We have nothing but the rocking chair to sit on. You may be sure that we won't forget our first day at St John's, and what led us to abandon our idea of remaining at Kapunda.

The pastor may have been aggrieved that the new work was outside his jurisdiction (being controlled by the Government and the Josephites), but he seems to have had second thoughts. He invited the Sisters to dinner and Mary was not slow to report his friendliness, although experience had taught her to be relieved that he had no hand in the management of the Home. Some light is thrown on the conditions at St John's by what Mary wrote to the mother of one of the Sisters who had been sent to staff it:

Every now and then she says, "Mother, what will they think of me at home—three changes already this year," and then, "Do write to Minnie and tell her it is not my fault etc. etc." Well, I may safely say that it is not her fault any more than that she is a good child and ever ready at the call of obedience to go to any place on the shortest notice. This is a new foundation and a most important one and the Sisters have to be persons of experience and tried virtue, so you see that in placing Sister Genevieve here, we are proving our trust and confidence in her.

The trouble Mary took to reassure this Mrs Wantstill about her daughter is typical of her kindly use of the pen. Letter-writing was never off her conscience. She was always at it, and always regretting that she could not do more. It enabled her to keep in touch with all the far-flung areas, separated by thousands of miles, where the Josephites were to be found. In Quirindi, in the north of New South Wales, the school debt had been paid off, and she was most grateful for that. But she did not let the town rest on its laurels. In her anxiety that it should have a worthy church, she wrote to tell them that their present one was a disgrace, and that to look at it no one would think there were so many good Catholics in the district. God's house, she said, should be the first care of his true servants.

Although she wrote to so many people, the Sisters always came first. She marked personal feast-days with a word of greeting, and she did what she could to be with each one on such an occasion, in spirit at least. As one who knew well what sickness meant, she was very practical in her advice to the ailing: "For God's sake take care of yourself," she told one, "and don't attempt to work too soon. Take the rest you require, and let the work wait."

She used the simplest language to encourage the Sisters to the highest ideals, suiting her advice to the character of the one she was writing to. Sometimes the encouragement is slipped in obliquely, as when she told Ethelburga she was saddened by a Sister who did not do her work cheerfully. On another occasion she had a more direct prescription for Ethelburga, who had a quick tongue: "Try to be very cool, patient, and charitable at Christmas. You know what I would wish you to be, what I would wish you to say and what to avoid saying."

Her news and comments were always personal, or concerned the convents and the schools. There are remarkably few references in her letters to the big events of the secular world about her. Even the Federation of the Australian Colonies does not feature in her extant correspondence. In this case, however, she could hardly have been indifferent to an event which vindicated her vision of Australia as one nation rather than a collection of adjacent colonies. She realised the value of writing about the routine events in the lives of the Sisters and those they worked with. The bonds of charity, she knew, were strengthened by a sharing of the many ordinary elements of human life. In this she anticipated the words of the Second Vatican Council when it said in 1965 that the way of love lies open to all and is "not something to be reserved for important matters, but must be pursued chiefly in the ordinary circumstances of life".

On various occasions she showed a detailed interest in the fabric of the convent buildings, the guttering, the water supply, the drainage (she often did this literal "dirty work" herself), and in domestic livestock such as chickens and ducks. From far away in New Zealand she was interested in the number of cows at the Kincumber orphanage, and whether the farm supplied them with "vegetables, butter, eggs, etc.". She was most decidedly against anything that smacked of luxury, but she was always concerned that the Sisters should be provided with healthy comfort, especially heating when the climate demanded it.

As early as August 1896 there was talk of sending a foundation to the more southerly part of the South Island of New Zealand. Mary wrote to the Provincial from Adelaide, "We are to send a community from here for Dunedin. I do not yet know who is to take them over." When the contingent was ready to travel fifteen months later, she herself was the one who took them over. Even towards the departure date, when the sense of expectancy was high, things were still uncertain because of money difficulties. The delay made Mary even busier, because the various convents were at her to come and see them just once more: "This from almost every house near Adelaide. God bless them."

Eventually, she was able to pen a quick last farewell to the Adelaide Sisters: "Goodbye and God bless you. I leave my heart with you all." In mid-October 1897 the party of four was on its way, first to Melbourne, and then by the vessel *Wakatipu* headed for Bluff in the very south of New Zealand. Mother Bernard was there to see them off, and as it turned out this was the last time she and Mother Mary saw each other in this life. One of the group, Margaret Mary Sexton, later wrote about the scene:

> Mother Bernard came on board to bid Godspeed to the little band and to say what proved to be her last goodbye to the Mother Foundress, for Mother Bernard died before Mother Mary's return to Australia. It was edifying to see Mother Mary's humility and reverence for the authority of Mother General and the latter's confidence in and love for Mother Mary.

Second Visit to New Zealand

"We were all very sick and only got to Bluff about 5 p.m. on Friday." These inauspicious words introduced Mother Mary's long letter to Mother Bernard about the Institute's arrival in southern Otago, Dunedin's hinterland, on 22 October 1897. In addition, it was raining heavily. But there was a heartening welcome awaiting them at Bluff, where they were met by Father Keenan, the pastor of remote Arrowtown. He had lodgings for the night ready for them at Invercargill, and arranged to accompany them on the train to Kingston the next morning. Mary's remark that he was "determined not to lose sight of us" was a significant one. He was not only being hospitable—he had taken possession. He was making sure he did not lose them to another parish. He had organised a welcome for them at Queenstown when they arrived after six hours by train to Kingston and a further three hours by steamer on Lake Wakatipu.

Finally on Monday, October 25, they set out on the historic journey to Arrowtown, fifteen miles away:

> When about six miles from here, a number of men and women on horseback met us; and nearer again, several in buggies. They cheered and cheered again. Such an entry as we made into the pretty town!

The two priests, Father Keenan and Father O'Donnell from Queenstown, were in the leading buggy, then came the four nuns in a large double buggy, and then other buggies and riders. Margaret Mary said what seemed to be the whole population came out to meet them—men, women, and children—some in spring-carts and buggies, others on bicycles or horses. One horse gave its girl rider some trouble, and when she had quietened him down Mary came over, patted the horse, and said to the girl: "You handled that well, dear." After this cavalcade and the rest of the excitement, the nuns were glad when finally they could "sit down to a quiet meal in our own nice little convent".

Father Keenan's presence on the wharf at Bluff had made the small party feel very welcome in the Dunedin diocese, but it had created a problem for Mary. She explained that there were only enough Sisters for one place, Port Chalmers, and that the pastor there could not be denied. But Keenan said that the bishop had promised him a community for Arrowtown, and that quarters had been ready for them there since June. Margaret Mary described how he pleaded so strongly for his little wayback children that Mary yielded and he carried off the whole company in triumph to the Cold Lake District in Central Otago.

At Queenstown, Father O'Donnell had known nothing of the work of the Josephites and thought it foolish to expect two or three Sisters to live in such an out-of-the-way place as Arrowtown. But later on he became one of the greatest friends and admirers of the Sisters, very impressed by their readiness to work away in the lonely mountains for the sake of a few children. When later conditions made it look as if they were to be withdrawn, he begged Mary to leave them, offering to provide their expenses out of his own pocket if necessary.

Mary remained a month with the pioneer "Arrow" Sisters, but she had to bear in mind that there was pressing business in Dunedin, Port Chalmers, and Rangiora. At first she thought she would have to break up the little group almost immediately, in order to help the priest at Port Chalmers, but he gave her a reprieve until after Christmas. As a result, when she left on November 22 she did not have to take a Sister with her. She was sensitive to the need of the three at Arrowtown to be reassured that their isolation in no way cut them off from the Institute, especially as they would be having their first real taste of loneliness at Christmas. She also wanted "to see that they have a proper Convent for the winter". So as soon as she had Sisters to staff the school at Port Chalmers, she returned to Arrowtown.

But when she arrived she found that things were moving very slowly in the building line. The church, school, and convent were all in the one block, and that was an advantage; and besides, the ground was high, clean, and dry. She insisted on a fence to give the Sisters some privacy. Realising from experience that she would have to exert a little pressure, she remained in the role of overseer until the last week in April although she had planned to be away in the first days of the month. She wrote that the people and the priest were most kind, "but noted, I believe, for procrastination," and she had to avail herself of the bishop's suggestion that she threaten to remove the Sisters unless they were in warm quarters before the winter.

She would have preferred to leave three Sisters there instead of two, as the need to study meant there was a danger they would not have time to prepare proper food for themselves and attend to the housework. Since she was not a regular teacher herself (though she took Catechism and also other classes when necessary), the household problem was solved while she was around. In order to have the meals up to standard, she sometimes had to ask the lady next door for advice and assistance, especially when the flounder she was cooking fell to pieces. The result of the lady's lesson made her "as proud of her success as if she were cooking for the queen instead of for two humble little professed novices". She washed the clothes, sometimes getting this done before the early morning call, and also took her share of washing up the dishes and sweeping, dusting, or gardening.

At first the two young Sisters felt a little shy about living in such a small community with the Mother Foundress, but her simplicity "very soon dispelled all feelings of restraint and they felt in her presence as free as they would have felt in that of a novitiate companion". Her government "allured to brighter worlds and led the way". The Rule was kept, but it was a kind and gentle discipline when she was around.

Once a Sister was hurrying after lunch to make the Way of the Cross. Mary quietly pointed out to her that her duty at that time was to see to the children's recreation in the playground and that on no account should this duty be set aside for religious devotion. She was sensitive to the "hierarchy of values" too where the rules were concerned, impressing on the Sisters the need to create a bright cheerful atmosphere in their little isolated convent. She said she would prefer to see Sisters who had to live in small communities in out-of-the-way places bright and cheerful, rather than strictly observing the rule of silence.

This southernmost foundation of the Josephites lasted half a century. In 1943 the decline in population made it impractical to continue, and there was general sadness when the Sisters withdrew. Throughout its isolated existence, the Arrowtown Convent was affected by the early influence of the foundress, and all those who had ever formed part of the community spoke of the little town with affection. The people still have vivid memories of the Sisters, and traditions are handed on—this one's mother was the one who prepared the tea the day the Sisters arrived; that one's mother was the one who was complimented by Mother Mary on the way she handled the bolting horse at the welcoming cavalcade; "the bowling club there is the building the Sisters used for their school . . . Mother Mary taught in there, it was then in a different part of town, but she taught in it. . ."; "that little old wreck of a stone shed was once the Sisters' house", and so on.

No place typifies the spirit of Mary MacKillop and the early Josephites better than Arrowtown—by Australian standards it is far "beyond the black stump", and by the standards of the rest of mankind it is on the edge of the earth; but it was not too humble, cold, or remote for the Sisters to go there to bring the knowledge and love of God to little children. This peculiar quality of the Josephite vocation impressed Father O'Donnell. "He venerated Mother as a saint," said Margaret Mary, "and after her death used to implore her intercession for his schools and parish." Mary herself, while pleased with the prospect of a house near Dunedin, regarded the readiness to go to the remoter places as "our real work". She wrote to Mother Bernard from Arrowtown that while it would be well to have a city house, "all the same our real work lies more in the scattered country parts—and I hope we shall never forget this."

In the providence of God, dedication nurtured by the Christian faith that had been brought by the MacDonalds and the MacKillops from the remote Highlands of Scotland had found its way to what was almost exactly the antipodes of Lochaber.

Writing from Arrowtown, Mary told of a family at Nokomai, not far away, which brought back memories of Penola: "A nephew of Uncle Cameron's and his wife are near us on the other side of Queenstown—the principal people of that part." When she was preparing to leave Arrowtown in November she wrote to this Mrs Cameron, the wife of the son of the King's brother Ewen:

> I shall be passing on to Dunedin on Monday next and should you be at home and it be convenient for you to send to meet me, would gladly spend one night with you. I must be in Dunedin on Tuesday evening as I am rather hurried. At the same time it would give me great pleasure to see you and your husband of whom as "Donald New Zealand" I used to hear so much long ago in Penola. I am very fond of all Highland friends, and though we are not cousins, feel almost as if we were for dear Uncle Cameron's sake . . . I take it for granted you know it is Mary MacKillop that was who is writing to you . . . . Yours very sincerely in J. M. J., Mary of the Cross.

She did go to Nokomai, and though she was with the Camerons for such a short time she left an impression that has remained with the family to this day—and indeed with the house—for there is a room there known as "Mother Mary's Room". The tradition grew that any child suffering from an indisposition had only to be put to sleep in "Mother Mary's Bed" to wake up normal in the morning.

Staying at the house at the time of Mary's visit was a little boy of five, Donald L. Cameron, the grandson of Donald Angus. Throughout his life he retained a vivid memory of the lovely lady with the wonderful eyes who had stayed a night at his grandfather's place, Glenfalloch Station, Nokomai. His frequent and enthusiastic repetition of the story had turned it into family folklore. This is attested by his daughter Margaret Marshall.

The Josephites had gone to Rangiora in 1887, and in the early years the story was a happy one. On her first visit in 1894 Mary had found them a happy and united community, living in a building that was very poor but properly furnished. The pastor, Father O'Connor, was extremely kind and helpful. During his last illness Mary showed constant concern from distant Australia, and at his death she wrote around asking for prayers for one who had been a devoted friend of the Institute. But his successor, Father Aubrey, had a different disposition, and while Mary was ill at Temuka in December 1897 she received an unpleasant letter from him. He had words of praise for their devotion to the late pastor in his illness, and their patience in living for eleven years in a wretched dwelling house, but had obviously little to say for them as teachers: "I am of opinion that the time of their usefulness in this parish is over and that a change of Order is imperiously demanded by the necessities of the place." He therefore asked for the Sisters to be withdrawn as soon as convenient.

This prompted quick action on the part of Mother Mary, in spite of the telegram that came from Father Aubrey on the same day saying: "Letter posted this morning kindly wait for another before taking any steps whatever." But he was dealing with somebody who knew how to analyse a situation and make a decision. Although quite unwell, she consulted the concerned parties and her local pastor, and sent the following reply:

> Rev. and dear Father, Your telegram and letter reached me yesterday. After due consideration and consultation with the Sisters, I feel that we must act upon the request made in your letter and so withdraw the Sisters for good at Xmas.

His promised second letter, just as unfortunate as the first, did nothing to induce her to alter the decision. The bishop had been in touch with him, he said, and he was modifying his demand. She might leave Sister Isidore, but would she kindly remove Gertrude and Mary Louis and replace them by somebody better. Otherwise she was to remove the lot. Mary told Annette all about it, remarking that up to that year the school had had a good report, and though this time it was not as good as before it had not failed. She sent copies of the correspondence to Bishop Grimes, who was in Europe at the time. Part of her own letter ran:

> You know, my Lord, that hitherto our Rangiora school has always received good reports from Father Goggan, and this year it might have been the same had Father Goggan had time to examine carefully. As it was, he could only give two and a half hours for the purpose, and he assures us that he would never have attempted it had he had the faintest suspicion that Father Aubrey would use his report as he did.

She assured the bishop that she had urged the Sisters of the Mission to take on the work at Rangiora and that they were happy to do so. The Josephites had tried to retire as quietly as possible, and there was plenty of work waiting for them in other places. She wrote gently of the pastor, and defended the Vicar General's behaviour during the episode. She was indeed sensitive to the feelings of the Sisters, and begged the bishop to reassure them in some way so that they would have more heart for their work "about which they are so much in earnest".

Bishop Grimes was just as unhappy with what had happened as the Josephites were. He wrote to Mary when she was again Mother

General, describing it as an outrageous act of injustice and begging her to send Sisters back to Rangiora. He described his request as a tardy but just act of reparation. Mary was prepared to send Sisters back, but found it quite impossible to fulfil her hopes of doing so. She told the bishop of her regrets, letting him know she appreciated his kind motive in urging his request.

Her further business in New Zealand in 1898 consisted of supervising the foundation of Port Chalmers, and visiting the communities and schools already established at Temuka, Kerrytown, and Waimate. A new convent was being built in Temuka to replace one that had become dangerous to live in. Those in the North Island she saw only briefly on her way home.

The New Zealand climate agreed with Mary, and in spite of the various problems she faced, her health seemed to improve. "I won't complain of the cold," she wrote, "to me it is simply delightful." She told Annette she thought it was the freedom from worry and the lovely climate that was responsible: "You would wonder to see how I can climb the hills without puffing." A few months later she told Annie the same thing, adding: "Would you believe that I am the most active Sister in this house."

She had, however, a thumb that gave her much trouble at this time, not only because it was painful, but because it made writing difficult. She told Mechtilde on March 10, "I can hardly write, my thumb being so painful that I cannot hold the pen properly." There was some improvement, but it was slow, and even in August the thumb was still giving trouble—"I dread it at times". A fortnight later she remarked: "My thumb has rather much work for its good."

She had been hoping to be back in Australia for the June Retreat, but business kept delaying her, and finally an attack of measles put her out of action for two weeks. In addition, Mother Bernard wished her to settle some difficulty in Auckland, so it was early August before she was ready to leave New Zealand for Sydney. A reference to a rough sea trip from Napier makes it clear that she visited the Meeanee Sisters on the way up to take the northern route home. We do not have much detail about her visits to the schools in the North Island. There is no reference to a visit to Matata, but as she mentions her intention to leave for Australia on the 15th, it is likely that she planned to visit there in the meantime but had to change her plans and leave for Australia at once.

In the last days of 1897 news had come from Rome that Cardinal

Moran was authorised to extend Mother Bernard's period of office until the Chapter scheduled to take place in 1902. There would thus be no election in 1898 as promised. Mary commented to Annette on this surprising turn of events: "Personally I am not disappointed or pained, but I am sorry for the disappointment of my dear good Sisters and oh, I am sorry for M. Bernard herself."

Seven months later, on 3 August 1898, there came another unexpected piece of news—Mother Bernard was dead. This was shortly after her last letter ("her last two letters to me were particularly nice ones") had arrived. So Mary had to make a quick change of plans:

> I had only reached Auckland on Sunday, received her *last* letter on Monday—Wednesday saw the Bishop and got back to find the cable of her death and had less than half an hour to catch the steamer for Sydney—the San Francisco mail.

THIRTY-ONE

A MOST

SUBTLE CROSS

The Generalate of Mother Bernard 1885–1898

During the years 1885–1898 Mother Mary played the role of consoling angel to people in many walks of life; but her energy was mainly devoted to encouraging her Josephite Sisters, and to assisting Mother Bernard with the management of the affairs of the widespread Institute.

What occasioned her the greatest concern, however, was the fate of the Institute under the rule of a Mother General who, for all her goodness, can only be described as weak, yielding and incompetent. That may seem a hard judgment to make on a fine woman like Mother Bernard, but the evidence is there. The impact of the situation on the foundress could be described perhaps as the most subtle cross of her life, posing at the same time a complex spiritual problem.

Mary had previously seen the Institute threatened by men in authority, but she had the law on her side when she defended it. In Brisbane, Bathurst and Adelaide, she knew that the bishops were acting outside their powers when they brought pressure to bear on the unity and independence of the Institute. Rome had always supported her, but in this present case the threat to the Institute was coming from a source sanctioned by Rome itself. Although the authorities there supported the Constitutions, they consented for a proposed seventeen years to a government that did not emerge from those Constitutions but from the will of Cardinal Moran. Mary recognised that the situation, however unhelpful to the Institute, was a legal one. She accepted it as the will of God, but she was also convinced that God willed her to do what she could, within the limits of obedience and charity, to minimise its negative effects.

In 1885, when Propaganda issued the directive that Mary was to stand down because her election in 1881 was invalid, Moran appointed Bernard temporary Mother General. In announcing the decision to the Sisters, Mary reminded them of the faith that lay at the foundation of their religious dedication, and of the charity that should animate all their endeavours: "Now, my own Sisters, be of good heart and be one with the Superior God has given through His Church." Bernard's kindness was remarked on by several in commenting on her appointment. Mary supported the choice, and a number of Sisters' letters expressed gladness that, if they had to have a change, Sister Bernard was the one. It seems that, like many another, her unfitness did not become apparent until the burdens of the office began to weigh upon her.

Nobody had been given much time to think about the choice, and in any case they understood that the appointment would only be effective until a Chapter was called (as soon as possible, said the Roman document of 8 May 1885) to elect a new Mother General. It was in the light of the fact that Cardinal Moran had been told to hold this election that Mother Bernard said: "There is comfort to me in the certainty that this trial will not last for long."

But, as it turned out, Moran's choice was not of someone to be in charge for the few months that would elapse before a Chapter could be held, but for: (1) the period until the Propaganda Decree of 1888, then (2) the period of ten years dating from that Decree, and (3) the period between the end of those ten years and the Chapter foreseen for the latter half of 1902. That would have amounted in all to nearly seventeen years, but Bernard died unexpectedly just as she completed the ten years of the second period, that is, after twelve years as Mother General.

Not long after her appointment, however, it became apparent that the new Mother General was not up to the demands of the office, and the situation did not improve with time. The result was not merely inefficient government, but a real threat to the welfare of the Institute, and indeed to its very existence. It will be seen from instances soon to be discussed that it was not only in matters of business that Mother Bernard was lost—such a situation could have found a remedy—but she seemed confused by the ordinary demands made on her and incapable of attending to the routine duties of her office. Letters demanded by administrative necessity, or simply by good manners, were frequently not written. Personal concern for the Sisters and attention to their ordinary needs seemed to escape her notice. Anything at all unusual seemed to paralyse her power of decision making; the consequent inaction was often fraught with dangerous possibilities.

In one matter at least, that of select schools, she was induced to allow something not only against the spirit of the Institute but contrary to its law. The foundations in New Zealand never seem to have gripped her imagination, and she showed no enthusiasm about implementing the decision of the Chapter to take up a mission among the Aboriginal people in Australia's north. Her inability to understand the situation in which she found herself left her open to flattery, as this gave her a temporary feeling of security. It was a hollow consolation, and the gulf between her thinking and that of the foundress became wider and wider. When confronted by a relaxation of discipline Bernard knew no way of tightening the reins consistent with her gentle character. Even open insubordination was a challenge she was unable to meet.

Bernard was not a great letter-writer. The style of her letters does not reflect a standard of literacy higher than ordinary, and what she has to say does not indicate that she was of more than ordinary intelligence. The style and tone of some early official letters bearing her signature are so noticeably different from her usual writing that they are apparently the work of some other hand. It would not be an easy thing to find materials for a *Life* of Mother Bernard, or for a full history of the Institute during her Generalate, nor is it within the compass of this present work to attempt such a task. The task here is, rather, to illustrate the problems confronting the Mother Assistant during those years, to show that she had real grounds for concern, and to reveal how she handled the trying situation. Thus, for example, the long story of the Institute's attempts to grapple with its financial problems in Adelaide in the late '80s, and of its harassment by Dr Reynolds during the last half-dozen years of his life, has its place in the history of Mary MacKillop only in so far as it throws light on her attempts to help the Mother General.

An interested observer of the scene was the Bishop of Port Augusta, John O'Reily. He expressed himself to Mother Bernard firmly on more than one occasion, and a study of his interventions provides light for a judgment on those of Mother Mary. The bishop was an intelligent man, well trained in theology and law, and well versed in spiritual principles. He knew the Institute's problems, and we know he discussed them with Mary, so it would not be rash to maintain that the two had agreed that it would be a sound contribution to the welfare of the Institute if Bernard were helped to some kind of intellectual grasp of her position. In a way that Mary could hardly do with propriety, O'Reily tried at various times to enlighten the Mother General about the principles underlying authority, both in regard to the exercise of her own and in regard to people claiming to exercise it over her.

One such attempt of the bishop to lend Bernard some strength occurred just before Moran's return to Australia with the final approbation of the Institute in 1888. On October 10 Reynolds told the Mother General she was not to leave Adelaide:

> I have been duly notified of the coming of His Eminence the Cardinal who will arrive (D. V.) in Adelaide about 12 of November. I therefore *direct you not to leave* this Colony, until he arrives, as an important interview shall take place, between us, and at which you shall be present.

Hearing of this order, O'Reily wrote to Bernard on October 19 that he was "decidedly of opinion" that Reynolds had no authority to issue such an order. On the contrary, the cardinal's directive that she return speedily to Sydney was a very serious reason for *not* remaining in Adelaide. In point of fact, she remained in Adelaide, but the cardinal did not even go ashore when his ship came in (perhaps he was annoyed that his instruction for her to meet him in Sydney had not been observed), and the important meeting referred to by Reynolds never took place. Instead, the cardinal sent Bernard another message to meet him in Sydney—a turn of events that could hardly have improved her confidence.

Moran's behaviour undermined the position Reynolds had taken up, and won him no favour in that quarter. O'Reily for his part, knowing his Adelaide colleague well, was aware that his own attempt to safeguard the due order of authority would not have won him any favour either. "But it will be worse," he wrote to Mary, "should it leak out what advice I gave to Mother General on the question of her departure or otherwise from Adelaide."

Later examples of O'Reily's attempts to help Bernard understand her position and to strengthen her hand occurred in two instances of insubordination among the Sisters in 1890–91. Writing of the first case, that of Sister Cyril, he told the Mother General that to allow this Sister's fault to pass unnoticed would be to proclaim to every member of the Sisterhood that if a discontented Sister could not have her way by asking, she could have it by taking the law into her own hands. Invoking Cyril's own interests, the interests of the Sisters in the diocese, the interests of the whole order, and the interests of obedience, he said she "*must be compelled* to return *forthwith* to the post which she has deserted, placing herself there in her Provincial's hands. If local authority is despised, contempt of central authority is not far off. When subordination fails, the Order itself is lost."

O'Reily said he wrote strongly because he felt strongly, and he felt strongly because of the injury done to an order which he esteemed so much. It seems that he wrote strongly, too, because he had reason to fear that the Mother General would react weakly to the challenge. This is made clear in the second instance of disobedience, a more serious one. In May 1891 Sister Borgia had refused to obey a repeated order of her Provincial, Calasanctius, to move to another place.[1] The bishop wrote to Bernard, stating explicitly that his fears about her timidity had induced him to write to her strongly about the case. Calasanctius had his full support, he said, and in the interests of religion, in the interests of the Institute, and in the interests of the offender, "Borgia's obedience must be insisted on and with that obedience an apology for her disrespectful letter to her Provincial." Milder counsels, he warned, would have lamentable, indeed fatal, consequences.

When Borgia said in defence that she was going to appeal to her higher superior, the bishop wrote again to Bernard, evidently convinced of the need to warn her of the danger of undermining the authority of a Provincial. He asked her not to do anything until she had heard from him, as he saw Borgia setting a painful example of avowed and persistent disobedience to the Provincial's orders. "If Sr Calasanctius is to be Provincial," he said, "she ought to be free to do Provincial's work." She should not be tied down to daily school duties, as this makes it impossible for her to give time to the business to which she is appointed. He would rather close a school than jeopardise the whole order by allowing her office to be treated this way.

He took up the theme again a few days later, in an instructive disquisition on government and obedience he sent to Bernard. Everybody has the right of appeal, he said, but nobody has the right to disobey commands in the meantime and insolently avow a determination to persist in that disobedience. In view of hints that he was interfering with central government, he made his own position clear, distinguishing it carefully from that of those bishops who had usurped authority within the Institute. He was issuing no orders, no directives of any sort, he was merely doing his duty to protect the authority of the Provincial, linked as it was so closely to that of the Mother General. "My right only, as my duty," he said, "is to see that the commands of her who has authority are obeyed—so far as my influence can secure such obedience." He pointed out that his appeal to Bernard could have no meaning if he did not respect central government.

As well as writing to Bernard directly about this disturbing matter, O'Reily asked Mary on one occasion to relay his views. She did so very plainly. She told Bernard that he deplored the rebellious disposition of some of the Sisters towards their Provincial, and regretted that her authority was not better maintained at headquarters. In this Mary said she agreed with him. Things were very serious as far as the spirit of discipline was concerned, and the work could not last if things continued that way. The Congregation would crumble away bit by bit without a spirit of obedience in its members. She concluded:

> Now, to sum up. Be careful. Dr O'Reily is a good disinterested friend—he has no *pettiness* about him—he likes the Sisters, sees their faults and their virtues. He does not interfere as long as he sees order maintained, and knows that the Poor Sisters are doing their best. But do not try him *too far*. For any other act such as Sister Borgia's—if repeated—he says he will follow up to the bitter end, that is, he will lay all before the Cardinal showing him the want of discipline and how it is—or will—ruin the Congregation if not checked.

This was serious business. A few months later Mary repeated the substance of the bishop's advice when she wrote again about the trouble in Port Augusta. She warned Bernard against undermining the authority of superiors by weakly encouraging disgruntled Sisters. Borgia was not the only one involved—a small group of discontents intended to apply pressure to have the Provincial removed. After questioning the Sisters, she had concluded that the two who were really behind the trouble (a third had been drawn in without being a prime mover) had created the false impression that everybody was unhappy with Calasanctius. Compared to the way O'Reily had repeatedly expressed his views to Bernard, Mary's words were very mild. But important values were at stake, and she wrote in her normal simple and forthright manner because she knew by experience how hard it was to convey a sense of reality to the distant Mother General. She wanted her words to be effective.

The financial crisis confronting the Institute in Adelaide in 1890 is another good example of the problems that faced the Mother Assistant. She could see that the pressure on the Adelaide Superior to meet the interest payments on the mortgages had become critical, and the Mother General in Sydney showed no signs of making a decision to face it in any way. The problem would not solve itself, the only conceivable reason for inaction being the possible hope that the ailing Archbishop might die. Veronica did indeed say twice in the course of one letter: "His Grace cannot live long." But as long as he lived it was clear that he was determined to make things hard for the Sisters, by preventing them from selling property and forbidding them to collect money to pay the interest. The mortgagees would before long be able to foreclose and sell Kensington over their heads.

It seems to have been the Archbishop's hope that in the final outcome of this transaction he would emerge as the sole owner of the property. One of the Sisters' worries was that scandal would arise when the people found what had happened. Critical tongues would not spare the Archbishop for such shabby treatment of a body of religious who had served the diocese so selflessly.

Mary intervened to help deal with the crisis. She had advised Bernard to send the General Treasurer, Veronica, to Adelaide with authority to act on her behalf, but the suggestion had not been taken up. She had asked Bishop Higgins, Moran's assistant, to approach the cardinal about the Institute's plight, but he had told her it was her duty to do this herself. So, knowing that her motive could be misunderstood and that her intervention could be seen as interference in the Mother General's office, she wrote a letter outlining the facts for the cardinal and begging him to help Mother Bernard with his advice in her trying position.

Sister Veronica was in fact sent to Adelaide. In the face of grossly discourteous treatment she handled the problem with great patience and competence. Although Reynolds had ultimately been forced to tolerate central government under pressure from Moran, it is clear that his bitterness pursued the Josephites. He expected to have his own way, as Mary was no longer in charge and Bernard was perplexed and indecisive. Veronica's letter to Bernard shows that the situation was serious and that it was a good thing she was there to deal with it. Reynolds sent her a message that it was necessary to inform him first in writing of the nature of her business and from whom she came. When she produced papers he would still not see her personally but made it clear through his messenger, Dean Nevin, that he was not going to cooperate. She bullied back a bit by asking why Mother Bernard was treated to silence when she wrote. She reported to Bernard that instead of helping the Sisters who were teaching in his schools, His Grace tied up their hands and would not allow them to do one single thing that would help them out of their difficulties. He was a hard master and very cruel. He was always talking about the good thing he did when he took his poor flock out of the hands of the Josephites.

"If I were you," she told Bernard, "I would give notice to the Archbishop on the 1st December saying that you would give up this place, the Sisters are no better than slaves, working for nothing, without time for even their prayers; it is unjust to the Sisters." In some of these small places they had to raffle cushions and do sewing to get the means of existence. "It is sad to see Sister Monica going out every day," she said, "and she not able, giving lessons for this Interest; it is nothing short of persecution. It will finish Sister Monica, so it begins and ends in this, there is nothing for it but to sell Kensington." One priest told her that Reynolds would crush the Sisters and drive them into further difficulties unless they took a stand. Other men she trusted told her that if the Sisters did make a stand they would not be as they were in Adelaide. "I will stand my ground," she said, "if you don't recall me."

Bishop O'Reily in Port Augusta was not at all happy with the attitude of the Archbishop of Adelaide, as Veronica told Mary:

> He thinks that permission to collect for the debt should be obtained from the Holy See. The people of Adelaide are only too willing to help the Sisters, and if their place is sold, there will be rebellion among the people; if others forget their work, the people don't.

On August 21 Veronica thought it necessary to put Bernard on her guard with a warning about the Sydney properties. "They can sue for any portion of their debt left unpaid . . . So, my dearest M. G. , be careful. We must know our legal position first and not rush on headlong and yet deeper into it." She was betraying misgivings about the Mother General's ability to grasp the situation and to take the necessary action: "If you wish me to suggest anything let me know, but be sure and answer this letter. Be sure and answer this, and don't be keeping things back." Veronica's letter to Mary on October 2 contains more than one hint that Bernard could not be relied on to take necessary or advisable action, and Mary is asked to urge her to it.

Monica's influence over the Sisters in Adelaide was most precious, and many would be lost without it, but in addition Mary should write to each Sister occasionally, as they are being tried so sorely.

The tendency to approach Bernard through Mary, as a surer means of stirring her into action than the direct approach, is evident also in some of O'Reily's correspondence. For example, to counter Reynolds' obstructionist tactics, he wrote to Mary in July 1889 about a plan for the Sisters' retreat. Then he made two remarks that were perhaps hints that all was not well from the point of view of administration. There were Sisters overdue for vows; and he hoped for "great good for the Order to be secured by the labour of the delegates" to the coming Chapter. He concluded: "Give my best wishes to M. B. and ask her to regard this note as one addressed to herself as well as to you." It seems that he had more confidence in getting some action by writing to Mary, but this would surely have made her heart sink, and it would hardly have reassured Bernard to read it.

The Leichhardt-Villa Maria episode is another illustration of the kind of thing Mary had to cope with. It concerned a change she made in Sydney during an absence of Bernard in 1888. On Monday April 30 Bernard wrote from Adelaide:

> I have heard that Sister Eulalia is in Sydney. Well it is better for her to stop there until I go back. On no account let her go to Villa Maria or we will be sorry. I have a place that will suit her to perfection.

On the next day, Tuesday May 1, before she could possibly have received this letter, Mary wrote to Eulalia at Leichhardt:

> You complain of the Leichhardt house and that you cannot teach much, and accuse your Superiors of favouring others at your expense. Well, dear Sister, you and Sister Maria are to go to Villa Maria, and Sister Agnes go to Leichhardt.

She had not wished to act hurriedly, so she had been in touch with Bernard herself, who had replied: "I know dear Mother you will know what is best." As she had also conferred with the Josephite Council and Cardinal Moran, the decision had clearly been made after more than adequate consultation, as well as with the conviction that the Mother General had given authority to decide what seemed best. On Saturday, May 5, however, the following telegram arrived from Adelaide for Mother Mary:

> Do not change Sister Agnes from Villa Maria leave them as I left them Leichhardt same will write particulars if changed bring back before Monday.

This was followed by an angry and temperamental letter from Mother Bernard. Some of its expressions are unkind and quite unfair. Its surprising tone suggests that she may have succumbed to the influence of Dr Reynolds, as well as to the pressure of business she could not handle. She was evidently quite out of touch, not only with the probity of her Assistant, but with the character of Cardinal Moran, as the latter never gave any sign that he was a man who would suffer words to be put into his mouth. She wrote:

> I am very sorry to hear that you have made the change at Villa Maria. I never thought you would do such a foolish thing. Why disturb a school like Villa Maria at the wrong time to please others . . . When I go back I will make the change again. If you wanted to change Leichhardt, why did you not send Sr Irene in there . . . [*etc.*, *etc.*] I see now why you wanted me to go to W. A. or not to be in a hurry home. The Industrial school was not in such a hurry. I received a telegram last week from you in which you said His Eminence agreed or some such word, but I think the word was put into his mouth. If I wished to speak I would tell you more than I would here. I have heard plenty but always hid it but will no longer. Your telegram last evening said all parties agreeable, but pardon me to say I fear not . . . You will say it is all temper. Such is not the case. I will still adhere to what I said and will do. I left all in happiness and the bills pretty well paid, so it was not much I asked you to do.

In May 1897 Mary sent on to Annette a letter from Bishop Grimes of Christchurch, with her own comment on the back of it:

> Dr Grimes is wild over the way Sr Isabelle has been treated. I know all now. Poor M. G. did wrong in listening to slanderers, and Sister's character would have been ruined only for the Bishop and Vicar General.

There is ample documentation on this episode. An accusation had been sent to Bernard by an outsider (an ex-Brother Peter) that Sister M. Isabelle was in the habit of seeing a Mr St George (a friend of the Sisters) in the evening after night prayers. Part of Isabelle's own account was that two of the Sisters had this Peter "over in the community room to recreation nearly every night, told him the whole trouble, made the Marist Fathers and their Bishop here a constant subject of ridicule and myself into the bargain because I would not side with them". Peter had been urged by these Sisters to write to Bernard, because Isabelle had disapproved of his being made too welcome in the community room of the convent. As for the accusation against herself, she told Father Cummings when he asked her if she saw Mr St George after night prayers: "I had a recollection of once during the Bazaar time that he called on a Sunday night; the Sisters were in the oratory, he had been to the presbytery and Father Regnault had given him a message for me. I couldn't remember any other time."

Bernard had reacted rashly to Peter's accusing letter. She did not enquire from anyone in New Zealand about his story, and she did not seek the opinion of her Assistant, one who knew the situation and the Sisters better than she did. Instead, she was credulous, and persisted in her own judgment even after the bishop and several priests had written in defence of Isabelle. Grimes' letter to Isabelle indicates the anger and frustration he felt at the Mother General's action:

> I will readily comply with your request to see the Rev. Mother General, though to speak candidly I had felt so disgusted that I had almost resolved not to go near the Mother House . . . Be assured though that I will not fail to say what I think when I go to Sydney.

Mary wrote to Bernard about the affair, reporting that the priests found the treatment of their communications inexcusable, and deploring that the bishop's letter had not received a reply. She urged her to believe good priests rather than hidden slanderers and suspicious Sisters, and concluded by stating her conviction that detraction was the besetting sin of the Institute.

When Bishop Luck was not happy with the way the Institute's affairs were being managed in Auckland, he wrote to Bernard firmly and with some feeling:

> It is not a pleasure to complain—but you must allow me on this occasion to make a complaint as to the manner in which you have *so far* carried out the agreement we arrived at whilst I was in Sydney.

He wished their relationship to remain as friendly as it had always been, but he expected agreements to be faithfully carried out. He also suggested that if she wished to preserve the bond of union and good will with the Sisters, she should not treat them the way she was treating Teresa.

Similar dissatisfaction was expressed by priests from time to time, and the evidence shows that there was good foundation for what they had to say. Mary Joseph in Temuka told in 1890 how Bernard had promised to send Father Regnault a community in Waimate within six months, and to come herself and discuss it with him within a month. She had neither come nor written. If she found it impossible to keep her promise, said Mary Joseph, "it would be better for her to write and say so than to treat him with silent contempt . . . We are quite ashamed because these French priests are so very polite, and they seem to be greatly surprised at being treated so impolitely."

The Institute's great friend, Father Fauvel, found it necessary to protest angrily to Mother Bernard about the way she had treated him and the New Zealand Sisters—so angrily that Mary wrote back on her behalf (Bernard was ill and could not manage any business) explaining that she felt it would upset her too much to see the letter, and asking him to agree that it be not shown to her, especially as part of his problem had been solved in the meantime. In the extant correspondence there are numerous such complaints about Bernard's failure to fulfil promises or to attend to necessary business. There are likewise examples of Mary's almost desperate attempts to prompt her into action, to warn her of pitfalls, and to help her cope with a delicate situation. Late in 1891 she wrote from Melbourne, "Now, dear Mother, I have said enough to put you on your guard when writing—and I beg that you do so at once to His Grace. Delay will irritate him."

For a long time the Sisters in New Zealand hoped that Bernard would fulfil her promise to visit them, but they were disappointed. Something always led to a postponement. This was not always without good cause, as Mary pointed out in defending the Mother General on one occasion: "Many urgent things occur to prevent the M. G. always carrying out things as she would wish." But for one reason or another it turned out that in all her years of office Bernard never visited New Zealand. She did, however, send Mary twice, and thus vicariously did much for the Sisters there. Even so it is plain enough that she did not always support the decisions of her Assistant, and this breaking of official promises was embarrassing to the Assistant. In such a situation only the personal presence of the Mother General would give the security that decisions demanded. Mary urged the Provincial in October 1892: "You should make one more effort to get M. General over to see you all."

The establishment of select schools—those other than primary schools for poor children—was one matter on which Mary could not approve of current policy in 1895. The Chapter of 1889 had said: "Only parochial and, where necessary, free schools are to be taught by the Sisters." But on her return from New Zealand in 1895 she was amazed to discover that select schools had already been approved and established. It seems that she became aware of this quite accidentally, hearing it from the captain of the ship on her way back to Australia. When he complimented her on the opening of a grand secondary school in Adelaide—"You are going to do wonders!"—she felt (she said later) as if her heart had ceased to beat. On arrival she expressed herself strongly: "They are against our Rule and spirit and *never* will have my sanction." The next Chapter voted the select schools out of existence. This all makes unconscious irony of a short interchange of question and answer at the Process in 1928. They asked Mother Laurence: "You don't think she ever swung away from the ideal of teaching poor children in the primary school?" She replied, "No, not at all. I know Mother was never happy while two schools were open that were called select schools." Archbishop Kelly cut in with: "Could the Pope have rebuked Mother Mary for not maintaining the Rule in this regard?"

Another of the things Mother Mary had found difficult to adjust to during these years was Mother Bernard's failure to show interest in the directive of the 1889 Chapter that the Josephites should undertake work with the Aboriginal people in the far north of Australia. Father Duncan McNab, the MacKillop cousin who had come to Australia from Scotland, had gone to Europe in 1879 to plead the cause of the Aborigines with both the Colonial Office in London and the Church officials in Rome. As a result of McNab's Roman visit, the Holy See called the attention of the Jesuit General to the needs of the Australian native peoples, and he in turn directed his men to take up missionary work in the Northern Territory. In 1882 they began at Rapid Creek, but after a few years the station was transferred to the Daly River, further inland, and the Jesuit missionary enterprise in the Northern Territory has come to be known by that name.

A brave effort was made to introduce agriculture at some distance from the white population, and to provide education and medical attention for the Aborigines. The approach was similar to the one that had succeeded in Paraguay in the seventeenth and eighteenth centuries, but Australian conditions were very difficult. Owing to the nature of the country and the nomadic habits of the people, progress was slow and reverse followed reverse. Eventually the obstacles proved too great and the whole enterprise was closed down in 1899.

One of the Jesuits who worked at the Daly River Mission was Father Donald MacKillop, Mary's brother. This fact no doubt had something to do with the application made by the Jesuit Superior to the Sisters of St Joseph in 1889 to provide Sisters for the Mission. The Chapter of that year directed that the Institute should provide a community for the Mission, and Mary eagerly looked forward to taking the first Sisters there and seeing them settled in the work. But year followed year and nothing was done. It sometimes looked as if Sisters were about to be sent, as when Father Donald came south at the end of 1892. But the Sisters never went. From New Zealand Mary commented to Annette early in 1898:

> I am sorry, sorrier far than I can say, that there should be such apathy about the Northern Territory mission. Mother General, naturally, or rather from the first, shrank from that work, but all are not of her opinion, and I am sure a community could be made up.

A few months later she was to write: "Poor M. Bernard's death was indeed sudden . . . I don't think there will be any fear for the Black mission now as far as we are concerned." As Bernard's former Assistant, she was in charge until the Chapter could elect a successor. She reassured her brother:

> I want to know for certain if the Sisters will be required for the Daly Mission next year. Whatever other plans may have to wait for Sisters, the Mission must be supplied if the Fathers are ready, and I want to be in a position to bring this strongly forward at our G. Chapter.

There can be no doubt about her positive enthusiasm for this mission, but when the Jesuits withdrew in 1899 the Sisters were left no base to work from. Total disaster struck when the Daly River flooded in March, destroying every vestige of building and cultivation, but it appears that the decision to withdraw had already been made. The question must remain forever unanswered: might the closure have been avoided if the Sisters had come? "We shall never succeed without Sisters," Donald wrote in 1888, "they are the want. I would ask for Sisters tomorrow if I had the means to support them and to prepare a nice home for them—something better far than we put up with." But his dream was never to be fulfilled, nor was Mary's, and it was many decades before the Josephites were to be seen in Australia's north and north-west.

These several instances have been given at some length to show that Mother Mary was by no means the only person who was disturbed by the shortcomings of the Mother General. Bishop O'Reily, Bishop Grimes and Bishop Luck each expressed his concern in no uncertain language, and felt constrained to offer stern advice; a number of friendly priests, such as Father Fauvel and Father Regnault, spoke critically to Mother Bernard about the way the Institute was being governed; and some Sisters in responsible positions, like Veronica, showed they had little confidence in their Mother General's competence.

Seeing as plainly as anyone that things were not going well, Mary was confronted by a personal dilemma. It would have been relatively easy to withdraw entirely, to give up, to preserve an absolute silence, to be uncritical and to allow the situation to deteriorate unchecked. The temptation to do this could have been based on the idea that the foundress, being no longer Superior, could thereby give an admirable example of self-abnegation and humility by her "non-interference" with the decisions of her successor. But was this the course dictated by prudence? Moreover, was it true obedience, and could she reconcile it with her duty as Assistant General? Above all, was it charity?

On the other hand, if the foundress were seen to be "interfering", or were known to be opposed to the policies of the Mother General, to be critical of her decisions or her inaction, it would have been only too easy to remark that one who had preached obedience had no idea how to submit to the authority of another, or how to keep her place humbly as a subject. Observers could even create the fiction of a clique centred on a disgruntled Mother Mary. Archbishop Carr once thought he had come across evidence of a "party" in her favour, and warned her not to "tolerate to the slightest extent the existence of such a fatal division in your ranks". This was good advice, no doubt warranted by the thoughtless observation of the Sister who had said to him, "Mother Mary is our real Mother though Mother Bernard may be our nominal one." But there is no evidence that Mary encouraged anything like a party in her favour, or was likely to tolerate it in any way. At the Process, Annette gave direct evidence to the contrary:

> A great many did not wish to have Mother Bernard but Mother Mary did not side with them. She was very much against parties. She paid every respect to M. Bernard. She never showed any lack of loyalty and did not show signs of desiring to return to office.
> She did everything for Mother Bernard. I did the management of business for her because Mother Bernard was no business woman. One day Mother Bernard cried to me saying, "If Mother Mary were here she would not allow the Sisters to speak so disrespectfully to me."

Remarks made by Veronica in her letters of August 1890—such as the suggestion that Mary should visit Port Augusta as the bishop wished, and that she should write to each Sister to encourage her—could easily be made to look like canvassing, or an attempt to have her set up in contrast to Mother Bernard. But the contrast did not need to be set up—it was obvious to all. Both Veronica and Mary were members of the General Council, one as Treasurer and the other as Assistant General, and the two were perfectly entitled to discuss the weaknesses of the Institute and the possible good that might result from a visit and some letters from the foundress. As far as Mary was personally concerned, the danger of a party was non-existent, as such a course would have been a violent contradiction of her whole cast of mind. If she had observed it in the minds of others she would have repudiated it vigorously, and sternly lectured those responsible. Bernard's authority was to be respected because her appointment was made by legitimate authority. Mary could not deny that it caused serious difficulties, but these had to be faced within the limits of obedience and charity.

There were two distinct elements in what the Sisters wanted, though they could appear superficially as one and the same. There was the strong desire to be free to elect their own superior according to the Constitutions, and there was the likelihood that their choice would fall again on the foundress. Although there is no documentary evidence to show why Cardinal Moran kept Mother Bernard in office, there is no reason to think that it was because he wanted her personally in preference to some other. It *is* clear that he had some reason for wanting Mother Mary kept out. However, he knew that if the Sisters were allowed a vote in Chapter they would most probably re-elect her. Hence, throughout the years when he imposed Bernard on the Institute, any suggestion that the Sisters should be allowed to observe their Constitutions by electing their own Mother General could be interpreted by unsympathetic minds as the plot of a clique intent on restoring the foundress as Mother General.

Mary was well aware of this tangled situation. She was disturbed by what she could see, and she was sensitive to the disadvantages of each of the alternatives open to her, action or inaction. The course she chose was to do her best to help the Mother General, and to encourage the Sisters to be faithful to their Rule and to respect the one placed over them.

Mary spoke her mind to Bernard when she thought it her duty to do so. She was not only the foundress with a reasonable right to call attention to deviations from the spirit and the law of the Institute, but she also had rules to keep as Assistant General and as a member of the Council. The Rules for General Guidance of the Sisters contain a section dealing with the duties of the members of the Council. Rule no. 1 says that "they must frankly give her the benefit of their opinion when duty requires it, even though that opinion may not accord with hers"; no. 9 of the same Rules prescribes the duty of the Assistant General:

> . . . humbly and charitably to admonish the Superior General of any faults against her office which may be seen in her conduct, and to make known to her what in her conduct gives either disedification or dissatisfaction to others, and this not to incense her against others, but simply that she may correct what is amiss in herself and better discharge the duties of her office.

This put Mary in an awkward position. Any act or word of hers intended as a fulfilment of this duty could be interpreted, by those seeking to do so, as an expression of resentment against the appointment of Mother Bernard. The irony of the situation is that she who saw to it that the duties of the Assistant were set down in the Rule, in the expectation that they would lead *her* Assistant to admonish her of her failings, found herself in a situation where it was *she* who had the duty to admonish another. She proceeded to do what any other Sister would have been bound to do as Assistant General.

She was well aware that in fulfilling this duty she was leaving herself open to the criticism that she was discontented with her subordinate position. But she was not in the habit of facing situations politically. She saw each moment simply as a challenge to find and follow the will of God. Decisions made according to this principle, she knew, did not always please everybody, but she saw this as a cross to be borne, not as a consideration to be allowed to influence her choice. What would be said of her today if it were known that she had remained silent in the face of a gravely deteriorating situation, and did not try to offer effective help to a struggling and clearly harassed Mother Bernard? Failure to be honest and courageous in pointing out deficiencies would have been a fault, more or less serious, on the part of the Mother Assistant.

The purpose of giving advice to the Mother General was not simply to be able to say that advice had been given, and that duty had thereby been done, but to see that it registered effectively on her mind. To ensure this, it was necessary to speak plainly, as is clear from what was said to Mother Bernard by Bishop O'Reily, Bishop Grimes, Bishop Luck, Sister Veronica, and the various priests who have already been cited. There is no reason to think that in expressing themselves strongly and clearly these people were moved by any other spirit than that of disinterested good will.

Mother Mary, honest by disposition and forthright by the necessity of the case, likewise spoke directly and clearly. But divorced from this context, and from the well-attested character of the writer, some of her words led one of the theological examiners of her writings to suggest in 1953 (January 15 in fact!) that she spoke sharply and bitterly, and that she lacked humility, magnanimity, generosity, sweetness, discretion, and a high level of charity. She seemed to be giving orders rather than advice, and if she had been truly selfless she would have found some better way of helping Mother Bernard. One sentence of Mary's, cited as questionable, was this:

> In any case I do not like the look of sending that transfer to strange lawyers. It should have come to me direct—and I could then see our own about it. I beg of you not to allow such a thing to be done again. I have too much reason to be on my guard—and also have you.

The critic was asking that the possibility of a negative interpretation of this be removed. The fact is that Mary had here been entrusted with conducting a delicate piece of business fraught with important consequences, and she found that without her knowledge lawyers other than the Institute's regular attorney had been brought into it. Worse still, the lawyer employed by the man who was seeking occasion to crush the Sisters had somehow managed to become their legal representative! Painful experience enabled Mary to recognise an explosive situation. Her warning to Bernard, perfectly reasonable in the light of the past history of the Institute, was expressed in words that reflected the seriousness of the danger. Her protest against this disastrous turn of events was in fact very restrained, and much stronger language would have been perfectly justified.

Two other reflections of the critic call for comment. He thought that it was possible to detect a certain bitterness in Mary's failure to congratulate Bernard on the extension of her time as Mother General, and that some of her utterances betrayed signs of ambition to be re-elected to the office herself.

After Mary heard in 1897 that Bernard's term of office had been extended for another five years, she wrote to her:

> The tidings from Rome came as a surprise—God's will be done. I

cannot congratulate you knowing what this must mean for you—but with all my heart I pray that God will strengthen you to be a kind and just Mother to those again committed to your care.

It is enlightening to recall what Mary had written to Dr Campbell about her own re-election in 1881:

It was with the deepest grief that I found myself re-elected. I had hoped that it would be otherwise and longed for that which it does not seem to have been God's will to grant me.

Mary MacKillop knew just what the burdens of the office meant to a Mother General. When the expression, "I shall not congratulate you," occurred in a letter she received from a friendly priest on this occasion of her own re-election, she had no doubt readily appreciated his sympathetic meaning. The words were meant to convey a feeling of good will and sympathy to somebody who has to shoulder a heavy burden. Mary's habit of using language in a forthright and direct manner, with no lip-service to empty conventional phrases, would have demanded that she refrain on this occasion from congratulations, which are meant to express appreciation for some personal achievement, or at least to signal the advent of some good fortune. Neither was appropriate on this occasion. She expressed her good will by assuring Mother Bernard of her heartfelt prayers and promising that she would give her all the help she could. To see bitterness in the words, it would be necessary to understand them in a sense quite contrary to what was meant by this straightforward Australian woman.

As for ambition, the only thing that Mary expected and desired was that, after the ten years set down in the Roman document of 1888, the Sisters would be allowed to observe their Constitutions and elect a Mother General. She even mentioned that they could elect Mother Bernard, and so far from desiring to be elected herself she said a number of times that she was willing to stand down so that there could be no possibility of it. Her ambition was totally confined to the welfare of the Institute—that it would be allowed to function constitutionally, and that the Sisters would be encouraged to excel in selfless love.

This trial was an intense one for her, and of long duration. Among the small handful of trusted senior Sisters to whom she spoke about it was Annette, who "did the management of business" for Bernard. Mary wrote to her after her illness in 1892:

All these things have pained me very much and have forced me to speak very plainly to M. G. Forgive me, dear, for grumbling and don't be shocked at my doing so. I don't think it can do any harm with you three, and I have told M. G. that I would have to speak to some of the old Sisters, and let them understand my position.

After the extension of Bernard's term of office:

Have patience and go on quietly with your work. It is God's work and you are doing it *for Him*. Personally I am not disappointed or pained, but I am sorry for the disappointment of my dear good Sisters and oh, I am so sorry for M. Bernard herself.

Mary's endeavours to assist Bernard during these years were constant and wearing, but she came to doubt whether for all her good will she was making much progress. By 1897 her doubts had become convictions. She told Bernard honestly that their views were not the same with regard to some important matters, and as she had a horror of contention and also of being placed in a false position, she begged to be left in New Zealand as long as possible. She confided in her brother Donald:

But oh, I do dread Sydney. You can have no idea of the falseness of my position there. I do not mean in the way of humiliations to myself, though there are plenty, but in what I am expected to do and remedy. I do not and cannot approve of things I see done, or undone.

There are things in some of the letters Mary wrote to her brother that indicate the pain, humiliation and perplexity she suffered during these years. References to conversations make it clear that she had spoken openly to her brother, as to a confessor or director, about her anguish. It was a most distressing situation for her, and it was a serious challenge to find a satisfactory way of handling her dilemma. She was acutely aware that there were serious problems in the Institute, and that the machinery to handle them was not operating. It was not just a matter of inefficiency. Ideals were being overshadowed in the counsels of those determining policy, and many Sisters were in serious need of encouragement and spiritual counsel that was not forthcoming. She described her own position as "false", since as Assistant she was unable to exert any effective influence in Sydney.

The most revealing of her letters was a long one written to her brother just after the extension of Mother Bernard's term late in 1897. She recoiled from anything that looked liked a lack of harmony with authority, but she did wonder that no one in authority could "represent the true state of affairs to Rome, and not leave all in the Cardinal's hands". She spoke plainly:

I am truly sorry that the Cardinal has done this as, unknowingly, he has done our poor Institute a great wrong. He simply does not know the utter unfitness for her position of the one he has placed over this widely spread Institute. May our good God help us not to fail in submission.

Mother Bernard seemed to be insensitive to the personal needs of the Sisters. Mary could not bear to see the sick without necessary medicines, and sometimes without food and clothing, so she went about procuring these things herself, and then was left to find money to pay for it all. "God only knows," she said, "the torture I have endured over such things, the murmurings and misery I have tried to lessen." But there were deeper reasons for disquiet:

Many do not trust M. Bernard because she has a way of insinuating all she can against both S. La Merci and me. You simply would not credit all we know in this way. I am so sorry to say it but, dear Donald, she is not my friend with the Cardinal. But oh dear, I am saying far too much.

We do not know exactly what she had said to Donald face to face, but it was enough to disturb him. She may have suggested that it seemed that God was allowing the Institute to fall apart and that this was a trial she had not foreseen. The treatment the Institute was undergoing at the hands of Cardinal Moran was legally justified by his mandate from Rome, but the situation brought about by having no firm and competent hand on the helm was disastrous. There can be little doubt that Mary discussed this when she consulted her brother. When she later spoke of how she had "desponded", it may be that in developing the theme she had suggested that the solution of her personal quandary was to withdraw completely from any attempt to influence the course of things, to allow her dream of the Sisters of St Joseph to fade away, and to bear this heavy cross in a withdrawn silence.

When all is said and done we can only guess at what it was that so upset Donald. We have no records of their conversations, and we have only a few sentences from letters which, after all, were very personal communications of a troubled soul to a brother who was in this instance approached as a trusted priest. She was aware that there were factors that he did not know about: "I suppose that when I told you of the horrible temptations I had in the past I should have told you more, and this would have saved you some of the anxiety." The many extant early Josephites' documents make it clear that any thought that occurred to a Sister inconsistent with "perfection" was called a *temptation*, even if there had not been the slightest suggestion or possibility that it be acted upon. It was often just a state of mind or a mood. So when Mary revealed to her brother her thoughts about the condition of the Institute—thoughts she could no more help having in her mind than she could help having eyes in her head—she described them as temptations. But it is significant that she reassured him: "I really did resist the temptations against submission and my vocation, though they were awful while they lasted." She was later to reassure him again when she recalled his horror and surprise on being told how she had been "tempted to give all up". Whatever this phrase was meant to cover, it was rejected as a temptation, but she later recalled the mood as something that would safeguard her humility in the future. When a flood of good will (even from Cardinal Moran and his Vicar General) burst on her after her re-election in 1899, she wrote to Donald: "I think you will say with me, it is good I have something to keep me humble."

Whatever went on, it might all be summed up by an analogy with her headaches. As these came against her will and were always painful—to apply her own phrase, "awful while they lasted"—so she was pained by the thoughts that came into her mind against submission and her vocation, also "awful while they lasted". From all the evidence we have, she was as little guilty in the one case as in the other. The only things of any substance at all of which she spoke of being guilty, were losing her temper once and not being able to convince herself that Bernard was just and fair. This was in her letter to Donald, 29 December 1897:

> Excepting that I lost my temper with M. G. on one particular occasion which I ever shall regret for I forgot what I owed to her in her position, and that I could not honestly feel that she was either true or just, I really did resist the temptations.

She had become used to the headaches, but this other thing was a painful experience that took her quite by surprise.

A few months after the intervention of divine providence that released the tension of these years, Mary reflected in a letter to Annette on the "hard bitter struggle" she had to keep the Institute together. Her only regret was that she had not made better use of the means God had given her to die to herself for his sake. She knew her ideals, but there was no posing: "I cannot say with God's faithful servants that I *love* humiliations, but I know they are good for me, and if He sends them I hope I shall be grateful. I do want with all my heart to be what God wishes me to be." Shortly afterwards she was able to look back on it all: "God is good and has brought light and help when all was very dark."

Footnote

[1] This was Francis Borgia, not the Mary Borgia Fay who has already come into this history as an honest and courageous defender of the Institute in the aftermath of the 1883 trouble.

PART X

Last Years

1899–1909

THIRTY-TWO

MOTHER GENERAL
ONCE MORE

On arriving in Sydney in August 1898, Mother Mary found herself temporarily responsible for the Institute. As Assistant she had the immediate duty to see to the election of a Superior General.

Although Cardinal Moran had always been kind and fatherly towards her, she had grounds for misgiving about his attitude to the Constitutions. He had shown himself nervous about allowing the Sisters of St Joseph to elect their own Superior, presumably because he thought they would elect her. According to the official interpretation of the 1881 Chapter, there had been no election of a Superior General since 1874. If Mother Bernard had not died, he had intended that this state of affairs should continue until at least 1902. His action in retaining her was not illegal, as he had Roman authority for it. If he was still determined to exclude Mother Mary, he could just as legally provide the Sisters with another non-elected General. Mary had no desire for office, but she was anxious that the Constitutions be observed, planning to declare herself unavailable for election if that might help. Such withdrawal would normally not be allowed, as the Rule said that a Sister was obliged to accept election; but as things stood, the cardinal had authority to do what he liked, and the freedom enjoyed by the Sisters if Mary's withdrawal were accepted would be a kind of compromise between no freedom and the freedom granted by the Constitutions.

To Mary's dismay the cardinal had let it be known that he thought she should continue as Acting General until 1902. His desire not to have her in authority was evidently not as strong as it had been, but his proposal meant that he was continuing to ignore the Constitutions. At all events, Mary was not very confident of the outcome of her first interview with him. But the sudden death of

Mother Bernard had given him the shock of his life, and things took a surprising turn. Mary described the momentous interview for Sister Patricia:

> He received me most kindly, spoke with great feeling of the sad event of her loss, and of the wonderful ways of Providence. Then he turned to me and said, "You, M. M. are Assistant General?" I simply said, "Yes." "As such you act in her place." Again, "Yes, Your Eminence." "And what do you purpose to do?" I could not speak for a minute and then told him that my duty as pointed out in the Constitutions was to call a General Chapter for the earliest opportunity. To my intense surprise, he said most *emphatically*, "*Keep to the Constitutions*," and something more I won't repeat now.

That is restrained writing. She was stunned, and as she wrote she still felt dazed at this turn of events. "God be praised," she said, "for indeed His ways are wonderful."

The Chapter required a great deal of organising. Delegates had to be brought to Sydney, so it was first necessary that they be elected in the various districts after a preparatory Retreat. As the end of the year was not far off, the timing of the school break-up had to be adjusted only a little to allow them to leave their work. The arranging of these matters did not leave Mary much spare time. But the cardinal had become most cooperative—"Yes," he said at once, "arrange as you see best." Yet for her the organising of detail was far from being the most important element in the preparation of the Chapter. Her circular letter reminded the Sisters that the Constitutions indicated the will of God for them. She put them in mind of the spiritual principles that gave meaning to the whole procedure, and urged them to pray for purity of intention and an unworldly wisdom.

Meanwhile the ordinary business of the Congregation demanded attention. What she called "country convent troubles" claimed a great deal of time. For the New Zealand retreats she was anxious to procure Donald as director. The hierarchy had invited him, and as his years in the far north had seriously affected his health, his sister thought that as well as helping the nuns he would benefit from the change and the opportunity of the mineral springs treatment at Rotorua. The retreats were appreciated, but the health cure was apparently not so effective. Before he left for New Zealand, Mary had passed on two cautionary words. There is stern realism in the phrasing of the first (probably vintage MacKillop): "Don't call Mrs H. anything but Hamilton, for it is only under that name that even Mrs Rigg or any of the Priests know her. She is hiding from her husband, for should he find her there would be murder, and we knew she had to fly to save her life. *He is no good*." The other was a discreet warning that Father Fauvel, whom Donald would find at Rotorua, disliked smoking but was too polite to say so.

The Chapter, held early in January, was evidently a source of great joy to all the Sisters. They could speak in a body for the first time since the events of 1883, and they spoke their opinion of Mother Mary with one voice. It seems that Moran and his secretary were happy too. Mary wrote to Donald:

> You will have heard ere this of the G. C. and its result as far as I am concerned . . . The election was unanimous, and the Cardinal was genuinely pleased. He complimented me upon it, and said many kind things. Dr O'Haran told some of the Sisters afterwards that he had never seen anything like it, and that he had been at many elections.

Donald for his part, having shared some of the secrets of his sister's suffering, shared in the general satisfaction. He had some affectionate prophesying to offer Mary of the Cross:

> Oh, when Heaven will come, dear Mary, what a reward may be yours! And this is little, how for all Eternity you may be able to pay back in His own choice gifts the love that has been showered, in crosses be it, upon you in time.
>
> I have never wished to see you without the cross—you never will be without it—no, not in eternity, but then it will be your joy and your crown, the constant reminder of all you were to your King and Spouse, the Master of all the hosts of Heaven.

The Chapter elected Sister La Merci as Assistant, and although some thought she was somewhat young for such an important office, Mary had every confidence in her. With the passing of the years, she proved a most valuable and faithful Assistant, especially when increasing bodily infirmities meant that the foundress's physical powers were no longer at the command of her noble spirit. "In the event of my death," Mary had told Donald, "so much would depend on her." It was indeed La Merci who announced Mary's death to the Congregation, but before five months had elapsed she was to follow her out of the vale of tears in which they had suffered together.

The Activities of a Mother General

Mother Mary's normal place of residence as Mother General was Mount Street, North Sydney, but before she was immobilised by illness she travelled extensively. Besides calling on the numerous establishments of the Institute around Sydney, she was often on visitation to the Sisters spread over New South Wales—between Tenterfield in the far north and Eden in the far south there was something like 600 miles.

The purpose of her visits was not only to solve particular problems, but to offer the Sisters the encouragement that was so vital to them. She sent periodical letters to the whole Institute, true, but she knew the value of the personal touch too. So when she could not be with them in person she kept contact by means of her pen, which never seemed to be out of her hand. Many Sisters had been with her in the early days, others had been her novices at North Sydney, and there were those younger still whom she was anxious to teach about the traditions and the spirit of the Congregation. A good number were not only far away, but were often isolated from the ordinary contacts that could have helped to keep their spirits up. She set herself a busy programme early in 1899: "I mean to visit each convent myself before mid-winter."

The evidence of these visits is scattered throughout her correspondence—"just back from Bombala", or Glen Innes or Kiama or Dapto or Lithgow or any number of such places. One July she wrote from Bungendore of her intention to visit Captain's Flat, Araluen, Candelo, Eden, and Bombala. This was by 3rd class train through snow country in mid-winter. When she was now and then unable to fulfil her own hopes of visiting some distant region, she was full of apologies to the Sisters. Thus, before leaving for New Zealand late in 1900, she wrote to the Sister in charge at Armidale, "It is only today that I had to give up any hope of getting *at least* to see you and the Bishop." The sort of schedule she followed is indicated in a note from Sydney to Gertrude in 1901: "Will leave here on Sunday next, arrive in Melbourne on Monday, and if able go to Broadmeadows that night, return next day, stay with you and see about the Providence on Tuesday, and leave for Adelaide on Wednesday."

In the period between her re-election and her stroke, that is, between the years 1899 and 1902, Mary travelled at least seven times to Victoria, extending four of these journeys to South Australia; and she went twice to New Zealand. During each of the two years before she went to New Zealand at the end of 1900, she paid two visits to Melbourne and one visit to Adelaide. In 1901 she was twice in Victoria and South Australia. After her stroke in New Zealand in 1902 she returned to Sydney, and it was more than a year before she ventured interstate. Then she made one prolonged visit to Victoria and South Australia in each of the years 1904 and 1905, but after that she remained in Sydney.

While asking the Sisters to pray that she might have the wisdom and strength to cope with the problems confronting the Institute, Mary frequently reminded them to be grateful for deliverance from past dangers. The current problems did not, as some past ones did, constitute threats to the very existence of the Institute, but they were demanding ones nonetheless. New foundations, together with the extension or relocation of old ones, occupied much of her time. In Sydney the termination under Government pressure of the work at the old Providence was counterbalanced by the constant demand for new schools, the building of the Free School at North Sydney to act as a Training School for the young Josephites, and the expansion of the work at the two orphanages at Kincumber and Lane Cove.

In Victoria, the extension of the work in these years involved a growing number of schools, the change of location of the Providence to Victoria Parade, and the major undertaking of the Foundling Home at Broadmeadows. In South Australia the establishment of a new Refuge and the building of a new convent at Kensington were concerns that added to the already considerable responsibilities of the Institute in its State of origin. The work in New Zealand continued to grow, Paeroa and St Benedict's in Auckland being the main additions. Finally, the second Bishop of Rockhampton, Dr Higgins, fulfilled the desires of the first, Dr Cani, in having the Sisters of St Joseph return to Queensland after so many years. They established a school at Clermont in 1900. Archbishop Duhig was later instrumental in having them return to Brisbane.

A number of these enterprises are referred to in Mary's letter for St Joseph's Day 1900. She gives some details of the new works—at Clermont, Paeroa in New Zealand, the North Sydney Free School, the Kincumber orphanage, and the new wing at Kensington where "a very kind friend had promised to pay"—the quiet hand of Mrs Barr Smith at work again. But Mary is more interested in the interior spirit of the Sisters than in statistics. It is almost as if she is saying that in spite of so much external progress there is more subtle danger in present spiritual deficiencies than there was in the open unfriendliness of ecclesiastical authorities in the past.

The opening of the Foundling Home at Broadmeadows, some ten miles north of Melbourne, was not without its problems, and Mary was grateful to have La Merci there in mid-1900 conducting negotiations. Teresa had gone in February to take charge, and the Archbishop was very favourable, but there were difficulties in the selection of a site, the finding of finance, and the bigoted opposition of some people in the community at large. Promised Government aid in the form of ten shillings a week for each child was not forthcoming. But there was something Mary regarded as more serious: "I would not mind external troubles," she said, "but I miss the spirit of generosity for such an undertaking in one or more of our own Sisters . . . they soon cry out when real difficulties arise." In spite of all she was confident because it was St Joseph's work.

In May they had a good trained nurse ready to work in the Home and a local doctor had promised to attend free of charge. But things did not run smoothly. By November the nurse had left, dissatisfied with the management, and the Archbishop had asked Mary to come and investigate matters. Her hopes of finding things not as hard as they were represented seem to have been fulfilled, as an excellent nurse was found and danger of the work collapsing was averted.

Great joy was brought to Mary and her Sisters when the Josephites from Bungaree in Victoria amalgamated with the Mother House; and shortly afterwards those from Wilcannia in New South Wales did the same. Mary never cast any doubts on the legality of the position of the diocesan Josephites (except the personal case of Sister Hyacinth) but she was saddened nevertheless by the division of the Josephite name. The Roman Decree of 1888 had stated that the Sisters of St Joseph were free to belong to one or the other group, but it seems that this choice was never communicated to many of the diocesan Sisters. When he received the decree Bishop Dunne in Wilcannia had asked Bishop Murray: "Will it be necessary to consult the Sisters in the Diocese as to their option?"

Twelve years afterwards, when the Sisters at Bungaree in the Ballarat diocese wished to join the Mother House, Mary wrote to Cardinal Moran:

> They knew nothing of the Decree of 1888 until they received the printed Rule, a copy of which I forward with this. Since then they have been very unsettled, recent events having made them more so.

There was an initial difficulty with Bishop Moore, who said he would never grant the permission, but he did eventually give his consent. Gabriel, one of the Sisters involved, left a memoir describing the experience, which the nuns thought was miraculous. How much she really understood is hard to say, but she told how Mary was full of confidence as she went to see the bishop, as God was all powerful, and soon came back with the permission. But what happened was most likely that Mary simply made the juridical position clear and the bishop was intelligent enough to see the point. It was not up to him to give permission or not—a Roman decision had been ignored for years, and it would not look so good if this were brought to the attention of the authorities there. But Mary would have put it very nicely. She stayed with the Sisters until they were ready to leave, and on their arrival at Mount Street saw to it that they were shown every kindness.

At first Mary thought it would be possible for the Institute to carry on with the school at Bungaree, but the bishop had already made other arrangements. He made some strange financial demands on Sisters who had laboured in his diocese for years for the love of God and very little else. Mary hoped he might be more generous and appreciative of what they had done, but when she approached him he said their financial affairs were their own business, not his.

During these years the wear and tear of a busy life took its toll on Mary's physical resources, but on the whole she was able to keep going remarkably well. She occasionally sent a report to her old nurse of January 1892, Sister Ethelburga, blending it with gratitude and some simple personal encouragement. She told her in March 1900: "I am well, often very tired, often longing for rest and getting none but thank God, keeping up and going on with the work day after day. I never forget your care for me in illness and sorrow." When she referred to her infirmities she treated them as matters of fact, like the weather, and as reasons for doing less than she had hoped. There were bouts of illness—colds, stomach catarrh, bronchitis, and the growing discomfort and pain of rheumatism—and it is only when one stands back and looks at what she was doing that it becomes clear how remarkably energetic she was. She was grateful to God for his sustaining help and to the Sisters for their prayers. She looked forward to the cold weather, as she felt it caused her to become "another being".

A typical schedule was the one she undertook in late April 1901. After a very busy time in Melbourne she went to Adelaide, where she had a similar round of duties, and shortly after her return wrote from East Melbourne: "Since my return from Adelaide this day week, I have been twice at Broadmeadows, one night at Surrey Hills, another at Williamstown, and the rest here, but out every day." From time to time her contemporaries commented on her remarkable stamina, and suggested something preternatural about it. She was aware of something strange too—"God seems to be giving me more than natural strength," she said in July 1901—but she saw it simply as a loving divine providence, and her only comment was a wish that some of her Sisters would stop expecting the impossible and realise she was human like themselves.

Mary was also aware of some strange contradiction within herself, as she had remarked in March: "I feel so strangely weak, and yet look so well, that I am a puzzle to myself. I feel that I require complete rest from worries, and some cheerful and cool change." She was well aware that she was not the only one in the Institute who had a lot to do and as a consequence ran the danger of damaging her health. She warned others directly, for example Annette: "Take care of yourself and *don't* work beyond your strength."

As the months went by, the Mother General became more aware of the effects of advancing age, and cf the burden of her office. But it was not such cares, nor ill health among the Sisters, nor even the frequent deaths that occurred, that was the cause of deepest concern to her. It was the lack of the proper Josephite spirit in some of the Sisters, who became so absorbed in the needs of their own work that they thoughtlessly demanded more help than was available; and not being prepared to make sacrifices for the general good, such people would begin to complain and demur. Mary told Annette: "I then get a queer crushed feeling that I cannot describe."

The Mind of the Mother General

It was not difficult for the Sisters to know the mind of their Mother General. In addition to regular personal contact with her, they had been reading her letters for years. After the Chapter of 1889, she had undertaken to write a circular letter every month. In these letters there is constant insistence on kindness and union, and there are strong warnings against murmuring and unkind gossip. "When you become hard, suspicious, or censorious," she warned, "then goodbye to being the children of St Joseph." Kindness—"charity"—was what she considered the heart of the Institute, not the business matters, or assignments, or other external matters, however important. There is a realistic acceptance of human limitation, but never a limit set to zeal for a more perfect service of God.

Josephites should work in a quiet unostentatious way. Trusting in God and living in inner peace, they should do what they can and leave the rest to him—"Don't try to do too much . . . *He* knows we cannot do impossibilities". Mary never tired of reminding them that the human troubles that are part of life on earth, sometimes amounting to heavy crosses, are to be seen in the light of faith as a precious sharing in the Cross of Christ. "If our intention is pure and we have charity in our hearts, we shall have God with us—and with Him on our side, what need we fear?"

The strongest of all her circular letters was a very long one written from Brisbane on 14 December 1890. It is a revelation of her own soul in the form of advice to others. As usual she proposes the highest ideals of living by faith, and makes a firm and confident call to the charity and obedience God expects of them. As a prelude to her message, she touches on some of the past history of the Institute and makes a very open and humble declaration of the human limitations of its members. God has made use of His servants, she says—"one in particular"—to try the Institute sorely, but its members had done much to bring this on. They had been using their tongues far too freely and too thoughtlessly. She blames herself for being too trusting in the past and not being more vigilant about the murmuring, fault-finding, petty bickering, and criticism of superiors that was widespread among the Sisters. She appeals to them now to make war on these things vigorously, firmly, and unitedly.

In August 1901, however, she was able to add in a letter to Raymond: "We have very little of it now, thank God." God will not ask you about those in authority, she said, but about how you have obeyed and in what spirit, so attend to that and let them get on with their work.

Letters to the whole Institute were expected at times like Christmas and New Year, before Lent, for the Feast of St Joseph, and in preparation for the annual Retreat. Personal letters were often written, especially to superiors, on the occasion of some crisis of greater or less importance. She saw the Retreat as a privileged time of grace, a time when God wished to speak to them in a special way. So she urged them to dispose themselves by excluding all other interests and occupations and to spend the full eight days at it.

She used the occasions of retreats and visitations to remind the Sisters of the high ideals of their calling. She urged them to bear with one another and to study the general good, putting their fancies and tempers aside. But her exhortations were never harsh or impersonal. However appropriate her words, it was her person that left the deepest impression. Laurence recalled at the Process: "From her discourses, her manner, her bearing, the impression of the holiness of her life could be gathered."

Although Mary held that a strict observance of the physical demands of the lenten fast would prevent the Sisters from doing their work, as Cardinal Moran had pointed out, she was anxious nonetheless that they be distinguished for the self-denial of the Gospel: "We can do this in many ways without weakening our health or rendering ourselves unfit for the ordinary duties." In describing how this could be achieved, she outlined a very demanding life: a programme of observance of the Rule, careful attention to school duties, and control of the tongue would be more than enough to keep them going.

She availed herself of the season of Christmas and the New Year to remind them of the same lessons, pointing out that they were not called to a mere exercise of asceticism, but to a loving personal service of their Lord, and selfless love of one another: "Help one another, bear with one another as God bears with each of us." These were no abstract precepts delivered from some distant impersonal source of moral and spiritual wisdom. That was not Mother Mary's style. Her letter to "dear old Temuka" at the end of 1901 was a cry from the heart: "I positively long for the restful quiet of a Xmas spent with my dear Sisters at Temuka. Well, thanks be to God who sees fit to deny this wish."

A secular chronicle of Mary's activities could give the impression that her main concerns were the founding of new institutions, getting jobs done, educating children, and rendering social service. These were not her top priorities at all. Her mind was that of the Gospel: "The greatest commandment is to love the Lord your God with all your heart, soul, strength and mind. And the second is like to this: Love your neighbour as yourself." It was "the soul", the life in Christ the Son of God, that came first with her; "the work", the love and service of others, came second, and had its true meaning as an expression of the first.

Mary MacKillop saw the work of the Sisters not as a public service, but as an element in Christian living inspired by the Spirit of Christ. Far from diminishing its value, this made it all the more precious and the need for it more urgent. This was an involvement in God's care for his beloved people, each of whom was graced with a divine dignity by the God who assumed human nature.

From time to time she was distressed to find that some priests who should have known better were guilty of an inversion of values, and she did not hesitate to use strong words to point this out. The Sisters were not workhorses. "I feel very strongly on this point," she wrote to Raymond, "and cannot understand how religious Priests are not more considerate." And to a priest:

> Are we not Religious *first*—Teachers *second?* I often think that those for whom we work are too exacting, and in their anxiety for the success of the schools, forget at what price that success is gained.

The Feast of St Joseph was for Mary an opportunity to remind the Sisters of the precious value of obedience, and she never tired of urging them to pray for a true understanding of this virtue. She was well aware of its contribution to smooth government, but she never proposed anything but motives of faith and divine charity for treasuring it, reinforcing her remarks from time to time with reminders of its rich fruits and its guarantee of heavenly blessings. The Sisters should keep before their eyes the will of God, not his human instruments—she even notes that sometimes it is channelled through "thoughtless superiors".

Knowing how easy it was to see only the human side of obedience and authority, she never tired of reminding them that it was the intervention of the divine into human affairs. It was God who had given each of them a personal call, and she was saddened to see human nature leading any one of them to think of her life as anything but a loving personal response to this call. Having left all that the world held dear—parents, home, relatives, and in many cases, country—they should not allow themselves to form new ties and become troubled when they are asked for some further sacrifice. The Sisters could not say they had never been reminded of the demands made by the service to which they were called. But they were reminded also that it was the privilege of a personal service rendered to the Son of God. The inevitable hardships in a life of religious obedience were not to be seen as unfortunate accidents resulting from carelessness or limitations on the part of superiors, but as invitations to share the cross of Christ. To the real motive of living with Christ, she added a little personal appeal, "and if I dare say such a thing, helping me to keep up under trying duties and failing health".

Mary rejoiced to see that the Church had a rich variety of

Sisterhoods, each called to the service of Christ in a particular manner. But she knew that each was expected to be faithful to its own call, not confusing the response by aiming at all possible good works and all worthy undertakings. The Josephites were called to the care of the poor and the neglected, and it distressed her that some Sisters seemed to be in danger of forgetting this. "Let others seek the better more remarkable places," she said, "but let St Joseph's true children remember their mission and seek first the poorest most neglected parts of God's vineyard."

Her words of encouragement, written and spoken, were reminders to the Sisters of the high standards of their calling. More powerful still was the example of her own life. Her manner, kindly and patient, recollected and calm, was frequently remarked on as a sign of her union with God. Laurence said she frequently spent many hours of the night in prayer. The simplicity of her personal lifestyle was another matter that spoke more powerfully even than her words. Laurence said:

> She hardly had a room at all. She used a table at a landing. Sometimes in a room called the library which was a common room. She used the common dormitory even when she was the General.
>
> At Kensington she had a very small room for herself. She had no office of her own but used the common room. Sometimes she interviewed the Sisters there, sometimes in a cellar underneath the house. When she came to Mount Street she did not have an office till the new wing was added.

Obedience laid its burden on Mary in the form of authority itself. As she saw it, both the person giving orders and the person carrying them out were obeying the same call to service and sacrifice. She revealed her mind on this aspect of religious life to Raymond, who was pleading to be released from the burdens of office in New Zealand. Urging her to accept in humility the cross of remaining in charge, Mary reminded her that among the most valuable contributions she could make to the general good was her own obedience and her handling of authority. She frequently called attention to this value, the *general good*. Although it has to be constantly considered by those in authority and looms large in their decision making, individuals engrossed in their own work can be inclined to forget it. On one occasion she said of a Sister who was disgruntled about some arrangement made by authority: "She simply does not know what she is talking about, nor the reasons our Superiors had for so acting."

This concept of authority as service in charity meant that Mary heeded the advice of the Apostle Paul and never lorded it over her subjects. She told a superior once, after receiving a letter from a Sister: "I could not *command* her to remain. I had *asked* her; she still wished to leave, and my duty to her soul was to consent." Whenever she had to refuse a request, as in the case of Raymond, she did it gently, with a reminder of how precious a truly obedient religious was in the eyes of God. The same gentleness and respect is evident on occasions when Mary felt (or "fancied") herself bound to speak a word of reproof.

Reminders that superiors had reasons concerning the common good that would not be generally known, implied that the superiors themselves had the duty to study all aspects of a situation before making a decision. Nothing could be farther from the mind of Mary MacKillop than the idea that it did not really matter what a superior decided, because whatever she decided was for the subject the will of God! Even less was she of the mind that anyone could carelessly lay heavy burdens on the shoulders of others on the plea that the more of the cross they had the better! Such twisted thinking was anathema to her. She saw it as the duty of those in charge to arrange things as well as possible, and to remove annoyances: "I would remove all undue care were it in my power." Only then could they ask people to view the unavoidable problems as crosses sent by God.

The same kind of thinking applied to lifestyle. Nobody was keener on a life of simplicity and poverty than Mary, but she was far from seeing this as a reason for those in charge to be unmindful of the health, comfort, or convenience of their Sisters. Waste and extravagance were to be avoided, she told them, "but mind that the Sisters have good wholesome food, and *plenty* of it, and warm clothing, beds, etc.".

What she wrote on the occasion of a difficulty with the pastor at Waimate is a good illustration of her priorities and her concern for the welfare of her Sisters. It showed too her appreciation of the value of obedience not only as a service to God but also as a help to human administration. This priest had been dissatisfied with arrangements at his school and Mary had told the Provincial to look into the matter. This the Provincial unfortunately did not do, and the pastor was in consequence blaming the Mother General. While giving him the details of the case, Mary reminded him of the proper order of authority: "Did I not do my duty in writing to her and asking her to report?"

Of course she let Raymond know at the same time that she was pained at her neglect, and pointed out the inconvenience caused by tardy obedience. Such a reminder was from time to time necessary if someone had neglected some duty, but generally Mary's support for her Provincials and local superiors was simply an application of what she had to say to all about obedience and religious subordination. In a letter which she called "precise and very determined", she told Raymond not to heed discontents and murmurers, but at the same time to provide herself with full information about each situation. Then no one could justifiably complain.

Careful to respect the authority of those under her, Mary made her suggestions to help rather than to cut across their decisions. She once told a superior that she did not recommend any changes, but should *she* have any reason to think any advisable, she was to use her own judgment and go ahead. Even when she lived in the same house, as at North Sydney, Mary left the one in charge to run the house, and only gave advice when she was asked for it. But she did have suggestions if they were called for, for example at Quirindi: "The girl in the kitchen might get on better under you. I think Sr M. Agnes is too exacting and these girls won't stand much of that." Matilda was asked to superintend the kitchen at the Providence, but as her health was giving so much trouble she was "not to work, only to see that the work is done". If this proved too much it could be changed. Another time, when ill health was seriously impeding a work, Mary told the one in charge not to hesitate to close the school for a while rather than attempt the impossible.

Charity in Small Things as in Great

"Charity unbounded, unlimited, in word, thought and action was Mother Mary's characteristic action," wrote Sister Patricia Campbell. The whole of Mary's life was an act of charity, every work of the Institute she directed was a work of charity, and she never ceased to urge the Sisters to charity and union with one another. But great themes can sometimes be best illustrated by examples on a small scale—a cupful in the hand will tell more of the freshness and coolness of water on a hot day than gazing over the vast expanse of a reservoir.

Mary's charity expressed itself not merely in the efficient government of a charitable Institute, but in a delicate sensitivity to the feelings of others in all sorts of small ways. On one occasion, when some problem made it necessary for a particular Sister to be with the Remuera community for a time, she wrote to the Superior, "I want you to invite Sr Celsus to stay a while with you. Make her *feel* that you are glad to have her."

The duties of the Mother General made it essential that she be deeply interested in the works of the Institute, but this never became the impersonal concern of a busy woman preoccupied with organising and directing. Her chief interest remained in people and their welfare, whether inside or outside the Congregation. She always kept an eye out for the spiritual needs as well as the physical distress of those close to her. Ethelburga remembered how Mary used to go into tough unsavoury areas to try to get people back to their religious duties and a better life.

An example was given by another Sister to illustrate "Mother's simplicity". It certainly showed that, and also what Uncle Peter once called her cheek. Cardinal Moran had asked her to run some Confirmation classes for adults six miles away. As there was no suitable place for this, she went out with Sister Irene one afternoon looking for somewhere. "We knew no one out there," said Irene, "but Mother saw a very pretentious looking mansion and said, 'They should have plenty of room.' I did not like the idea of asking, but Mother said we are doing God's work and He will help us." The people were Presbyterians, but for some months their large drawing room was used by a crowd of about thirty Catholic men and a couple of nuns, to whom every kindness was shown.

Education and works of charity can grow to a grand dimension, but Mary never lost touch with what "the work" was about. It was people, poor people, little people. Lucy later recalled:

> She had driven some miles in a snow storm, but her first wish was to visit the school. There was a poor little bare-footed and ragged boy standing in class. Mother went straight to him, and putting her arms around him she kissed him saying, "Ah, Sister, these are the children I love."

She had a keen eye for those who were grieving over a personal loss, and she always hastened to send a few words of condolence or make a personal visit. She had a special predilection for the sick. Her letters often give or ask for details about Sisters who are ill, always adding a word of sympathy. This interest in the sick was not confined to sympathy if there was anything more she could do. Mechtilde said: "When my father was dying she said we could remain there all night if we could be of use . . . She could not do too much for the Sisters and for the families of those who were bereaved." Thus, when she heard that Philippa had to go to hospital in Melbourne, she told Gertrude Mary to tell Mother Berchmans: "I would rather she would look after S. M. Philippa for me than anything she could do for myself."

It was not only her Sisters whose illnesses concerned her. When she was within reach of some friend who was sick or troubled, she tried to pay a visit, sometimes at great personal inconvenience. Ethelburga told that:

> One day Mother had business in Sydney and elsewhere. It was a scorching hot day. She called at St Vincent's Hospital to see a patient, and from there she was told to go home and to go to bed, as she was threatened with a serious illness.

Perhaps Mary's most memorable journey to visit the sick was when one of her Sisters was dying in great agony at Port Augusta as a result of a kerosene lamp exploding. Mary had got as far as Mount Remarkable and hoped to find some kind people to drive her the rest of the journey. Sister Patricia Campbell continued the story:

> Several farmers were in with their wheat but all shook their heads at the prospect of the long distance to Port Augusta. The farmers then adjourned to the hotel for refreshments, and Mother Mary walked in and said: "Gentlemen, one of my Sisters at Port Augusta is dying, and is constantly asking for me. If one of you will lend me a horse I will ride there." Chivalry was not quite dead in those Celtic hearts. Two or three jumped up, got a pair of horses and a buggy, and drove her on that afternoon, and she arrived in time to console the last moments of the dying Sister.

In 1925 Mother Laurence asked some old Sisters to write down their recollections of Mother Mary, and the manuscripts survive. Some of the writing is unsteady, but the memories are not. One of them wrote, on her second page of large writing, "I am sorry dear Mother that I cannot relate other incidents completely except that our dear Mother was good humble charitable and kind to all."

She had a special love for the orphans at Kincumber. Patricia gave a vivid picture of her usual mode of arrival for a visit. These were a joy to "the boys who met her at Woy Woy with a small open boat, rowed her across the Brisbane Waters, one little chap being employed all the time bailing out the water from the leaky boat. This happened frequently and on dark nights, when the splash of the oar only could indicate the Orphanage wharf." Once a little boy dying at the orphanage asked as a last wish to see Mother Mary. When she was told of this, she set out at once in the worst of weather to be with him. She stayed until he died, and walked in a violent storm to the cemetery and recited the Rosary at his grave.

A story recalled by old Sister Genevieve shows that the image of the grand and distant Mother General did not fit Mary in the least:

> When I was a young professed Sister another young Sister and I were sent to the country. The train left about 7 p.m. and we would not reach our destination until about 11 p.m. We left Mount St without tea; somehow Mother found out, and a few minutes before the train left she arrived at the train almost breathless, with some lunch in a paper bag, also some fruit. When she saw our distress on account of her coming she smiled gaily and said "She could not have her children without anything to eat until after 11 p.m." I said, "But Mother there are people in the compartment with us." She answered, "No matter, dear, and both of you are to eat all I have given you, it is a necessity."

Mary's best lessons were taught by example. One of the most memorable incidents among the reminiscences written down for Mother Laurence occurred in a country convent thirty years before, on a day it was visited by one whom Mary saw as a "poor old man—perhaps some father" that the world had not been kind to. Sister M. Borgia should be allowed to speak for herself:

> When she arrived our midday meal was over, and as we had in this place a very small school, only 30 day pupils no boarders etc, so you may guess we had very little to spare. When Mother came I was the only Sister in the convent as the other two Sisters were at school, one being the Superior. "Oh, dear child, are the Sisters at school? I am on my way to see my poor Sister at the next convent. I had to leave very early this morning, and had only time to take a cup of tea. I am very tired and hungry. So prepare something for me whilst I will run over to see the Sisters in the school. I will not be long as the train leaves at 3 p.m."
>
> I got ready what I could—only a little steak that was left, etc, as quickly as possible. Mother was back in a few minutes, and after a little delay the meal was set before her. Just as she was about to sit to the table a knock came to the door. I went to see who was there, and a poor, half-starved, badly clothed old man stood before me. "Would you give me a bit to eat, Miss?" he said. "I can get no work in this town, nor anything to eat. I am very weak." Mother followed me to

the door, and when she saw the man, "Sister dear," she said, "give to that poor creature what you have prepared for me. The very look of him would draw tears from a stone," she said, "a cup of tea and a slice of bread and butter will be sufficient for me. It will do me more good to give him a dinner."

THIRTY-THREE

UNCOMPLETED CURE
AT ROTORUA

Urgent business was pressing in New Zealand at the end of 1900, but the Mother General knew she could not be absent from Australia for long. She knew she would not be able to visit her favourite remote places like Arrowtown, but she could look forward to meeting all the Sisters assembled in more accessible locations.

She did not want the ones back in Australia to feel they were being neglected at Christmas, so, besides leaving directions that concerts, displays, and prize-givings were to be very simple, she apologised to Armidale that she could not go there at the moment, gave instructions about those coming to Sydney for the Retreat, and wrote a special Christmas message for South Australia. Reminding them to return God love for love, she asked for prayers for herself: "Be true and generous, and pray hard for poor me."

In April 1884, the year after they first came to New Zealand, the Josephites began a school in its largest city, Auckland. This was the "butcher's shop school" in Karangahape Road in the Newton parish, previously conducted by a Miss Kirby, with classrooms improvised out of an old shop next to Brophy's Hotel. To get to it the nuns had to walk west about a mile along a rough road from their residence in Gladstone Street near St Benedict's. One of them wrote: "I can quite understand now why Father Sullivan suggested the necessity of strong boots. I wish you could see the roads." The 41 pupils at the start grew to 110 by May, and 200 by September. The building was unsuitable, and it was too far from the convent, but the spirit of the teachers was good.

There were difficulties at the Gladstone Street cottage too, arising mainly from the attitude of the lay teacher, and it became imperative for the Sisters to find better accommodation. After moving for a short time to Brophy's Hotel, and then to rented lodgings, they were able in June 1885 to buy a property in Sussex St, Surrey Hills, west of the shop-school and somewhat closer to it. Later that year, work was begun on a church-school in Tennyson Street next door to the Sussex Street residence, and in 1886 they were able to move out of the shop-school and begin teaching in these more handsome quarters. They had wished very much to see Mother Mary in Auckland during these difficult times, but times were even more difficult for her in Australia just then, and the New Zealand Sisters were disappointed in their hopes. Mother Bernard often seemed to be on the point of coming, but she never did. When eventually Mary arrived as Mother Assistant in 1894, it was at this Surrey Hills address that she stayed.

In 1902 a large wooden convent building was erected in Sussex Street, and when in 1917 the school was established in a new location further west, on the Great North Road, Grey Lynn, the convent was physically transferred to the new location. It was destroyed by fire in 1921.

Remuera, where the Josephites established their second school in Auckland, was destined to play a part in Mary's personal history, as it was in the convent there that she spent six months convalescing after her stroke in 1902. Since 1885 there had been a school conducted by a laywoman in the Newmarket-Remuera area at the eastern end of the parish, but shortly after the district was transferred to the Parnell parish in 1889 the Josephites were asked to take over. Until they acquired the Remuera convent in Middleton Road, they had to walk the couple of miles from Surrey Hills to reach this Newmarket school. But in 1890 a generous benefactor, Miss Mary Consitt Stevenson, transferred Lot 13 in Middleton Road to them by deed of gift, and the school, with a chapel, was built there. The Sisters also acquired as their convent the house on the corner of Middleton Road and Lauriston Avenue. This is the house, no longer in the hands of the Josephites, but easily recognisable from photographs, in which Mary was convalescent in 1902.

It has been seen that the Josephites' first Auckland school had three successive locations. All were in the western end of the parish of Newton, in a district known then as Surrey Hills and later as Grey Lynn. The second school was at the eastern end, in the Remuera-Newmarket area, and was in fact in another parish by the time they moved in. Although the Sisters had at first resided in a cottage in Gladstone Street, near St Benedict's at the centre of the parish, it was not until 1901 that this area saw them return to open a school.

After the Surrey Hills school moved to Sussex Street, the shop-school was not completely abandoned. Miss Shelvin continued to teach there for a short time before moving back to Gladstone Street to open a school near St Benedict's. She was assisted by two Misses Coffey who later took over from her. In 1898 the bishop built a hall to replace the building in which they were teaching. But he also planned to ask the Sisters of St Joseph to take charge. This was the "St Benedict's business" that Mary went to New Zealand to negotiate in December 1900.

The bishop was going ahead with a larger school building next to the parish hall, and this was the reason for his importunity in asking for Sisters. It would make a very bad impression if the building were finished and there was nobody to staff it. In spite of her earlier conviction that she would not be able to comply with his wishes, Mary eventually managed to supply nuns for St Benedict's. In fact, they had to begin classes in the hall because the school was not completed as the bishop expected! Finding a suitable residence was a problem. For a time it looked as if they could have an old presbytery at a reasonable price, an offer that looked too good to be true. But wanting "no trouble later on", Mary eventually took up a second option and had the Gladstone Street cottage refurbished.

Five years later, the Mayor of Auckland, while laying the foundation stone of a new convent on the block adjoining the cottage, gave a laudatory address to a large gathering about the history of the Sisters of St Joseph in Australia and New Zealand. He also wrote to Mother Mary on the occasion, in appreciation of her "life's work in the cause of education" and her care for the poor and neglected. In 1910 an upper storey was added to the school, and some years later the old cottage was demolished to make way for extensions to the convent. The history of St Benedict's over the subsequent decades was a credit to the Josephites, and Mary's "worries and anxieties" in seeing it established were well compensated.

Paeroa is on the Waihou River some eighty miles south-east of Auckland, on the way to the goldfields, about halfway to Matata. When the genial pastor, Father Hackett—"The Dean"—had come in 1894, there was already a church and presbytery on a five-acre property. Though there was no school, a substantial legacy had been left for the purpose of building one. The Dean set about it and at the same time approached Mary for Sisters. We can glean from the correspondence something of the sense of eager expectation with which the arrival of the Josephites would have been awaited in many a district in Australia and New Zealand.

A large house had been engaged at a cheap rental for the nuns' residence and a big event for Opening Sunday had been planned. The Dean wrote Mary a most appealing plea, pointing out how ruinous it would be to have a fine school ready but no Sisters available for it in the new year: "May I say one of the greatest blessings they are waiting for is to have 'manners' taught to their children." But there were delays and frustrations, and after all his urging Father Hackett had to write apologetically on December 28 to say that the building would not be ready for school until after Easter. It would have been no hardship for Mary to hear this.

When three Sisters for Paeroa eventually arrived in Auckland, they spent some time in the convent at Surrey Hills before undertaking the eight hours steamer trip by sea and up river to their mission. They were in time to be embarrassed by the high expectations expressed by Father Hackett in his welcoming sermon on Palm Sunday. The people were told that the Sisters were among the best teachers from the Sydney Training College, with a system of education that embraced a graduated course of studies including a thorough knowledge of all branches of an English education. They would regard the moral training of the pupils as a most important duty, and they would endeavour to make the teaching of manners and good conduct their constant aim.

Whatever Mary's reaction may have been to the part about "English education", she certainly would have been pleased to hear his remarks about morals, manners and good conduct. The opening ceremony was held on the following Sunday, and school began the next day, 23 April 1900, with eighty-four pupils. Though the school got away to a good start, Mary found that the convent arrangements were not at all satisfactory. After long discussions with the priest and the committee, it was decided to build as soon as plans could be drawn up. Planning went ahead, but it was not until February 1902 that the convent, destined to become a landmark in the district, was at last begun.

In the meantime the saga of the "Paeroa cow" had unfolded, showing that Mary had much to cope with besides matters of historic moment. Though petty enough in itself, it was important to the people concerned, and she did what she could from Sydney not only to get the new convent built but also to solve this problem about a cow. Sister Liguori had objected to going to the presbytery to milk the cow for Miss Hackett. Mary told Sister Pierre she was wrong to ask a Sister to do this, as orders had been given that none of them was to go alone to the presbytery. If the cow had been sent to the convent, they could have milked it there; but they should not have been asked to ignore standing orders. "I don't care who the Priest's housekeeper is," said Mary, adding that she could not see why Miss Hackett could not learn to milk the cow herself. However, the Sisters should have obeyed the local superior for the time being, telling her that they would meanwhile appeal to the Mother General.

Much of Mary's time during this two months' sojourn in New Zealand was occupied trying to solve the problem of accommodation at Paeroa. It followed her home to Australia when she received a letter from Pierre asking for permission to mortgage the deeds of Remuera to pay for Paeroa. She showed herself a perceptive businesswoman in her caution and in the careful legal questions she put before she would consent to the idea. She had in the meantime assured Pierre: "You know how anxious I was about you in Paeroa, and how I wished to get you in a suitable Convent. It was impossible for me to do more than I did, and I am as anxious now as I was then for your health, comfort and happiness." The convent, from which a fine school with a friendly tradition was conducted for seventy-four years, was replaced by a more modern building in 1976, but it did not perish. It became a landmark in a new location, after being cut up, transported, and reassembled by its new owner.

Mary had planned to make her retreat with the northern Sisters in Auckland, but her time was so packed with the business of the north that she changed her plans and switched to the retreat of the southern Sisters at Temuka. These two retreats had been organised, one before Christmas and one after, so that she could meet all the Sisters in spite of the fact that she did not have the time to visit the remote convents.

She had intended at the beginning of this visit to New Zealand to avail herself of the natural medicinal baths at Te Aroha in the North Island for her growing rheumatic condition, but they were too far from Paeroa and her busy schedule did not allow it. Not only was the rheumatism no better, but after returning to Sydney she was aware that the trip had made great demands on her health and energy. She told Gertrude Mary: "My own health has failed very much, but I dare say when the great heat is over I shall be all right again. I had a hard anxious time of it in Auckland."

Rotorua, New Zealand, 1902

Mother Mary returned to New Zealand under doctor's orders two years later "for rest and change", and to submit herself to a rigorous programme at the famous medicinal baths at Rotorua. She followed the directives of her doctors, although she had misgivings about her status as a "poor beggar". She certainly spoke to Cardinal Moran about it, as we know from her letter to Monica on 18 April 1902 that he gave her an "injunction" to write as little as possible while taking the treatment.

A few days before leaving Australia on 28 January 1902, she told the Sisters she was leaving all business to Sister La Merci, and asked them to help her by making her duties light. Soon after arriving in Matata she told La Merci that she was having a grand rest: "No words can describe the restfulness of the place." It was much better than Remuera would have been, as many callers would have come there. A week later she wrote that her rheumatism was troublesome, especially in the right hand, and that she hoped the Rotorua Springs recommended for it would not be too strong for her.

It has been said of Rotorua (about 120 miles south of Auckland) that "it has intrigued, awed, mystified and thrilled almost every person who ever moved among its wonders".[1] The diversity of natural phenomena in the area is truly astonishing, and the curative powers of the water from the natural springs have long been known. It is not certain just when Mary arrived, but she was writing letters from there on March 16. These continued until May 9. Her condition often made writing physically difficult, but at least fifteen of her letters from Rotorua are extant. Besides reassuring the Sisters about her progress, she was at pains to offer the encouragement she knew was so important to them. She was especially careful to show her confidence in her deputy, La Merci, by speaking of it in so many words, and by leaving her for the most part to herself in the management of the Institute. At the same time she was sensitive to the need not to overburden her.

During her stay at Rotorua, Mary resided at a guest house called *Thirwell House* with her sister Annie and Sister Winifride. Annie's cooperation seems to have been taken for granted. She said: "Mother La Merci telegraphed to me to come to Sydney and there I found that our passages had been booked and I was to look after her." She described it as a nice private house, with a priest resident and very nice boarders. The very nice boarders included at one period the Archbishop of Wellington, Dr Redwood, whose demands on Annie to accompany his violin playing lost nothing in her later telling. As will be seen, the same Annie lets us know that the landlady was not always as polite as we may be led to believe by her sister's kind words. The place came to be known as "the Convent" as there were so many priests and religious to be seen around it.

The patient reported to her deputy in March that the baths were doing her good. The rheumatism in her knees was becoming less troublesome and she could walk easily. She had trouble writing, not only because of her hand but because of the effect on her head when she bent over. But she had great hopes. Her condition naturally reminded her of her illness in Melbourne ten years previously, and led her to think often of Ethelburga, her nurse at that time. Owing to her difficulty in handling a pen, she often asked Annie to do the writing, and added a short postscript herself. Annie contributed some scientific details Annie-style:

> She so often thinks of you when I am helping her at her baths . . . She does look comical . . . as only her head is to be seen and we always have a cold wet handkerchief tied around it, and a dry towel round her neck to keep the hot air from escaping. She has to sit in a place like a large wooden box, shut in all round with a very solid door and lid, you close first one side and then the other. The lids are very heavy. As soon as she is settled in it, we call the attendant who regulates the heat, counts the time and prepares the "douche" which is like a shower bath, only that it comes down like a *stream* instead of like a *shower*. They seem to be doing her a lot of good. The heat comes up from underneath and is very strong with "sulphur" (in the Vapour ones I mean). The Sanatorium grounds are beautifully laid out and full of hot springs of clear water, muddy water, and all kinds of heat up to boiling.

At the end of March, Mary joined the Auckland Sisters for Easter, but then returned to Rotorua. She told Raymond that she intended to remain there until the end of April, after which she had plans to visit all the houses in the South Island.

Annie was never idle in Rotorua. She not only had duties with regard to Mary, helping her at the baths and writing letters for her, but she busied herself also helping a sick priest. In addition to all this, there was that other demanding call on her resources which Mary described for Monica. If we learn to read her, we can detect the MacKillop family style under a tight rein:

> We have Archbishop Redwood and several Priests staying here. His Grace is very kind to me and to Annie whom he instructs to keep all worry from me, and cheer me up as much as possible. He discovered a new boiling mud pool in a very secluded part of the gardens, and brought us to it, offered me the use of his sitting room in which there is always a fire, and other little kindnesses. Annie is kept busy practising for, and playing his violin accompaniments, no easy matter you may suppose but she pleases him and that is saying a good deal. They have musical evenings every night and, as mine is next to the drawing room, I come in for great treats. He plays beautifully and has a splendid violin, a real 'Strad'. So she does not get much time to write.

At the beginning of May the "cure" was nearing the end of its course. It had helped, but there were still problems. Mary told Annette on May 9 that she was taking the strongest baths and they were doing her good. The rheumatism was not cured but there was good hope. The weather was cool and there were no hills to climb, so she could walk for miles on a level road. What she does not say is that the long walk to the church and back was done on a complete fast, even from water, and that they sometimes went to one of the baths between Mass and breakfast.

There is a positively hopeful note in Mary's letters early in May, and it is clear that she fully expected to be on the move by the 16th, and soon ready for duties in Australia. But divine providence had other plans. The story can best be told in the words of various witnesses, the first being Annie MacKillop. In addition to what she set down in her memoir and stated in evidence at the Process, she gave an account of the events of Sunday 11 May 1902 in a letter written to George O'Neill on 29 October 1926:

> The Dr had ordered *perfect quiet* and the woman of the boarding house came up to our room and was very impertinent about a woman who came to see Mary. She called while we were out, and went away, but came back when she saw us going in at the front door and came straight up to our room. When she left, Mrs W. (landlady) came up and gave us a talking to [*according to another version of Annie's, she was in a towering rage about the lady's impudence*] about the impertinence of this visitor walking into *her* house and upstairs to our room without knocking. Poor M. said nothing, but I *gave it back*, and M. said afterwards that she was so glad I did, as she couldn't.

That woman caused poor Mary's stroke, by sending a rush of blood to her head. She got the stroke the following Sunday. On Sunday as we were going to the baths she walked slowly as if she could scarcely move (we had walked a mile to Mass), and then it was a good walk to the baths after breakfast and home again. I left her with the landlady and hurried upstairs to get ready for dinner. I heard her coming up and somebody assisting her, so opened the door. She lay down at once and as I took off her gimps (linen face bands) she said to get the Priest and the Doctor.

Later on, Annie used to say of Mary's stroke: "she got it in Rotorua through the impudent talking of the boarding-house keeper." In an earlier memoir she had written about the bath:

It was very hot and severe. She would never let me try it. Then he ordered her the Vapour bath, another very trying one even for strong men . . . We met the Dr one day in the Sanatorium grounds, and I suggested that those baths were rather trying for her. He drew himself up and said, "But I approve and I'll have her take the 'Postmaster' yet." So he did, and she liked it very much—the water was so buoyant that she felt quite light when in it.

Ethelburga was summoned to Sydney and told to go to New Zealand. "We have a feeling," they said, "that you will bring her back alive." Another of the "rescue squad" sent from Australia was Patricia, who wrote to La Merci from Remuera:

We arrived at Rotorua about 8.30 on Monday night and were met at the station by the Bishop and two priests who carried our luggage and took us to where our dearest Mother was staying, which was only five minutes walk from the station. Mother cried when she saw us but on the whole all kept very quiet, His Lordship [Bishop Lenihan of Auckland] having prepared her beforehand. We then went into the sitting-room where the Bishop, two local priests, and three Vincentians were assembled, also the Doctor. His Lordship startled us by saying he had made arrangements to get Mother to Newmarket on Wednesday.

Sisters Clement and Pierre stayed up that night, the former having arrived on the previous Thursday morning—1 a.m., after twelve hours in an open trap and pouring rain all the time. Except Meeanee which is too far, all the Convents in the North Island were represented by a Sister from each when we arrived. Tuesday was spent in making preparations. The Bishop telegraphed for a special invalid carriage to the Railway Department, and arranged with Dr McLoughlin to accompany Mother up to the city. To tell you all the Bishop has done would take pages and pages. He absented himself from his cathedral on Whit Sunday, brought down his portable altar and said Mass in her room the four mornings he was there. He was in and out at all times with her like one of the Sisters. I can only say he is the nicest and kindest Bishop I ever met.

They will leave Auckland by this mail. Try and see them and thank them all. They took her up so gently from the bed to the ambulance; four priests carried her down very steep straight stairs, directed by the Bishop and the Doctor—and then on to the station, so gently. But it looked so sad. Mother was in a flannelette dressing-gown, a soft black shawl wrapped round her head and the Bishop's gold cross (with a relic of the Holy Cross within) which he placed around her neck on his arrival at Rotorua, and where it still remains. The whole side of the carriage opened and the Priests lifted her from the stretcher on to the bed prepared for her. We had a lavatory attached and another long carriage at the end all to ourselves. We were quite a large party coming up—the Bishop, three Priests, Doctor Annili and seven Sisters besides our darling Mother. The Doctor and Bishop came in at various stations along the line and were delighted to see her improving all the way up; she actually got us to prop her up to have a look at some of the lovely scenery along the line. The Sisters had a spirit lamp, made tea and coffee and boiled an egg for her lunch. In fact we were all able to have a cup of hot tea, Bishop and Doctor included.

Of course she is very helpless as her right side is quite powerless. At first the doctors gave no hopes; but now are more pleased with the progress she is making. Keep on the prayers and with God's help she will soon be all right again.

When we arrived at the Newmarket station, Fathers Henry and McCarthy were again to the fore—removing Mother from the bed to the ambulance. Our carriage had to be detached, the Fathers going on to Auckland by a later train. Father Henry was so kind-hearted; he would say, "Doctor, come here and show us how we are to lift Mother and how we are to place her." The Bishop had four men to carry her to the Convent, Sister Augustine and I walking at each side. The Bishop's carriage was there to take the bed, bedding and parcels, himself packing all in. The men put the ambulance down in the hall and the priests again carried Mother into bed a little tired after her 171 miles but far better than when she left in the morning. Doctor Purchase was at the station to meet her and to him Doctor McLoughlin consigned the best patient he ever had and remained the night with his Lordship and returned to Rotorua next morning.

Mother still wears the gold cross—and we were able to tease her a little about all her vanity and levity. She is a wonderfully good patient. Two of us have always to be with her—she can do nothing for herself, not even turn in the bed. I asked Doctor McLoughlin when he thought we could with any safety take her to Sydney, he said not before a month at all events, Dr Purchase laid down such strict regulations the night of her arrival that I am afraid to approach him on the subject . . . Mother's intellect is clear and sharper than ever—she sends her fondest love to each and all.

This invalid carriage is not traceable, but the Railways Department has been able to provide a photograph of it. The words "Special Invalid Car" are painted on the outside. It is quite possible that Mary was the first patient to be conveyed in it, as it went into service at the beginning of May 1902. There exists also a fine group photograph taken at Remuera at this time. On the verandah is Mary in a wheelchair, assisted by Nurse Glasheen, with Ethelburga, Raymond, Patricia, and Ambrose. Standing on the ground below are four more Sisters, and seated in front with another Sister is Annie MacKillop.

Annie said later: "From Rotorua I took her to Auckland." If there were no other evidence we might conclude that she had the job of taking Mary up to Auckland. In fact there were in the party seven Sisters, a doctor, three priests, and a bishop. In Auckland the patient got much worse, in Annie's opinion, because they insisted on taking her out in the fresh air every day. "I don't think she was afraid of death," she said, "she tried to live when she heard she was in danger, but she prepared for death. She was always cheerful and never gloomy. I never heard her complaining."

Footnote
1   Don Stafford, *The Romantic Past of Rotorua*, Reed, Wellington, 1977. The Railway from Auckland was completed in 1894.

THIRTY-FOUR

THE END OF THE
PILGRIMAGE

I n Sydney Mary "recovered a little and was able to move about
with help". In these simple words Annie MacKillop summed up
her sister's changed condition on returning from New Zealand at
the end of 1902. Whatever the future held, it was clear that she would
be much less active than in the past. But as she entered her twilight
years, those around her had a chance to see her inner life reflected
more steadily, unhurried as she was now by the crowded activities and
dramatic events that had passed into history. Mechtilde made a
perceptive remark about what she had observed in Mary even at the
busiest of times: "You never felt that she was losing herself in mirth or
in duty."

People could now see her as Mother Mary of the Cross, not as the
initiator of bold schemes, the organiser of new works, the negotiator
of earthly business for the purposes of heaven. She was no longer
constrained to defend the rights of the Institute—its status was now
more stable and did not demand such active watchfulness. Battles and
business of that sort were not now her vocation. Nor could she any
longer be the travelling consoler and encourager of her daughters
throughout Australia and New Zealand, from Port Augusta to
Tenterfield to Arrowtown.

The question in everybody's mind was, to what extent would she
recover her active powers? For his part, Donald was not content with
simply wondering what was going to happen—he made a spirited
appeal to his sister to recover her strength, reminding her that there
would be plenty of time for heaven later on. Reflecting on her title,
"Mary of the Cross", he rejoiced with her that she was privileged to
be so close to her Saviour:

How you must have suffered! And how much, perhaps, have you still
to suffer even if God wills to spare you to us. Mary of the Cross! What

a glorious name, my sister. How true, too, in your eventful life. I hope
in Heaven you will not be too proud for, you know, some of us would
like to get near you sometimes.

They both knew she had suffered deeply, but he reminded her: "You
have won also the love of Australia." She had certainly won the heart
of Mrs Barr Smith. When this lady received Donald's message about
Mary's illness, she replied immediately with a letter full of affectionate
memories: "All the past rises before me," she said, "Oh dear Father
Donald, I wish I could see her again! Pray for me that we may all meet
in the Kingdom beyond."

At first Mary made gradual progress, so that she could move about
with a stick or leaning on someone's arm, or even walk a short
distance unaided. Though normally at Mount Street, she spent a good
deal of her time in 1903 at the Gore Hill orphanage a few miles away.
By 1904 she was well enough to visit Victoria and South Australia.
She wrote from Adelaide in March that she was "daily gaining
strength". In September, after her return to Sydney, she wrote good
news in her first typed letter: she was sleeping much better and
moving about freely, with assistance. During another visit to Adelaide
the following year her health took a bad turn. She received the
sacrament of anointing, and it was feared that she might not survive.
But she was soon announcing calmly to the Sisters that she was much
better.

In the course of time, however, she was compelled to use the
wheelchair. Patricia remembered being told on one occasion, when a
slight mistake had been made about a postulant: "Sister, if I could get
out of this chair I would go down on my two knees and beg your
pardon." She was still a familiar figure visiting the schools in the
Sydney area. In 1985 an old Mercy Sister at North Sydney, Margaret
Mary, was able to cast her memory back eighty years to her school-
days at Naremburn. When Mother Mary came to visit she could not
leave her buggy because of her paralysis, but she talked with the
children in a lovely way from her chair, told nice stories, and produced
sweets from her tin ("Stedman's, they were"). But most of all, old
Margaret Mary remembered her eyes.

A priest who came to know Mary at this time survived to give
evidence in 1951. Francis Clune was not a garrulous witness, but he
obviously had a vivid memory of a very holy woman:

I have some devotion to Mother Mary. My first impression was that
I met an extraordinary person. So different from other people. Most

spiritual person I had ever met. I hope she will be canonized. Each time I met her I was more impressed. From the depth of my soul I believe she will be beatified.

He repeated a number of times how impressed he was with her union with God, her calmness and patience, and her complete lack of bitterness towards those who had injured her.

Mary never lost her mental powers; her speech, though it grew gradually weaker and gave trouble for short periods, was under her control until near the end. Only in the last weeks was it restricted to monosyllables. But her other great means of communication, letter-writing, was severely limited by her infirmity. Speaking of her use of the pen, she said simply: "It is not as easy to do so as of old." The fact was, she could not use her right hand. She took up writing with the left, with mixed success because the "good" hand was badly affected by rheumatism. She apologised once in a letter of condolence: "Words must be few—my left hand is unsteady and I cannot guide the pen." However, she took a simple pleasure in what she could achieve. "Good news," she wrote to her brother in June 1903 in a spidery scrawl, "I ventured to write like this to the Cardinal." In 1905 she started to practise writing left-handed in a copybook like a small child. Telling Bishop Lenihan of this, she promised that her next letter would be better.

Mary's references to her infirmity were always matter-of-fact, as though she were talking about the weather. The reason she mentioned it at all was the need she felt to apologise for not writing to somebody, or to explain why her letters were so short and undistinguished in appearance. God's will was always the reference point, whether it was a question of her illness or of prayers for her recovery. She feared some might think their devotion was being wasted and their prayers unanswered if they saw her going further into decline. "Let me beg that no one will think so," she pleaded, "The prayers will all be heard—if not as we wish—as God sees best."

She loved to receive letters from the Sisters. Her replies, however brief, were always full of gratitude. She kept her correspondence going by the use of the left hand, by dictating to the nuns helping her, and also by her own tedious one-handed efforts on a typewriter. But the letters were fewer and much shorter than was her custom and inclination. Towards the end they consisted of hardly more than a few sentences. But in a way they were, for all that, a more valuable indication of her mind. Having few words to spend, she made sure she laid them out on valuable merchandise. Charity was supreme—kindness and union with one another, bearing with one another, forgiving one another, watching the tongue. Then came the hidden virtues of St Joseph: humility, poverty, and obedience—obedience for its own value, but also as a form of charity to those in charge.

St Joseph's day each year was an occasion for a special reminder from the foundress that the true spirit of the Rule was to be found in charity and humility, the constant theme of her letters anyhow. She believed that as Patron and Protector Joseph had done much for the Institute, and she urged the nuns to let their gratitude take the form of working with generous hearts in fidelity to the Rule:

> Guard the spirit of charity, the spirit of charity so dear to him . . . Let us try to prove ourselves grateful children by closely imitating his hidden virtues, particularly his wondrous humility and obedience. In every difficulty, whether in school or Convent, apply to him with confidence, and you will never be disappointed.

In homage to the patron saint, Mary was able at this time to carry out a plan she had had in mind for some years—to publish a little periodical. Within a short time *The Garland of St Joseph* was spreading religious information and fostering devotion among thousands of people connected with the Josephites. In asking the Sisters to promote it in 1906, she said that one of its aims was to keep up the spirit of unity among the schools and the children.

The foundress was not the only one of the pioneer Sisters who was nearing the end of her earthly pilgrimage at this time. The beloved Josephine McMullen, first of the Adelaide Josephites and Number 4 on the Register, died on 24 April 1904. During her last illness, her old friend of thirty-seven years sent her a number of consoling messages, full of feeling: "You are seldom from my thoughts," Mary told her, "and I think of you as bearing your suffering in union with *Him* who suffered for us." When Josephine died, Mary said simply: "Poor but happy Sr Josephine is at rest, R. I. P. I envy her."

At this time the ordinary government of the Institute was in the hands of the General Assistant, La Merci. Mary's appreciation of her was expressed from her heart on a number of occasions in words of generous praise. She herself was in touch with all the houses and Provinces, and was no less able than previously to make judgments and decisions, but the heavy routine work was entrusted to her faithful deputy. One change noticeable at this time is the inclusion of "music money" in the reports. Conditions in Australia had changed over the course of thirty years. Consequently, accepting the decision of a Chapter on the matter, Mary wrote: "By decision of the General Chapter the music money should come to the Mother House."

An example of realistic leadership was the advice she gave the Sisters after the formation of the Australian colonies into a single Commonwealth in January 1901. This political development was not the sort of thing that normally found its way into her letters, but since it involved a civic duty she called the Sisters' attention to it. They were to make sure they were registered to vote. If they needed advice they could get it from wherever they chose, but they should keep their voting secret. Then a warning: "Every so-called Catholic is not the best man."

The General Chapter of 1905

The most important single piece of business during these years was the Chapter of March 1905. Mary's correspondence on the subject shows that she had a firm grip on the Institute's affairs. In September of the previous year she urged the nuns to pray that St Joseph would "obtain for us the graces we require to be faithful to the beautiful spirit of his Institute". They were to pray to the Holy Spirit that great unity might prevail, that charity and a holy unworldly wisdom might influence every word and act. A month or two later she repeated this insistence on the need to pray for a pure intention. The bishops of the dioceses where the Josephites were working were also approached for prayers and advice.

When the Chapter eventually assembled, it voted overwhelmingly that Mother Mary should continue in office. The delegates have not left us their reasons for re-electing an invalid, but we really do not have to look far. There were a few who evidently thought she should be relieved of the burden, but the choice showed that it was the foundress' spirit that was valued above all. Criticism has sometimes been levelled at the Chapter for re-electing Mary, and at Mary for accepting the decision. As far as she was concerned, her Rule bound her to accept election if the delegates decided they wanted her. As for the delegates, they were not voting from a distance—they were on the spot, and were quite capable of observing the limitations imposed by her infirmity.

As far as mobility was concerned, the pope of the time was for political reasons far more restricted in his movements than Mother Mary was. Whereas he was confined to the Vatican, she could travel over a thousand miles to South Australia, as well as around Sydney. Her mind was as good as ever. As for being unable to write her own letters, she had a good precedent in Catherine of Siena, Saint and Doctor of the Church, who for a different reason had to dictate all her writings.

The Josephites' esteem for their foundress, not only for what she had been in the past, but for what she was as she sat among them, was a healthy indication that they had their values right. They were not looking for efficiency, nor for smooth business administration; in any case, that side of things was not being neglected while La Merci was there. But they knew that what the Institute needed most was the guiding spirit of one who was close to God, and they had such a one, pre-eminently, in Mother Mary of the Cross. They would not have her much longer, everybody knew, and there would be time enough to look around for another when God withdrew the gift of her inspiring presence.

A memorable event in the history of the Institute in Adelaide was the completion of the convent at Kensington, with the wholehearted support of the Archbishop, in 1906. Mary's visit in 1905 was clearly the occasion for finalising plans for this building. More importantly, her friends the Barr Smiths—who were seeing her for the last time, but continued to pursue her with their generosity—made a donation that eased the burden of expense. The stages of the work can be followed in Mary's letters to the Sisters over ten months. In August 1905 she told them that the kindness of the Barr Smiths had enabled the building to go ahead. In April 1906 progress was excellent, and they should remember to pray for their benefactors, among whom was the Archbishop. A month later the work was all but completed. She was so glad for the sake of the "poor old Sisters who have worked and waited so long".

The opening was planned for 24 June 1906, just thirty-nine years from the day the first Sisters of St Joseph arrived in Adelaide from Penola. Mary introduced her appeal to benefactors by recalling this event, allowing herself to remark that "since then the Sisters have lived in very inconvenient places, with the scantiest accommodation". She was discreetly hoping that some Catholics might be stimulated by her announcement that the newly completed convent was due to "the liberality of a non-Catholic friend". She never tired of reminding the Sisters of what they owed to people who had been kind. With them she was much more specific, reminding them that without Mrs Barr Smith "we would be without our present comfortable home".

In the same year there were two welcome Josephite initiatives in Western Australia. One was a school at Southern Cross, 200 miles inland from Perth, where "water is scarce, milk is 8d a quart". Then there was another foundation made at New Norcia, the famous Benedictine enterprise eighty miles from Perth. In addition, far away across the Tasman the native people in the north of New Zealand welcomed another Josephite foundation, at Whangarei.

In 1906 the Archbishop of Melbourne, Dr Carr, wished to open a Receiving Home for unmarried mothers-to-be in Carlton, just outside the city centre. Mother Mary, who had never seen anybody in trouble without trying to help, had reassured him: "In that matter, as in all others, we shall be only too glad to meet Your Grace's wishes." The Home functioned for many years, and it was there that Annie MacKillop died on 11 January 1929.

"Proclaim the message, welcome or unwelcome, insist on it." This advice of Paul to Timothy was certainly taken up by Mother Mary. Her several "epistles" to the Sisters in 1906 spoke of gratitude for past blessings as a motive for fidelity to the spirit of the Institute: "Be kind towards each other, bear with each other, bear with the faulty as you hope God will bear with you." Such an appeal for charity must have become familiar to them—reminders about kindness, unity, harmony, peace, and the forgiving of faults; while obedience, humility, and confidence in God were topics never far away. "Let us be ready to give way," was her theme, "we are never sure we are right—and even when we are *nearly* sure, let us not contend."

It was becoming clear that Mary's service of God was henceforth to be expressed in suffering rather than in activity. Late in September 1906 she revealed her mind and heart in words that showed she was not interested in efficiency for its own sake, nor in suffering as though it were a good thing, but in doing and suffering all things for God:

> My own dear Sisters, let us refuse nothing to God's love. He humbled Himself and suffered for us—Let us be glad to show Him we are willing to suffer whatever He deigns to ask of us.

The Years of Dying 1907–1909

In 1907 Mary sent the Sisters a spiritual message in the form of "An Appeal of the Sacred Heart to a Weary, Disappointed Soul", a document she had composed in 1870. In words placed on the lips of

Jesus Christ, she appealed to them to live their lives in loving union with him. She did not speak in terms of fidelity to a philosophy, or a morality, or a theology, but in the language of love. Her words were an epitome of how she looked on her own life, and in particular the suffering that played such a prominent part in it. It is her version of Augustine's "You have made us for yourself, O Lord". She sent a copy to Mrs Barr Smith, who replied: "Ah, dearest Mother Mary, we are all weary and disappointed when we get old. Well for us if we have some hope of life beyond this. I like your little paper so much. It speaks to my heart and I envy you the life you have been able to live."

In 1908–09 Mary was not the only one of the MacKillop family who seemed to be dying. Annie's health was not good at all—in fact she was taking the New Zealand cure—but she seemed the healthiest of the three. Donald was in Victoria, fretting over his inability to work because of severe neuritis. A move to Sevenhill did little to improve his health or raise his spirits. Still, he realised that Mary's condition was more serious than his own. When he wrote in February 1909, her reply was very sympathetic. She added something about her own condition, and made an enquiry about Annie, who was still in New Zealand. Annie went to her side early in July, and wrote later: "She knew she was dying, but was not at all afraid of death. I think she was quite content."

By the middle of the year Donald began to have the feeling that Mary was not long for this world, and he put in an early bid for prayers from heaven. He asked her to come back and cure him so that he would be fit for some more years of work. It was clear that his own health was wretched, as he had just told her: "I said Mass for you on Sunday—the fourth Mass that I have been able to say since I came here nearly two months ago." His condition had made him more sensitive to what his sister had been suffering for years, and inspired him to reflect on her life:

> Every day I understand more what your sufferings must have been during the past seven years, and although none too patient of my own smaller cross, I do feel happy when I think of the reward you have won by yours. Mary of the Cross for 40 years and more, aye and long before! Surely the God of love will be kind to you!

His prayer was answered. After Mary's death he recovered his power to work, and lived on for another sixteen years.

As the visiting Sisters were leaving Mount Street after the Retreat in January 1909, Mary sent them a message from her sick room. It was brief, but they could recognise it as hers:

> Whatever troubles may be before you, accept them cheerfully, remembering Whom you are trying to follow. Do not be afraid. Love one another, bear with one another, and let charity guide you in all your life.

During the last months of her life she was visited by many priests and prelates, including Cardinal Moran and his secretary Dr O'Haran. One of her nurses later said: "I think that many looked on her as a holy person. I used to notice the way they entered." Among these bishops was James Duhig, the young Bishop of Rockhampton, who retained a vivid impression of the holiness of the dying woman and gave evidence at the Process fifty years later, when he was the aged Archbishop of Brisbane. He related how he had asked Mary for some nuns for Cloncurry. She said to La Merci: "We must do what we can for Dr Duhig, even if it means a great sacrifice." La Merci said, "Mother, how are you going to give the nuns? You have no nuns to give!" Mary replied, "God will see to that." She died in the following August, Duhig commented, thus releasing about half a dozen nuns.

Mary shared her thoughts about her condition with her old friend Annette. Though she scarcely knew any rest from her suffering, she was perfectly resigned to God's will. But she was, as usual, factual about her condition:

> It is just seven years since the hand of God was laid so heavily upon me, and I often wonder how long more I shall be left in this weary world, but a thousand times welcome be His most holy will.

Those who attended her said that her sufferings were great, and that her patience and calmness were heroic. Her whole life had borne witness to the source of this inner strength—union with Jesus Christ crucified. Ignatia, who nursed her during her last eighteen months, and was therefore able to observe the intensity of her suffering, wrote in a memoir:

> I was privileged to help to nurse her during that time, and on one occasion she said, "Have you ever had a toothache, dear?" I replied, "Yes." "Well, dear," she added, "the pain throughout my body is similar to a severe toothache."

Another Sister who nursed her for twelve months said: "She was a lovely patient, and after I left I often said she was a saint. She was no trouble as a patient." The nuns were aware that no ordinary person was dying, as Ignatia testified:

> I thought that a very holy person had died. That seemed also to be the feeling of the older nuns who had been with her a long time. I

remember that a number of the older nuns came along with rosary-beads to touch her hands with them before she died.

The novices, too, were united in prayer with their revered foundress. One of them wrote later, full of gratitude for the memory of it all, that she knelt with the other novices outside Mary's window, and they were allowed to enter two by two and hold her hand.

In her message to the Congregation after Mary's death, La Merci spoke of the kindness of so many friends, Sisters from other orders, and priests—three Jesuits came at once a few days before the end when the message went out that she was dying. On Tuesday August 4, Cardinal Moran visited her for the last time. Sister Celsus told how he read the prayers for the dying, and gave Mary the Last Blessing, while the Sisters knelt around. He was quite moved, and, placing his hand on her head, he said: "Dear Mother General, God is about to take you to your reward. Have confidence and courage. You have a rich harvest before you and St Joseph will be there to meet you. Pray for me, dear Mother, and I will also pray for you. We will meet again in heaven. God bless you." Mary tried hard to speak, but could not utter a word. As Dr O'Haran took her hand and spoke to her "her expression bespoke her deep gratitude for the kind visit". The cardinal sensed that history was being made, as he said, "Her death will bring many blessings, not only on yourselves, and your Congregation, but on the whole Australian Church." And he added as he left the convent, "I consider I have this day assisted at the deathbed of a saint."

On the first Friday of August, two days before the end, Mary received Communion for the last time. Writing about it later that month, La Merci gave some details about this memorable event, quietly convinced that there was something out of the ordinary about the patient's sudden ability to speak so clearly. La Merci herself was certainly very surprised. Mary had been speaking only in monosyllables for days and was unable to swallow even a drop of water, let alone the sacred host. La Merci wrote:

> Hoping against hope I said, "Mother, do you think you can receive Holy Communion? It is the First Friday, you know." She looked at me very intelligently and said quite clearly and audibly, "Yes, dear." To be perfectly sure, I said again, "Did you say Yes, Mother?" "Yes", she repeated.

After hurried preparations, the sacrament was brought to the sick room and the patient received it without difficulty. But before this, another small thing impressed them all:

> A path of flowers was made all the way from the Oratory to the room; the Sister who carried the vases had let the flowers fall out on the way, though unaware of the fact. When I saw them I really thought one of the Sisters had strewn them to honour the Blessed Sacrament.

Mary lingered for two more days, until Sunday. Ignatia, one of those on nursing duty at the time, said that towards the end she was in a sort of coma, and died very peacefully in bed in a sitting position. Annette said:

> There was no struggle at her death. As we said prayers her lips used to move in unison. She was conscious up to the moment of her death, and was able to press my hand. The blessed candle was in her hand all the time.

Before the day was done, La Merci had written to the Sisters throughout Australia and New Zealand:

> This news will not be a surprise to you as we were all in expectation of the end for some days past. It came calmly and peacefully about half-past nine this morning. The change appeared about four o'clock . . . Of course we were all around her, praying all the time. She seemed to be a little easier for a while, but at the hour mentioned she gently passed away, so quietly that we were hardly aware of it although all were watching.

A great number of Masses were being celebrated for Mary at the moment of her death, as it occurred just at a popular Mass time on Sunday morning. Father Smith, who had watched with her so faithfully, was one of these celebrants. In Donald MacKillop's memoir we read that by calculating the time he had concluded that his sister had died between the prayers for the living and the prayers for the dead at his Mass, thus getting the benefit of both.

But the most memorable Mass being celebrated at the time of Mary's death was that of Father Thomas Lee in Adelaide. The story was told by six witnesses at the Process, although of the six only Xavier was present at the Mass. Three had it from Father Lee—Laurence, Annette, and Leonard, who said: "I told him of what I had heard, and then he told us the incident just as we had heard." The others had it from an eye witness—"I heard this from Sister Mary John who was Sacristan," said Mechtilde—or from the Josephite tradition about it—"an incident that was told me", said Monica. Father Lee himself had died in 1916, a decade before the Process opened. Xavier gave this account:

> On the morning that Mother Mary died Father Lee was saying Mass

at Brompton Church. He stopped at the Consecration and I thought he was sick. He afterwards told the Sisters that he saw Mother Mary above the altar. That afternoon a telegram came to say that Mother Mary had died about the time that Father Lee was saying Mass. Father Lee was a great friend who had helped her in financial difficulty.

The difficulty was more than financial! Lee was the man who had rescued Mary from the Archdeacon and Sister Clare when they were plotting to land her in gaol for the debt over Mr Birmingham's boots. Annette's version of the story of the Mass was this:

> It was related to me by Father Lee who was celebrating Mass in Adelaide when Mother died, that he paused at the Consecration and at the right side of the altar he saw Mother Mary standing in her habit and smiling most beautifully at him. When he arrived in the sacristy after Mass the Sisters came and asked him if he had been ill. He replied, "No. Mother Mary is dead." "How do you know?" they asked. "I saw her," he said. This hesitancy was seen by all the Sisters, and the lay congregation assisting at the Mass and was testified to by them afterwards.

She uses the term "hesitancy"; Leonard says "very excited". Whatever it was, it was obvious to everybody.

At Mount Street itself the death of the foundress, though not unexpected, caused a great stir. The memoir of Celsus, at the time a novice, was obviously based on a clear memory of the event:

> I had the privilege of bringing groups of little ones, and lifting them up to look at the dear face of one who had loved and done so much for them. I have her features in my mind very clearly. She seemed quite different to when she was in her chair. The Sisters said at the time she was more like what she was in health.

Fifty years later, Sister M. Campion, Secretary and Archivist of the Josephites, recalled that day. Celsus may not have been her guide, but she was there, a schoolgirl of sixteen:

> I came from Monte Sant'Angelo when she died, as a representative of the Sisters of Mercy and the Children of Mary, and we were taken to the room where Mother's corpse was lying. A large number of nuns were there, praying and weeping.
>
> I always think that I got my vocation from that scene, as previously I had given no thought to the Sisters of St Joseph. The scene made a very deep impression on me.

It was a Sunday when Mother Mary died. To the surprise of the nuns, Cardinal Moran let them know late on Monday afternoon that he had arranged to celebrate the Requiem Mass and officiate at the obsequies on the Tuesday. This meant that the pace of the preparations at Mount Street had to quicken considerably, but they had everything ready, and all went well.

When the Sisters and children accompanied the remains to the church, the streets were crowded with people on both sides. Nothing seemed to be forgotten, at least according to La Merci's account of it, but Annie would not have agreed. She had been promised a reserved place at the Mass, but the church was so packed that there was not a seat available in the whole place. She was not happy about it at the time, but as the years went on she treasured the inconvenience as an illustration of the extent of the public interest in her sister.

Annie noted also the extraordinary respect shown for everything connected with Mary: "People generally got all I had of her as relics." She had been disturbed when the nuns were touching her sister's hands with their holy objects while she was still alive, fearing it would be a temptation to her (poor Mary had handled worse crises than that in her time), but she had no misgivings about it once she was in the coffin. They were touching her body with rosaries and other objects, and quite a lot of soil was later scooped up from around her grave by relic-seekers.

It was no surprise that the dead foundress was featured widely in the various organs of the Catholic press, but the secular press also treated her as somebody special. Mechtilde remarked that the reason the Sisters looked on her with veneration and the outside world had such an interest in her was her personal virtue rather than her achievements.

Cardinal Moran gave a solemn address, beginning with the words of the prophet Daniel: "They that instruct many unto justice shall shine as stars for all eternity." After touching on the excellence of the religious vocation, he dealt specifically with Mary's response to God's call to instruct the ignorant and minister to the poor. Moreover, she did this at a time when everyone seemed to be engaged in the pursuit of wealth, when "it appeared as if the whole world had set its heart on worldly goods".

Though refraining from any reference to the Father Founder, Moran traced the early history of the Sisters of St Joseph from the stable at Penola, and saw in the extraordinary growth of the Institute the hand of divine providence. Mary and her Sisters, he said, witnessed to Christ by living lives based on the Gospel, in direct contradiction to the ostentation of wealth and the pursuit of pleasure that absorbed the powers of so many around them. He concluded:

God has given the summons, and I trust she has received her crown;
and, if our prayers can add lustre to that crown, we shall pray God to
bestow every blessing that can be bestowed on his devoted servant.

It was a fine panegyric but his language was formal and his tone was
ecclesiastical rather than personal. This did not allow him to say that
she was a lovely person, warm, and kind, and interested, gracious and
self-effacing, very intelligent but not parading it, very determined but
only when the rights of the defenceless were at stake—all of which he
must have known from his long years of dealing with her. But the
facts shone through, and people were moved to tears because they
knew who he was talking about. They had seen her goodness.

The qualities of goodness were described by the Apostle Paul in
the thirteenth chapter of his first letter to the Corinthians, and Mary
had them all. She had more than enough grievances to brood over,
and what she endured would have provoked a stone to anger. Yet she
made allowances for the grossest behaviour, excused the inexcusable,
and repaid unkind treatment with sweetness that astonished those
who witnessed it. She had moved freely among the highest classes of
society, civil and ecclesiastical. Lord and Lady, Countess,
Marchioness, Baron, Duke, Duchess, Pope, Cardinal, Archbishop,
Bishop, and Mitred Abbot, appear frequently in the story of her life.
She dealt graciously with them all.

But the world's ratings did not impress her, titles and rank did not
awe or embarrass her. She respected all, high and low, because every
person she met had an unspeakable dignity as a son or daughter of
God, redeemed by Christ. Those at the lower end of the social scale
were given no less attention and respect than the highest. In fact, it
was the outcasts of society that were her specialty, poverty-stricken
children, orphans, the homeless, the old and friendless, girls in
trouble, prostitutes, jailbirds, murderers, the most unappealing
characters. It was the untitled poor who had first place in her heart,
people of flesh and blood and dirt and squalor, children who had
never known love.

In boyhood and early manhood Patrick Francis Moran had lived
for a quarter of a century in a town where there was a saint on every
corner, but they were all dead and entombed. Later, when he crossed
the world and spent another quarter of a century in a country which
had been a wilderness when these people were living out their
sanctity, he had the privilege of rubbing shoulders with a living saint.
It took him some time to realise it, because people who were not saints

483

had been busy with their tongues; but the evidence was eventually too clear to ignore. Although the published texts of his address at her funeral do not contain the remark, there is strong contemporary evidence, as Sister Campion put it, that "Cardinal Moran in his funeral address said that one day he hoped she would be raised to the Altars". There are a number of other independent witnesses who said he made the remark both at the convent and from the pulpit.

It is possible that he used the expression "the honours of the Altar" in the pulpit, and that it was omitted from the published text. Or it may be that his words about *prayers adding lustre to her crown* were understood as a discreet man's way of saying the same thing. Such a phrase is not the usual kind of language used by Catholics about the departed. Possibly Moran explained it later as referring to canonisation, and this gave rise to the tradition. The tradition was certainly a strong one. His two successors, Kelly and Gilroy, both alluded to it explicitly more than once in their formal documents.

Mother Mary was laid to rest in the cemetery at Gore Hill, a mile or two up the Pacific Highway from North Sydney, but it would be false to call her grave there a "last resting place". Before five years had passed, a Memorial Chapel had been built at Mount Street, and on 27 January 1914 her body was exhumed from Gore Hill and translated amid solemn ceremonial to a place of honour near the sanctuary of the new chapel.

Cardinal Moran had died in 1911, and his successor, Dr Kelly, had been invited to lay the foundation stone of the chapel in January 1913. Twelve months later the building was finished and free of debt. The Archbishop returned to dedicate it, and to preside over Mother Mary's return, in the presence of a crowded congregation. On the following Feast of St Joseph in March, the chapel was consecrated by Dr O'Connor, the Bishop of Armidale, Torreggiani's successor and a good friend of Mother Mary.

The vault, before the altar of the Mother of God, was most fittingly the last gift of Mary MacKillop's generous Presbyterian friend and admirer, Joanna Barr Smith. This lady had written to her shortly before her death: "Oh, my dear friend, I wish I could see you again, or hear your voice . . . Living or dying—my beloved friend—I am ever the same to you and am proud to look back on nearly forty years of unbroken friendship. My husband and I send dearest love."

At the Process in 1959 Sister Campion spoke of the frequent visitors who came to pray before Mary's tomb. Since that time the custom has grown more and more common, and organised pilgrimages have long been a regular thing. The visitors come not only from distant parts of New South Wales and the other States of Australia, but also from New Zealand and beyond. The most distinguished of them was Pope Paul VI in 1970.

August in Heaven

Though a historical work concerns only earthly activity, Christian faith reveals something of the truth that lies beyond the veil of death. And while it can say nothing about the manner of our union in Christ, it points with confidence to the reality of it. St Augustine reflected:

> There are, then, two ages. The first is the present age, which consists of the temptations and tribulations of this life; the second is the future age, which consists of everlasting peace and rejoicing.

Temptations and tribulations enough have been narrated in this story, so it may not be idle to spend a moment surmising the reunion and rejoicing of Mary Helen MacKillop with the loved ones who had shared her earthly pilgrimage.

There would have been so many of them: Julian Tenison Woods, now sure of finding the will of God, and relieved that one of his prophecies—his best—had been so gloriously fulfilled in "Mary of the Cross"; Josephine, Teresa, and Bernard, pioneers all, at the head of scores of faithful departed Josephites, rejoicing in their Mother's homecoming; the thousands of "ordinary folk" (maybe with the executed "wild beast" Fagan and the Magdalen's friends leading the band, with the eccentric old Rodriguez, the prophet of Portland, at hand) welcoming the one who had not seen them as ordinary or contemptible or strange, but as beloved children of God; those "not of this fold" like the Jew Emmanuel Solomon and the Protestant Doctor Benson, who had extended the charity of Christ to a sister in need; Uncle Peter and Aunt Julia shocked into admiration; Dr Sheil with his early intelligence and memory restored; Dr Reynolds, balanced now and confident; Charles Horan and Patrick Russell, the two "bad advisers" of bishops, finding in God's merciful providence a way to join the gladness; the Quinns, knowing the limits of episcopal authority and no longer concerned about it; Dr Kirby of the Irish College, proud of befriending the lonely young Sister in Rome, and free of his later gullibility to calumny; Dr Grant and Dr Campbell, late of the Scots College, Rome, delighted to see the triumph of

Highland blood; Roger Bede Vaughan, ever the English gentleman, quietly pleased that others could now see what he had seen from the first; Dr Torreggiani and Dr Cani, singing "L'anima mia magnifica il Signore" for the exultation of the lowly; Patrick Bonaventure Geoghegan, giving thanks for the fruit borne by his kindness to the young mother in Melbourne in 1841, and by his baptising of her infant the following year; Cardinals Barnabò, Franchi, Bilio, Simeoni, and Howard, eminently happy to see their judgment vindicated; Anton Anderledy, Josef Tappeiner, and other Jesuit friends and advisers (even poor Father Polk, hoping he might not be noticed) praising God that his word had been so faithfully heard and kept by their protégée.

And dearest of all, there was the family rejoicing in the child of grace who had grown in their midst—Grandpa MacDonald, amazed how his "gnothach miadhail" had grown since she was five; Mamma, praising God that her firstborn had clung with such determination to "the adorable Will you first taught me to love and venerate"; and young Alick and John and Maggie and Peter and Lexie, startled at the exaltation of the sister they loved; and at their head poor Papa celebrating success at last, his life (such a disaster, people said) now gloriously justified for eternity. He is Alexander, the father of Mary MacKillop.

INDEX